A New History of Documentary Film

ALSO AVAILABLE FROM CONTINUUM:

Peter Bondanella,
Italian Cinema: From Neorealism to the Present, Third Edition

Rémi Fournier Lanzoni,
French Cinema: From Its Beginnings to the Present

Paul Gulino,
Screenwriting: The Sequence Approach

Chris Jones and Genevieve Jolliffe,
The Guerilla Film Makers Handbook

Joseph G. Kickasola,
The Films of Krzysztof Kieslowski

Alyn Shipton,
A New History of Jazz

Isolde Standish,
A New History of Japanese Cinema

A New History of Documentary Film

Jack C. Ellis and Betsy A. McLane

continuum

NEW YORK • LONDON

2006

The Continuum International Publishing Group Inc
80 Maiden Lane, New York, NY 10038

The Continuum International Publishing Group Ltd
The Tower Building, 11 York Road, London SE1 7NX

www.continuumbooks.com

Printed in the United States of America

Library of Congress Cataloging-in-Publication Data

Ellis, Jack C., 1922–
  A new history of documentary film / Jack C. Ellis and Betsy A. McLane.
    p.   cm.
  Includes bibliographical references and index.
  ISBN 0-8264-1750-7 (hardcover : alk. paper) — ISBN 0-8264-1751-5 (pbk. :
alk. paper)
  1. Documentary films—History and criticism.   I. McLane, Betsy A.   II.
Title.
  PN1995.9.D6E46   2005
  070.1'8—dc22

                                                              2005013290

Contents

PREFACE

This book grows out of another book published in 1989, *The Documentary Idea*, the title of which was an homage to a man named John Grierson. It was Grierson who arrived at the concept of the documentary film as we think of it today: not to tell a story with actors but to deal with aspects of the real world that had some drama and perhaps importance—that we might do something about a particular situation or at least should be aware of it. How he chose to define this kind of film was "the creative treatment of actuality."

Grierson first applied the term *documentary* to a film entitled *Moana*, made by a man who would become his friend and verbal sparring partner. *Moana* was a record of life in Samoa in the 1920s as Robert Flaherty saw it and understood it. Grierson thought, "That's all very well, but why couldn't we bring that kind of filmmaking back to the mines and factories, the society and institutions, the problems and shortcomings of modern-day industrialized/urbanized life in Britain?" So, the mission of the documentary film began—part record of what exists, part argument about why and in what ways it should be changed. It's the history of this film form, following these diverging, sometimes conflicting, purposes —recorder on the one hand, agitator on the other—that this book chronicles.

This study deals mostly with the English-language documentary because this is, in fact, a mainline of the documentary tradition Grierson set in motion. It is concerned essentially with what might be called the *social documentary*; what's being excluded, for the most part, are nature, scientific, ethnographic films, educational films, and other types of the nonfiction form. It extends from the origin of documentary—which was also the beginning of the motion picture itself— with the Lumière brothers' record of their workers leaving the factory—to as near the present as can be gotten, given the inevitable delay between the writing and the publication of a book. Before commencing that history, some attempts to describe and define documentary are considered, and the intellectual contexts and historical precedents of documentary are examined.

Documentary proper originated in the 1920s in North America, the Soviet Union, France, Germany, and Holland. These sources were drawn upon by Grierson at the end of the twenties in his formation of the British documentary movement. British documentary of the 1930s then became a model for develop-

Workers Leaving the Factory (France, 1895, Louis Lumière). **National Archive Stills Library**

ment elsewhere. This chronicle follows the development of the documentary in Great Britain, the United States, and Canada. The bulk of the book concerns the evolution of documentary functions and forms.

Also surveyed are some developments out of aesthetic and political modernism beginning in Europe and spreading elsewhere, in which filmmakers have attempted to create new forms by mixing documentary actuality with narrative fiction and avant-garde experimentation. The latter part of the book includes developments in economics, technology, aesthetics, politics, and newer theories of documentary practice.

Listed at the end of chapter one are books relating to the general history of documentary and to documentary theory. Each subsequent chapter concludes with a list of documentary films that seem most valuable or interesting in the national period under consideration, and of additional books dealing with it.

Permission to use quoted material has been granted by the following institutions and persons: The Regents of the University of California, for John Grierson, "Postwar Patterns," *Hollywood Quarterly* 1, no. 2 (January 1946) and for Alan Rosenthal, *The Documentary Conscience: A Casebook in Film Making*. The British Film Institute for Gavin Lambert, "Free Cinema," *Sight and Sound* 25 (Spring 1956). Michelle Citron, for interview conducted by Mimi White, "Exploring

What We Take for Granted," *Afterimage* (December 1984). "Buffalo Bill's" is reprinted from *Tulips & Chimneys* by e e cummings, edited by George James Firmage, by permission of Liveright Publishing Corporation; copyright 1923, 1925, and renewed 1951, 1953 by e e cummings; copyright 1973, 1976 by Trustees for the e e cummings Trust; copyright 1973, 1976 by George James Firmage. And to General Publishing Co. for R. Blumer and S. Schouten, "Donald Britain: Green Stripe and Common Sense," in *Canadian Film Reader*, edited by S. Feldman and J. Nelson.

Chapter One

Some Ways to Think About Documentary

D ocumentary is one of three basic creative modes in film, the other two being narrative fiction and experimental avant-garde. Narrative fiction we know as the feature-length movies we see in theaters on a Friday night or on TV or video; they grow out of literary and theatrical traditions. Experimental or avant-garde films are usually shorts shown in nontheatrical film societies or series on campuses, in art museums, or available in a few video anthologies; usually they are the work of individual filmmakers and grow out of the traditions of the visual arts.

Description

Characteristics documentaries have in common that are distinct from other film types (especially from the fiction film) can be thought of in terms of: (1) subjects; (2) purposes, viewpoints, or approaches; (3) forms; (4) production methods and techniques; and (5) the sorts of experience they offer audiences.

As for **subjects**—what they're about—documentaries focus on something other than the general human condition involving individual human feelings, relationships, and actions: the province of narrative fiction and drama. For example, a British documentary made by Paul Rotha entitled *The Fourth Estate* (1940) was about a newspaper, *The* [London] *Times*, whereas Orson Welles's *Citizen Kane* (1941) is more concerned with a character modeled on William Randolph Hearst, the powerful American press lord, than with the publishing of newspapers. The National Film Board of Canada's *City of Gold* (1957) was made by Wolf Koenig and Colin Low from still photographs taken in Dawson City, in the Yukon Territory, in 1898 set within a brief frame of live-action actualities in present-day Dawson. In terms of library catalog headings, *City of Gold* would be listed under "Canada. History. Nineteenth century," "Gold mines and mining.

1

Yukon," "Klondike gold fields," and the like. On the other hand, if Charlie Chaplin's *The Gold Rush* (1925) were a book in the library it would be shelved in the Cs (alphabetically by author) under the general heading "Fiction." Though its recreation of the file of prospectors climbing over Chilkoot Pass is remarkably painstaking, *The Gold Rush* is not really about the Klondike gold rush as much as it is about loneliness and longing, pluck and luck, failure and success, friendship and love. Generally documentaries are about something specific and factual; frequently they concern public matters rather than private ones. People, places, and events in them are actual and usually contemporary.

The second aspect—**purpose/ viewpoint/approach**—is what the filmmakers are trying to say about the subjects of their films. They record social and cultural phenomena they consider significant in order to inform us about these people, events, places, institutions, and problems. In so doing documentary filmmakers intend to increase our understanding of, our interest in, and perhaps our sympathy for their subjects. They may hope that through this means of informal education they will enable us to live our lives a little more fully and intelligently. At any rate, the purpose or approach of the makers of most documentaries is to record and interpret the actuality in front of the camera and microphone in order to inform and/or persuade us to hold some attitude or take some action in relation to their subjects.

Third, the **form** evolves from the formative process, including the filmmakers' original conception, the sights and sounds selected for inclusion, and the structures into which they are fitted. Documentaries, whether scripted in advance or confined to recorded spontaneous action, are derived from and limited to actuality. Documentary filmmakers limit themselves to extracting and arranging from what already exists rather than making up content. They may recreate what they have observed but they do not create totally out of imagination as creators of stories can do. Though documentarians may follow a chronological line and include people in their films, they do not employ plot or character development as standard means of organization as do fiction filmmakers. The form of documentary is mainly determined by subject, purpose, and approach. Usually there is no conventional dramaturgical progression from exposition to complication to discovery to climax to denouement. Documentary forms tend to be functional, varied, and looser than those of short stories, novels, or plays. Often they are more like nonnarrative written forms such as essays, advertisements, editorials, or poems.

Fourth, **production method and technique**, refer to the ways images are shot, sounds recorded, and the two edited together. One basic requirement of documentary is the use of nonactors ("real people" who "play themselves") rather than actors (who are cast, costumed, and made up to play "roles"). The other basic requirement is shooting on location (rather than on soundstages or studio back lots). In documentaries no sets are constructed. Lighting is usually what exists at the location, supplemented only when necessary to achieve adequate exposure, not for atmosphere or mood. Exceptions to these generalizations occur, of course; but, in general, any manipulation of images or sounds is largely confined to what is required to make the recording of them possible, or to make the result seem closer to the actual than inadequate technique might.

Finally, the **audience response** documentary filmmakers seek to achieve is generally twofold: an aesthetic experience of some sort, on the one hand; and an effect on attitudes, possibly leading to action, on the other. Though much beauty exists in documentary films, it tends to be more functional, sparse, and austere than the beauties offered by fictional films. Also, documentary filmmaking offers more that would be described as professional *skill* than as personal *style*; communication rather than expression is what the documentary filmmaker is usually after. Consequently the audience is responding not so much to the artist (who keeps undercover) as to the subject matter of the film (and the artist's more or less covert statements about it). Generally the best way to understand and appreciate the intentions of documentarists is to accept the precept of the Roman poet Horace that art should both please and instruct.

Definition

The English-language documentary could be said to start with American Robert Flaherty's *Nanook of the North*, shot in Canada and released in the United States in 1922. In making his first film, Flaherty's intention was not unlike that of today's home moviemakers: he wanted to show the Eskimos, whom he had gotten to know in his travels, to the folks back home. To accomplish this he fashioned a new form of filmmaking. The success of *Nanook* drew Flaherty away from exploring, which had been his profession, and into filmmaking. His second film, *Moana* (1926), prompted John Grierson—then a young Scot on an extended visit to the United States (exploring in his own way)—to devise a new use for the word *documentary*. He introduced it casually, as an adjective, in the first sentence of the second paragraph of his review in *The New York Sun* (February 8, 1926): "Of course, *Moana* being a visual account of events in the daily life of a Polynesian youth and his family, has documentary value."

Now, documentary has as its root word *document*, which comes from the Latin *docere*, to teach. As late as 1800, according to the *Oxford English Dictionary*, *documentary* meant "a lesson; an admonition, a warning." When Grierson wrote that *Moana* had "documentary value," he would have been thinking of the modern meaning of document—that is, a record, which is factual and authentic. For scholars, documents are "primary sources" of information; for lawyers "documentary evidence" is opposed to hearsay or opinion. Perhaps Grierson was also thinking of the French use of *documentaire* to distinguish serious travelogues from other sorts of films including mere scenic views. In any case, he would move the term from his initial use of it back to the earlier one of teaching and propagating, using the "documents" of modern life as materials to spread the faith of social democracy. Flaherty, for his part, continued to document the subjects of his films as he saw them and, to some extent, as they wanted to present themselves to the world and to posterity.

Grierson carried the word and his developing aesthetic theory and sense of social purpose back to Great Britain. His definition of documentary became "the creative treatment of actuality." Beginning with his own first film, *Drifters*, in 1929, British documentary advanced to become an established movement. Most of the characteristics we associate with the term *documentary* and see evident in the films to which it is applied were present by the mid-thirties.

Documentary, then, as an artistic form, is a technique and style that originated in motion pictures. There are still photographic precursors and analogues, to be sure: the Civil War photographs of Mathew Brady, the remarkable photographic documentation of turn-of-the-century New York City by Jacob Riis, and the photographs made during the Depression years for the United States Farm Security Administration by Walker Evans, Dorothea Lange, Ben Shahn, and others. Documentary radio began in the early thirties in pioneering broadcasts of the British Broadcasting Corporation and in "The March of Time" weekly series on the Columbia Broadcasting System; documentary television (which usually means documentary film or video made for television) is prevalent. In literature the concept of documentary established itself as the nonfiction novel (Truman Capote's *In Cold Blood* and Norman Mailer's *The Prisoner's Song*), and in newspaper reporting in the late 1960s and early 1970s as the "new journalism" (Tom Wolfe's *The Electric Kool-Aid Acid Test*, Hunter Thompson's *Hell's Angels*, or Norman Mailer's *The Armies of the Night*). More recently, television courtroom and survival programs and other "reality" entertainments have become popular. In fact, the documentary idea is by now pervasive. But Webster's *New Collegiate Dictionary* offers as the primary meaning of documentary: "*n*. A documentary film."

Intellectual Contexts

Though various forms of nonfiction film preceded and existed alongside the story film, the latter early became the main line of both film art and film industry. In aesthetic terms, the fictional feature film is an extension of nineteenth-century artistic forms: the novel, drama, and photography. The documentary mode appeared, was invented in a sense, to meet new artistic and communication needs arising in the twentieth century. Documentary is purposive; it is intended to achieve something in addition to entertaining audiences and making money. This purposiveness is reflected in the four traditions identified by Paul Rotha in his seminal book of theory and history, *Documentary Film* (1935), as feeding into documentary: naturalist (romantic), newsreel, propagandist, and continental realist.

The beginning of the **naturalist (romantic)** tradition, exemplified by the films of Flaherty, roughly paralleled the development of anthropology as a social science. Sir James Frazer, a Scot who lived from 1854 to 1941, was the pioneer. His monumental survey of the evolution of cultures, *The Golden Bough*, was published in 1890 in two volumes; the twelve-volume edition appeared between 1911 and 1915. (Flaherty began to film the Eskimos in 1913.)

Almost exactly contemporary with Frazer was Franz Boas (1858–1942), a German-born American anthropologist and ethnologist. Boas maintained that the immediate task of anthropology should be to record endangered cultures that might vanish. He stressed the specifics of each culture and taught that only after extensive data had been collected through fieldwork could any theories be put forward. Fieldwork has been the foundation of anthropology ever since. (Though Flaherty had no training as an anthropologist, he approximated field-work more closely than any filmmaker preceding him, living with and observing the Inuit of the Hudson Bay region many years before filming them.)

Boas's work was followed by that of Polish-born Bronislaw Malinowski, who lived from 1884 to 1942. (Flaherty's dates were 1884 to 1951.) Malinowski's *Argonauts of the Western Pacific* was published in 1922 (the year *Nanook of the North* was released). It is about the people of the Trobriand Islands, located off the coast of New Guinea. Margaret Mead (1901–1978) published her *Coming of Age in Samoa* in 1928. (Flaherty's *Moana*, dealing with Samoans, was released in 1926.)

The **newsreel** tradition came out of the phenomenal expansion of journalism in the twentieth century. The beginning of mass circulation newspapers (and a practicable theory for radio transmission) arrived at about the same time as the movies—1896. The popular press, with its dramatization of the news, functioned not only as dispenser of information but as informal educator for millions of avid readers. Newsreels appeared in movie theaters in regular weekly form from 1910 on. They were simply an extension into motion pictures of equivalents to the rotogravure (photographic) sections of the tabloids.

The concept and term *propaganda*, Rotha's third tradition, goes back at least to the *Congregatio de propaganda fide* (Congregation for propagating the faith), a committee of cardinals established by Pope Gregory XV in 1622. A subsequent use of propaganda grew out of the revolutionary theory set forth by German political philosopher and socialist Karl Marx (1818–1883). Propaganda became a key concern of Russian communist leader Vladimir Ilyich Lenin (1870–1924). Following the October revolution of 1917, the new government in Russia—the Union of Soviet Socialist Republics (U.S.S.R.)—was the first to make sustained, extensive, and coordinated peacetime use of film propaganda. Modern interest in propaganda is related to the intellectual disciplines of sociology, social psychology, and political science.

Rotha's final tradition, **continental realist**, emerged as part of the European avant-garde of the 1920s, headquartered in Paris. One of its preoccupations was finding artistic means for dealing with the interrelatedness of time and space. This modern understanding, originating in the physical sciences, was enunciated by Max Planck in his quantum mechanics, by Albert Einstein in his theory of relativity, and by others beginning about the turn of the twentieth century. Another preoccupation of the avant-garde was with expressing the understanding of the unconscious human mind offered by Sigmund Freud, Carl Jung, and others in the new psychological science at about the same time.

Pre-documentary Origins

Depending on how one defines documentary, it could be said to have begun with the birth of film itself. The filmed recordings of actuality in the experiments of technicians at the Edison laboratory in West Orange, New Jersey, might qualify. For example, the sneeze of an employee named Fred Ott was filmed in 1893, and two of the Edison workers dancing to phonograph music can be viewed during an attempt to synchronize sight with sound in 1896. Closer in content and approach to subsequent documentaries are the first films made by Louis Lumière and projected for paying customers in Paris on December 28, 1895. They included *The Arrival of a Train at the Station, Feeding the Baby*, and *Workers Leaving the Factory*. A member of the audience at this showing is supposed to have exclaimed of the film being projected, "It's life itself!"

In the first years of the motion picture that followed, films were mostly similar brief recordings showing everyday life, circus and vaudeville acts, and skits. Only Georges Méliès used specially conceived narrative and fantasy to any extent in the films made before 1900, and even he began by recording snippets of life on the streets of Paris (*Place de L'Opéra, Boulevard des Italiens*, both 1896). Gradually, as the novelty of the moving photographic image began to fade, the actualities recorded by filmmakers were selected for extra-cinematic interest.

Foreign and exotic subjects had a strong appeal. Traveling projectionists and cameramen of the Lumière organization roamed widely, showing "scenic views" of the Eiffel Tower and the Champs Elysées to Russians or Spaniards, for example. While in Russia they photographed troika rides and Cossacks, and in Spain flamenco dancing and bullfights, to be shown to audiences in France and elsewhere. In addition to such early travelogue forms—*Moscow Clad in Snow*, 1909, is a surviving French example (produced by Pathé Frères); *The Durbar at Delhi*, 1911, a British one—were filmed reports of exploratory and anthropological expeditions, more serious in purpose and educative in effect—*With Scott in the Antarctic*, 1913 is a British example, made by Herbert Ponting; *In the Land of the Head-Hunters*, 1914, is an American one, produced by Edward S. Curtis. About the Kwakiutl Indians of the Pacific Northwest, the latter was the most ambitious experiment of its sort up to that time. Curtis was not only a professional photographer but a trained and experienced ethnologist. Although working quite sepa-

Production still taken during shooting of *In the Land of the Head-Hunters*, aka *In the Land of the War Canoes,* Curtis is operating the camera (U.S., 1914, Edward S. Curtis). Thomas Burke Memorial Washington State Museum

rately from Flaherty, he was headed in a similar direction. Flaherty met Curtis and saw his film in 1915.

The newsreel tradition may be said to have begun in France with Lumière's *Excursion of the French Photographic Society to Neuville*, 1895. Called "interest films" at first, the subjects quickly became events of greater newsworthiness. Many of them featured heads of state and ceremonial occasions. Some examples are: the crowning of a czar (*Coronation of Nicholas II*, 1896), the campaign of a presidential candidate (*William McKinley at Home*, 1896), and the final rites for a queen (*The Funeral of Queen Victoria*, 1901). Warfare was another frequent subject. The Spanish-American War (*Dewey Aboard the "Olympia" at Manilla, Tenth U.S. Infantry Disembarking*, both 1898), the Boxer Rebellion (*The Assassination of a British Sentry, Attack on a China Mission*, both 1900), and the Russo-Japanese War (*The Battle of the Yalu, Attack on a Japanese Convoy*, both 1904) had films made about them—though these were mostly reenactments rather than actualities. Among other examples that have lasted down to the present are *Launching of "H.M.S. Dreadnought" by King Edward VII* (U.K., 1906) and *Suffragette Riots in Trafalgar Square* (U.K., 1909). The newsreel in weekly form was begun by Charles Pathé of France in 1910.

Isolated examples of what might be called propaganda films, in Rotha's sense of the term, appeared before the outbreak of World War I in 1914. In the United States, the Department of the Interior produced and distributed motion pictures as early as 1911 to entice Eastern farmers to move to the newly opened agricultural areas of the West. The Civil Service Commission used a film, *Won Through*

President McKinley's Inaugural Address (U.S., 1896, probably the Edison Company).
Museum of Modern Art Film Stills Library

Merit, in a recruiting campaign in 1912. In the same year the city of Cleveland had a movie made as part of a program to alleviate slum conditions.

When America entered the war in 1917, training films were produced to instruct troops in certain activities. Propaganda films were intended to instill in military personnel and civilians alike hatred of the enemy and desire for victory. *Pershing's Crusaders, America's Answer,* and *From Forest to France* were used to boost morale and the sale of war bonds. Newsreels took on propaganda dimensions and the filmic documentation of warfare became much more comprehensive and skillful (and actual) than in preceding wars. *The Battle of the Somme* (1916), made by J. B. McDowell and Geoffrey Malins, and *The Western Front* (1919) are two British examples.

The continental realist tradition, as Rotha called it, was an aspect of the avant-garde movement of the 1920s. Only a few earlier films (perhaps *Romance of the Railway*, 1907, by Charles Urban) might be related to that creative line.

Of Rotha's four traditions—naturalist, newsreel, propaganda, continental realist—it is with the naturalist tradition and the work of Robert Flaherty that the next chapter begins. Newsreel and propaganda follow in chapter 3, and continental realist is covered in chapter 4.

Books on Documentary Theory and General Histories of Documentary

Theory

Barsam, Richard Meran, ed., *Nonfiction Film Theory and Criticism.* New York: E. P. Dutton, 1976.

Benoit-Lévy, Jean, *The Art of the Motion Picture.* New York: Coward-McCann, 1946.

Coles, Robert, *Doing Documentary Work.* London: Oxford University Press, 1997.

Corner, John, *The Art of Record: A Critical Introduction to Documentary.* Manchester, UK: University of Manchester Press, 1996.

Grant, Barry Keith and Jeanette Sloniowski, eds., *Documenting the Documentary: Close Readings of Documentary Film and Video.* Detroit: Wayne State University Press, 1998.

Grierson, John, *Grierson on Documentary,* ed. Forsyth Hardy. Berkeley: University of California Press, 1966.

Hughes, Robert, ed., *Film: Book 1: The Audience and the Filmmaker.* New York: Grove Press, 1959.

Hughes, Robert, ed., *Film: Book 2: Films of Peace and War.* New York: Grove Press, 1959.

Levin, G. Roy, *Documentary Explorations: 15 Interviews with Film-Makers.* Garden City, NY: Doubleday, 1971.

Macdonald, Kevin and Mark Cousins, *Imagining Reality: The Faber Book of Documentary.* London: Faber and Faber, 1996.

Nichols, Bill, *Introduction to Documentary.* Bloomington: Indiana University Press, 2001.

Nichols, Bill, *Representing Reality: Issues and Concepts in Documentary.* Bloomington: Indiana University Press, 1991.

Newsreel in wartime London (U.K., 1917). From Strichting Nederlands Filmmuseum

Plantinga, Carl R., *Rhetoric and Representation in Nonfiction Film*. New York: Cambridge University Press, 1997.

Rabinowitz, Paula, *They Must Be Represented: The Politics of Documentary*. New York: Verso, 1994.

Renov, Michael, ed., *Theorizing Documentary*. New York: Routledge, 1993.

Renov, Michael and Jane Gaines, eds., *Collecting Visible Evidence*. Minneapolis: University of Minnesota Press, 1999.

Rosenthal, Alan, *The Documentary Conscience: A Casebook in Film Making*. Berkeley: University of California Press, 1980.

Rosenthal, Alan, *New Challenges to Documentary*. Berkeley: University of California Press, 1987.

Rosenthal, Alan, *The New Documentary in Action: A Casebook in Film Making*. Berkeley: University of California Press, 1972.

Rothman, William, *Documentary Film Classics*. New York: Cambridge University Press, 1997.

Warren, Charles, ed., *Beyond Document: Essays on Nonfiction Film*. Hanover, NH: University Press of New England, 1996.

Winston, Brian, *Claiming the Real: The Griersonian Documentary and Its Legitimations*. London: British Film Institute, 1995.

Wright, Basil, *The Use of Film*. London: John Lane, 1948.

History

Baechlin, Peter and Maurice Muller Strauss, *Newsreels Across the World*. Paris: United Nations Educational, Scientific and Cultural Organization, 1952.

Barnouw, Erik, *Documentary: A History of the Non-fiction Film*. New York: Oxford University Press, 1993.

Barsam, Richard Meran, *Nonfiction Film: A Critical History*. Bloomington: Indiana University Press, 1992.

Barsam, Richard, guest ed., *Quarterly Review of Film Studies* 7 (Winter 1982). Special issue on documentary.

Jacobs, Lewis, ed., *The Documentary Tradition*. New York: W. W. Norton, 1979.

Hertogs, Daan and Nico De Klerk, *Nonfiction from the Teens*. Amsterdam: Stichting Nederlands Filmmuseum, 1991.

Leyda, Jay, *Films Beget Films*. New York: Hill and Wang, 1964.

Manvell, Roger, ed., *Experiment in the Film*. London: Grey Walls Press, 1949.

Rotha, Paul in collaboration with Sinclair Road and Richard Griffith, *Documentary Film*. New York: Hastings House, 1952.

Waugh, Thomas, ed., *"Show Us Life": Toward a History and Aesthetic of the Committed Documentary*. Metuchen, NJ: Scarecrow Press, 1984.

Chapter Two

Beginnings: The Americans and Popular Anthropology, 1922–1929

The Work of Robert Flaherty

Between 1910 and 1915, at the time Edward Curtis (mentioned in chapter one) was making *In the Land of the Head-Hunters* in western Canada, another American, Robert J. Flaherty, was exploring and mapping the Hudson Bay region. He was employed to search for iron ore by Sir William Mackenzie, the great developer of the northern wilderness ("the Cecil Rhodes of Canada," Flaherty called him). Though Flaherty found some ore, the deposit was not rich enough to tempt anyone to try to mine and transport it. In the course of his travels Flaherty discovered the main island of the Belcher group, which was named after him. But the most important discovery of his expeditions was how to make a new kind of motion picture. Through this discovery he would reveal to the rest of the world the far north country and its inhabitants, the Inuit, upon whom he depended for his very existence.

It was on his third expedition, in 1913, that Flaherty, encouraged by Mackenzie, took along motion picture equipment to record what he saw. He shot some 70,000 feet of 35mm film (almost twelve hours) of the Inuits, their activities, and their surroundings.

While editing this mass of material in Toronto, he dropped a cigarette onto a pile of film on the floor. Since it was the highly flammable cellulose nitrate stock of the time, it went up in a great flash of flame, nearly taking Flaherty with it. Though the original negative footage was almost totally destroyed, an edited positive work print survived and Flaherty showed it around a bit. John Grierson, who subsequently managed to see it, reported his reaction as follows: "In the first version Flaherty was still with the old travelogue of Hale's Tours, and planning learning from the ground up, not to mention the backs and fronts of sledges."

Evidently Flaherty had agreed with Grierson's unenthusiastic assessment. Another novice might have given up filmmaking altogether following such a disas-

Nanook of the North (U.S., 1922, Robert Flaherty). **Museum of Modern Art Film Stills Library**

trous entry into the field; Flaherty not only persisted, he learned from the experience. In the initial version, though it seems he had faithfully recorded aspects of Inuit existence, his feelings for the people and their way of life had not been expressed in a form that would permit audiences to share them. When his interest in filmmaking began to take precedence over exploring, he obtained backing from the fur company Revillon Frères for a return to the North to make another film. What resulted from his shooting between 1920 and 1922 was the *Nanook of the North* we know.

When Flaherty took the completed *Nanook* around to film distributors in New York City, one by one they turned it down. "Who would want to see a movie about Inuits, a movie without a story, without stars?" they seemed to be asking. It was Pathé Exchange, a firm with French origins (like the sponsoring Revillon Frères), which eventually undertook distribution. No doubt much to the surprise of Pathé and perhaps to Flaherty, this new kind of movie received an enthusiastic reception by the critics and became a substantial box office hit. Apparently a lot of moviegoers wanted to see a movie about Inuits. In this un-precedented feature-length film ordinary people reenacted things they did in

Robert Flaherty, photographed on Vancouver Island, circa 1908, by Frances Hubbard before she became Mrs. Flaherty. Thunder Bay Historical Museum Society

everyday life—working, eating, sleeping, traveling, playing with their children—doing for the camera what they would have done if the camera hadn't been there.

Following the success of *Nanook*, Flaherty was approached by Jesse L. Lasky of Famous Players-Lasky (which later became Paramount Pictures), the first firm to have turned down distribution of *Nanook*. Lasky offered Flaherty what amounted to a blank check. He was to go anywhere in the world and bring back "another *Nanook*."

Flaherty had become interested in the peoples of the Southwest Pacific through the eloquent descriptions of a friend, Frederick O'Brien, who had written a popular book about the area: *White Shadows in the South Seas*. O'Brien urged Flaherty to go to Samoa to record the lovely culture of its gentle people before it was further eroded by the incursions of foreigners and disappeared altogether. With his wife, Frances; three small daughters; their nursemaid; and his brother David, Flaherty set sail for the South Seas.

Flaherty was aware of what Hollywood expected from him—another box office success—and wondered what he would find in Samoa that could provide the drama of human survival contained in *Nanook*. (Two years after that film was released Nanook died of starvation, as many of his people had.) On the way to Samoa, Flaherty learned that a giant octopus had been sighted from another ship. Maybe enormous sea creatures threatened human life on Samoa.

Once there he found no sea monsters. On the contrary, Samoan existence seemed to provide no drama at all. Nature was munificent beyond belief; if you weren't hit on the head by a falling coconut you might live forever. For weeks a dejected Flaherty sat on the veranda drinking apple beer, gloomily contemplating what form he might give to a film about Samoans.

Through his informal investigations into their culture Flaherty had learned of a practice no longer carried out that interested him. Formerly, young Samoan men had been initiated into manhood by undergoing elaborate and intricate tattooing over much of their bodies (the knees being particularly painful), which took some weeks. Flaherty had concluded that because there were few physical threats to their existence, the Samoans had invented a test of endurance involving considerable pain. He revived this custom for the purposes of his film and organized it around the initiation of one Samoan youth named Moana. Preceding and paralleling the scenes of tattooing are scenes of the gathering of food—in the jungle, from the sea, and along the shore—the making of clothing and ornaments, the preparing and cooking of a feast, and the dancing of the *siva* by Moana and his intended bride. When the tattooing was completed there was a ceremonial drinking of *kava* (a fermented beverage made from the crushed root of a shrubby pepper) by the chiefs and a celebratory dance by the men of the village in honor of Moana's courage.

In his first two films—*Nanook* and *Moana*—Flaherty's subjects and purposes led him (one might almost say forced him) into innovations in film form. He found a means other than the plotted story, or simple topical organization of

Moana (U.S., 1926, Robert Flaherty). **Museum of Modern Art Film Stills Library**

newsreels and travelogues, to present real people and their everyday lives on the screen. Unlike other documentary pioneers whose work will be discussed later (Dziga Vertov or John Grierson, for instance), Flaherty was no theorist. Rather, he was intuitive and pragmatic. He tended to talk about the subjects of his films—the Inuits, the Samoans—rather than the nature of the medium. Nonetheless, he made profound contributions to film aesthetic and technique and to the uses to which films could be put.

The organizing structures of Flaherty's films involve loose narratives set within natural chronology. (Subsequent documentarians would move away from narrative toward exposition and argument.) *Nanook* extends through almost a year, beginning in late spring and ending in deep winter. *Moana* covers the period of its hero's initiation rites, from preparations through festive conclusion—somewhere between a month and six weeks (the tattooing itself takes three weeks, we are told).

The separate sequences within the overall time spans describe the various kinds of work, ceremony, children's play, and other activities most characteristic and distinctive of these peoples. We see Nanook spearing fish, catching and rendering walrus, hunting seals, and building an igloo. Moana and his family are seen snaring a wild boar, collecting giant clams, gathering coconuts, capturing a huge tortoise, making custard, scraping breadfruit, and baking little fish. What

Flaherty chose to show are traditional skills and customs that, while different from "civilized" modern ways, are rooted in common sense we can appreciate. Nanook's kayak appears an extremely serviceable craft for navigating the ice-clogged waters of the far north; the igloo he builds seems an efficient and comfortable home. In Samoa, clothing made from the bark of the mulberry tree and outriggers of carved wood and spars bound together with vines seem good use of what is readily available and well suited to tropical climate and rolling surf.

What Flaherty offers mainly is visual description of unfamiliar human activities and artifacts, of exotic flora and fauna—a purpose achievable by and perhaps sufficient for a maker of silent films. (Spoken commentary would be needed to deal with significant implications or non-manifest aspects of these lives, but Flaherty seems to have had little interest in such analysis and interpretation.) His films are all virtually silent films. When sound became available, he used it essentially as an accompaniment to the images, filling in another sensory dimension of reality with natural sounds, adding emotional color with music. Dialogue is used sparingly in Flaherty's two major sound films—*Man of Aran* (1934) and *Louisiana Story* (1948)—especially in the former. Mainly it serves to characterize the timbre and style of his subjects' speech and to suggest their attitudes, more than to convey information or reveal psychological motivation.

Those who spent long evenings in Flaherty's company remembered him as a teller of tales, a consummate raconteur with a sure sense of drama. In all his films the dramatic conflict is achieved with human beings against or at least in relation to nature. In *Nanook* it is the Inuits against the arctic cold and desolation. In *Moana*, amid the warm soft abundance of a tropical paradise, it is Samoans against invented pain. In Flaherty's later *Man of Aran* it is people against the infertile rock of a barren island off the west coast of Ireland and the towering waves of the North Atlantic. And in *Louisiana Story*, with the most complex conflict of the four major films, it is still human beings in ecological relationship with nature—a boy and his raccoon moving amid the secrets and dangers of a primordial swamp, and an oil-drilling crew wresting treasure from deep beneath its surface.

If Flaherty was a storyteller, he was also a teacher. His pedagogy employed mystery and suspense to arouse our curiosity, to make us want to learn about the subjects that fascinated him. One of many similar instances of this method occurs early in *Moana* when Moana's younger brother, Pe'a, climbs a palm tree. First we see him midframe, on a section of the trunk. He is allowed to climb up out of frame; then the camera tilts up to re-center him. Pe'a again climbs out of frame and is again pursued by the camera. On the third climb-tilt the uppermost part of this majestic tree is revealed. By that time we are not only craving to see the top, we are prepared to accept this as the tallest palm in the world. In another scene from the same film we see Pe'a looking at something, and a title tells us he has come upon "a telltale bit of evidence—an empty coconut shell." We do not learn what it is evidence of, however, and the mystery deepens as Pe'a scrambles

Maggie in *Man of Aran* (U.K., Robert Flaherty). International Film Seminars

about the rocks, peers in the crevices between them, tries to move one, and starts a small fire accompanied by smoke until a creature emerges. Only then does a title say, "Ah, Mr. Robber Crab, you won't climb my father's coconut trees anymore." Also, Flaherty's visual exposition is generally exemplary in its simplicity and clarity. Nanook's construction of an igloo is presented so clearly and simply we feel we could go out and build one, given enough snow. Much the same can be said for the making of soil in *Man of Aran*.

The dramatis personae of the Flaherty films are the nuclear family structured along conventional lines. He did not acknowledge the polygamy practiced in traditional Inuit culture nor the looseness of the Samoan family arrangement described by Margaret Mead in *Coming of Age in Samoa*. A Flaherty film family usually has: a strong, mature father; a gentle but heroic mother devoted to him, to their children, and to the concerns of the family; and a son who is learning his way into his cultural and natural surroundings. The women in Flaherty's films are subordinate and supportive of the men in the struggle for existence, assisting them in domestic and ceremonial activities. (Maggie, in *Man of Aran*, is somewhat unusual in her demonstrated strength of character, independence, resourcefulness, and bravery.) We might take the Flaherty film family as deriving from what he thought his own to have been like as he was growing up, the son of a mining engineer in northern Michigan and Canada before the turn of the century. In this view the young boys of his films become surrogates for the young Flaherty himself. Water, small boats, and fishing are prevalent in the life of his films, as they would have been in the life of the region in which he grew up.

The families were artificially created for the films, for the most part, with considerable care given to the casting. Those selected to become father, mother, son, sister, and the rest are physically representative of the culture and also attractive—not necessarily handsome or beautiful but best of type. Community life is scarcely acknowledged. The sudden appearance of numerous Inuits, Samoans, or Aran Islanders for the trek to the fur trader's, the performance of a tribal dance, or the hunt for basking sharks seems incongruous with the prevailing intimacy and isolation of the central family. Ages and stages of life are present— early childhood through maturity—but little attention is given to old age or infancy. There are no human deaths or births in Flaherty's films.

What he seeks out among his peoples are their consistent patterns of physical behavior—activities related to obtaining food, clothing, and shelter—rather than aberrations of human psyches and antisocial actions that are the basis for Western drama from the Greeks on. Flaherty may ultimately have been most concerned with the human spirit, but what he chose to show are its basic material manifestations. He pays no attention to how his societies govern themselves. Nor is there anything in his films about the spiritual life of the people he is depicting. Religious beliefs and practices are absent—remarkable considering the importance of religion in the cultures he chose. We see neither anger nor grief. While affection is quite evident—of his subjects for one another and (implicitly) of the filmmaker's for his subjects—there is no sex. (The relationship of Moana to his betrothed, Fa'angase, might be mistaken for that of brother and sister.) Personal feelings, the emotions of individuals, are not central to Flaherty's concerns. Rather, more generalized notions of what a man, a woman, and a child do are operative. What it means to survive, to exist in the culture and in the environment one is born into, are the stuff of which his films are made.

Shooting in remote places in the way Flaherty did was unprecedented—at least in feature filmmaking up to that time. His methods of conception and production were especially original and unusual in two respects. One was what was characterized by his wife and coproducer, Frances Flaherty, as "non-preconception." Rather than approaching a society with an idea of the film he wanted to make about it, Flaherty chose to live with and observe the people, to discover their essential story, like the Inuit sculptor who cuts into the ivory tusk until he finds the seal figure it contains. The other, corollary characteristic was Flaherty's practice of shooting tremendous amounts of footage on the aspects of the people and their environment that struck him as significant, or beautiful, or interesting. That initial lack of fixed intention and seemingly random shooting were accompanied by long evenings of screening, looking for the essences of the culture in

Filmmaker Martin Johnson (right) poses in the Solomon Islands, circa 1906. Johnson served as a crewmember aboard the *Snark* for writer Jack London.

the images, seeking the particular rhythms and graces of the life being shown. His subjects and members of his family and crew screened the uncut footage with him and discussed it. But the final decisions about what to include were always made by Flaherty.

As innovative as his production methods were, his use of film language followed accepted practice. Flaherty's camera was always mounted on a tripod. His nonactors were directed to reenact things he had observed them do and to repeat their actions in multiple takes. They became "performers" to a degree that is no longer usual in documentary. The conventional continuity editing evidently rested on some sort of postproduction script that formed in Flaherty's head during the repeated screenings. (He seems never to have used written scripts, only scribbled notes.) Though occasional lapses and "errors" are evident, the sequences are constructed with long shot-medium shot-close-up, matching action and sight lines, and consistent screen direction.

Yet, shooting in out-of-the-way locations required considerable technological improvisation and ingenuity. In the studio it is comparatively easy to adjust the technology to the filmmaker's needs. If movement of the camera is limited by its size and weight, it can be placed on a dolly or crane; if the film emulsion is not sensitive enough to the light available, more klieg lights can be added to the set. In the field, the filmmaker has to adapt to existing conditions. Many technological advances and alterations of technique have come about through filmmakers working outside the studio, trying to get close to unaltered real life.

Though he tended to profess ignorance of technological matters, Flaherty seems to have been a natural and perhaps superb technician. For his first filming in the north in 1913 he used a 1912 Bell and Howell studio camera, adapting it to his needs. Later he would use the Akeley, a sophisticated gyroscopic camera employed by newsreel cameramen, and then the Newman Sinclair, which became a standard camera for documentarians. On *Nanook* Flaherty began his practice of developing and printing film in the field, necessary if he was to see what he was shooting while still on location. His Inuit helpers cut holes in the ice to obtain water for processing, carried it in barrels to the hut, and strained out the deer hair that fell into it from their clothing. The "printer" was a rectangle of clear glass left on a window painted black. It corresponded to the 35mm film frame in size and dimension. Through it the low arctic sun shone. That such a system worked at all is amazing; that the quality of images in *Nanook* show little sign of the crudity of the "laboratory" involved is even more astounding.

For *Moana* Flaherty was the first to use Eastman Kodak's new panchromatic film. Though black and white (before practicable color was available), panchromatic film is sensitive to all colors of the spectrum, unlike orthochromatic film then in standard use. While orthochromatic film did not respond to red and was prone to harsh contrasts, *Moana* offers a Samoa in rich and varied shades of gray. It was also on *Moana* that Flaherty first began to make extensive use of long (telephoto) lenses. Almost all of *Moana* was shot with lenses of six inches focal length and upward (two inches being standard). Their use had the obvious advantage of permitting the filming of distant and inaccessible subjects—the outrigger on the surf, for example. Also, Flaherty found that his subjects were less self-conscious and therefore behaved more naturally if the camera was some distance away from them. And he also thought certain special photographic qualities resulted from the use of long lenses: "The figures had a roundness, a stereoscopic quality that gave to the picture a startling reality and beauty," he wrote, "alive and real, the shadows softer and the breadfruit trees seemed like living things rather than a flat background."

For *Man of Aran*, Flaherty's first sound feature, recording sound on the Irish island of Inishmore would have been next to impossible with the cumbersome optical equipment then in use. (Magnetic recording was not yet available.) To solve this problem Flaherty postrecorded in a London studio a sound track made up of music and noises and fragments of speech, laying it over the images in a complex and poetic blend unlike—far in advance of aesthetically—the synchronous sound track standard on fiction films of the time. *Louisiana Story* was the first feature shot with the 35mm Arriflex camera, which had through-the-lens viewing capability developed from the 16mm combat model used by the Germans in World War II.

The Flaherty Way

In considering Flaherty's overall significance, what seems most important is his special use of the film medium, which grew out of his creative impulse and began one main line of documentary. Stated simply, Flaherty used film to show people he loved and admired to the rest of us. He was not an anthropologist; he idealized and interpreted as an artist does, a visual poet, in his case. The view he offers is his view, admittedly. In some respects his films are as much about him—his pleasures, his prejudices, his convictions—as about the people he was filming. Often he set them back in time to recapture and preserve cultures that were disappearing; and he always presented them at their finest, simplest, and noblest, gaining their cooperation to achieve this presentation. *Man of Aran* especially—in which the hunting of basking sharks was recreated from past practices, and the urgent present economic problems of Aran ignored—has been criticized for its "distortions." But Flaherty did not invent or glamorize. His films were not created from make-believe or fakery; all that he shows did happen or had happened in the lives of the people. (*Louisiana Story* is the exception; though based on actuality, it is a story, as its title announces.)

True, Flaherty usually stuck to so-called simple peoples in far corners of the earth and dealt with the essentials of their traditional existence. But this is not exoticism à la "Hollywood" (as in *Tabu*, 1931, which Flaherty made with F. W. Murnau in Tahiti but which became Murnau's film replete with love story, villainy, and scary superstitions). In Flaherty's films there are neither "colorful na-

Robert Flaherty with a Newman Sinclair camera, England, 1930s. Museum of Modern Art Film Stills Archive

tives" nor "native color." Instead, he was attempting to show how other cultures are like our own; how understandable they are, rather than how different and strange. When *Nanook* ends with a close-up of Nanook's face, we may think, "There's a man I've enjoyed getting to know. If I were in his situation, I hope I would be able to do things as well as he does."

Flaherty frankly liked and felt comfortable with people living close to nature; he was raised in the north woods with Native Americans and miners as companions. Also, his choice of "primitive" peoples and traditional cultures followed from what he wanted to say. An artist concerned with the conditions of survival—work for subsistence, family for procreation—the timeless and universal requirements of humankind, may do better to stay away from the complex and sophisticated in order to see the essentials more clearly. Incidentally, the people Flaherty chose to make films about led a physical life and reveal themselves more fully through external action, visible work and ritual, than would modern city dwellers. Most of us would have a hard time explaining through images alone how we earn our livings.

To patronize Flaherty as a "romantic," as Paul Rotha and others did in the 1930s, seems to miss the point. One can see what Rotha is thinking of if the people and settings Flaherty selected and the way he chose to present them are linked with the noble savage of Jean-Jacques Rousseau and the idealized landscapes of early nineteenth-century painters. But Flaherty's films have little to do with the romanticism of the romantic movement, resting as it does on individual imagination and heightened emotions. On the contrary, his work might be said to be "classical," as the term is generally used in the romantic/classical dichotomy; it is spare and uninvolved with individual psychologies. His view suggests that of a genial pagan or a pre-fall Adam—lacking interest in Christian notions of sin and guilt in any case.

Flaherty worked with what he understood and said what he had to say. Like many artists of substance this was essentially one thing. The French director Jean Renoir once remarked that a filmmaker spends his whole life making one film over and over again. What Flaherty said throughout his work was that humankind has an innate dignity, and beauty dwells in its patterns of existence.

Let this discussion of the Flaherty way end with a substantial quotation from a talk given by Frances Flaherty, who became an eloquent spokesperson for her husband's views after his death.

> Robert Flaherty loved primitive peoples, he loved their simplicity and their dignity, and the way they were free to be themselves. He loved the courage and generosity he found absolute in Eskimo life. But because he made his films of primitive cultures and cultures that are dying, and because he was not interested in their dying but only in them when they were most alive, he has been called a romantic and an escapist. Actually what he was deeply concerned with in these pictures of machineless people was the emergence of the machine. What he is saying in *Nanook, Moana* and *Man of Aran* is that the spirit by which these peoples came to terms with Nature is the same spirit by which we shall come to terms with our machines—that the continuity of history throughout its changes is written in the human spirit, and we lose sight of that continuity at our peril.
>
> Robert Flaherty seldom talked about his work. Yet he never, never for a moment was away from it. His dedication was more, however, than the dedication of an artist to his art; it was rather a dedication to his vision of the new power and new values that this new medium had brought into the world AS ART. All he cared about his films was that they should show this power and these values, that they should be great enough so that people would see, see the importance of an approach to this medium that gave them life and love and a deeper communion and greater awareness, so that they would see that this approach was the true greatness of the medium, its *art*.

Offshoots from Flaherty

Though a school or movement never formed around him, Flaherty's example was followed in a general way by other Americans who worked along popular anthropological lines. Merian C. Cooper and Ernest B. Schoedsack were two of them. Their first film, *Grass* (1925), records the migration of 50,000 Bakhtiari tribesmen in central Persia (Iran) who cross a wide river at flood stage and a 12,000-foot mountain to reach pasture for their herds. *Chang* (1927), which followed *Grass,* is Cooper and Schoedsack's concocted account of a family in the jungles of Siam (Thailand) struggling for survival against hostile animals—tigers, leopards, and elephants.

In the 1930s the husband-wife team of Martin and Osa Johnson made a number of popular travel/expedition pictures with meretricious "educational" trappings and condescending asides about the natives: *Wonders of the Congo* (1931), *Baboona* (1935), and *Borneo* (1937) are among them. Frank Buck, in much the same vein, filmed his expeditions to capture wild animals in Africa: *Bring 'em Back Alive* (1932), *Wild Cargo* (1934), and *Fang and Claw* (1935).

A much more significant offshoot from Flaherty's nonfiction form was the application of it by John Grierson and the British documentarians to purposes and subjects quite different from Flaherty's. The British were concerned with people in an industrialized, interdependent, and predominantly urban society. Their interests were social and economic (and political by implication), and will be returned to in chapter 5. But Grierson, in a moving "Appreciation" published in *The New York Times* at the time of Flaherty's death in 1951, said of his old friend and ideological adversary, that perhaps he had been right after all in pursuing the timeless rather than the timely. Flaherty's films may even have contributed as much to social well-being as had Grierson's own, he conceded, in spite of his (Grierson's) concentration on improving the conditions of living in the here and now. After explaining Flaherty's seminal importance in the history of film, Grierson concluded with a quote from e e cummings in loving tribute to what Flaherty had meant to him personally:

Buffalo Bill's
defunct
        who used to
        ride a watersmooth-silver
                        stallion
and break onetwothreefourfive pigeonsjustlikethat
                                Jesus

he was a handsome man
                        and what I want to know is
how do you like your blueeyed boy
Mister Death

Films of the Period

1922

Nanook of the North (U.S., Robert Flaherty)

1925

Grass (U.S., Merian C. Cooper and Ernest B. Schoedsack)

1926

La Crosière noire (*The Black Cruise*; France, Léon Poirier)
Moana (U.S., Flaherty)

1927

Chang (U.S., Cooper and Schoedsack)
Voyage au Congo (*Voyage to the Congo*; France, Marc Allegret and André Gide)

Books on the Period

Barsam, Richard, *The Vision of Robert Flaherty: The Artist as Myth and Filmmaker*. Bloomington: Indiana University Press, 1988.

Brownlow, Kevin, *The War, The West, and The Wilderness*. New York: Knopf, 1979.

Calder-Marshall, Arthur, *The Innocent Eye: The Life of Robert J. Flaherty*. London: W. H. Allen, 1963.

Flaherty, Frances Hubbard, *The Odyssey of a Film-Maker: Robert Flaherty's Story*. Urbana, IL: Beta Phi Mu, 1960.

Griffith, Richard, *The World of Robert Flaherty*. New York: Duell, Sloan and Pearce, 1953.

Holm, Bill and George Irving Quimby, *Edward S. Curtis in the Land of the War Canoes: A Pioneer Photographer in the Pacific Northwest*. Seattle: University of Washington Press, 1980.

Imperato, Pascal James and Eleanor M., *They Married Adventure: The Wandering Lives of Martin and Osa Johnson*. New Brunswick, NJ: Rutgers University Press, 1992.

Murphy, William T., *Robert Flaherty: A Guide to References and Resources*. Boston: G. K. Hall, 1978.

Rotha, Paul, *Robert J. Flaherty: A Biography*, ed. by Jay Ruby. Philadelphia: University of Pennsylvania Press, 1983.

Chapter Three

Beginnings: The Soviets and Political Indoctrination, 1922–1929

Paralleling the nonfiction films of Flaherty and others in the United States in the 1920s were those of Soviet filmmakers. After the Revolution in 1917 one of the first acts of the new Communist government was to set up a film subsection within the Department of Education. It was headed by Nadezhda Krupskaya, wife of Vladimir Ilyich Lenin, principal architect of the Revolution. In 1919 the film industry was nationalized and the State Institute of Cinematography (VGIK) established in Moscow to train filmmakers. The theme of sponsorship sounded by *Nanook,* which would become crucial to the economy of documentary, was greatly amplified—from public relations for a fur company to communication by a national government to its citizens.

In Russian the word *propaganda* was said to lack the pejorative connotations it acquired in English. Soviets working in the media understood that ideological bias operated in the selection and presentation of content of all information and entertainment, and that it was naive or hypocritical to pretend otherwise. Those whose work will be considered in this chapter came to documentary and related realist forms as dedicated Marxists with a desire to help educate and indoctrinate the Soviet people in ways that would be useful to this first socialist state.

Lenin had said, with remarkable foresight given the uses of film generally up to that time and the negligible czarist film production, "Of all the arts, the cinema is the most important for us." He instructed Soviet filmmakers to begin with newsreels and other nonfiction short films. This seemed advisable at the time partly because of the drain on resources that production of fiction feature films would have represented. Even more important was the urgent need to communicate the experience and spirit of the Revolution to the still largely uninformed and apathetic public. Three types of Soviet nonfiction films were prominent in the 1920s: newsreel-indoctrinational series, compilations of archival footage tracing recent history, and epic-scale celebrations of contemporary Soviet achievement. They were paralleled by fiction features based closely on past or present conditions and events.

Nonfiction

Reportage

Among the most active and influential of the pioneer Soviet filmmakers was a young man who called himself Dziga Vertov. Actually his name was Denis Arkadievitch Kaufman. He had two brothers who became filmmakers as well: Boris, a famous cameraman who worked with such directors as Jean Vigo, Elia Kazan, and Sidney Lumet; and Mikhail, also a cinematographer, for Vertov, and then a documentary maker in his own right. Dziga Vertov translates as "spinning top," which characterized well his unstoppable energy. While his talent and originality are unquestionable, he seemed a whirling dervish to some, an eccentric fanatic to others. Before becoming a filmmaker Vertov had been an experimental poet and writer of fantasy and satire. In 1918 he joined the staff of "Kino Nedalia" ("Film Weekly"), the first newsreel produced in Soviet Russia.

What attracted Vertov to cinema was what he saw as a close relationship between the filming process and human thought. (Sergei Eisenstein, whose work will be discussed shortly, would develop much the same idea in his theories of montage.) Also, Vertov saw human perception as having limitations compared to the more perfectible "machine eye" of the motion picture camera. (Flaherty, too, thought of the motion picture camera as a seeing machine, like the telescope or microscope, offering "a sort of extra sight.")

In his delight in the scientific and mechanical bases of cinema, Vertov was consistent with the great emphasis being placed on the machine in Soviet life and art. The government felt the need to bring the Soviet Union up to a level of industrial production comparable to that of the Western nations, and to use modern technology to harness the vast natural resources of the country. The aesthetic movement of futurism, prominent in Russia in the 1920s, was marked especially by an effort to give formal expression to the dynamic energy and movement of mechanical processes.

As a corollary, Vertov's aesthetic position demanded antinarrative, antifictional forms. His iconoclasm was intended to free film from bourgeois obfuscations of story and the effete pleasures of theatrical performance in order to arrive at the truths of the actual world. Vertov eschewed the exotic subjects sought by Flaherty and chose, instead, to stay close to home and contemporary reality.

In 1920, during the continuing warfare between the counterrevolutionaries and the Communists, which threatened the very existence of the new state, Vertov worked on "agit trains" and made *agitka*. Agit is short for agitation; sometimes the term *agitprop* was used, for agitation and propaganda. *Agitka* were little political propaganda pieces. The agit trains were variously equipped with small

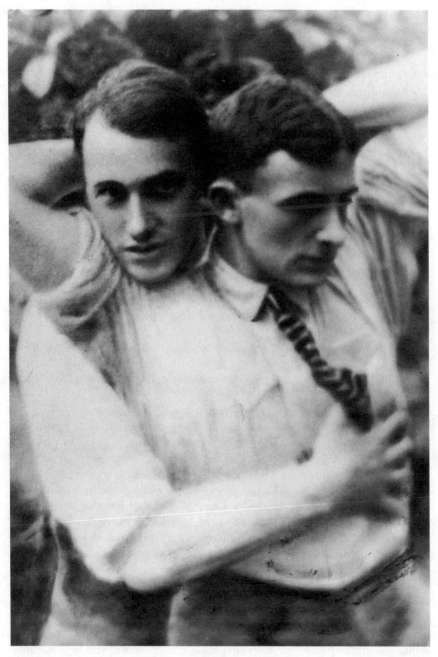

Dziga Vertov (right) with brother Mikhail Kaufman. Museum of Modern Art Film Still Archive

printing presses, actors who gave live performances, filmmaking and processing equipment, and other means of entertainment and communication. They would travel to the far-flung battlefronts to instill the troops and peasants along the way with revolutionary zeal.

In 1922 (the year *Nanook of the North* was released) Vertov began to produce the "Kino-Pravda" series of short films. *Kino pravda* means, literally, film truth; *Pravda* was the name of the Soviet daily newspaper, central organ of the Communist party. The film series was released irregularly for twenty-three issues until 1925. It was a precursor to "The March of Time" series in the United States (1935–1951) and to the technique known as direct cinema or *cinéma vérité* (which began around 1960; the French term, also meaning film truth, was an homage to Vertov). These two subsequent developments are dealt with in chapters six and fifteen, respectively.

In "Kino-Pravda" the newsreel and propaganda traditions merged. Each issue, running about twenty minutes and frequently comprising three or more reports on separate subjects, was intended to inform and indoctrinate Soviet audiences regarding the necessity for and the values and progress of the Revolution. The sampling of "Kino-Pravda" available in the United States begins and ends with a sequence portraying methods used for exhibiting the films. The beginning contains images of a reel of film, a projector being threaded, and a poster announcement sharing a split screen with an overhead pan of a city. The ending is of a mobile projection unit setting up a screen (with a mosque in the background), generator, and projector in a city square. This reflexivity would become increasingly characteristic of Vertov, culminating in *The Man with a Movie Camera* (1929).

The available example of "Kino-Pravda" contains six separate reports. The first is on the renovation and operation of the Moscow trolley system, with rails being laid, electric lines installed, meters measuring power, and trolley cars running. Second is the building of Khodinka Airport, with army tanks pulling graders to level the landing field. The third deals at some length with the trial of the Social Revolutionaries (i. e., Social Democrats, members of the immediate post-czarist government under Alexander Kerensky that had been replaced by the Bolsheviks, that is Communists, led by Lenin). Fourth is the organizing of peasants to form communes. Fifth is a sanitarium for crippled children at the town of Gelenzhik. Last is a report on starving children at the Melekes rail junction.

The subject matters of all six reports are of a practical, immediate, and materialistic nature: social, economic, and political problems being solved and things remaining to be done. Vertov's purpose in "Kino-Pravda" seems to have been to inform the citizens about what is going on in their country: to show various activities to the public at large; to awaken interest in what militant citizens are doing and gain respect for government progress; to engender pride in contemporary achievements, and occasionally to encourage action (*Save the starving children*, a title in the last report exclaims).

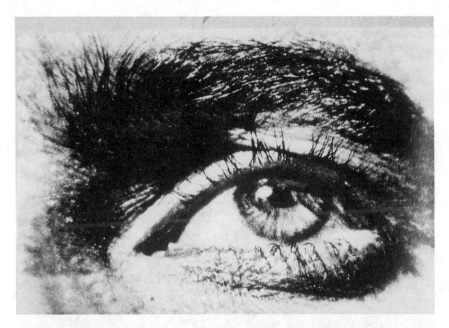

The Man with a Movie Camera (U.S.S.R., 1929, Dziga Vertov)

In the persuasions accompanying the information, Vertov contrasts the new with the old. For example, in the collectivization sequence a shot of Czar Nicholas II reviewing his troops, in stiff, formal military elegance, is preceded by an intertitle that reads, *Before we never had enough animals for individual needs.* The shot of the czar is followed by the title *Now in the communes we work together with machines,* and subsequently Lenin is shown wearing a soft worker's cap, appearing without emphasis in a group. Or, in the sequence on the building of the airport, the (czarist) tanks are no longer being used as instruments of destruction. *Tanks on the labor front* a title announces, making a propaganda point that would not have been lost on the audience at the time.

There appears to have been no overall organizational form to the "Kino-Pravda" issues. Each offered merely a collection of a few quite separate reports, vignettes, slices of life, not unlike the subsequent "March of Time" in this respect. Some of the reports in the available sample are organized in a slightly narrative way—the one on the Moscow trolley system, for example. Mostly they are descriptive. An issue of "Kino-Pravda" was much less shaped than Flaherty's work—overall or even within its parts.

Initially Vertov's production method did not involve recreation or direction, as did Flaherty's. Vertov confined himself, for the most part, to capturing what he could of undirected action as it was occurring—"Life as it is" and "Life caught unawares" were his slogans. "All people must continue to act and function in

"Kino Pravda" newsreel series (U.S.S.R., 1922–25, Dziga Vertov). Museum of Modern
Art Film Stills Archive

front of the camera just as they do in everyday life," he wrote. This strategy of
shooting became a principle that has remained at the core of subsequent theories
of documentary filmmaking. Vertov insisted that the camera "strive to shoot
events 'unnoticed' and approach people in such a way that the cameraman's
work does not impede the work of others"; and, conversely, the cameraman was
not to hide when people reacted to the camera even if they expressed displeasure
at being photographed.

To be sure, in "Kino-Pravda" there are some exceptions to these generalizations. In the sequence about the trial of the Social Revolutionaries, for example,
the selling of newspapers on the streets and the reading of newspapers in a moving trolley obviously have been enacted for the camera. But even if Vertov generally confined himself to recording what was happening in front of the camera
without intervention, he felt free to manipulate this filmed actuality. He edited
as fully as he chose in order to make clear and emphatic the meanings he wished
to communicate to his audience. Like Flaherty in not using a script, Vertov was
unlike Flaherty in doing his shaping much more by editing than by directing or
shooting. The brevity of the shots in "Kino-Pravda" may have been necessitated
in part by the shortage of available film in the Soviet Union at the time, which

would have required the use of odds and ends of raw stock. On the other hand, the rapid cutting is consistent with the new editing theory and technique Vertov was developing. In either case, there is much more intercutting between bits of related action within a single scene in "Kino-Pravda" than can be found in Flaherty's silent films (the only ones he edited). Vertov's use of editing marked the beginning of Soviet montage and would lead to the work of Esfir Shub, Sergei Eisenstein, and others to be discussed presently.

Most people would find the aesthetic experience offered by "Kino-Pravda" less satisfying than that of *Nanook* or *Moana*. Vertov's images are more restricted and didactic in intent than are Flaherty's. At the same time they seem less carefully composed, even cluttered and unlovely. The editing continuity is rougher, the action fragmented. The resultant style could be called naturalistic nitty-gritty—as opposed to naturalist (romantic), as Rotha called Flaherty's work. If "Kino-Pravda" is less an artwork than are Flaherty's films, the cause was not that Vertov was incapable of achieving artistic expression—he would gravitate toward it. Rather, for the kind of filmmaking represented by "Kino-Pravda," beauty would be thought of as a distraction.

Instead of aesthetic pleasure, "Kino-Pravda" offered its audience close relationship with ongoing events that affected them more or less directly. One title announces *The Trial of the Social Revolutionaries will be continued in the next issue of Kino-Pravda*. A final title instructs the viewers *For inquiries regarding traveling film shows / For inquiries on all film and photo work / Write to Kino-Pravda, Moscow*, and then provides the street address. Vertov clearly intended a direct and active connection with his audience, what might be thought of as "interactive," as the term is currently used in referring to a viewer-medium relationship.

What Vertov contributed with "Kino-Pravda" was a new kind of screen journalism through which he could communicate directly and dynamically with the people. And, incidentally, through his emphasis on the visual, he was able to transcend the problem of illiteracy then prevalent in his country. "Kino-Pravda" conveys the drama and optimism of the time—a sense of a new society being built. The brief reports are socially purposeful; there are no beauty parades or animals at the zoo, ubiquitous in the newsreels of other nations. Also, emphasis was placed on work being done and on working people rather than celebrities and state occasions. The reports are not all sweetness and light, either—they include seemingly honest, hard-hitting exposés—but the tone is generally inspirational: There's a job to be done. Reporting on one geographic location or one aspect of national life to the nation at large was a mission that would be picked up by the British documentarians in the 1930s.

Vertov's film practice was accompanied by his steadily developing film theory. In a 1925 article, "The Basis of 'Film Eye' [*Kino Glaz*]," he explained his conception. Deciphering "life as it is" began with the direct recording of facts found in real life. "Film Eye" had to act not through the medium of theater or literature, since they were "surrogates of life," but on its own terms. (This bias stimulated Vertov's followers, called *kinoks*, to become extremely antagonistic to drama and fiction as well as to "pay little attention to so-called Art.") This authentic film material ("life facts") was then reorganized into cinematic structures ("film things") to give a new unity with a particular ideological meaning. According to the Marxist view, the world could not be known through naive observation because its operation is hidden. The empirical world is the starting place (the source of raw material) for the "scientific" (that is, Marxist) analysis of the world. This reorganization was to be multileveled and perfected during the process of montage, the final step of the "Film Eye" method. The completed film would thus help the audience perceive reality as they otherwise never could. Vertov repeatedly pointed out that the "deciphering" of life through cinema "must be done according to the communist view of the world." Consequently the "Film Eye" method combined an aesthetic concept of un-staged film with an ideological attitude toward art in general.

A contradiction may seem to exist in Vertov's demand that the *kinoks*, on the one hand, record "life as it is" without beautifying it, while, on the other, they were to propagate the communist worldview. Vertov did not believe that these two commitments excluded each other; rather, he maintained that they reflected the dialectical process of the evolution of a socialist society. The true communist artist, Vertov claimed, must face reality "as it exists," neither hiding from facts nor masking problems.

But Vertov's artistic impulse eventually proved stronger than his social one. (He would have denied that the two impulses could be separated, and argued that his formal innovations were superior means of persuasion in support of the Revolution.) Though maintaining their basis in recorded actuality, his films moved ever more toward aesthetic, psychological, even philosophical preoccupations. In his feature-length *Kino-Eye* (1924), opening titles announce it as *The First Exploration of "Life Caught Unawares"* and *The First Non-Artificial Cinema Object, Made Without a Scenario, Actors or a Studio*. What follows is a succession of vignettes and anecdotes suggesting investigative journalism not unlike that of CBS-TV's *60 Minutes* cut together to achieve a structural symmetry. The subtitles of his next two features, *Stride, Soviet!* and *A Sixth of the World* (both 1926), suggest the direction his artistic development was taking: *A Symphony of Creative Work* for the former, *A Lyrical Cine-Poem* for the latter.

Vertov's *The Man with a Movie Camera* (1929) is one of the densest, most complex and experimental films ever created. An impressionistic montage of Moscow life from dawn to dusk, it more easily fits among the "city symphonies" being made in Western Europe at the time (discussed in chapter four) than among the works of most other Soviet filmmakers. Even in the company of avant-garde work, its examination of filmic illusion in relation to reality and its employment of an amazing range of special effects within a complicated overall structure, constitute a daring innovation that places great demands on the

The Fall of the Romanov Dynasty, a compilation film (U.S.S.R, 1927, Esfir Shub). Museum of Modern Art Film Stills Archive

viewer. Like Eisenstein, Vertov was essentially a formalist, a term that became a rebuke in the 1930s as the rule of Joseph Stalin tightened and "socialist realism" became the only acceptable artistic style.

Compilation

A major new genre of documentary was introduced by Esfir (Esther) Shub. A consummate editor, she influenced Vertov and Eisenstein; she also, admittedly, learned from their work, insisting that she was, "in the final instance, Vertov's pupil." Beginning in film in 1922, Shub was shortly inspired by Eisenstein's full-blown use of montage in *Battleship Potemkin* (1925) to begin her work on compilation films. In her first three features she reconstructed recent Russian history through editing together shots taken from earlier newsreels, home movies, and other sorts of record material she somehow managed to locate. *The Fall of the Romanov Dynasty* (1927) covered the period 1912 to 1917, *The Great Road* (1927) 1917 to 1927, and *The Russia of Nicholas II and Leo Tolstoy* (1928) 1896 to 1912. The first of these is the only one currently in distribution in the United States.

The Fall of the Romanov Dynasty is in four parts: pre-World War I, preparations for war, the war, and the Revolution. Throughout, narrative intertitles in the past tense are used to identify images and give them emotional coloring, frequently ironic. It begins with *Czarist Russia in the years of the black reaction*. There are short sequences on *The Kremlin of the Czars, Moscow of the priests, Police*, and the legislative body: *In St. Petersburg the State Duma, obedient to the Czar, was in session*. We then see a prosperous-looking rural Russia of clergy and landed aristocracy. There is one shot of village huts, with peasant women at a well, and a scene of *Yoked peasant labor on the lands of the gentry*; but there is much more of court nobility, senators and officials, and the military (army units and the fleet). In a sequence of pointed contrast between aristocrats *on an outing at sea* dancing the mazurka aboard a warship and laborers doing various sorts of manual work, a title makes a small joke about sweating being involved in each activity. This is just one instance of a steady intercutting of contrasts between the ruling classes and the people in factories, on farms, and in mines. A surprisingly substantial industrial economy is documented, while *Landless peasants, driven by need, left their homes. The Czarist regime's prisons [which] made short work of those who rose up and fought*, and *Forced labor and exile*, are also shown.

Speculators, Banks, Gold, and *Capitalists* are identified as factors leading to war. Following the title *All countries were preparing for war*, we see military training, munitions being manufactured, and warlike activity in various countries. *Czarist Russia marched in step with world imperialism*, we are told. With the threat of war *The mobilization took workers from their machines and peasants from the fields*.

Scenes of mobilization are followed by dramatic combat footage of World War I, much of it of French and British forces, and some of German, it would appear from the uniforms. There is also material taken on the Russian front. *Grain fields were burned by retreating armies*—presumably the czarist Russian army retreating from the Germans.

Following a title that proclaims simply *1917* is extensive coverage of the uprising that put Kerensky in power in February of that year. This is shown as a popular revolution, but *The bourgeoisie, striving to use the revolution for its own purposes, seized power*, a title explains. Emphasis is given to the continuing dissidence and the parallel government of Soviets of the Workers and Soldiers. Lenin's slogan of "Bread! Peace! Freedom!" is introduced. A title informs us that on March 4 the people learned of the abdication of Nicholas II. We see torn-down czarist emblems and then *Kerensky, leader of the Social Revolutionaries [Social Democrats] and Minister of Justice*, along with the leader of the Mensheviks. (The latter were a wing of the Social Democratic party who believed in the gradual achievement of socialism by parliamentary methods as opposed to the Bolsheviks led by Lenin.) Kerensky is shown pursuing the war; Lenin is shown speaking from a platform to a huge crowd in a square. The final shot is of Lenin in a locomotive tender, shaking hands with someone and smiling happily.

Two immediate reactions to *The Fall of the Romanov Dynasty* seem likely. One is to wonder how in the world Shub managed to obtain all that remarkable footage. An enormous amount of work, including, no doubt, much ingenuity and persistence must have gone into locating it, even before the cataloging and creative assembling could begin. The other reaction is amazement and pleasure in the vivid sense of time and place, even of the personalities, caught by the camera. It is an astonishing document, full of life and Shub's lively response to that life.

Even though she is clearly justifying the Revolution through showing the background out of which it came, the humanity of the people photographed still comes through, regardless of which side they were on politically. A scene of an aristocratic celebration in Moscow of the 300th anniversary of the Romanov reign is fascinating for its interplay of relationships among family members and friends caught and preserved, in some instances without any apparent awareness on their part that their images were being recorded. Imagine how changed our understanding of ancient Rome and the Romans might be if a similar moving picture record had been made then and there. Nothing like Shub's films had existed before them, and her work remains among the finest examples of the compilation technique.

Shub's contributions were influential in the United States. In the early 1930s leftist filmmakers made what they called "synthetic documentaries" out of newsreels edited for propaganda purposes. This kind of filmmaking would be picked up and used later in "The March of Time" (1935–1951) series, in the "Why We Fight" (1942–1945) indoctrination series made during World War II, and in countless compiled documentaries made for television following the great success of *Victory at Sea* (1952–1953). A book by Jay Leyda devoted to this kind of filmmaking has the apt and engaging title *Films Beget Films* (1964). The legacy of Shub will be discussed in chapters six and twelve.

Epic

The final Soviet documentary pioneer to be considered here is Victor Turin. Only one film of his demands attention: *Turksib* (1929), a large-scale seminal feature about the building of the Turkestan-Siberian railway.

Prior to making it Turin had been sent by his well-to-do family to America, where he moved from the Massachusetts Institute of Technology to the Vitagraph Company in New York City before returning to the Soviet Union and entering filmmaking. After the great success of *Turksib* Turin was rewarded by being given a studio production post, organizing other people's films.

The introductory titles of *Turksib* set forth the economic-geographical problem with which the film and the activity it documents are concerned. Cotton can be raised in Turkestan but "Cotton for all Russia" could be grown there if the wheat needed for the Turkestans' subsistence could be shipped from Siberia, thus permitting Turkestan land planted in wheat to be planted in cotton. The film is constructed in five "acts."

Act I deals with the importance and scarcity of water in Turkestan. Shots of the parched land are followed by a famous irrigation sequence as the snow melts in the mountains and water flows down into the valley. Trickles become streams, which become torrents. (This sequence was imitated in the United States in King Vidor's fictional *Our Daily Bread*, 1934, and in Pare Lorentz's documentary *The River*, 1937.) Though there is enough water for wheat, there is not enough for cotton.

Act II deals with transportation under the existing outmoded system: camels and mules in Turkestan (with another splendid set piece of a sandstorm [simoon]), and horse-drawn sleds in the snow of Siberia. A way must be found to transport Siberian grain south 1,000 miles to Turkestan, we are told.

Act III presents the work of surveying the route: the surveyors, *the advance guard of the new civilization*; a nomad village and its reactions as they arrive; and the work at headquarters in Alma-Ata of planning the route.

In Act IV, *The attack is launched at last*; *Civilization breaks through*. It shows actual construction across the desert, including the removal of a huge rocky obstruction (*But still more stubborn is man and the machine*), the frozen north, and nomad tribesmen on their mounts racing alongside a locomotive on the completed track.

Act V recapitulates what has gone before and concludes in a pulsating exhortation that the railroad be completed by 1930, the final year of the First Five-Year Plan.

Turksib combines documentary ingredients that had proven effective with others appearing fully for the first time. It includes the distant and exotic, the Flaherty heroic struggle of humanity against nature. But, whereas Flaherty recorded and celebrated tribal cultures, Turin urged WAR ON THE PRIMITIVE (as the large intertitle shouts). For Flaherty, technology represented a threat to what is most human; for Turin it was an extension of human power (*Forward the machines*).

Turksib has the same timeliness as Vertov's work. Released before the completion of the railway, it was designed to enlist enthusiasm and support for that effort. It has the vastness of scale of the American epic westerns (*The Covered Wagon*, 1923; *The Iron Horse*, 1924), which John Grierson, in Britain, would find related to the documentary impulse. And the roots of its epic struggle are in the economics of the modern industrialized world, as are those of Grierson's own first film, *Drifters* (1929), about commercial herring fishing in the North Sea. No wonder he especially valued *Turksib*; it was Grierson who prepared the English-language version.

But *Turksib* seems even more to look ahead to the documentaries of Pare Lorentz in the United States, to be dealt with in chapter six. *The Plow That Broke the Plains* (1936) and *The River* (1937) have much more in common with the epic sweep of *Turksib* than do the British documentaries of the thirties.

Fiction

If generally it seems possible to separate documentary from fiction, hybrids do exist. For example, Gillo Pontecorvo's *The Battle of Algiers* (Italy, 1966) is a fictionalized account of a major clash in the Algerian struggle for independence from France, which draws upon actual people and events as the basis of its story. Shot on location, using nonactors almost exclusively, it gives the impression that events are being recorded as they occur. A similar example is *The War Game* (U.K., 1966), Peter Watkins's imagined but horrifyingly credible account of nuclear holocaust. In addition to such individual films, certain national styles and movements fall into a gray area containing a bit of both documentary and fiction. The British semidocumentaries of World War II (to be dealt with in chapter seven) are one such body of films. The Italian postwar neorealist films are another. The first of such bodies of fused fiction-documentary work would be the Soviet silent features.

The basic factor setting all Soviet cinema apart from that of the rest of the world was its state support. Filmmakers had to answer not to bankers and the profit motive but to government administrators and the presumed needs of the populace. This difference, if basic, may not have been as great as it appears. Capitalist as well as communist films embodied ideology. Both attempted to attract large audiences. The control of contents and forms in both instances was exerted by a "front office," whether those behind the desks were called bosses or commissars. The success of all Soviet films, however, was measured in terms of how well they conveyed the sponsor's message—the extent to which they succeeded in affecting audience attitudes and behavior in conformance with the sponsor's wishes. In this respect they were profoundly different from films of the West up to that time. Given government sponsorship and indoctrinational goals, even Soviet fiction films contained many aspects of subject, purpose, form, production method, and resultant aesthetic experience and social effect that would come to be associated almost exclusively with documentary elsewhere.

If there were sufficient space, the documentary aspects in the fiction films and theoretical writings of the three greatest Soviet silent film masters—Sergei Eisenstein, V. I. Pudovkin, and Alexander Dovzhenko—could be considered. Since there isn't, the work of one of them will have to suffice. Eisenstein's is exemplary and the most influential of the three. It is also closest to documentary.

Eisenstein started his artistic career in the theater, coming under the influence of a renowned experimental director, Vsevolod Meyerhold. He bounced out of theater into film after he produced a play in 1924 entitled *Gas Masks*, performed by workers and staged in a real Moscow gas factory. Instead of replacing "art" with "life," as he had intended, Eisenstein found that the industrial setting and the performances of nonactors showed up the artificiality of conventions that would have seemed perfectly at home in the theater. He then turned to film as the medium in which art could be made out of materials much closer to life than in the other arts.

What are the documentary-like characteristics of Eisenstein's silent films? First, their subjects are all related to actual life lived recently or presently being lived. They are about people in relation to their institutions. Their concerns are

Battleship Potemkin, a fiction film based on historical fact of the 1905 abortive Russian revolution (U.S.S.R., 1925, Sergei Eisenstein). Museum of Modern Art Film Stills Archive

social, economic, and political. *Strike* (1925) deals with a labor protest and the smashing of it in czarist Russia. *Battleship Potemkin* (1925) is based on the mutiny of the crew of an armored cruiser in the abortive 1905 revolution. *October/ Ten Days That Shook the World* (1928) is a recreation of the Bolshevik seizure of power in St. Petersburg, the storming of the Winter Palace, and the takeover from the Kerensky government. *The General Line/Old and New* (1929) is about an agricultural collective in the new state; it is like an expansion of a "Kino-Pravda" report (with the same emphasis on machines, in this case a tractor and a cream separator).

The purpose of these Eisenstein films is to inform and involve emotionally the Soviet public regarding: (1) the conditions and events leading to and justifying the Revolution; (2) the heroic struggle of the Revolutionary forces during it; and (3) the positive and constructive efforts of the new state following it. The appeals are perhaps first to a general humanism and then to national pride. Their aim is to persuade the people to support the efforts of their government, to make them think as Communists—for brotherhood, collective effort, and material progress, and against everything that stands in the way of those goals.

Large in scale, the four films are structured along distinctive epic lines. Their plots consist of events that affect the whole nation. Their characters represent classes and localities more than individual human beings—the masses become the hero. As with *Turksib*, *Potemkin* has five acts. If that makes it like a classical tragedy, as Eisenstein suggested, it is a tragedy with only a chorus; it is not about particular men or women of high station as in the Greek plays. (Incidentally, the acts are one reel in length [about fifteen minutes], allowing the pause for reel change to come at the end of each should no changeover projector be available.)

As for Eisenstein's production method, he shot on location and used non-actors. Though he started with actuality, he submitted it to extreme formalistic control and shaping. His work seems to represent a fusion of the contributions of two American pioneers: David Wark Griffith and Robert Flaherty. He acknowledged his indebtedness to Griffith; it isn't known whether he saw Flaherty's films. But Eisenstein began with something close to Flaherty's natural material and applied to it a highly developed Griffith directing and editing technique.

According to his theory of *typage*, Eisenstein would select the person to play a priest, or a ship captain, or a foundry worker whose appearance suggested most strongly that he might perform such a function. What Eisenstein needed was different from Flaherty's getting Nanook to play himself driving a dogsled, however; performances in Eisenstein's films had to be created according to script requirements. Flaherty could capture his sort of action in sustained wide-angle takes. Eisenstein had to cut his nonactors' performances into bits and pieces to omit evidence of embarrassment and of being out of character. Not only did montage, as Eisenstein conceived it, match the Marxist dialectical process—shots cut together equaling thesis, antithesis, synthesis—rendering it ideal for polemical purposes. In his sort of filmmaking extensive editing was required in order to create performances from the behavior of nonactors.

The aesthetic experience and social effects offered by Eisenstein's films finally move them outside the realm of documentary. Take *Potemkin*, for example. For all its documentary elements, it is essentially historical recreation and spectacle—superior Cecil B. DeMille (and Eisenstein's direction of crowds is at least equal to DeMille's). Or, consider *Old and New*, his last silent film. In it Eisenstein is dealing with a fully documentary, contemporary subject matter, and the actual people on their actual land. Through his imposition of formalism and aesthetic concerns onto this material, however, the film comes to resemble a fairy tale, a kind of lighthearted myth (and its final intertitles call attention to its happy ending, in reference to Hollywood, surely).

Of course Flaherty had to blend his art with entertainment in order to make a profit, just as did fiction filmmakers. But if the art of Vertov, Shub, and Turin, of Eisenstein, Pudovkin, and Dovzhenko, might include entertainment and earn a profit, it was intended ultimately to make a better-functioning country. Almost all of the great Soviet silent films of the 1920s share documentary impulses and characteristics as defined in this book. The relationship between government and documentary established in the U.S.S.R. would be picked up later not only by Fascist Italy and Nazi Germany but in the English-speaking democracies of Great Britain, the United States, and Canada, as will be seen.

Films of the Period

1922–1925

"Kino-Pravda" series (Dziga Vertov)

1924

Kino-Eye (Vertov)

1926

Mechanics of the Brain (V. I. Pudovkin)
A Sixth of the World (Vertov)
Stride, Soviet! (Vertov)

1927

The Fall of the Romanov Dynasty (Esfir Shub)
The Great Road (Shub)

1928

The Russia of Nicholas II and Leo Tolstoy (Shub)

1929

The Man with a Movie Camera (Vertov)
Turksib (Victor Turin)

Books on the Period

Feldman, Seth R., *Dziga Vertov: A Guide to References and Resources*. Boston: G. K. Hall, 1979.
Feldman, Seth R., *Evolution of Style in the Early Work of Dziga Vertov*. New York: Arno Press, 1977.
Kenez, Peter, *Cinema and Soviet Society*, 1917–1953. New York: Cambridge University Press, 1992.
Lawton, Anna, ed., *The Red Screen: Politics, Society, Art in Soviet Cinema*. New York: Routledge, 1992.
Leyda, Jay, *Kino: A History of the Russian and Soviet Film*. New York: Macmillan, 1983.
Roberts, Graham, *The Man with the Movie Camera*, "Kinofilm Film Companion," 2. London: L. B. Tauris, 2000.

Shlapentokh, Dmitri and Vladimir Shlapentokh, *Soviet Cinematography, 1918–1991: Ideological Conflict and Social Reality*. New York: Aldine de Gruyter, 1993.

Taylor, Richard and Ian Christie, eds., *The Film Factory: Russian and Soviet Cinema in Documents, 1896–1939*. Cambridge, MA: Harvard University Press, 1988.

Taylor, Richard and Ian Christie, eds., *Inside the Film Factory: New Approaches to Russian and Soviet Cinema*. New York: Routledge, 1991.

Youngblood, Denise J., *Soviet Cinema in the Silent Era, 1918–1935*. Austin: University of Texas Press, 1991.

Zorkaya, Neya, *The Illustrated History of Soviet Cinema*. New York: Hippocrene Books, 1991.

Chapter Four

Beginnings: The European Avant-Gardists and Artistic Experimentation, 1922–1929

I t is a curious historical coincidence that at almost exactly the time Flaherty in America (*Nanook of the North*) and Vertov in Russia ("Kino-Pravda") began laying the groundwork for documentary, the avant-garde film was starting in Western Europe. Thus, by the early nineteen twenties documentary and experimental had emerged alongside fiction to establish the three main aesthetic impulses of film art, its principal modes. Although not a direct part of the English-language tradition, these Soviet and Western European films, along with Flaherty's, became sources for the documentary film as it would develop in Great Britain at the end of the 1920s. And the avant-garde as well as documentary started as rebellion against the fiction film, which had become the predominant artistic as well as commercial form.

Aesthetic Predispositions

What caused this rebellion was the feeling on the part of devotees of both new artistic tendencies that the conventions of the fiction film were limited and limiting. Someone once remarked that the artistic experience offered by the Hollywood movie was equivalent to a performance by someone playing a grand piano with one finger. The documentarists and avant-gardists shared a desire to explore more fully the capacities of film as a medium—to do what only film could do, or only what film could do best. They wanted to create films different from literary stories told through the theatrical means of actors and sets. They also agreed that the fiction film was telling lies about life. They did not agree on much else, however. For the documentarists, conventional fiction films were not realistic enough; for the avant-gardists, they were too realistic. The former wanted external (objective) facts presented fully and accurately; the latter wanted formal (aesthetic) patterns and inner (subjective) truths presented poetically.

The creative predilection of the documentarians extended out of the detailed verisimilitude the photographic image offered; the illusion of motion in the cinematographic image permitting the recording of yet more of visible reality—more than was attainable in any other means of communication or form of art. With the motion picture, material and physical life could be captured as it was being lived. The *actualités* of Louis Lumière (*Workers Leaving the Factory*, 1895) were the filmic antecedents of the documentary.

The avant-gardists, on the other hand, extended out of modern painting. They valued the apparent movement of the moving picture for allowing their visual imagery to become more complex and consistent with twentieth-century conceptions of time as a fourth dimension. In addition, movement in time enabled the avant-gardists to follow the workings of the mind into dreams, hallucinations, fantasies, which jumble an incongruous succession of images in a stream of consciousness. Through film they could both present abstract patterns in motion and represent dreamlike perceptions. Their filmic precursor was Georges Méliès (*A Trip to the Moon*, 1902), who offered the marvelous, decorative, and painterly world of set designers' unreality and magicians' illusion.

In the traditional arts the interrelationship of space and time was already being explored. In painting, Marcel Duchamp's *Nude Descending a Staircase* (1912) offered an abstracted, stroboscopic view of a person and her activity. The practice of cubism, Pablo Picasso's *The Violin* (1913), for instance, rests on the notion of an observer moving about to view a subject from various distances and angles. The separate views are then overlaid to try to suggest looking at the subject from different positions all at once. In literature, Marcel Proust, in his multivolume *Remembrance of Things Past* (1919–1925), assumed that the past is always present and that places experienced earlier join with places experienced later. James Joyce, in *Ulysses* (1922), intermingled what is happening to his characters in various parts of Dublin on June 16, 1904, cutting back and forth among them as a filmmaker would, trying to convey a sense of simultaneity and interaction of events and persons.

Avant-Garde and Documentary

The first of the avant-garde films were along lines of abstraction and nonobjectivity. In 1921 two painter friends living in Berlin each began work on short films that might be thought of as the beginning of avant-garde cinema. Influenced by such artistic movements as futurism and cubism, Viking Eggeling, a Swede, and Hans Richter, a German, had been attempting to bring a sense of motion approximating animation into their paintings. Their preoccupations led them from picture scrolls to the moving picture, and Richter's *Rhythmus 21* (1921) and Eggeling's *Diagonal Symphony* (1925) were the first results. "Rhythm in painting" is what they said they were after. Richter's film comprises an interacting set of square and rectangular shapes in white, gray, and black; as they change sizes, they seem to be moving toward or away from the viewer. Eggeling's consists of white abstractions shaped like lyres in shifting relationships with one another against a black screen. These two films might make one think of Piet Mondrian paintings in motion.

Some of Mondrian's nonrepresentational, geometric canvases resemble aerial photographs of a city taken from extremely high altitudes so that all we see is the grid of streets, a block of color that may be a park, and so on. In 1921 two Americans, Charles Sheeler and Paul Strand—the first a painter, the second a photographer—made a film that offered a somewhat similar view of New York City. In their *Mannahatta*, shot mostly looking down from skyscrapers, the city becomes abstract. The streets and buildings appear as patterns of light and shadow. The people, flattened and seen at a great distance, exist only as part of the design. Though shown very little in the United States, *Mannahatta* appeared in Paris in a Dadaist program that included music by Erik Satie and poems by Guillaume Apollinaire. It was said to have received an ovation on that occasion, and might be thought of as an embryonic beginning of the "city symphony" films that link avant-garde with documentary and are the main subject of this chapter.

Another seminal film that could be added to the works of Richter, Eggeling, and Sheeler and Strand is one by the French painter Fernand Léger. With technical assistance from an American named Dudley Murphy, Léger made *Ballet mécanique* (1924), exploring the rhythmic relationships of images in motion. In it, the capacity of film for mechanical repetition and its power to animate the inanimate (kitchen utensils, mannequin legs, Christmas ornaments, bottles, printed words, and geometric shapes) are strikingly exploited. Marcel Duchamp's *Anemic Cinema* (1926) is somewhat similar in its intentions.

The second line of avant-garde creation was inspired by psychoanalysis and gave rise to the artistic *ism* of surrealism, with its preoccupations rooted in dream and the unconscious. In painting, Salvador Dalí, who subsequently worked occasionally and briefly in film, painted in the surrealist manner. This generally involved more or less realistic representations of objects and persons placed in strange juxtapositions with each other. In literature Proust, though no surrealist, also relates to this psychoanalytic tendency, with the past affecting the present, as does Joyce, in *Ulysses*, especially in the use of stream of consciousness and in the Nighttown dream play. In film Luis Buñuel and Salvador Dalí's *Un Chien andalou* (1929), Buñuel's *L'Age d'or* (1930), and Jean Cocteau's *The Blood of a Poet* (1930) are celebrated examples of these dreamscapes.

Even among Rotha's realist (continental) precursors of documentary there is evidence of these two avant-garde styles. Abstractionism appears in Dutchman Joris Ivens's first significant film, *The Bridge* (1928). It is related to modernist movements such as cubism, futurism, and constructivism. Like much of the later

Vertov, whose work influenced Ivens, *The Bridge* converts machi
Camera composition and movement and edited relationships of
signed to bring out the functional and also aesthetic essence of
railway bridge in Rotterdam. Few people appear in the film—a workman climbing a ladder and a bridge tender answering a phone and starting machinery that
raises and lowers the bridge—and it ends with animated squares à la Richter's
Rhythmus 21.

Surrealism might be thought evident in Jean Vigo's *Jean Taris, champion de
natation* (1931). This study of the aquatic style of a celebrated French swimmer
is notable for its beautiful underwater cinematography in slow motion and a
dive back out of the pool onto the diving board at the end. Jean Lods's *Le Mile*
(1934), about a runner, employs "ether music," slow motion, and superimposi-
tions. Buñuel's *Land Without Bread* (1932) forces us to look at the devastating
actuality, the poverty of the Las Hurdes region of Spain, in a way that might be
described as having the intense irrational reality of a dream—that is, of being
sur real.

But it was a third line of avant-garde filmmaking, developing near the end
of the twenties, that fed most directly into documentary. Its aesthetic *ism* was
impressionism, and its origins went back to the French impressionists at the turn
of the century. The style of impressionism also placed emphasis on the space/
time relationship; impressionist painting was like looking at life from a fast-
moving railway carriage, it had been said. (Of course film provided this actual
opportunity; see, for example, Jean Mitry's *Pacific 231* [1949], about a powerful
locomotive rushing through the French countryside.) The impressionist films
resemble the earlier paintings through their quick views and concentration on
surfaces and light. What they offer mainly are collected glimpses of city life during a passage of time. Joyce's *Ulysses* might again be thought of as a literary
precedent. Eisenstein wrote of that novel, "What Joyce does with literature is
quite close to what we're doing with the new cinematography, and even closer
to what we're going to do." He further said that if *Ulysses* were ever made into a
film, the only man capable of directing it would be Walther Ruttmann or Sergei
Eisenstein.

Eisenstein's qualifications for such an assignment were discussed in chapter
three. Ruttmann directed one of the early "city symphonies," *Berlin: Symphony
of a Great City* (1927). It was preceded slightly by *Rien que les heures* (*Only the
Hours*, 1926), about Paris, directed by Alberto Cavalcanti. *Rain* (1929), Joris
Ivens's film about Amsterdam followed. Most of the remainder of this chapter
will be devoted to these three seminal works: *Rien que les heures*, *Berlin*, and
Rain. It must be acknowledged, however, that the line they started includes Jean
Vigo's *À propos de Nice* (1930), a scathingly satirical study of the famous resort
in the manner of Honoré Daumier paintings, Ralph Steiner and Willard Van
Dyke's *The City* (U.S., 1939, to be dealt with in chapter six), Arne Sucksdorff's

A youthful Joris Ivens with editing equipment used at the time. Museum of Modern Art Film Stills Archive

Symphony of a City (1947), about Stockholm, and John Eldridge's *Waverly Steps* (1948), about Edinburgh. Many other films could be added to this list.

Three City Symphonies

Alberto Cavalcanti was a Brazilian emigré who became part of the Parisian avant-garde in the early 1920s. He began his film career as an innovative set designer for Marcel L'Herbier on such features as *L'Inhumaine* (1923), in collaboration with Fernand Léger, and *The Late Matthew Pascal* (1925), in collaboration with Lazare Meerson.

Rien que les heures is a curious and fascinating mixture of the aesthetic and the social. It deals with Paris from predawn to well into the following night—roughly twenty-four hours. Opening titles promise that we will not be looking at the elegant life but rather at that of the lower classes. Thus the social viewpoint is established. But a philosophical thesis concerning time and space is also introduced and returned to. At the conclusion of the film we are asked, after we have seen what the filmmaker has shown us of Paris, to consider simultaneously Paris in relation to Peking (Beijing). The titles assert that, though we can fix a point in space, arrest a moment in time, both space and time escape our possession—that life is ongoing and interrelated, and that, without their monuments, cities cannot be told apart.

Rien que les hueres (France, 1926, Alberto Cavalcanti). **Museum of Modern Art Film Stills Archive**

Mainly the film is devoted to contrasting scenes and changing activities of Paris during the passing hours. In early morning we see all-night revelers still out on deserted streets with the first workers on their way to work appearing; later, workers at labor; then lunchtime. In the afternoon some people are swimming; work ceases, and rest and recreation occupy the evening. Among the views of unstaged actuality are brief, staged fragments. Three slight narratives are developed. The protagonists of all three are female—an old derelict (drunken or ill), a prostitute, and a newspaper vendor—all of them pathetic figures. The overall mood of the film is a bit downbeat; there is a sweet sadness, a sentimental roughness about it.

Still, Cavalcanti's attitude may be one of detachment, perhaps cynicism: *"c'est la vie,"* he seems to be saying. Though some attention to social matters is evident, the considerable number and variety of highly stylized special effects—wipes, rapid match dissolves, multiple exposures, fast motion, revolving images, split screens, freeze frames—seem to confirm that Cavalcanti's greatest interest was in artistic experimentation.

Like Cavalcanti, Walther Ruttmann came out of architecture and painting into avant-garde filmmaking in the early 1920s—specifically, in his case, to abstract, geometric forms in motion like those of his mentor, Viking Eggeling. A

A collage of images from *Berlin: Symphony of a Great City* (Germany, 1927, Walther Ruttmann). Museum of Modern Art Film Stills Archive

Poster for *Berlin: Symphony of a Great City*.

fascination with design is even more evident in *Berlin: Symphony of a Great City* than in *Rien que les heures*; and, incidentally, the former was released so soon after the latter that there can be little question of one influencing the other. Unlike *Rien*, *Berlin* emerged from mainstream commercial cinema. Produced for Fox-Europa Film, its scenario was written by Ruttmann and Karl Freund, based on an idea by Carl Mayer. (Mayer had written scripts for *The Cabinet of Dr.*

Caligari [1919], *The Last Laugh* [1924], *Tartuffe* [1925], and other notable German silent features.) The cinematography was supervised by Freund (who was director of photography on some of the great fiction films of the period including *The Golem* [1920], *The Last Laugh* [1924], *Variety* [1925], and *Metropolis* [1927]); three camera operators are credited. Original music was composed by Edmund Meisel (who had created a famous score for the German exhibition of *Potemkin*). The editing was done by Ruttmann. Though the camerawork of *Berlin* is dazzling, it is above all an editor's film, and Ruttmann is credited as its director. We see Berlin, true enough, but it is Ruttmann's Berlin that we see.

The overall organizational basis is temporal; occasionally clocks show the time: 5:00, 8:00, 12:00. The major sequences comprise very early morning (the city coming to life), morning (work and general activity), lunchtime (eating and repose), afternoon (work ceases, recreation takes place), and evening (entertainment and various sorts of diversions). Intertitles indicate "acts" up through four (though a fifth would seem to be intended), but they are much less clearly structured than the five acts of *Potemkin* or *Turksib*.

The criteria for selection and arrangement of material within these acts rest heavily on visual similarities and contrasts. Ruttmann is fascinated with the way things are shaped, the way they move. At any given time the organizing principle may be kinetic (things going up, things coming down; things opening, things closing) or shapes that look alike (people in a crowd walking, a herd of cattle moving, a troop of soldiers marching).

There are also topical groupings: workers going to work; children going to school; women cleaning and scrubbing; the various means of transportation; people eating lunch; animals feeding at the zoo. The pattern for each scene or subsection within the major sequences/acts is frequently that of an activity starting, increasing in tempo, then coming to a halt. The people are treated much as the objects; both are subjects for visual examination.

Some of the action is staged: a group of merrymakers in the early morning returning from a party; an argument between two men that attracts a group of watchers; a woman jumping from a bridge to drown, apparently. But mostly life is caught unawares. Much influenced by Vertov, Ruttmann did not follow Vertov's dictum about advancing a social point of view, though at the time he was identified with the political left.

In *Berlin* the rich and powerful are seen in contrast to members of the working classes but no social comment is made as in *The Fall of the Romanov Dynasty*. Much less attention is paid to individual persons in *Berlin* than in "Kino-Pravda." Machines are as important for Ruttmann as they are for the Soviets, but in *Berlin* they are not shown to have social utility as they are in *Turksib*. Instead, they exist as fascinating, intricate, moving objects. The film's opening proceeds from abstractions of water to what look like polarized images of fast-moving locomotive wheels and railroad tracks, beginning a protracted, elaborately-cut evocation of a train's early-morning approach to a Berlin terminus, which climaxes in a huge close-up on one of the engine's now stationary piston wheels after its arrival. Later, the image of a typewriter keyboard is set spinning and metamorphoses into a whirling animated design. *Berlin* strikes most viewers as brilliant and cold, an exercise in cinematic virtuosity.

The exclusively aesthetic concentration of Ruttmann represented a severe limitation not only from the Soviet point of view but from that of subsequent British documentarians. Yet *Berlin* may have more value as a *document* than do those *documentary* films made with more explicit social biases and programs. Though composed according to artistic insights and intuitions and the requirements of form, what it offers essentially is a visual description. From this film we can learn a great deal about the appearance of life in Berlin in 1927.

Joris Ivens, like Louis Lumière, came out of the photographic business. His grandfather was a pioneer Dutch photographer; his father owned a chain of camera shops. After serving an apprenticeship at the Zeiss camera factories in Germany, Ivens returned to Holland in 1926 to become manager of his father's Amsterdam branch.

His *Rain* (1929) is a short, like *The Bridge* (both run 10 to 15 minutes) and unlike *Rien* or *Berlin*, which are short features (45 and 70 minutes, respectively). Perhaps *Rain* is a city sonata. It presents Amsterdam just before, during, and immediately after a shower. Ivens's play with light and shadow and the compositional relationships of shots becomes much more important than in *The Bridge*. *Rain* is impressionist rather than cubist, lyrical rather than analytical. Its shapes and textures tend to be round and soft rather than straight and hard. It seems a very tactile film.

It begins with shots of canals and harbor, roofs, sky, an airplane, streetcar and traffic, sheets hanging on clotheslines, and awnings. The first person we see extends his hand, palm up, to feel raindrops, then turns up his coat collar. An umbrella is opened; a window is closed. Throughout, Ivens seems to be asking us to examine images in everyday life—rain on windshields, puddles in streets, umbrellas, reflections—to see the "artistic" in the actual. Fernand Léger once observed that before the invention of the moving picture no one knew the possibilities latent in a foot, a hand, or a hat. Ivens makes something as commonplace as an umbrella or a bare window a thing of uncommon loveliness and significance.

End of the Avant-Garde

The avant-garde was killed in part by the expensiveness, complexity, and cumbersomeness of sound, added to the motion picture in the late 1920s. It was no longer possible for individuals or groups of friends to shoot on weekends, registering images as they found or created them, cutting them together in the evenings using only a pair of rewinds and a splicer, and screening the completed film at a local ciné-club. Now the big studios, with soundstages and synchronous

Rain (Holland, 1929, Joris Ivens). **Museum of Modern Art Film Stills Archive**

sound recording apparatus, exercised complete domination, and not only over production but over distribution and exhibition as well.

Perhaps at least as contributive to the death of the avant-garde were changing intellectual and artistic interests and attitudes. If the twenties were "roaring" and frivolous, they also nurtured aesthetic innovation. The notion of art for the sake of art, with emphasis on formal experimentation, prevailed in influential circles. The intellectual preoccupations of the thirties, in contrast, were markedly social and political. This decade included a worldwide depression, the rise of fascism, and other misfortunes that culminated in a second world war. In the thirties, art for the sake of society became a rallying cry, and the documentary film replaced the avant-garde film at the center of intellectual and artistic life in a number of countries.

Before making *Rain*, Joris Ivens had been involved in the politics of the international student movement and had participated in workers' demonstrations, which strengthened his leftward leanings. In his subsequent films Ivens moved away from formal experimentation toward social problems posed in a realistic style. In 1929 and 1932 he visited the Soviet Union. From that point on his films would be made in support of projects on the political left. His work will be encountered again in subsequent chapters, especially chapter six.

Ruttmann, too, moved from the avant-garde to the political, but in a different direction. In the late 1930s he lent his talents to the Nazi propaganda ministry. He served as adviser to Leni Riefenstahl on the editing of her massive *Olympia* (1938), which celebrated the Olympic games held in Berlin in 1936 and subtly supported certain aspects of Nazi mythology. In 1940 Ruttmann made *Deutsche Panzer* (*German Tanks*) and recorded on film the German occupation of France. The following year he was killed while covering the Russian front for a newsreel.

But of the three city-symphonists, Alberto Cavalcanti is the most neatly symbolic figure of transition. He moved from the French avant-garde of the 1920s to the British documentary of the 1930s. Cavalcanti's documentary work will be dealt with in the next chapter.

In concluding this chapter two points can be made about the relationship between British documentary and the avant-garde. One is that in its time, British documentary was considered avant-garde, too, and included much experimentation with new forms and techniques as well as with new subjects and purposes. The other is that if it is thought of as an artistic movement, as it can be, British documentary is remarkable within the history of twentieth-century art movements for lasting some twenty years, its influence spreading internationally and extending down to this day. The formal experimentation was encouraged partly to attract artistically talented young persons to documentary filmmaking and partly to find ways in which social arguments could be made most appealing and persuasive. British documentary continued the avant-garde experimentation with shapes in movement; the emphasis of the Soviets and the avant-gardists on machines continued in Britain. While the addition of sound helped end the continental avant-garde, it increased the potency of documentary, spoken commentary becoming one of its hallmarks. British documentary led the way in the creative use of sound in relation to image.

Films of the Period

1921

Mannahatta (U.S., Charles Sheeler and Paul Strand)

1926

Melody of the World (Germany, Walther Ruttmann)
Ménilmontant (France, Dimitri Kirsanoff)
Rien que les heures (France, Alberto Cavalcanti)

1927

Berlin: Symphony of a Great City (Germany, Ruttmann)
The Bridge (Netherlands, Joris Ivens)

1928

La Tour (*The Eiffel Tower*, France, René Clair)
La Zone (France, Georges Lacombe)

1929

Finis Terrae (France, Jean Epstein)
The Man with a Movie Camera (USSR, Dziga Vertov)
Rain (Netherlands, Ivens)

Books on the Period

Aitkin, Ian, *Alberto Cavalcanti: Realism, Surrealism and National Cinemas.* Trowbridge, Wilts.: Flicks Books, 2000.

Bakker, Kees, ed., *Joris Ivens and the Documentary Context.* Ann Arbor: University of Michigan Press, 2000.

Böker, Carlos, *Joris Ivens, Film-Maker: Facing Reality.* Ann Arbor, MI: UMI Research Press, 1981.

Delmar, Rosalind, *Joris Ivens: 50 Years of Film-making.* London: British Film Institute, 1970.

Ivens, Joris, *The Camera and I.* New York: International Publishers, 1969.

Manvell, Roger, ed., *Experiment in the Film.* London: Grey Walls Press, 1949.

Rees, A. L., *A History of Experimental Film and Video.* London: British Film Institute, 1999.

Chapter Five

Institutionalization: Great Britain, 1929–1939

While documentary filmmaking was beginning in the 1920s—in America with films about tribal societies (*Nanook of the North* and *Grass*); in the Soviet Union with indoctrinational newsreels ("Kino-Pravda") and epics (*The Fall of the Romanov Dynasty* and *Turksib*); and in Western Europe with the city symphonies (*Rien que les heures* and *Berlin: Symphony of a Great City*)—the conceptual origins of British documentary were also being formulated—but not in Britain, and not in film. John Grierson later remarked that "The idea of documentary in its present form came originally not from the film people at all, but from the Political Science school in Chicago University round about the early twenties."

Background and Underpinnings

Grierson, founder and leader of the British documentary movement, was a Scot. Born in 1898 and raised near Stirling, he was strongly influenced from an early age by the Scottish labor movement and what was then called "Clydeside socialism," emanating from the working-class district along the Clyde River in Glasgow. Most of World War I he spent in the navy. When he was mustered out in 1919 he entered Glasgow University with other returning veterans.

Upon graduation in 1923 Grierson taught briefly in Newcastle-on-Tyne. While there he obtained a Rockefeller fellowship to pursue graduate research into public opinion and the mass media in the United States. He set sail for America in 1924.

He had chosen the University of Chicago as his base because of its distinguished social science faculty. He also knew and admired the work of Chicago writers such as Sherwood Anderson, Ben Hecht, and Carl Sandburg. He was fascinated by the newness and originality of American culture and by the ways in which Europeans were being changed into Americans.

John Grierson in the 1930s. Museum of Modern Art Film Stills Archive

This assimilation of the foreign-born into American culture, and the role the popular press played in their education, occupied much of Grierson's attention. He spent more time on Halsted Street, with its polyglot population of Germans, Italians, Greeks, Russians, and Poles, than on the Midway campus of the university, he liked to say. As Grierson came to understand the matter, the tabloid newspapers—the Hearst press, like Chicago's *Herald-Examiner* and its imitators—provided more of these immigrants' education into citizenship than did the schools, churches, or government.

A book that strongly influenced his thinking at the time was Walter Lippmann's *Public Opinion*, published in 1922. In it Lippmann described how the earlier ideals of Jeffersonian democracy had been rendered inoperative. Originally the Virginia gentleman sitting on his veranda reading the two-week-old newspaper brought by packet from Philadelphia could make up his mind about the issues facing the nation and vote for a candidate running for public office who would represent his views. Since that time government had gotten big, distant, and complex. The citizen, feeling he could not keep abreast of the information necessary to participate in the decision-making process, had disassociated himself from government. Lippmann thought education was the only solution to the problem, but that it was too late for it to take effect in time to keep the democratic system viable. Grierson postulated that what was needed was to involve citizens in their government with the kind of engaging excitement generated by the popular press, which simplified and dramatized public affairs. As he traveled around the country, Grierson eventually met Lippmann. It was Lippmann, Grierson frequently acknowledged, who suggested to him that, rather than the press, he look into the movies. Perhaps they were the form best suited to turn citizens' attention to the decisions that needed to be made in common, and to provide them with a basic education in the factors to be considered.

Clearly the entertainment film was not readily available for these purposes. Two filmmakers and films not part of the Hollywood industry suggested to Grierson a way to harness the motion picture to the job of educating citizens. One filmmaker was Sergei Eisenstein. Though Grierson would not meet Eisenstein until a few years later, he did gain intimate knowledge of and respect for his *Battleship Potemkin* (1925) by helping prepare it for American release. The other filmmaker, Robert Flaherty, Grierson met sometime in 1925. It was to Flaherty's second film, *Moana* (1926), that Grierson first applied the term *documentary*.

When Grierson returned to England in 1927 he approached another man who would become enormously important in the development of the documentary film: Stephen (later Sir Stephen) Tallents, Secretary of the Empire Marketing Board. The EMB had been established in 1926 to promote the marketing of products of the British Empire and to encourage research and development among the member states. The broader purpose implicit from the outset was to substitute for the decaying military and political ties of empire the economic ones of a commonwealth of nations. Tallents saw quickly that the motion picture might be a valuable tool in this unique new governmental public relations endeavor, and that Grierson was exceptionally well qualified to initiate its use.

Employed at first in an unofficial advisory capacity, Grierson surveyed and reported on the use of film by governments abroad. He also set up for EMB personnel screenings of films that seemed to him to provide some suggestions

***Drifters,* Grierson's first film (U.K., 1929, John Grierson). Museum of Modern Art Film Stills Archive**

for what would become the documentary film. Along with straight informational and instructional shorts, there were the features of Flaherty, with their detail of the life of traditional cultures. There were the films of the U.S.S.R., which dramatized revolutionary events in order to indoctrinate and educate the Soviet people. There were the Hollywood super-westerns, *The Covered Wagon* and *The Iron Horse*, for example, which had attracted Grierson's attention as offering a kind of American screen epic. And, finally, there were the city symphonies of the European avant-garde, which made impressionist art out of urban realities.

The System

Empire Marketing Board

Following Grierson's research into film activities of other governments and the EMB screenings, he and Tallents succeeded in talking the Department of the Treasury into funding production of a film by the Empire Marketing Board. *Drifters* (1929) was the result, written, produced, directed, and edited by Grierson. A short feature in length, it dealt with herring fishing in the North Sea. Rather than follow its substantial success with another and then another film of his own, as he certainly might have done, Grierson chose to establish a collective filmmaking enterprise, a sort of workshop and schoolhouse, out of which the British documentary movement would emerge.

In 1930 the Empire Marketing Board Film Unit was established, with Grierson as its head. During the four years of its existence it made over one hundred films. Two of them still in active distribution will be discussed later.

Grierson's catchphrase for what the EMB films were designed to do was "to bring the Empire alive." He pursued this purpose by showing one and then another part of the empire (one region of Britain, one of its colonies, one of its industries) to the rest. He hoped that films of this sort would help citizens of the empire to more fully understand and appreciate one another, to perceive their interdependencies and value them, and to create a more coherent civic whole.

In the production of the EMB films Grierson involved dozens of young people, mostly upper middle class and well educated (many at Cambridge University), who were used to being listened to, as Grierson once put it. They learned not only filmmaking but the sort of social commitment that motivated Grierson. What he wanted films to do was to make the state and the society function better. He thought that collective effort, cooperation, and understanding could lead to a better world—not only better food and better housing, better teeth and better schools, but a better spirit—a sense of being part of a valuable society with space still left for individual satisfactions and eccentricities.

Those who came through this informal but rigorous schooling at the Empire Marketing Board included, roughly in the order of their hiring, Basil Wright, Paul Rotha, Arthur Elton, Edgar Anstey, and Stuart Legg. Harry Watt came later, as did Humphrey Jennings. Alberto Cavalcanti joined the group as a sort of coproducer and coteacher with Grierson. They were paid so little it was laughable, or perhaps weepable at the time, but they were all caught up in the excitement of art put to social use. Each had special talents and interests: Wright's were poetic, Elton's technological and scientific, Legg's political, and so on. After absorbing what Grierson had to offer and developing deep and lasting loyalties to his causes and to himself, they could (and did) move out into the world filming for other sponsors, forming other units, training other filmmakers, while still working for a common cause.

Concerned with creating filmmakers, Grierson was also concerned with creating audiences for his kind of film. Though documentaries were sometimes shown in theaters, theatrical showings were limited. The film industry resisted government filmmaking; distributors and exhibitors said the public didn't want documentaries. In answer, Grierson developed a method of nontheatrical distribution and exhibition. It began with afternoon screenings at the Imperial Institute in London, expanded to include the Empire Film Library for the free loan of 16mm prints of films by mail, and, later, at the General Post Office, came to include traveling projection vans going out into the countryside.

In order to build audience support, film critics on the major papers were recruited on behalf of the movement, and Grierson and his colleagues wrote and lectured tirelessly. They were instrumental in founding and guiding three successive journals—*Cinema Quarterly, World Film News*, and *Documentary News Letter*—which served as house organs for the documentary.

If Grierson didn't do it all himself, it was mainly his leadership and his manifold activities that brought British documentary into being and caused it to grow in its influence. The movement developed a powerful, coherent energy, with Grierson able to direct, to a remarkable extent, the uses to which that energy was put.

General Post Office

In 1933, at the depth of the Depression, the Empire Marketing Board was terminated on grounds of necessary government economy. Tallents moved to the General Post Office as its first public relations officer, on condition that he could bring the EMB Film Unit and the Empire Film Library with him.

A vast enterprise, the GPO handled not only the mail but the telephone, wireless broadcasting, a savings bank, and a whole host of government services. Here the subjects of the films were reduced from the exoticism and drama inherent in the far-flung reaches of empire available at the Empire Marketing Board to such subjects as the picayune detail of mail delivery (*Six-Thirty Collection*, 1934; *Night Mail*, 1936). "One remembers looking at a sorting office for the first time," wrote Grierson, "and thinking that when you had seen one letter you had seen the lot."

Designed to increase respect for the work of the GPO, by the population at large and by the GPO workers themselves, one approach the GPO Film Unit took to fulfill its obligations to its new sponsor was to stress the fact that post office services provided the means of modern communication. And some drama was found, though occasionally by stretching beyond what might properly be seen as post office concerns (*Song of Ceylon*, 1934; *Coal Face*, 1935). Out of the more than one hundred films made by the General Post Office Film Unit came some lovely and lasting ones. Major British documentaries of the thirties will be discussed shortly.

Private Sponsorship

Growing restive within the constraints of government budgets and departmental requirements, Grierson began to reach out to private industry as an additional source of funding. He must have been remarkably persuasive in talking industrial leaders into taking his own broad view. Not only did he find sponsors, he convinced them to eschew advertising in favor of backing films in the public interest—that is to say, films whose subjects Grierson thought needed attention. The oil industry was especially receptive.

Out of a report he made for Shell International on the potential uses of film came the Shell Film Unit, highly regarded for its films on scientific and technological subjects. Edgar Anstey was first head of the Shell Unit. He was succeeded by Arthur Elton, who maintained a lifelong connection with films sponsored by the oil industry and developed great skill as a maker of expository films on technical subjects.

Grierson also succeeded in getting the gas industry to back an annual film program. The group of films resulting were intended to increase general awareness of problems of pressing concern, to provoke discussion of them, and to suggest attitudes that might contribute to their solutions (*Housing Problems*, 1935; *Enough to Eat?*, 1936). Some of them will be discussed in the following section.

With documentary growing apace, private units were being formed by alumni of the EMB and GPO units to make films for the emerging nongovernment sponsors. In 1937 Grierson resigned from the GPO to set up a central coordinating and advisory agency to put sponsors in touch with producers (and the other way around), oversee production, plan promotion and distribution, and the like. Film Centre was the organization he (with Arthur Elton and Stuart Legg) established for that purpose in 1938.

The British system of documentary financing, production, and distribution became a model for subsequent developments in other countries. Many foreign visitors came to London to look into this new use of film—especially from the commonwealth nations and the colonies—and in 1937 Paul Rotha went on a six-month missionary expedition to the United States to show British documentaries and spread the documentary gospel. At the New York World's Fair of 1939 British documentaries were shown to sizable audiences with evident success.

The Films

Some sixty filmmakers working within what is here called the British documentary system made over three hundred films between 1929 and 1939. Three main lines of subject/purpose/style emerged roughly in the order in which they are dealt with below. First, following *Drifters* (1929), were the documentaries that undertook to interpret one part of the empire—or one region of Britain, one of its industries, or one of the government services—to the population at large. Often poetic and experimental, this group included such films as *Industrial Britain* (1933), *Granton Trawler* (1934), *Song of Ceylon* (1934), and *Coal Face* (1935).

Drifters, Grierson's first film, was the only one of the hundreds of films with which he was associated in one way or another that he completely controlled creatively. It has a simple narrative structure. The herring fishermen board their trawlers in the harbor, sail to the North Sea banks, lay the nets, haul in the fish in the midst of a storm, and race homeward to auction the catch at quayside. Rather than evidence of creative genius, it more nearly represents the work of a brilliant synthesist who had absorbed what was at hand to make the kind of film he wanted to see made. In it are reflections of Flaherty's *Nanook of the North*, with brave men eking out their existence in the face of the elements. Eisenstein's *Battleship Potemkin* is even more heavily called upon. In *Drifters*, the loving long takes of a Flaherty are cut up and banged together in Eisensteinian montage to provide a modern dynamism, and the individual accomplishments of Nanook are replaced by the collective efforts of a crew, as in *Potemkin*.

It is unlike both sources in certain respects, however. Instead of the exotics of Flaherty or the heroics of the Soviets, the drama of *Drifters* is in the everyday workday. By ending the film with the fish being sold at market, Grierson sets the fishermen's work firmly within the context of economic actualities of contemporary Britain. It was an unusual, perhaps unique, instance in British cinema up to that point in which work had been given this sort of importance and members of the working class presented with dignity rather than as comic relief.

Industrial Britain establishes its thesis at the outset: Though traditional ways of work have changed over the centuries, the success of British industry rests on the skill of its craftsmen. "The human fact remains, even in this machine age, the final fact," the commentator intones. To produce it Grierson invited Flaherty to England. Though given a lot of film, Flaherty shot it all on the lovely images of traditional craftsmen (glassblowers) and ancient crafts (pottery). The individual faces and gestures that appear ("Look at those hands," exclaims the commentator) are like *Moana* in fragments. Then an intertitle in large letters, *STEEL*, advances toward us, accompanied by portentous music. This unexpectedly announces what becomes in effect a separate film, making the point of bigness, collectivity, and internationalization—clearly Grierson's contribution. If *Industrial Britain* represents the contrast between these two filmmakers' approaches, the commentator's stilted delivery and the clichéd stock music (including bits of Beethoven) are at odds with both. It was made before the film unit had its own sound recording facilities. Nonetheless *Industrial Britain*, along with *Drifters*, was the most successful and generally liked film to come out of the Empire Marketing Board.

Granton Trawler can be thought of as a shorter version of *Drifters*. It, too, is about herring fishing but lyric rather than epic in its intentions and form. Grierson himself shot it on a busman's holiday in the North Sea. Edgar Anstey edited it under Grierson's supervision (as he had *Industrial Britain*). Later Cavalcanti added sound. The sound track is made up of the rhythmic thumping of the ship's engines, the creaking of its rigging, the cries of gulls, the harsh metallic noise of a winch playing out cable, muffled shouts of the men as they pull in the nets, a repeated fragment of a plaintive tune played on an accordion and another whistled, and random and mostly unintelligible comments from members of the crew. There is no commentary. The sounds were all postrecorded, imitated, in fact, in the studio. (One of the "fishermen's" voices is Grierson's.)

Granton Trawler (U.K., 1934, John Grierson). **Museum of Modern Art Film Stills Archive**

Simple as it is, the track is a remarkably strong component of the picture. This montage of seemingly natural sounds arbitrarily modified and arranged is what would come to be called *musique concrète*. Sounds are laid over a succession of impressionistic views of parts of the ship, the fishermen's activities, and the shifting horizon, which becomes vertiginous in high seas. It is as if the makers of the film, and therefore the viewers, are standing on the trawler looking about as their eyes are led to one thing or another while their ears register certain sounds. Not only was it an aesthetic experiment ahead of its time, it represents the kind of filmic poetry that can be achieved by a stylized rendering of reality completely controlled by the maker(s).

Song of Ceylon, Basil Wright the principal creator, is one of the accepted masterpieces of documentary. Sponsored by the Ceylon Tea Propaganda Board (Ceylon today is Sri Lanka), it is first of all remarkable in being so fully and freely a work of art while doing so little to sell the sponsor's product, perhaps even subverting its main goals. It may be even more remarkable, within the body of early British documentary, as a highly personal work, which, furthermore, emphasizes matters of the spirit. It is a moving hymn to a native people, their

The Song of Ceylon, Wright's account of the culture in the country now called Sri Lanka, is a work of art that perhaps subverts the sponsor's intended purposes (U.K., 1934, Basil Wright). **Museum of Modern Art Film Stills Archive**

work, their ways, and their values in conflict with imposed requirements of modern commerce.

Formally, in aesthetic terms, *Song of Ceylon* is the most complex and sophisticated artwork of British documentary of the 1930s. Though it contains exquisite images of a golden time and place, not unlike those of Flaherty's Samoa in *Moana,* Wright's discovered Eden has a discordant note accompanying it.

The commentary is drawn from a 1680 book on Ceylon by the traveler Robert Knox. It provides an appreciative description of traditional life, which we see and also hear in reverberating gongs, native music, and rhythmic chanting to the dancing. In the third sequence, entitled "The Voices of Commerce," the discord erupts. Images of the indigenous and traditional are here accompanied by deep whistles of seagoing freighters, Morse code beeping on the wireless, English voices dictating business letters and listing stock market quotations. This medley of sound, plus a musical score suggesting an Eastern modality composed and conducted by Walter Leigh, was supervised by Cavalcanti. In addition to Wright's principal role, Leigh, Cavalcanti, and Grierson, to one extent or another, were all involved in the creation of the whole, which can astonish and delight audiences as much today as it did when first shown.

Coal Face (U.K., 1935, Alberto Cavalcanti). At a time when coal mining was the basic industry of Britain, Brazilian-born Cavalcanti offers a sense of the lives dependent on the mines in an experimentation of sight and sound.

Coal Face, mainly Cavalcanti's creation, continued the formal experimentation with sound in relation to sight, though this time as an exalted tribute to the lives of British miners. Added to Grierson and Cavalcanti on its crew were the poet W. H. Auden and the composer Benjamin Britten, who worked together and separately on subsequent documentaries. *Coal Face* is an evocative combination of factual information laid over haunting images drawn from the coal-mining regions, of harsh modern music with piano and percussion prominent, of choral speech, which at one point ascends into a kind of keening, and of snatches of miners' talk and whistling. The drabness and hardship that mark the men's lives are evident, along with their resilience, courage, and dignity—all heightened by the poetry of Auden recited and sung by the women's chorus. Though the commentary ends with the statement "Coal mining is the basic industry of Britain," the last images we see are of an individual miner walking against a background of mining village and pithead at evening.

The second line of British documentary, which began in the mid-thirties, consisted of calling public attention to pressing problems faced by the nation; of insistence that these problems needed to be solved; and of suggestions about their causes and possible solutions. Such matters sometimes involved differing

Housing Problems (U.K., 1935, Arthur Elton and Edgar Anstey). **Museum of Modern Art Film Stills Archive**

political positions and in any case did not relate directly to the concerns of the Post Office. These were the films for which Grierson stepped outside the GPO to enlist sponsorship from large private industries. The subjects included slums (*Housing Problems*, 1935), malnutrition among the poor (*Enough to Eat?*, 1936), air pollution (*The Smoke Menace*, 1937), and the shortcomings of public education (*Children at School*, 1937). These films consisted of reportage and argument. Making much use of stock shots and newsreel footage, they were given coherence and rhetorical effectiveness through editing and voice-over commentary.

Unlike the earlier British documentaries, these films are journalistic rather than poetic; they seem quite inartistic, in fact. Yet they incorporate formal and technical experiments. Most notable among these is the direct interview—with slum dwellers in *Housing Problems*, for example—presaging the much later cinéma-vérité method.

Sponsored by the British Commercial Gas Association, *Housing Problems* was made by Arthur Elton, Edgar Anstey, John Taylor, and Ruby Grierson (John's youngest sister). It begins by presenting the problems and what they look like— "a typical interior of a decayed house"—with a housing expert commenting (voice-over) on how badly the housing functions. Then the film commentator (also voice-over) says, "And now for the people who have to live in the slums." The man we see (no interviewer appears; the interviewees talk directly to the camera) observes that where he lives they "haven't room to swing a cat around" and describes how uncomfortable and unhealthy his apartment is; two of his children have died. A Mrs. Hill tells us "the vermin in the walls is wicked [shots of cockroaches crawling on walls are cut in] and I tell ye we're fed up!"

The commentator says, "The more enlightened public authorities have been applying themselves to clearing away slums with energy." We see models of new types of housing, one of them of a housing development at Leeds. "And now let's have a word with Mrs. Reddington," who is living in one of the new housing developments. She tells us how pleased her family is with their new quarters; they especially like the new bathroom.

Set forth in this bald way *Housing Problems* may not seem the innovation it in fact was. Its combination of voice-over housing authority and film commentator with onscreen interviews, of stock footage with models and fresh-shot material, established the basic format and technique of much later television documentary. The spoken word is used to provide information and analysis and to allow persons to reveal themselves more fully and colorfully than was altogether possible in silent film. The intentions of *Housing Problems,* and certainly its effect, are quite different from those of *Nanook.* "Kino-Pravda," on the other hand, would have benefited from spoken commentary and spontaneous dialogue.

Released shortly after *Housing Problems,* it was *Night Mail* (1936) that started the third trend—the narrative. Cavalcanti and Harry Watt were the leaders in this new tendency. Watt would go on in a direct line of increasing narrative elements. In *The Saving of Bill Blewitt* (1937) he shaped documentary ingredients of location shooting, nonactors, and sponsor's message into plot, character, and theme. With *North Sea* (1938) he reached a peacetime height in realistic use of story. This line led directly to the wartime British semidocumentary feature, a fusion of fact and fiction. Essentially a contribution of the 1940s, it is dealt with in chapter seven. Judging from the evidence of Watt's subsequent films, it is his directorial style that is dominant in *Night Mail,* though he shares director's credit with Basil Wright.

Night Mail is the most celebrated of Watt's prewar films. Following the passage of a postal train from London to Glasgow, it is a prime example of "drama on the doorstep," to use the Grierson phrase—everyday and close to home, yet engaging and lasting. It may be the ultimate blend of Grierson's ethic (social purposes) and aesthetic (formal properties). In any case, it is a paradigm of propaganda so intertwined with art that the viewer experiences pleasure while absorbing the message (painlessly, effortlessly, and probably even unconsciously). What this film is saying is simply that (1) mail delivery is a large and complicated undertaking requiring the attention of the national government on behalf of all of us; (2) this government service is a splendid thing involving speed, efficiency, and intricate processes faultlessly learned and carefully regulated; and (3) the government employees who perform these multifarious and interesting tasks for us are a pretty good bunch—patient and caring but not without an occasional irritability or a little joke.

Within this slight odyssey of a working journey, expository and poetic sequences alternate. The poetic interpolations include the rhythmic montage of mailbags being discharged and picked up by the speeding train, and the climb up into Scotland, "Past cotton grass and moorland boulder, shoveling white steam over her shoulder." These latter words are from bits of verse written by Auden. (Grierson himself speaks two sections after the train enters Scotland, including the final one; Stuart Legg speaks the rest.) As in *Coal Face*, the words are combined with music by Britten; sound supervision is again by Cavalcanti. Interlaced with Auden's poetry is a factual, statistical commentary, as if from the General Post Office itself, and the dialogue of the postal workers' conversations with one another while doing their jobs. This mélange of sound, almost as diverse in its components and complex in its assemblage as that of *Song of Ceylon*, accompanies the visuals in a manner that makes *Night Mail* a lively and seemingly effortless description and explanation of the workings of the postal train on its nightly run.

Grierson and Flaherty

In eighteenth-century England the essayist Joseph Addison, in his *Lives of the Poets*, complimented Alexander Pope by observing of his poetry that "New things are made familiar, and familiar things are made new." In the films of Robert Flaherty it seems clear that he was attempting to make the unfamiliar familiar; to discover and reveal, as he put it, what was distant and past. In the films produced under John Grierson, on the other hand, the attempt was to find new meanings and excitements in the familiar through applying the creative treatment of actuality, as Grierson said, to the close-to-home workaday modern world. Flaherty and Grierson represent two poles in the documentary tradition between which any documentary filmmaker still has to find a place. Incidentally, both men—the Irish American whom Grierson once described as "a sort of handsome blond gorilla" and the small wiry Scot—had considerable personal magnetism and charm. How extraordinary yet somehow appropriate that these two should have become friends and antagonists, loving each other while hating each other's ideas. Their archetypal arguments were carried on in long evenings of talk and drink on what Grierson once described as "a dialectical pub crawl across half the world."

Flaherty, the artist, was a practical man in many ways. Determined and persuasive, he could talk big business and big government into financing his artistic statements. His concern was with showing the world as he saw it, which is one way of understanding the artist's job; it is sometimes argued that this is the only thing the artist should be expected to do. The artwork may lead to social change but it is not created to effect that end. So it was with Flaherty.

Grierson, for his part, said, "I look on cinema as a pulpit, and use it as a propagandist." He was, however, an extremely discerning and sophisticated propagandist who realized the utility of beauty in selling ideas—and recognized it when he saw it, incidentally. He early wrote about painting and his reviews of fiction films are exceptionally perceptive, well informed, and articulate—including especially those of popular Hollywood features. Grierson's own film-making, however, was primarily concerned with social engineering—with making the institutions of society function better on behalf of all of us—and he used every means available, including art, to achieve that end. Artistic creativity in British documentary of the 1930s appeared mainly when it could contribute emotional depth to intellectual argument.

Grierson's goals were always social, economic, and political. He saw British documentary from the beginning as an antiaesthetic movement. Art for him was "the by-product of a job of work done"; not beauty as a good in itself or aesthetic experience as enriching and broadening. Nor was he much interested in documentaries that offered information or insights along with beauties, which, while they may have contributed to sympathetic understanding, did not attempt to lead the viewers to action.

Perhaps an understanding of the fundamental aesthetic divergence between the Flaherty and Grierson positions can be amplified by a short quotation from Frances Flaherty, acting as her husband's medium, and a long one from Grierson, summing up the relationship between Flaherty and himself as he saw it. Here is Mrs. Flaherty:

> A Flaherty film is not a documentary, because a documentary film is precon-ceived. The great documentary movement fathered by John Grierson is all pre-conceived for educational and social purposes. Hollywood preconceives for the box office. None of these is simply and purely, freely and spontaneously, the thing itself, for its own sake. In other words he had no axe to grind.

It is interesting, of course, that the films of the man frequently called the father of documentary are disassociated from that mode altogether by Mrs. Flaherty. The matter of whether Flaherty in fact had no preconceptions, no axes to grind, was discussed in chapter two.

Now to Grierson, and his views of Flaherty's position in relation to his own:

> The history of the documentary film so far as I personally have been concerned with it has derived in part from my own theoretical deviation from Flaherty; but I ought also to add that we have been the closest of friends for twenty years and that no difference of opinion has affected our complete dependence on each other. In the profoundest kind of way we live and prosper, each of us, by denoun-cing the other.

Flaherty's approach to documentary in *Nanook* and *Moana* in the early twenties was a naturalist's approach. He was in revolt against the synthetic dramas of Hollywood. He believed that the film camera was denying its destiny in shutting itself up inside the studios; that its destiny was to get about on the earth, and be the means of opening the end wall of the theater on the whole wide world. . . . All this, of course, was very sensible and exercised an enormous influence on those of us who were thinking our way to the film of reality.

The influence of Flaherty's outlook was the greater because of the highly refined personal talent he brought to his observation. No eye was clearer, nor, for that matter, more innocent. He was by nature a poet . . . He could see things with great simplicity, and everything he touched found added grace at his hands. . . . In any estimate, Flaherty has been one of the greatest film teachers of our day, and not one of us but has been greatly enriched by his example—and I shall add, but has been even more greatly enriched by failing to follow it.

I have said that Flaherty was innocent. He was all too innocent. His revolt was not just against the synthetics of Hollywood; there was at the same time a revolt more dangerous: against the very terms of our actual and present civilization. Flaherty's choice of themes was significant. It was primitive man in Labrador or primitive man in Samoa or primitive man in the Aran Islands, or primitive man in industry, or primitive man, in the significant person of romantic youth, taming elephants in India. Flaherty would be shocked all over again to hear me say so; for he would maintain, with his usual great distinction, that the beauties they enact are age-old beauties and therefore classical. I merely make the point that his people and his themes are noticeably distant from those which preoccupy the minds of mankind today, and that if they were not so notably distant Flaherty would make them so.

But there is a problem of the Eskimo that is all too close to our own problems, as our technological civilization marches northward in Asia and America and takes him in. His hunting grounds today are scientifically observed, and his economy is progressively planned. He is subjected to the white man's misunderstanding of polygamy. His clothes and his blankets most often come from Manchester, supplied by a department store in Winnipeg, which, incidentally, has the public health of the Eskimo on its conscience. Some hunt by motor boats, and some travel by air. They listen to fur prices over the radio, and are subjected to the fast operations of commercial opportunists flying in from New York. They operate tractors and bulldozers, and increasingly the northern lands, and with them the Eskimos who inhabit them, become part of our global concerns.

Our contrary approach to documentary has been so different as to appear sometimes all too practical and all too materialistic and, in the sense of plainsailing, all too plain. We have not denied the fine first principles of Flaherty's, though, but rather have given them a different application. We have struck out against every temptation, and not without a grim measure of self-discipline, against the attraction of both romance and commerce, to the here and now of our own society. We have sought not the residuum of the ancient beauties, but the beginnings of new ones in the somewhat unlikely milieu of the chaotic present. We have believed with persistence that the first and last place to find the drama of reality is in what men today are doing and thinking and planning and fighting for. We have indeed found our field of observation and the rough patterns of our work in the clash of forces inside our own metropolitan community.

Like Flaherty, who had been a geologist and explorer, Grierson came to film from another field: social science. Whereas Flaherty wanted to use film to discover and reveal little known people and places, Grierson wanted to use it to enlighten and shape the modern, complex, industrialized society in which he lived. Flaherty was a highly personal filmmaker who worked alone initially and always attempted to control every phase of the production of his few films. Grierson, who directed only one film himself, established documentary units within which dozens of other films were created. In *Industrial Britain* (1933), the credits for which read "Production Grierson-Flaherty," Flaherty came into brief contact with the early stage of British documentary. Then he went his individual way to make *Man of Aran* (1934), a project Grierson helped set up, incidentally, leaving Grierson to the production of and supervision of a host of other documentaries.

Grierson's Contribution

It is for his multifaceted, innovative leadership that Grierson is to be most valued. As a theoretician he articulated a basis for the documentary film, its form and function, its aesthetic and its ethic. As an informal teacher he trained and, through his writing and speaking, influenced many documentary filmmakers, not just in Britain but throughout the world. As a producer he was eventually responsible to one extent or another for thousands of films and played a decisive creative role in some of the most important of them. And for most of his professional life he was an adroit political figure and dedicated civil servant. Even when not on government payroll, Grierson's central concern was always with communicating to the people of a nation and of the world the information and attitudes he thought would help them lead more useful and productive, more satisfying and rewarding lives.

More than any other person, Grierson was responsible for the documentary film as it developed in the English-speaking countries. The use of institutional sponsorship, public and private, to pay for his kind of filmmaking, rather than dependence on returns from the box office, was one key innovation. A second, that complemented the first, was nontheatrical distribution and exhibition—going outside the movie theaters to reach audiences in schools and factories, union halls and church basements, and eventually on television.

The three hundred or so British documentaries made during the ten years between *Drifters* and Grierson's departure for Canada in 1939 and the system that spawned them became models for other countries. If many of those films were dull and transient in their significance—only the exceptions have been dealt with here—such an opinion would not have disturbed Grierson. His strategy involved a steady output of short films presenting a consistent social view—a constant reinforcement of certain attitudes, not unlike the approach of today's makers of television commercials. Each film dealt with a small piece of the larger argument. It may seem ironic that conservative institutions were talked into paying for what was overall and essentially the presentation of a socialist point of view. But the desperateness of the economic situation during the Depression had to be acknowledged even by the Tories in power. Perhaps the subject matter of the films about work and workers that Grierson talked them into sponsoring was, or was made to seem, obligatory.

The attitudes of those films were always positive; problems could be solved by combined good will and social action. Though never acknowledged publicly, it seems to be true that the films were seen primarily by the middle and upper classes rather than by the working classes whom they were mostly about. Opinion leaders were thus reached who may have been persuaded or at least encouraged by the films to take a Griersonian view of the world.

One of the requisites for the success of the Grierson enterprise was the notion of consensus. The documentary films did not advance partisan political positions; they stayed within what the two major political parties, Conservative and Labour, might agree upon. Nor did the documentary filmmakers attach themselves publicly to a political party. At the same time, the subjects and viewpoints evident in the steady flow may have contributed to some extent to the sweeping Labour victory in 1945, at the end of the war.

In any case, Grierson once hinted that he thought documentaries of the thirties had helped prepare the British people for the collective strength soon to be required of them in wartime. Perhaps without the documentary movement there might have been responses other than the heroic national effort that began once the bombs started to fall. Before dealing with World War II in Britain, however, let's have a look at the parallel, if ultimately contrasting, documentary development in the United States during the 1930s.

Films of the Period

1929

Drifters (John Grierson)

1933

Aero-Engine (Arthur Elton)
Contact (Paul Rotha)
Industrial Britain (Grierson and Robert Flaherty)

1934

Granton Trawler (Grierson and Edgar Anstey)
Shipyard (Rotha)

Song of Ceylon (Basil Wright)
Weather Forecast (Evelyn Spice)

1935

B.B.C.—The Voice of Britain (Stuart Legg)
Coal Face (Alberto Cavalcanti)
Housing Problems (Anstey and Elton)
Workers and Jobs (Elton)

1936

Enough to Eat? (Anstey)
Night Mail (Harry Watt and Wright)

1937

Line to Tschierva Hut (Cavalcanti)
The Saving of Bill Blewitt (Watt)
We Live in Two Worlds (Cavalcanti)

1938

North Sea (Watt)

1939

Men in Danger (Pat Jackson)
Transfer of Power (Geoffrey Bell)

Books on the Period

Aitkin, Ian, *Alberto Cavalcanti: Realism, Surrealism and National Cinemas*. Trowbridge, Wiltshire: Flicks Books, 2000.

Aitken, Ian, ed. *The Documentary Film Movement: An Anthology*. Edinburgh: Edinburgh University Press, 1998.

Aitken, Ian, *Film and Reform: John Grierson and the Documentary Film Movement*. London: Routledge, 1990.

Anstey, Edgar, "Development of Film Technique in Britain," *Experiment in the Film*, ed. Roger Manvell. London: Grey Walls Press, 1949, 234–265.

Arts Enquiry, The, *The Factual Film*. London: Oxford University Press, 1947.

Beveridge, James, *John Grierson: Film Master*. New York: Macmillan, 1978.

Commission on Educational and Cultural Films, *The Film in National Life*. London: George Allen and Unwin, 1932.

Ellis, Jack C., *John Grierson: A Guide to References and Resources*. Boston: G. K. Hall, 1986.

Ellis, Jack C., *John Grierson: Life, Contributions, Influence*. Carbondale: Southern Illinois University Press, 2000.

Grierson, John, *Grierson on Documentary*, ed. Forsyth Hardy. Berkeley: University of California Press, 1966.

Hardy, Forsyth, "The British Documentary Film," *Twenty Years of British Film 1925–1945*, eds. Michael Balcon et al. London: Falcon Press, 1947.

Hardy, Forsyth, *John Grierson: A Documentary Biography*. London: Faber and Faber, 1979.

Hogenkamp, Bert, *Deadly Parallels: Film and the Left in Britain 1929–39*. London: Lawrence and Wishart, 1986.

Lovell, Alan and Jim Hillier, *Studies in Documentary*. New York: Viking Press, 1972.

Low, Rachel, *The History of the British Film 1929–1939: Documentary and Educational Films of the 1930s*. London: George Allen and Unwin, 1979.

Low, Rachel, *The History of the British Film 1929–1939: Films of Comment and Persuasion of the 1930s*. London: George Allen and Unwin, 1949.

Macpherson, Don, in collaboration with Paul Willemen, eds., *Traditions of Independence: British Cinema in the Thirties*. London: British Film Institute, 1980.

Orbanz, Eva, *Journey to a Legend and Back: The British Realistic Film*. Berlin: Verlag Volker Spiess, 1977.

Petrie, Duncan and Robert Kruger, eds., *A Paul Rotha Reader*. Exeter, UK: Exeter University Press, 1999.

Rotha, Paul, *Documentary Diary: An Informal History of the British Documentary Film, 1928–1939*. New York: Hill and Wang, 1973.

Rotha, Paul, *Rotha on the Film*. London: Faber and Faber, 1958.

Sussex, Elizabeth, *The Rise and Fall of British Documentary: The Story of the Film Movement Founded by John Grierson*. Berkeley: University of California Press, 1975.

Swann, Paul, *The British Documentary Film Movement, 1926–1946*. Cambridge: Cambridge University Press, 1989.

Watt, Harry, *Don't Look at the Camera*. London: Paul Elek, 1974.

Chapter Six

Institutionalization: United States, 1930–1941

I n Great Britain, documentary began in order to meet certain needs of the government. Alongside the Grierson movement was a small production effort carried out on the political far left. In 1934 the (British) Workers' Film and Photo League was formed. It produced "Workers' Newsreels" (which lasted to a fourth edition before ending in 1935), *March Against Starvation* (1936), and subsequent "story documentaries." This production never attracted the attention of a wide public, nor did the filmmakers become involved with the mainline documentary movement for the most part.

In the United States the situation was different. From its outset American documentary was deeply involved with political positions, generally on the left, and faced up to the central issues of the 1930s, including the Depression, unemployment and poverty, unionism, and the growing threat of fascism abroad. U.S. Marxist groups began making films in the early thirties. In the mid-thirties "The March of Time" series, an offshoot of *Time* magazine, began. At the same time federally sponsored documentary production commenced. In the late thirties large-scale nongovernment documentaries took their place alongside the government ones. These four developments will be dealt with in this chapter.

Film on the Left

In 1930 the (U.S.) Workers' Film and Photo League was established in New York City. Its goal was to train filmmakers and photographers to produce media material that would present the "true picture" of life in the United States, that is, from the Marxist point of view—a picture not revealed by the news services, the newsreels, or the capitalist press. Among its listed advisors or associates were Margaret Bourke-White and Ralph Steiner, photographers, the former subsequently worked for *Life* magazine, the latter became a documentary filmmaker;

77

Elia Kazan, actor and later stage and screen director; Elmer Rice, playwright; Burgess Meredith and James Cagney, actors; and Slavko Vorkapich, film theorist and montage expert. The Film and Photo League (it dropped Workers' from its title, as did the League in London) produced such topical films as *Winter* (1931), *Hunger* (1932), and *Bonus March* (1932).

An increasing schism in this leftist group developed between those who wanted to stick to straight agitprop newsreels and polemical films and those who thought the cause of revolution (or of social progress—political aims varied from person to person) could best be served by films with greater aesthetic value and emotional appeal. The latter contingent argued that through film artistry they might in fact be able to persuade the un-persuaded, whereas the standard and obvious forms of propaganda being used were mainly preaching to the already converted.

In 1934 three key members—Leo Hurwitz, Ralph Steiner, and Irving Lerner—left the Film and Photo League to form Nykino (evidently a Russianized abbreviation for New York cinema; a leftist film organization named Kino existed in London). Its *Pie in the Sky* (1934), by Elia Kazan, Molly Day Thatcher, Ralph Steiner, and Irving Lerner, became its first publicized release. It is a whimsical spoof of the promises of religion for life in the hereafter in place of food for present hunger on earth. Nykino would subsequently become Frontier Films, whose work will be dealt with later under Nongovernment Documentaries.

The March of Time

Like those developments on the political left that began with the Workers' Film and Photo League, another development, on the political right (or center at least), stood apart from the mainstream of American documentary but would be highly influential in relation to it—and to British and Canadian documentary as well. Entitled "The March of Time," this monthly film series offered a new and distinctive kind of screen journalism, a cross between the newsreel and the documentary. Sponsored by Time-Life-Fortune, Inc., headed by Henry Luce, it was preceded by a weekly radio series of the same title. Roy Larson, of *Time* magazine, was responsible for the initiation of both series. Louis de Rochemont became the principal creator of the film series. It was the American prototype for the "compilation documentary," pioneered by Esfir Shub in the Soviet Union (see chapter three).

"The March of Time" had the most substantial and sustained success of any documentary-like material prior to television. It was announced on movie marquees, sometimes appearing above the feature title. At its peak, in the late 1930s and the years of World War II, it was seen in the United States by over twenty million people a month in 9,000 theaters. It was distributed internationally as well.

League of Nations, from "The March of Time" series (U.S., 1936, Louis de Rochemont). Museum of Modern Art Film Stills Archive

Though originating from a conservative organization, the MOT was identified with a liberal stance, more so than *Time* magazine. This was particularly true on foreign affairs; on domestic issues the films tended to be more conservative or erratic. Still, while fiction features in the thirties ignored or dealt only covertly with the Depression, MOT acknowledged the breadlines, unemployment, and the political demagoguery it gave rise to (for example, *Huey Long,* 1935; *Father Coughlin,* 1935; *Strikebreaking,* 1935; *Unemployment,* 1937). Internationally, while the newsreels avoided controversial political and military developments, MOT tackled the machinations of Hitler, Stalin, Mussolini, and Tojo (as in *Nazi Conquest—No. 1,* 1938; *The Mediterranean—Background for War,* 1939; *Japan—Master of the Orient,* 1939; *Newsfronts of War—1940,* 1939).

Along with its energetic innovations, the success of "The March of Time" was fueled by the controversy it aroused and by its press-agentry. One of the most politically controversial films in the history of American cinema was MOT's *Inside Nazi Germany* (1938). In its sixteen minutes it examined in some detail the regimentation of the German people, the control and consolidation of national allegiances, and the preparations being made for future military and economic expansion. This was at a time when the majority of the American public was still strongly isolationist and the government maintained a careful impartiality.

The makeup for each issue of "The March of Time" was worked out in its early years and varied little, regardless of subject. The fixed format may have been necessitated by the pressures of monthly production with modest resources; it must also have come to seem desirable given the considerable popularity of the series in the form in which it was offered. One of the most important ingredients was the voice and delivery style of its commentator, Westbrook Van Voorhis. His "Voice of Time" (sometimes irreverently referred to as the "Voice of God") was deep and commanding, ominous and reassuring at the same time. Spoken words carried the weight of the communication; the footage (largely stock), music (obvious and clichéd), and sound effects (sparse and highly selective) were cut to them. Often the images were given their meaning by the words as part of "the dramatization of the news" that MOT practiced. An extreme close-up of part of a face and a mouth at a telephone becomes *An angry refusal*; laid over a wide-angle shot of a city street at night with only a few electric signs visible are the words *That evening Shanghai is tense* (both examples from *War in China*, 1937). Editing was the key. The pace is fast, with a hard rhythmic impact; a great deal of information is presented dramatically to capture the attention of the popcorn-munching Friday night audience.

Structurally, every issue has four parts, with titles announcing each part. The first establishes the magnitude and urgency of the problem being dealt with. The second offers a historical survey of its origins and causes. Part three presents the immediate complications, confirming its newsworthiness. The concluding part looks to the future, stressing that the problem is a matter for continuing and serious concern.

No doubt its unchanging style and approach (along with the competition of television and the rising costs of production) had something to do with the series's eventual demise in 1951. "The March of Time" remains, however, a noteworthy phenomenon in the history of American popular culture. Its influence has extended to much of the documentary and public affairs programs on television today.

Government Documentaries

The Film and Photo League and "The March of Time" were precedents of sorts, but documentary in the institutional or Griersonian sense—engaging and educating citizens in the affairs of the nation—began in June 1935, in Washington, D.C. At that time Rexford Guy Tugwell, head of the newly established Resettlement Administration, made a decision to use motion pictures to interpret the organization's program and objectives.

A former University of Chicago professor, Tugwell was one of the "brain trust" assembled by President Franklin Delano Roosevelt to implement his New Deal. Roosevelt gathered around him the best minds he could find—many of them from universities—to help solve the problems presented by the Depression. They were placed in a number of separate agencies, which often overlapped and competed with one another. The "alphabet soup" of those days included the

Pare Lorentz in the 1930s

NRA (National Recovery Administration), PWA (Public Works Administration), WPA (Work Projects Administration), and CCC (Civilian Conservation Corps). The Resettlement Administration was one of the entities clustered around the Department of Agriculture. It was intended to aid those farmers who were being forced off their land by low crop prices compounded by the dreadful drought in the West and Southwest that had caused the Dust Bowl.

Into Tugwell's office came a movie critic named Pare Lorentz, whose wife was vaguely related to the president. Lorentz was a combination of New York liberal (where he was established) and West Virginia populist (where he had been born and raised). He convinced Tugwell that what was needed was a new kind of dramatic/informational/persuasive movie. (Lorentz disliked the term *documentary* and much of Grierson's work in England as being too schoolteacherish. "Films of Merit" was Lorentz's label for what he would produce.)

Out of that conversation came *The Plow That Broke the Plains* (1936), an indictment of the lack of planning that had caused the Dust Bowl. In its present twenty-minute version, *The Plow* shows the historical origins of the problem and its then current magnitude and urgency. Originally an additional final sequence dealt with the "beltville communities" being proposed by the Resettlement Administration. These beltvilles were to be established adjacent to industrial towns and cities, such as Detroit. The idea was that the rural dispossessed, when moved there, would be able to farm small plots of land and work part-time in the factories. Shortly after the release of the film, the Resettlement Administration became part of the Department of Agriculture; subsequently its name was changed to the Farm Security Administration. The beltville concept was never fully realized and the final sequence of the film dealing with it was deleted.

Lorentz, who had no prior film production experience, wrote and directed *The Plow*. As cinematographers he hired Paul Strand, Ralph Steiner, and Leo Hurwitz. Strand and Steiner had backgrounds in still photography; all three had been active in the Film and Photo League. When they began shooting out in the field, with Lorentz remaining in Washington, they were frustrated by the lack of clarity in their instructions. To compensate for this, and to give them some guidelines for shooting, they drafted a script. The film as they conceived it was to be about the devastation of the land caused by exploitative capitalism. This was not an economic-political stance Lorentz was prepared to take (nor would the government have welcomed it) and dissension and cross-purposes resulted.

Lorentz hired an editor, Leo Zochling, to assist him, and with his help he learned to edit. He assembled the footage according to a rough outline and began writing the commentary. Virgil Thomson, whom he had known in New York, was hired to compose the score. Working together, in hours upon hours of shaping and reshaping, they combined images and music with spoken words and sound effects. It was Thomson's idea that his music should have an operatic balance with the rest of the filmic elements. In fact, his score—which exists virtually as he wrote it for the film as a suite in standard orchestral repertoire—tends to outweigh the visuals. Thomson was in full professional stride; Lorentz was learning filmmaking. Some of the score is drawn from traditional music, and the majority, which was newly composed, is in a style appropriate to the time and indigenous to the place being shown. Over the final sad spectacle of the caravans of Okie jalopies moving westward, a sort of sad passacaglia played by the brass is underscored by a slow tango beat, acknowledging the Hispanic heritage of the Southwest.

Unlike Grierson, who always determined in advance how his films would reach their audience, Lorentz had failed to set up distribution for the completed film. In his innocence he evidently had assumed that if he created a fine piece of work, a film of merit, others would be eager to acquire it for distribution. He might have been forewarned of the Hollywood film industry's resentment of government film production by the resistance he encountered in trying to obtain footage from fiction features of covered wagon trains. (It was finally only with the help of veteran director King Vidor that he obtained what he needed.) Accordingly, *The Plow That Broke the Plains* was not shown as widely as it might

The Plow That Broke the Plains (U.S., 1936, Pare Lorentz). **Museum of Modern Art Film Stills Archive**

have been. What distribution it had it received because of glowing reviews. Theater patrons would ask local exhibitors when the film was going to be shown. The Rialto Theatre in New York City publicized its showing by proclaiming it "The picture they dared us to show!"

Lorentz was discouraged by the inadequate distribution, exhausted from the hard work and frustration of production, and in debt for money he (and his wife) had invested in the film to complete it. (His original bid on the cost was an unrealistic $6,000.) In that dismal mood, he went to Tugwell's office to say good-bye. As part of his farewell he suggested another film he thought should be made—one about flooding in the Mississippi Valley. Lorentz's enthusiasm for this project convinced Tugwell to allow him to produce yet another government film, *The River* (1937), backed by the Farm Security Administration.

While the Resettlement Administration, which had sponsored *The Plow*, had intended to relocate people forced off their land, the Farm Security Administration was attempting to keep them on their farms. *The River* became a compelling plea for national flood control and soil conservation. Whereas *The Plow* originally offered the beltville communities as alternatives to Dust Bowl deserts, *The River* showed the Tennessee Valley Authority as a way to make ravaged land and economically depressed regions viable. The latter film also counteracted the public relations campaign being conducted by private utilities to keep government out of electric power. While it is now generally agreed that the TVA was a remarkable and salutary instance of the government undertaking an activity hitherto in the hands of private corporations, it remains an experiment that has never been repeated.

Lorentz again wrote and directed. For *The River* the cinematographers were Stacy Woodard, Floyd Crosby, and Willard Van Dyke. Woodard had been producing a series of nature films entitled "The Struggle to Live." Crosby had worked on the Murnau-Flaherty *Tabu* (1931), would have a long association with Lorentz, and went on to fiction features (including *The Brave Bulls*, 1951, and *High Noon*, 1952). Van Dyke, who had studied still photography with Edward Weston, was marginally involved with political filmmaking on the left and would become a fine documentary maker in his own right. Though there was no political contention this time, there seems to have been the same uncertainty on the part of the cameramen (and maybe on the part of Lorentz) as to exactly what kind of footage was wanted. The score was again by Thomson, based almost entirely on hymns ("Yes, Jesus Loves Me"), folk songs ("Go Tell Aunt Rhody"), and popular tunes ("Hot Time in the Old Town Tonight"). The orchestral suite arranged from *The River* is less often performed than *The Plow* suite, possibly because its music is more fully integrated with the visuals; the edited visuals are its equal in aesthetic weight.

Lorentz's lyric commentary for this film became classic. (Its free verse litany of names of rivers and towns has often been imitated and sometimes parodied.) For example:

> We built a hundred cities and a thousand towns:
> St. Paul and Minneapolis,
> Davenport and Keokuk,
> Moline and Quincy, Cincinnati and St. Louis, Omaha and Kansas City. . . .

Or, again:

> Down the Judith, the Grand, the Osage and the Platte;
> The Rock, the Salt, the Black and the Minnesota;
> Down the Monongahela, the Allegheny, Kanawha and Muskingum;
> The Miami, the Wabash, the Liking and the Green;
> The White, the Wolf, the Cache, and the Black;
> Down the Kaw and Kaskaskia, the Red and Yazoo.
> Down the Cumberland, Kentucky and the Tennessee. . . .

It seems possible that *The River* has been seen by as many people as any film ever made. Lorentz this time took pains to set up proper distribution and it was shown in more than 5,000 theaters. It has remained in active nontheatrical distribution ever since—shown in schools, to various sorts of adult groups, and on public television—not just as a historical curiosity but as a significant statement about an ongoing ecological problem and as an epic poem. The only negative criticism, leveled at it frequently, is that following its moving evocation of

A scene from *The River* **(U.S., 1937, Pare Lorentz)**

the history of this big country, its people, and its natural resources, it adds a commercial. The last six minutes on the TVA are much weaker; even the photographic quality drops, with some stock shots being used. Unlike the best of the British documentaries, in which the propaganda becomes an indissoluble part of the whole, here the sponsor's message seems tacked on. The first twenty-four

A devastation scene in *The River*. **Museum of Modern Art Film Stills Archive**

minutes are unrivaled, however. Lavishly praised at the time of its release, *The River* has come to be considered a masterpiece of the screen.

On the basis of its success Lorentz was able to persuade the Roosevelt administration (with the backing of the president himself, who is reported to have loved the film) to set up the United States Film Service in 1938. It was intended to make films propagandizing the policies and activities of all departments of government.

The first of the U.S. Film Service productions was *The Fight for Life* (1940), produced for the U.S. Public Health Service. Written and directed by Lorentz, it was based on a book by Dr. Paul de Kruif, a writer who popularized scientific and medical subjects. It is about the work of the Chicago Maternity Center in providing prenatal care for mothers and delivering babies in the homes of poor families. It was photographed by Floyd Crosby. The music, composed by Louis Gruenberg (who shortly before had written the score for John Ford's *Stagecoach*), was innovative, including the use of blues while the young doctor wanders the city streets at night. Its cast mixed nonactors with actors, including Will Geer (subsequently of the long-running television series *The Waltons*).

Feature-length, half dramatic and half documentary, *The Fight for Life* is what would come to be called a semidocumentary. It was made a little before Harry

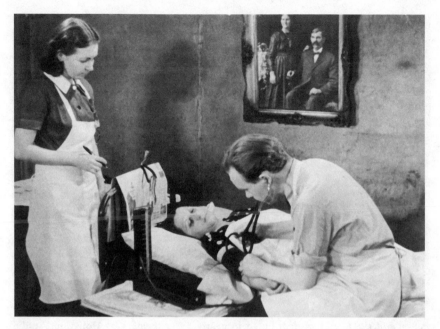

The Fight for Life (U.S., 1940, Pare Lorentz). **Museum of Modern Art Film Stills Archive**

Watt's *Target for Tonight* (1941), the British wartime prototype for the form (dealt with in chapter seven). It might be considered a precursor to Hollywood postwar semidocumentaries such as *The House on 92nd Street* (1945), *Boomerang* (1947), and *Call Northside 777* (1948). In attempting to heighten the drama and engage the emotions, Lorentz inadvertently made childbirth a frightening experience. When the film was completed and rushed to the White House for viewing on New Year's Eve 1939, Franklin Roosevelt showed little enthusiasm for it. Eleanor Roosevelt is said to have remarked in her gentle way, "Surely there's something good to be said about having a baby," having given birth to a number of sons herself. It was not very widely shown. In Chicago it was banned by the police censorship board, though it had been made there.

On the other hand, *Power and the Land* (1940), the next production, was distributed by RKO to nearly 5,000 theaters. It was so well received that it continued to be reissued nontheatrically into the late 1940s, with its maps being updated to show the continuing increase in the number of farms receiving electric power. It was produced for the Rural Electrification Administration and the Department of Agriculture. Joris Ivens, the Dutch documentarian living in the United States, directed, and Helen van Dongen, his then wife and expert documentary editor, edited. Cinematography was by Floyd Crosby and Arthur Ornitz; the commentary was written by poet Stephen Vincent Benet; musical score was by Douglas Moore, composer of the folk opera *The Ballad of Baby Doe*.

Power and the Land was distributed to nearly 5,000 theaters by Hollywood studio RKO (U.S., 1940, Joris Ivens). Museum of Modern Art Film Stills Archive

Power and the Land pursues its objective of persuading farmers to organize rural cooperatives to obtain government power by showing the Parkinson family on their farm in southwestern Ohio. We see them at work, before they have electricity and then afterward. The contrast in the greater ease and comfort electric power provides these decent and hardworking people with whom we have become acquainted is a simple and effective argument. At the same time, Ivens offers an affectionate picture of this family and their farm as it would strike a sensitive and sympathetic visitor. With deft and poetic strokes he documents for other cultures and future generations a kind of life and economy that no longer exists.

The next production, *The Land* (1941), was conceived and directed by an even more famous documentary pioneer, Robert Flaherty, returning to America after a decade in Britain. It, too, was edited by Helen van Dongen. Cinematography was by Irving Lerner, Douglas Baker, Floyd Crosby, and Charles Herbert; the music by English composer Richard Arnell; the commentary was written and read by Flaherty.

Produced for the Agricultural Adjustment Agency (AAA) of the Department of Agriculture, this became what the French would call a *film maudit* —a cursed film. Its initial purpose was along the lines of *The Plow That Broke the Plains* and *The River*: to encourage the careful and controlled use of our agricultural resources. During its production, United States foreign policy shifted from a strict

The Land (U.S., 1941, Robert Flaherty). **Museum of Modern Art Stills Archive**

neutrality in the beginning of the Second World War to support of the British standing alone against German aggression. A lend-lease program had been initiated and our promise to become "the breadbasket of democracy" required that agricultural production be increased by every means available. *The Land* works against itself (not unlike the earlier *Industrial Britain*, with Flaherty pursuing one line, Grierson another). The commentary argues that intelligent and scientific practices and modern machines will make the land ever more productive. The images, however, of the despoliation created by cutting down the timber and cultivating all of the available land, like those of *The Plow That Broke the Plains*, carry the dramatic weight. The visuals may represent Flaherty's true uneasiness concerning what he had discovered about the land and the people on it in this first film about his own country.

In any case, before *The Land* was completed, Congress—now alienated from the New Deal by Republican victories at the polls in 1940—decided that government film production was needless and, indeed, un-American. The U.S. Film Service was not exactly abolished, since it had never really been approved. It had worked out of the administrative branch, with funds allocated for individual films. Now, not only were no funds for the Film Service appropriated by Congress, legislation was passed that forbade tucking film production costs into other budgets. *The Land* was never shown in the theaters. Its single source for nontheatrical distribution was the Museum of Modern Art Film Library, where it could be obtained for film study purposes only—like the Nazi propaganda film *Triumph of the Will*.

The reasons offered by film scholar Robert Snyder in *Pare Lorentz and the Documentary Film* for the termination of the United States Film Service are these: (1) antagonism and antipathy in Congress toward the New Deal; (2) lack of support from the executive branch (Roosevelt was now preoccupied with international issues); (3) opposition by the public and Congress to propaganda activities by the government (portrayal of southwestern and western states as deserts in *The Plow That Broke the Plains* provoked considerable outcry at the outset); and (4) opposition from Hollywood.

In summarizing Lorentz's contributions, a number of things can be said. He established American precedent for the government use of documentaries, which would be continued during World War II (by the armed forces and the Office of War Information) and afterward (by the United States Information Agency). From Lorentz's efforts five large and important films resulted, the first three of which he directed: *The Plow That Broke the Plains, The River,* and *The Fight for Life.*

In *The Plow* and *The River* Lorentz developed an original personal style of documentary that also became a national style. (Similarities can be seen in films by others: *The City* [1939] and *And So They Live* [1940], for example, to be dealt with in the next section.) In his two mosaic patterns of sight (carefully composed images shot silently) and sound (symphonic music, spoken words, selected noises), no single element says much by itself. Together they offer a form and content resembling epic poems. They seem close to the attitudes of American populism and are rooted in frontier tradition. The sweeping views of a big country and the free verse commentaries with their chanted names and allusions to historic events make one think of Walt Whitman. The use of music is quite special, with composer Virgil Thomson participating more fully than usual in the filmmaking process.

In contributing two lasting masterpieces to the history of documentary, Lorentz joins a very select company: the artists of documentary. (Flaherty and Humphrey Jennings, the latter to be considered in chapter seven, would be other Anglophone members of such a group.) Some would argue that *The River* is the finest American documentary to date—aesthetically and in terms of expressing the American spirit. Lorentz's limitations appear most sharply in the light Grierson occasionally cast upon them. First, Lorentz relied on the impermanent partisan support of the party in power. He had the backing of President Roosevelt and the films were associated with the Democratic program. When the balance in Congress shifted to Republican, the United States Film Service was not allowed to continue. Second, even within that New Deal context, Lorentz opted for a few big films sponsored by agencies related to one department of government (four of the five films are on agricultural subjects) rather than many smaller films from

The City was a hit at the 1939 New York World's Fair (U.S., 1939, Ralph Steiner and Willard Van Dyke). Museum of Modern Art Film Stills Archive

various departments that would have broadened the base of sponsorship and made for a steady flow of communication. Third, he was creating art at public expense—making personal films à la Flaherty—with no real commitment to public service. Finally, Lorentz remained aloof in Washington. He made no efforts to seek sponsorship for documentary filmmaking outside the government. He had little connection with the New York City documentarians responsible for the nongovernmental documentaries of the 1930s (to be dealt with in the next section) even though some of them had worked with him on goverment films.

On the other hand, the situation here was not the same as in Britain. The government of the United States *is* highly partisan; one does not find the centuries-old tradition of public servants working outside the party in power as in England. If Lorentz could not establish an enduring film unit, he could not follow through on the other things Grierson called for. It is not clear whether Grierson could have done better in the U.S. than Lorentz did; Grierson's criticisms tend to ignore the central differences of government structure and practice.

However one chooses to look at the matter, the closing of the U.S. Film Service proved a great waste and inefficiency. Shortly after its demise, the United States entered World War II and government filmmaking on a vast scale had to be restarted from scratch.

Nongovernment Documentaries

Paralleling the work of Lorentz and the United States Film Service were the documentaries of private and commercial sponsorship. "The March of Time," already dealt with, was the most conspicuous success, playing in theaters from 1935 on with unrivaled popularity. In 1937 Nykino, discussed at the beginning of this chapter, metamorphosed into Frontier Films, which would represent those committed to art on behalf of social action rather than the more doctrinaire party-liners of the Film and Photo League.

Among the persons associated with Frontier Films, either actively or as advisors, were John Howard Lawson, Elia Kazan, Leo Hurwitz, Herbert Kline, Ralph Steiner, Joris Ivens, Malcolm Cowley, John Dos Passos, Lillian Hellman, Archibald MacLeish, Lewis Milestone, Clifford Odets, Willard Van Dyke, and Paul Strand. The mainstays were Strand, Hurwitz, and Steiner. Frontier Films intended to be an alternative to "The March of Time." Films produced under its auspices will be considered shortly.

The nongovernment documentaries of the 1930s offer a catalog of the most significant problems and issues of the time—with a bias to the left in their selection and treatment. The largest block of privately-sponsored documentaries exceeded "The March of Time"'s concern with the growing menace of fascism in Europe and of Japanese imperialist conquest in Asia. A number of films were made about the Spanish civil war (1936 to 1938), in which General Francisco Franco's Moorish legions, backed by Nazi Germany and Fascist Italy, were pitted against the Republican Loyalists aided by Communist Russia and volunteers from many nations. All of the American films supported the Loyalist cause. From Frontier Films came *Heart of Spain* (1937, Herbert Kline and Geza Karpathi) and *Return to Life* (1938, Henri Cartier-Bresson and Herbert Kline). From Contemporary Film Historians, Inc., formed by a group of writers that included John Dos Passos, Ernest Hemingway, Archibald MacLeish, and Lillian Hellman, came *The Spanish Earth* (1937).

The most ambitious and widely seen of the Spanish civil war films, *The Spanish Earth* was a short feature in length (54 minutes). Directed by Joris Ivens, cinematography was by John Ferno (born Fernhout), editing by Helen van Dongen. Narration was written and read by Ernest Hemingway; music arranged by Marc Blitzstein (composer of the opera *The Cradle Will Rock*) and Virgil Thomson, from Spanish folk melodies.

A slight narrative links the village of Fuentedueña to Madrid. A farm boy, Julian, serving in the Loyalist army, returns home from the city to the village on a three-day leave. The front—extending along a line west of the two locations—has different kinds of terrain and fighting: the open countryside of hills and farmland with infantry and tanks moving forward; Madrid, with artillery shelling by Loyalists and Rebels (as Franco's forces are called throughout) and aerial bombardment by the latter; and the road connecting Madrid and Valencia, with a crucial bridge subjected to attack and counterattack. The political positions represented are dealt with midway in the film, largely through commentary and paraphrasing of military and civilian leaders speaking to Loyalist gatherings in Madrid and Valencia.

The narration for the film is quite distinctive. Hemingway talks about the images we are seeing as if we were sitting together watching home movies. "I can't read German either," he says, as we see embossed words on pieces of a Junker bomber shot down by a Loyalist fighter plane. The Loyalists are identified as *the people*, as opposed to Franco and his foreigners—Germans, Italians, Moorish mercenaries, and the Civil Guard. Hemingway's words are supported by shots of people with close-ups of faces: soldiers, weeping women, children. The informality and democratic nature of this citizen army are evident, as well as their camaraderie and solidarity. We never see the Rebels; they remain a faceless enemy.

As for films dealing with China's defense against Japanese aggression, which began with the invasion of Manchuria in 1931 and continued until 1945, Frontier Films made *China Strikes Back* (1937). Harry Dunham directed; Jay Leyda and Sidney Meyers were among others involved in its production. This film offered sustained coverage of the Chinese 8th Route Army, its guerilla tactics, educational program, relations with the peasants, and efforts toward the unity of Free China against the invading Japanese. (This was the Communist force, with Mao Ze Dong among its leaders. At the time, the only Chinese political entity Americans knew of was Chiang Kai-shek and his supporters.) Contemporary historians produced *The Four Hundred Million* (1939), its title referring to the size of China's population. It was directed, shot, and edited, respectively, by the Dutch trio—Ivens, Ferno, and van Dongen. Commentary was written by Dudley Nichols (best remembered for his scripts of films directed by John Ford) and spoken by Fredric March. Music was composed by Hanns Eisler (who would flee the U.S. for East Germany in 1950).

Films were made about the Munich crisis of 1938, which was resolved by Prime Minister Neville Chamberlain of Great Britain agreeing with Reichkanzler Adolph Hitler that Germany might annex the Sudetanland section of Czechoslovakia—without interference from Britain. *Crisis* (1938), produced and directed by Herbert Kline, was codirected by the Czech Alexander Hackenschmied (who would become Hammid after emigrating to the United States). The same pair created *Lights Out in Europe* (1938). In 1940 "The March of Time" released a feature-length compilation entitled *The Ramparts We Watch*, summarizing the European situation.

As for nongovernment documentaries on domestic subjects, most of those had "progressive tendencies" and dealt with issues of particular interest to the political left. The 1930s were years of considerable labor unrest and progress, of union building and busting, and a number of films were made in support of unionism. For example, three were produced by Frontier Films. *People of the*

Native Land was the swan song of the American documentary on the political left
(U.S., 1942, Leo Hurwitz and Paul Strand). Museum of Modern Art Film Stills Archive

Cumberland (1938) is about an isolated community of pioneer English and Scottish ancestry working in the coal mines of Appalachia and their emergence from
poverty and backwardness to social consciousness and action. The work of Miles
Horton and the Highlander School is featured. The film was directed by Elia
Kazan and photographed by Ralph Steiner. *United Action* (1939) is a record of
the organization of the United Auto Workers-Congress of Industrial Organizations (UAW-CIO) and the strike against General Motors in Detroit in 1939.

The feature-length *Native Land* was Frontier Films' magnum opus (and swan
song). Production of it began in 1939 but it wasn't released until 1942. Based
almost entirely on the investigation and conclusions of the U.S. Senate Robert
Lafollette Committee on Civil Rights and on other labor documents, it dealt with
workers' rights and unionism, and was part actuality footage and part dramatization. Direction and script were by Leo Hurwitz and Paul Strand; cinematography
was by Strand; music by Marc Blitzstein. Paul Robeson narrated. Howard da
Silva, among the actors in the cast, played a pitiable labor spy in the pay of
management.

Municipal planning was another subject dealt with. *A Place to Live* (1941) is
a cogent little film about slum clearance in Philadelphia. *The City* (1939) is a

Willard Van Dyke (left) with Ralph Steiner in 1980 during the filming of *Conversations with Willard Van Dyke*, a film by Amalie R. Rothschild.

trenchant large one. A hit at the New York World's Fair of 1939, it was produced for the American Institute of Planners by American Documentary Films, set up by Ralph Steiner and Willard Van Dyke, who codirected and cophotographed the film. (When Van Dyke and Steiner left Frontier Films on ideological grounds this sponsored project left with them. That incident caused a serious and lasting breach among various filmmakers who had been involved with Frontier Films.) The scenario was by Henwar Rodakiewicz from an original outline by Pare Lorentz; the commentary was written by cultural historian Lewis Mumford and spoken by actor Morris Carnovsky. The music score was by Aaron Copland.

The City promotes the concept of the planned greenbelt communities detached from urban centers. It has a five-part historical organization: (1) In the Beginning—New England (a rural community dating from the eighteenth century); (2) The Industrial City—City of Smoke (Pittsburgh); (3) The Metropolis—Men into Steel (Manhattan); (4) The Highway—The Endless City (Sunday traffic congestion in New Jersey and the environs of New York City); (5) The Green City (shot in Radburn, New Jersey, and Greenbelt, Maryland).

John Grierson, who was himself working on a film about city planning at the time (*The Londoners*), much admired the keenness of observation, the rhythm, and the energy of *The City*. In "the sort of analysis one producer expects of another," he had this to say about its weaknesses:

Steiner and Van Dyke, under suasion no doubt, try to tell us they are all against metropolitan madness, that they are sick of its nervousness, its wasted energies, its dangers, its damnations. They describe what they say is their road to heaven. It is, first of all, the rural paradise we have lost; and it is true enough that the rustic swinging with the seasons produced a harmonious art of life. But there is something wrong about the Steiner-Van Dyke paradise. There are fine shapes but no applejack. Van Dyke, as an old villager himself, might at least have remembered the smells that go with it.

The road to heaven twists. What is it now but a Washington suburb—neat and clean and tidy and utterly antiseptic, with all the citizens practicing to be acrobats? No smells here either. . . .

What I am getting at is that I do not believe Steiner and Van Dyke believe a word of it any more than I do; and I have the proof of it the moment they shoot these children on the sidewalk, those domestic jalopies on the metropolitan road, the clamor of the industrial scene, or the open sesame of the automat. Like myself they are metropolitans. Their cameras get an edge on and defeat their theories.

The Depression and joblessness are touched upon in a number of films. *Valley Town* (1940) concerns the problem of technological unemployment. Sponsored by the Sloan Foundation, it was produced jointly by the Educational Film Institute of New York University and Documentary Film Productions. Willard Van Dyke directed. Cinematography was by Roger Barlow and Bob Churchill, editing by Irving Lerner. The score was composed by Marc Blitzstein. A dark view of a depressed American community, it has an English predecessor in *Eastern Valley* (1937), a film made by some of Grierson's coworkers.

Aesthetically and technically *Valley Town* is remarkable for several reasons: the extraordinary force and effectiveness of its images for one, and its daring use of soliloquy, even sung soliloquy, in an effort to heighten the feeling of its contents for another. It makes one think of the words and music of Bertolt Brecht and Kurt Weill in *The Threepenny Opera* and their other music dramas with social meanings.

Valley Town offers a partial solution to the bitter problem it examines. But, as with many of the American films of this era, the hopeful ending seems like whistling in the dark, added to meet the sponsor's requirements without much conviction on the part of the film's makers. The impression that remains after viewing it is of the terrible meaning in individual human terms of a vast and impersonal economic system that has somehow broken down.

From the same sponsor and producers as *Valley Town* came *And So They Live* and *The Children Must Learn* (both 1940). Their subject is the kind of education needed to alleviate some of the hardships of poverty-stricken rural areas of Appalachia. The former was directed by John Ferno and Julian Roffman, the latter by Willard Van Dyke. In *And So They Live* the filmmakers' affection for the Appalachian family, chosen as exemplary of many such families, shines through. There is a beguiling simplicity in their brief: what this family has is in touching contrast to what they need. The sparse commentary suggests merely that life ought to be made better for these gentle people.

But perhaps the beauty and dignity of this family and of their behavior with one another undercut the argument—particularly in the lengthy and lovely final scene of the family together in their cabin in the evening. Their situation might have looked somewhat enviable—like that of Flaherty's people—to persons feeling harassed by complex lives and unsatisfactory relationships. The film may be stronger as a document (like Flaherty's work) than as a documentary for social change (like Grierson's). Perhaps this is true of many U.S. documentaries.

Another, somewhat related film, *One Tenth of a Nation* (1940), is about the need for better schooling for the Southern Negro. It was the most widely seen of several films dealing with the problems of black Americans. Henwar Rodakiewicz and Joseph Krumgold coproduced and codirected.

In concluding this section a number of generalizations can be made about the nongovernmental American documentaries of the 1930s. First of all, if the filmmakers often took bold positions on social matters, they had continuing difficulty finding backing for their statements. The pattern was one of a big, fine film for which funding was somehow obtained, followed by inadequate distribution and exhibition, leading to the sponsor's disenchantment and the filmmaker's having to scramble to try to find sponsorship for the next film.

Second, because of the uncertainty of sponsorship, there was no steady flow of smaller films reaching interested audiences and little reinforcement of the ideas presented. Too frequently only those persons who already agreed with the filmmakers' positions saw the films or even learned of their existence.

Third, and related to the second point, rarely is the propaganda mixed with the artistic form in a smooth blend. The sponsor's message may obtrude. On the other hand, sometimes the pleasures of form seem to be working against the content and evident intention of the film. The liveliness and humor of the New York City sequence in *The City* is much more engaging than the blandness of its greenbelt sequence; the loveliness of much of *And So They Live* makes the Appalachian situation seem one that should be preserved rather than changed.

Though he never contributed to organizing American documentary filmmakers, Robert Flaherty may have been their unacknowledged bellwether. Often they seemed to be following the Flaherty way more than the Grierson one.

American and British Differences

Documentary other than Flaherty's films didn't really begin in the United States until seven years after documentary in Great Britain. American documentary did not grow out of British documentary, though it may not have begun when it did if there had not been the British precedent. Connections between the two national groups of documentary makers were not made until the late thirties. Some have felt that it would have been better if the Americans had learned from the

British. Given the differences in their geographies, histories, and national temperaments, perhaps they couldn't have.

Filmmakers

One striking difference was that in Britain there was a single production center; out of London came films of all kinds, and documentary was part of general film activity. In the United States there was Washington, D.C., where the government documentaries were produced; New York City, where the nongovernment documentaries were produced; and Los Angeles, which produced all of the fiction entertainment films but virtually no documentary. The filmmakers in the three production centers had comparatively little contact with one another.

There were also differences in leadership. In the United States, Pare Lorentz was the only one in a position to be a Grierson. Louis de Rochemont, the other possible candidate, wasn't really a maker of documentaries and identified himself more with the newsreel and the theatrical film industry than with the documentarians. But Lorentz was not Grierson. In spite of a shared capacity for drink and talk late into the night—prerequisites, generally, for documentary making it sometimes seems—Lorentz was more of an individual filmmaker. He demonstrated no particular aptitude for administration or political maneuvering. As in Britain, many of those who would become American documentarians had developed their craft working on government films. The credits of *The Plow* and *The River* contain many of the significant names in American documentary of the 1930s. But Lorentz never attracted a band of loyal colleagues. Without strong leadership, the filmmakers competed with one another in trying to obtain financial backing for their productions. No firm sense of collective endeavor developed in the U.S. as it did in Britain.

Political persuasions took on different importance and different forms in the two bodies of filmmakers as well. American documentarians were highly political, and sectarian squabbling divided the New Dealers from socialists, Trotskyites from Stalinists, and so on. In one sector there was a running contention regarding whether to follow Communist party discipline, which was antiaesthetic and exclusively in favor of the agitprop, or to move along lines that permitted more individual and artistic freedom. In general, American documentarians seemed not to consider the need for collective effort sufficiently; instead, each stood on principle and—as in French politics, with a party for every point of view—they remained fragmented, never achieving the unity of purpose of the British documentary movement.

Sponsorship and Distribution

No one in the United States systematically developed industrial sponsorship for documentary as Grierson had done. It was as true in the U.S. as in Britain that business and industry money was really the only money outside government accessible and sufficient for a program of film production; and industry, like government, had reason to communicate with the public. American industry could see the value of advertising goods and services and of promoting corporate images. But the idea that private corporations might back films in the public interest or support worthwhile causes seems never to have occurred or been persuasively presented to business and industry leaders.

Instead, American nongovernment documentaries depended on support from a few philanthropic foundations and, even more, on contributions from individuals, mostly on the left politically and frequently in the arts. As a result, production of documentaries in the United States in the 1930s was limited and sporadic. The filmmakers seem to have sometimes been irresponsible in regard to the sponsors' interests, following their own notions of what was needed once the money was obtained. A wake of ill-feeling on the part of the sponsors was left behind a number of productions.

After their films were made—some big and fine, as has been indicated— American documentarians seemed strangely indifferent to or inept at obtaining adequate distribution for them. Their sense of achievement too often seemed confined to the satisfactions of making the films. Nor had an effective system of nontheatrical distribution-exhibition been established (as it had in Britain). Documentaries were shown for the most part in art-type theaters in a few big cities.

Films

The major differences between American and British documentaries of the thirties seem to have grown mostly out of contrasting political positions. The American films are rooted in populism, the British in socialism. The populists, represented in the People's party around the turn of the century, felt that government should control tendencies toward monopoly (the monopolistic and exploitative excesses of capitalism) but that its function should end there. Populism began among American farmers in the country, socialism among factory workers in European cities. Agrarian subject matter and influence are very strong in the American films (this despite the fact that by the mid-thirties the majority of Americans were living in cities); urban and industrial subjects predominate in British documentary. In the American films, the importance of the people and the sacredness of the individual receive considerable emphasis. In the British films, collective effort through government, with government leadership, is stressed.

Certain other differences—some of which stem from these fundamentally different political stances—are evident in the films described in the past two chapters. The American films are more romantic, more emotional in the appeals used. The appeals of the British films, in comparison, seem more reasoned and objective, rooted in evidence and argument. The work and working class of the

British films seem to be thought of differently from the labor and people of the American films. Perhaps the latter are somehow related to populist leader William Jennings Bryan's famous "Cross of Gold" speech given in the House of Representatives in 1894, in which he declared: "I shall not help crucify mankind upon a cross of gold. I shall not aid in pressing down upon the bleeding brow of labor this crown of thorns."

The romantic and emotional led to the poetic rather than the expository. In general, American documentaries of the thirties may have been more "aestheticky," to use a Grierson dismissive term, than the British. "The March of Time" is, of course, an exception to this generalization. Grierson seemed to value it (he imitated it, in fact, in films he produced in Britain and later in Canada) more than he did *The River* and *The City*.

Perhaps also related to populism is the tendency of American films to be large in scale. Ours is a big country, Americans seem to be saying, so we make big statements in big films. We employ hyperbole rather than the understatement characteristic of the British. After all, America is the culture of the legendary giant lumberjack, Paul Bunyan, who could cross Minnesota in a single stride. In *The River* the vistas of the land are vast; in *Night Mail* the countryside appears cozy by comparison. Even *The Fight for Life* suggests a city and problems larger than those of *Housing Problems*. *North Sea* reduces the terrors of the Atlantic to the domestic situation aboard a crippled trawler and in the wireless station at Wick.

Another difference is that American documentaries tended to gravitate toward the historical and to use before-and-after arguments. *The City* moves from eighteenth-century rural New England to twentieth-century urban Pittsburgh and New York, *Power and the Land* from the farm before electricity to the farm after it. Frequent reference is made to folk history and customs. It may be that Americans felt themselves lacking in tradition; after all, education, art, and even fashion looked to Europe. In the 1930s people began to discover what it was to be American, that, in fact, there was such a thing as a national heritage. The murals painted by WPA artists in post offices across the country confirm this impulse. Also, the New Deal, accused in some quarters of being a kind of creeping socialism, tended to attach itself to established American values and virtues, suggesting that the cooperation with government it embodied was as American as apple pie.

As for contemporary subjects, as has been pointed out, American films faced the Depression, rising fascism, and Japanese conquest head on. Some fine, strong films were made on those subjects. With Grierson's dependence on consensus, sponsors couldn't be found to finance such statements. It seems unlikely that he tried, because they were divisive subjects. Coherence and continuity were important in Grierson's conception of what British documentary and Britain itself needed. In spite of talk about films being in the forefront of policy, mainline British documentarians made no directly *political* films. Rotha's little "poster film," *Peace of Britain* (1936), supporting the League of Nations, would be the exception that proves the rule.

Finally, there are the sorts of aesthetic experiences and effects on social attitudes being offered. On the aesthetic side the United States certainly need not be apologetic. *The Plow That Broke the Plains, The River, Power and the Land, The City*, and *And So They Live* are as lovely and lasting as anything the British made. On the side of social and educational effectiveness, however, what Grierson called *propaganda*, perhaps none of these matched *Night Mail* or *Housing Problems*. Though there is no way to test such an opinion empirically, American documentary as a whole seems to have had less influence on national life than British documentary. "The March of Time" might make a claim in this respect. But the MOT was not consistently advancing anything in particular except, perhaps, an antifascist, prowar international position beginning in the late 1930s.

Denouement

At the end of the 1930s some efforts were made to organize American documentary along British lines. Mary Losey (sister of feature-film director Joseph Losey) was a key figure in them. On a trip to London in 1938 she had met Grierson and been stimulated by his achievements. On her return Losey "set to work after the Grierson pattern to organize the jangling sects of American documentary into a purposeful group," as Richard Griffith put it. An Association of Documentary Film Producers (its British model the Association of Realist Film Producers) was established in New York City in 1939. The ADFP membership included, "with the conspicuous exception of Pare Lorentz," Losey noted, "all the producers of documentary today"—some sixty full members, roughly the same number of documentary makers as in Britain. Even Flaherty became part of this group on his return from Britain in 1939 to begin production of *The Land*.

A year earlier Losey had established an American Film Center, modeled after the Film Centre in London, with support from the Rockefeller Foundation (with which Grierson had close ties). Her intention was to use it as a base "to attack the citadels of sponsorship and distribution," said Griffith.

Alas, those efforts were too little and too late. Following the United States' entry into World War II in late 1941, the members of the Association of Documentary Film Producers were scattered about the globe. That organization disbanded in 1942. American Film Center was discontinued in 1946 owing to lack of financial support and differences in point of view among producers and Film Center personnel. "What a people, what a people," Grierson once remarked about Americans, in a mixture of affection and exasperation.

With the war, the groups on the far left that had culminated in Frontier Films lost their principal reason and means for being. The political situation was now that of a common cause, with the United States fighting fascism alongside Communist Russia. During the war there was a virtual cessation of private documentary production, and documentary filmmakers instead made government films of one sort or another. In 1943 Frontier Films ceased to exist.

The war would profoundly affect British and American documentary. Since the British were first into the war, as they had been first into documentary, we will return to Britain in the next chapter. But before that we should look at another manifestation of the documentary impulse in the 1930s.

An Aside to Conclude

Though this history is mostly of the English-language documentary, we would be remiss here if we did not recognize some non-Anglophone developments, in this case in Germany. Early in 1933, with curious simultaneity, Franklin Delano Roosevelt became president of the United States while Adolf Hitler, leader of the National Socialist Party, came to power in Germany. In Britain the Labour party had been succeeded in 1931 by the National Government (made up of a coalition of the Conservative, Labour, and Liberal parties), with Prime Minister Ramsay MacDonald followed by Stanley Baldwin in 1935, and Neville Chamberlain in 1937.

Paralleling John Grierson in Britain and Pare Lorentz in the United States was Leni Riefenstahl in Germany. In 1936 Grierson (and Watt and Wright) made *Night Mail*, Lorentz *The Plow That Broke the Plains*, and Riefenstahl *Triumph of the Will*. All three films were sponsored by their governments to try to rally support for current activities, programs, and policies. Politically the films could be characterized, implicitly at least, as socialist, populist, and fascist.

Triumph of the Will was made to commemorate the sixth Nazi rally in Nuremberg in 1934, the first such gathering after Hitler had come to power. Produced by order of the führer, it was intended to show the German people the power of a resurgent Germany united under a Nazi party. The event itself was staged as a ceremony—a religious ritual—elaborate, powerful, and penetrating, with mass emotion overcoming individual reason. Its key image is the molding of tens of thousands of human beings into artistic patterns—stationary and solid masses in the huge stadium or moving with deliberation and vigor in endless parades. What *Triumph of the Will* offers, rather than a ride on that smoothly humming mail train, or a part in a vast sweet-sad epic saga, is the joining of self into—the losing of self in—the mass: in total dedication to an ideal of a strong and united nation, to supermen and superstate—a transcendence. Riefenstahl's other masterpiece, *Olympia* (1938), similarly edited from an enormous amount of footage covering a huge public event, the Olympic Games of 1936 held in Berlin, also, though much more subtly, articulates Nazi ideology in cinematic terms. Taken in this light they can be seen as contributing to the *Zeitgeist* that accompanied the Holocaust and World War II.

Films of the Period

1935

"The March of Time" series began (Louis de Rochemont)
The Wave (Paul Strand and Fred Zinnemann)

1936

The Plow That Broke the Plains (Pare Lorentz)

1937

China Strikes Back (Harry Dunham)
Heart of Spain (Herbert Kline)
The River (Lorentz)
The Spanish Earth (Joris Ivens)

1938

Crisis (Kline)
The Four Hundred Million (Ivens)
People of the Cumberland (Elia Kazan)
Return to Life (Kline)

1939

The City (Ralph Steiner and Willard Van Dyke)
Lights Out in Europe (Kline)

1940

And So They Live (John Ferno and Julian Roffman)
Power and the Land (Ivens)
The Ramparts We Watch (de Rochemont)
Valley Town (Van Dyke)

1941

The Fight for Life (Lorentz)
The Land (Robert Flaherty)
A Place to Live (Irving Lerner)

1942

Native Land (Leo Hurwitz and Paul Strand)

Books on the Period

Alexander, William, *Film on the Left: American Documentary Film from 1931 to 1942.* Princeton, NJ: Princeton University Press, 1981.

Böker, Carlos, *Joris Ivens, Film-Maker: Facing Reality*. Ann Arbor, MI: UMI Research Press, 1981.

Campbell, Russell, *Cinema Strikes Back: Radical Filmmaking in the United States, 1930–1942*. Ann Arbor, MI: UMI Research Press, 1982.

Delmar, Rosalind, *Joris Ivens: 50 Years of Film-making*. London: British Film Institute, 1979.

Fielding, Raymond, *The March of Time, 1935–1951*. New York: Oxford University Press, 1978.

Ivens, Joris, *The Camera and I*. New York: International Publishers, 1969.

MacCann, Richard Dyer, *The People's Films: A Political History of U.S. Government Motion Pictures*. New York: Hastings House, 1973.

Rother, Rainer, *Leni Riefenstahl*. London: Continuum, 2002.

Snyder, Robert L. *Pare Lorentz and the Documentary Film*. Norman: University of Oklahoma Press, 1968.

Zuker, Joel Stewart, *Ralph Steiner, Filmmaker and Still Photographer*. New York: Arno Press, 1978.

Chapter Seven

Expansion: Great Britain, 1939–1945

On September 1, 1939, German panzer divisions rolled across the Polish border and Stuka dive-bombers took to the skies. On September 3, Prime Minister Neville Chamberlain announced over BBC radio that a state of war existed between Great Britain and Germany. (His announcement was followed by the accidental setting off of air-raid sirens.)

At the time, the British entertainment film industry was dominated by Americans. Gary Cooper, Greta Garbo, James Cagney, and Bette Davis commanded the popular audience. French and, to a lesser extent, Soviet films attracted the discriminating in London. British features lacked distinction and a specifically national tradition such as French poetic realism or the American genres of western, gangster, and musical. Of course there were isolated exceptions—films of Alfred Hitchcock (*The Lady Vanishes*, 1938), or Anthony Asquith (*Pygmalion*, 1938), or a young Carol Reed (*Bank Holiday*, 1938), for example. But in general the public took British features as second best to Hollywood, and the intellectuals were completely indifferent to them.

Documentary, on the other hand, though relatively small in terms of money and audience, had established film as a means of social and scientific communication with hundreds of short films of fact and opinion. It had prestige among the educated classes and fit in with thirties' ideas about art in relation to society. A movement with trained and skilled workers, it offered a distinct style as well as purpose and innovations in form and technique that are arguably Britain's most important contribution to the development of the motion picture.

Further, with the outbreak of war, when the needs of the country were paramount, British documentary's identification with government from its beginnings became especially significant. The film unit at the Empire Marketing Board and then at the General Post Office had been training ground and trendsetter, and had offered means of national expression in an exact sense. With the war, the GPO Film Unit became the Crown Film Unit, serving all departments of government. Wartime documentaries would be made by veteran documentarians plus new recruits.

Following the declaration of war (in spite of the accidental air-raid sirens) it was some time before Britain was engaged in actual combat. There was a period of "phony war," as it was called—the "sitting war" or "Sitzkrieg," as someone dubbed it in reference to the Germans' *Blitzkrieg* (lightning war). Poland was defeated before either France or Britain, bound to it by mutual defense treaties, could come to its aid. Six months passed between the fall of Poland and the beginning, in Denmark and Norway, of the German drive in Western Europe.

Early Days

The first film job, immediately evident, was to record the events of war. For that purpose the five English newsreel companies pooled their resources for what would soon become a mammoth task. This provided for the free exchange of material to limit redundancy in the use of personnel and permit a maximum amount of war activity to be covered. Exceptional work was done by newsreel and armed forces combat cameramen throughout the war. The casualty rate among them was high. In battle situations where troops could dig foxholes, those who had to move about aboveground—platoon leaders, medics, and still pho-tographers as well as cinematographers—were most vulnerable.

To deal with the background as well as the foreground of war, documentary was needed. Those first months were marked by a worrisome complacency; the British didn't yet realize their danger. Evidence of naive overconfidence is offered in a feature film Alexander Korda produced for the government at his own ex-pense entitled *The Lion has Wings* (1939). Directed by Michael Powell and star-ring Merle Oberon and Ralph Richardson, it combines newsreel footage with fictional material. Its climax occurs when a German air attack on London is thwarted by the height of the barrage balloon. The earlier *Things to Come* (1936), also produced by Korda, from H. G. Wells's science-fiction novel, had been much closer to what enemy attacks on London would actually be like. In it hundreds of large, dark planes thunder over the city and rain destruction upon it.

In September of 1939 the Ministry of Information was established to take overall charge of the creation and dissemination of news and propaganda. Its Films Division was first headed by Sir Joseph Ball, who had been in charge of Conservative party publicity, and then by Sir Kenneth Clark, art historian and director of the National Gallery. The film advisers to the Chamberlain govern-ment were distrustful of the documentary people because of their leftward tend-encies. Instead of the documentarians, filmmakers from the entertainment film industry were called upon. The documentary group vented their frustration by grousing to each other and writing letters to *The Times*. Without any real autho-rization, let alone relevance to Post Office activity, the GPO Film Unit, on its own, made *The First Days* (1939) shortly after war broke out. Harry Watt, Hum-phrey Jennings, and Pat Jackson collaborated on it.

In January 1940 Prime Minister Chamberlain appointed Sir John Reith as Minister of Information. Reith, first and long-lasting head of the British Broadcasting Corporation, was a dour Scot who seemed to feel that God had entrusted him with the responsibility for uplifting the British people. When Winston Churchill became prime minister in May, he transferred Reith to the post of Minister of Transport and subsequently named Brendan Bracken, his close associate, Minister of Information. Bracken in turn appointed Jack Beddington head of the Films Division. Beddington, public relations officer for the Shell Oil group who had been instrumental in the establishment of the Shell Film Unit, understood the aims of the documentary movement and had a feeling for the film medium. His first act at Films Division was to request a paper from Film Centre explaining how to use films in time of war. Former Grierson associates Edgar Anstey, Arthur Elton, and Basil Wright wrote it.

Throughout the spring of 1940 the government documentaries were aimed chiefly toward what was called the "spiritual arming of the people." A series of short story films begun under Clark were completed. Some of these were by veteran feature directors. One example, *Men of the Lightship* (1940), was directed by David MacDonald. It is what today would be called a docudrama. A true story reenacted by actors, it concerns a lightship in the Thames estuary that was bombed and machine-gunned by German planes. Its crew took to boats and attempted to row thirty miles through heavy fog to reach shore. Only one man survived. *Channel Incident* (1940), produced and directed by Anthony Asquith, is a reenactment of an event in the evacuation of Allied forces from Dunkirk.

Produced at about the same time was an MOI series of shorts made in collaboration with the French to demonstrate solidarity. In regard to their French allies, a strategic problem existed for the British. If they sent large numbers of troops across the Channel and France fell, Britain would be left unprotected. The Germans took advantage of this dilemma in their propaganda directed at the French. "Where ARE your British Allies?" they asked, or predicted that "Britain will fight to the last drop of French blood."

After the summer of 1940, when France had fallen, the greater part of Western Europe was overrun by Germany. Britain was now a besieged island constantly under the threat of air attack. The documentarians reacted to these changed circumstances and became the interpreters of the British mood at war.

Another series of short factual films followed—half newsreel, half pictorial comment, and highly charged with the spirit of the time. *The Front Line* (1940), directed by Harry Watt, recorded life in the Channel port of Dover under air and artillery bombardment by long-range German guns. *London Can Take It* (1940) pictured life in the capital during the great night raids of the Battle of Britain. Directed by Watt and Humphrey Jennings, its commentary was written and read by American correspondent Quentin Reynolds. Cool images of actuality combined with hot journalistic prose are the basis of its style. Reynolds could

Squadron 992 (U.K., 1940, Harry Watt). **Museum of Modern Art Film Stills Archive**

say things about the English under fire that they couldn't modestly say about themselves.

With Beddington in place, the documentary old guard entered the wartime filmmaking effort. *Squadron 992* (1940), produced by Alberto Cavalcanti and directed by Harry Watt, was made by the GPO Film Unit for the air force. About the training of a barrage balloon unit that then moves up into Scotland, it ends with a simulated German air raid on the bridge over the Firth of Fourth. There is less attention to how things are done than is usual in documentaries and more to mood and imagery, with lovely shots of the bridge, countryside, and sea. The humor is noteworthy as well—including mild kidding of the Scots. (Watt was Scottish.) We see at a distance one of the soldiers knocking on the door of a house. A woman opens it, listens to him, and shouts back over her shoulder, "Willie, there's a man here who wants to put a balloon in our garden."

As the war got fully underway, hundreds of training and orientation, scientific and medical films were produced for military and civilian audiences. There were films that enabled aerial gunners to test the accuracy of their aim, or which taught pilots the use of their controls. Short films—"trailers," the film industry termed them—encouraged civilians to conserve fuel and water (*The Burning Question*, 1945, on fuel economy), to collect salvage (*Salvage with a Smile*, 1940, paper for cartridges, household waste for pig food), and the like. Each month the MOI presented a fifteen-minute film on the progress of the struggle: the conquest and rehabilitation of Naples (*Naples Is a Battlefield*, 1944), or the devastation created in Walcheren by Allied bombing of the dykes (*Broken Dykes*, 1945), for instance. The scientific and medical films included one dealing with the National Blood Transfusion Service (*Blood Transfusion*, 1942), a film for doctors on diagnosis and treatment of a skin disease caused by parasites (*Scabies*, 1943), and another on a new antibiotic drug (*Penicillin*, 1944).

In addition to these more directly utilitarian films, three major types of British wartime documentaries emerged between 1941 and 1945. They were (1) the semidocumentary indoctrinational features, (2) a continuation of the peacetime social documentary with new subjects and forms, and (3) the records of battle.

Indoctrination

Alberto Cavalcanti, who had followed Grierson as producer in charge of the GPO Film Unit, left for Ealing Studios in August 1939. He was succeeded by Ian Dalrymple, a successful screenwriter with no documentary experience. By the end of the year the name of the unit was changed to Crown Film Unit and it became responsible to the Ministry of Information rather than an appendage of the General Post Office. Under Cavalcanti and then Dalrymple (and subsequently J. B. Holmes and then Basil Wright) the aesthetic aspects of documentary were nurtured. Harry Watt would continue to develop the narrative line he had begun with *Night Mail* (1936), *The Saving of Bill Blewitt* (1937), and *North Sea* (1938). Humphrey Jennings would add impressionist poetic elements (evident early in *Spare Time*, 1939), becoming a sort of film laureate of wartime Britain.

Evidently the Ministry of Information decided that the best sort of support and inspiration for the population at large could come from showing British men and women going about their wartime tasks with resolution, efficiency, and quiet courage. In taking this approach a main line of British indoctrination films

Target for Tonight (U.K., 1941, Harry Watt)

moved toward Flaherty, and also toward fiction features, in depicting the drama of survival inherent in war. It was Watt in *Target for Tonight* (1941) who created the prototype for the feature-length semidocumentary indoctrination films that would come from Crown and be made by commercial studios as well, Ealing particularly.

Target for Tonight concerns a Royal Air Force bombing mission into Germany to destroy an oil refinery and storage and distributing center at Freihausen. After covering the preparation for the raid, it follows a Wellington bomber and its crew. The bomber is hit by flak over the target, one of its crew is wounded, and it limps back to base on one engine. The action is a composite representation of how such an engagement would actually be carried out. It has the real setting of airfield and airplanes and is acted by real airmen. Through our direct involvement with the crew members, it comes alive in a way associated with story films. The deft characterizations, dialogue that seems to fit the men and the situation, and bits of wry humor are all engaging. In the Crew Room before takeoff one of the airmen says to the young Scottish navigator, "Listen, Jock, who was it who didn't know whether he was over Hanover or Hampton Court?" Jock, not amused, explains indignantly to the others, "That's a joke." In giving these airmen a chance to be themselves, Watt was the first to depict the human undercurrents of war at a depth documentary had not previously attempted.

Following *Target for Tonight* out of Crown was *Coastal Command* (1942), a sort of companion piece. Directed by J. B. Holmes, with a score by Ralph Vaughan Williams (William Walton had written the music for *Target for Tonight*), its theme is cooperation between shore-based RAF aircraft and the navy in defending convoys at sea. In this case our identification is with the crew of a Sunderland flying boat.

Fires Were Started (1943), directed by Humphrey Jennings, is about the work of the Auxiliary Fire Service during the devastating German fire raids on London. By using the narrative device of a new recruit, Jennings can let us see through his eyes and learn not only about the functioning of this fire-fighting service but about the diverse and likable personalities brought together in it. When the raid begins in the evening we are able to follow the tactics of the firefighters without aid of commentary through their actions and conversations, the phone calls from headquarters, the maps with pins stuck into them, the lists of equipment chalked on a blackboard. Among other things, *Fires Were Started* is a model of exposition without didacticism.

But where its true greatness lies is in the way it informs, persuades, and moves us all at the same time. In this film Jennings goes beyond other of the semidocumentaries in differentiating and developing characters of his real/non-actor firemen. *Fires Were Started*, together with two of his shorts—*Listen to Britain* (1942), an impressionistic audiovisual poem about the country in wartime, and *A Diary for Timothy* (1945), a fusion of the impressionist/symphonic approach with (in this case multiple) narrative—comprise Jennings's masterpieces. His qualities as a filmmaker involve especially his formal experimentation, the intricate patterns of interwoven sights and sounds. The individual images Jennings selected are rich in symbolic expressiveness, evoking peace as well as war, past as well as present, in combination and contrast. English tradition and English spirit saturate his films. Jennings celebrates cultural heritage with a warmth that encourages us to share his feelings.

Western Approaches (1944, titled *The Raider* in the U.S.) was directed by Pat Jackson, who had assisted Harry Watt earlier (as had Humphrey Jennings before him). It is an account of the convoys of merchant vessels that left Halifax, Nova Scotia, to transport supplies to Britain and of the submarine warfare in the North Atlantic that they faced. It narrows down to the story of twenty-four men, survivors of a torpedoed freighter, who spend fourteen days adrift. Their lifeboat is used as bait by a lurking U-boat to attract an Allied ship.

This is the largest in scale, the most ambitious, and the most difficult technically of the British wartime semidocumentaries. Along with the documentary essentials of nonactors, location shooting, and description of process (how convoys and submarine attack and defense function), there is a high degree of skillfully handled artifice. The use of tightly scripted dialogue, synchronous sound recording on location, and shooting with the cumbersome Technicolor camera

Listen to Britain (U.K., 1942, Humphrey Jennings). Museum of Modern Art Film Stills Archive

on the high sea are all impressive. With its carefully plotted suspense and familiar characterizations, documentary here moves very close to fiction.

The semidocumentaries from the Crown Film Unit (*Merchant Seamen*, 1941, and *Close Quarters*, 1943, are others) were paralleled by semidocumentary features from the commercial studios. *In Which We Serve* (1942), codirected by Noël Coward and David Lean and based on the events experienced by an actual British destroyer and its crew commanded by Lord Louis Mountbatten, was the first of these. (It was also Lean's first directorial credit.) It was followed by some twenty or so others including *The Foreman Went to France, One of Our Aircraft Is Missing, Next of Kin* in 1942; *San Demetrio London, Nine Men* (which Watt directed after he followed Cavalcanti to Ealing), *We Dive at Dawn, Millions Like Us* in 1943; *The Way Ahead* in 1944; *The Way to the Stars* and *Journey Together* in 1945.

Two indoctrinational intentions of the British wartime semidocumentaries are apt to strike a viewer. One is their emphasis on togetherness. Over and over again the people are shown, civilians as well as military, working together to get the job done. Though microcosms of English society are frequently offered— with various identifiable regional and class accents, and a Scot or perhaps Canadian thrown in—no tensions between regions or among classes are shown. In fact, such differences, very real in Britain, are minimized. Everyone is doing his or her work; all are working equally hard to win the war.

The other distinctive characteristic is the lack of violence shown and the lack of hatred toward the enemy expressed in either dialogue or narration. Rather than digging coal or working for an advertising agency or attending university, the job now is to destroy the (unseen) enemy to keep them from destroying us. If bombs fall from the night skies, it's as if they were an act of God, a natural disaster like an earthquake. The thing to do is to put out the fires, clear away the rubble, attend the wounded, and bury the dead.

While one might think these two attitudes were part of general wartime propaganda strategies, they appear to be very British, maybe even more specifically English. Nothing quite like them is present in the wartime films of Canada or the United States.

Social Documentary

Notwithstanding the national peril, the social documentary survived. In fact, some interesting innovations of subject and form were added to it. In the wartime social documentary a common goal was put forward: not simply that the war should be won, but that it should be won to some purpose; that life should hold better opportunities for everyone after it. This attitude even appears in the Crown/Jennings indoctrinational *A Diary for Timothy*. When the Welsh miner is injured in an accident, the commentary, written by E. M. Forster and read by Michael Redgrave, adds, "It's pretty shocking that this sort of thing should happen every day though we've been cutting coal for five hundred years." As he is recuperating, the miner reminds his wife of the gains in health services made by labor since the end of the First World War. "Surely, if we can do that during that period," he says, "nothing can stop us after this war." If postwar opportunities was a frequent theme in British wartime documentaries, it was probably at least partly a response to working-class feelings that their great sacrifices and losses of World War I had not resulted in sufficient benefits for them.

World of Plenty (1943), Paul Rotha's compilation argument film, begins with the breakdown in international food distribution before the war—surpluses in some countries, starvation in others. The system of fair distribution by rationing enforced nationally in Britain during the war is then presented. It is suggested as a worldwide model for the future. Rotha always insisted (as did Grierson less stridently) that documentaries had to deal with the economic underpinnings of any subject tackled. At the same time, economic abstractions are much harder to present in the language of motion pictures than are specific actualities. In attempting to solve this problem Rotha introduced a number of experimental elements. Diagrams, interviews, and trick optical effects were added to stock footage. The remarkable animated representations created by the Isotype Insti-

World of Plenty (U.K., 1943, Paul Rotha). **Museum of Modern Art Film Stills Archive**

tute, a firm producing animated films, add clarity and drama to statistics of food production and distribution. Especially original is the argumentative dialogue between an offscreen voice speaking for the audience to onscreen actors and among onscreen actors, in roles of persons in various parts of the world, speaking to each other.

Children of the City (1944), produced by Rotha and directed by Budge Cooper, takes on the narrative aspects of the semidocumentaries to deal with juvenile delinquency in a Scottish city. While the problem was not an exclusively wartime one, it had been exacerbated by the strains on families caused by fathers in military service and mothers working in war plants. *Children of the City* offers case studies of three boys who break into a pawnbroker's and are apprehended by the police as they are emptying the till. Not only the boys and their quite different family backgrounds but the social workers, the court officials, and the judicial and penal system within which they work are all observed.

As a final example of the wartime social documentary there is *When We Build Again* (1945), about housing and city planning. Sponsored by Cadbury Brothers, Ltd., makers of chocolates, it was produced by Donald Taylor and directed by Ralph Bond. Dylan Thomas wrote and read the poetic portions of the commentary. The film begins with a slight narrative of three returning servicemen (who

Desert Victory (U.K., 1943, Roy Boulting). **Museum of Modern Art Film Stills Archive**

are subsequently dropped). The music sounds like and is used in the manner of dramatic films. Inner-city slums, suburbs, and new towns (like the greenbelt town of *The City*) are surveyed. Interviews, statistics, visual demonstrations of existing housing, and models for the future are employed. "No private interest to stand in our way," intones the commentator, who calls people "the greatest capital—the future belongs to them." This film could be thought of as *Housing Problems* ten years later. It was made in the year of Labour's victory at the polls.

Records of Battle

Desert Victory (1943)—with production by the Army Film and Photographic Unit and the Royal Air Force Film Production Unit, direction by Roy Boulting, and music by William Alwyn—is about the British Eighth Army's campaign in North Africa against the German forces under the command of Field Marshall Erwin Rommel. In this kind of filmmaking, with filmmakers working with miles of footage shot by combat cameramen, two creative problems are uppermost. The first is to give clarity to the mass of confusing, technical detail. The second is to give it dramatic form. These problems are the same as those faced by Esfir Shub in *The Fall of the Romanov Dynasty* (1927), discussed in chapter 3. In *Desert*

Victory, the first problem was solved by the use of animated maps to establish the overall patterns and movement of the campaign and by a carefully planned narration. As for the second, all of the nonartistic material with the irregularity of history inherent in it was organized into a coherent story told chronologically with beginning, middle, and end. In addition, the irrelevancies of the sponsor's requirements—to show each branch of the armed forces, the civilian workers, the presence of U.S. aid, and the like—were fitted into the whole without warping it out of shape.

Desert Victory starts at the lowest point of the campaign. The British, who had retreated across the Sahara, pursued by the seemingly invincible Afrika Korps, are halted just sixty miles from Alexandria, deep inside Egypt. Then there is the fierce battle of El Alamein, with the British emerging victorious. From there the film follows the triumphant 1,300-mile pursuit of the German army to the final victory at Tripoli. To organize these events so they would appear both clear and dramatic, the filmmakers contrived an alternation of cause and effect. To personalize the mass action and gain empathy, a number of close-ups of individual soldiers (some of them obviously recreated, particularly in the night attack sequences) are inserted. Generals Alexander, Montgomery, and Wavell, and Prime Minister Churchill are introduced as well.

In comparison with the indoctrinational semidocumentaries, which tended to make the violence of war part of a job of work to be done, *Desert Victory* is singularly bloodthirsty. Perhaps these filmmakers weren't inclined to conceal their elation over this first major British victory following the battering Britain had received in the desert fighting and from the air blitz. It was hugely successful at home and abroad, receiving an Oscar as the year's most distinctive achievement in documentary features.

Tunisian Victory (1944), a British-American coproduction, was also directed by Roy Boulting, plus Frank Capra. Commentary is spoken by Bernard Miles and Burgess Meredith; music composed by William Alwyn. It carried the North African story from the American landings in November 1942 to the annihilation of the German forces at Cape Bon. *Burma Victory* (1945), Roy Boulting again, may have been prompted partly by a Hollywood feature, *Objective Burma* (1945), directed by Raoul Walsh, that offended the British. In it Errol Flynn, as an American paratrooper, pretty much single-handedly mops up the Japanese enemy. *Burma Victory* succeeds in making clear the confusing phases of the Burma campaign, which was essentially a British operation, between 1942 and the end of the war with Japan.

The True Glory (1945) was produced jointly by the British Ministry of Information and the U.S. Office of War Information. It was codirected by Englishman Carol Reed and American Garson Kanin, fiction film directors of considerable distinction. William Alwyn composed the score. It covers the final phase of the war in Europe, from the preparations for the D day landings in Normandy through the fall of Berlin, to the establishing of contact between the Western

The True Glory was a triumphant record and hymn to Allied victory in Europe. (U.K and U.S. co-production, 1945, Carol Reed and Garson Kanin). Museum of Modern Art Film Stills Archive

Allies and Soviet troops at the Elbe River. Made from 5.5 million feet of combat footage shot by five hundred American, British, and other Allied cameramen, it is a vast panorama, yet intensely human, even intimate at moments.

Emotional involvement is gained largely through the experimental use of commentary. The words are complementary to the images, sometimes in humorous or ironic counterpoint to them. Alternating with free verse choruses are multiple voices representing soldiers involved with the particular action being shown. The generals' version, spoken by Dwight D. Eisenhower himself, supreme commander of the Allied forces in Europe, is irreverently interrupted by simulated voices of enlisted men who were there—New York cab driver, cockney Londoner, member of the French Maquis, and others. One marvelous moment occurs when a black American MP directing military traffic at a crossroads explains that the situation is tough, that the invasion forces are bottled up in the Caen Peninsula. "Then we heard that the Third Army was taking off," he says. "They'd pulled a rabbit out of a hat—and what a rabbit! A rabbit with pearl-handled revolvers." As he utters these last words a tank bearing an erect General George S. Patton roars by.

The True Glory was the final triumphant record and hymn to Allied victory in Europe. The occasion permitted a kind of boasting and self-congratulation without it appearing to be so. Pride is expressed in the massiveness and efficiency of the military machine and in its democratic character. The participation of many nations is indirectly reiterated without explicit statement being required. The Allied attitude toward war is presented as being purposeful and matter-of-fact, its violence accepted as part of the job, as in the British semidocumentaries. Unlike the semidocumentaries, however, dislike and distrust of the German enemy are strongly stated. The horrors of what the advancing forces discovered at the Belsen concentration camp are included. An American GI, talking about guarding German prisoners of war, says, "I just keep 'em covered. . . . It wasn't my job to figure 'em out. . . . But, brother, I never gave 'em more than the Geneva convention, and that was all." Finally, though, it is the positive corollary of the GI's attitude that receives the strongest emphasis. What The True Glory is saying mostly is that this was a just and necessary war and that on the Allied side everyone can all feel proud of winning it.

Films of the Period

1940

London Can Take It (Harry Watt and Humphrey Jennings)
They Also Serve (Ruby Grierson)

1941

Merchant Seamen (J. B. Holmes)
Target for Tonight (Watt)

1942

Coastal Command (Holmes)
The Harvest Shall Come (Max Anderson)
Listen to Britain (Jennings)

1943

Desert Victory (Roy Boulting)
Fires Were Started (Jennings)
The Silent Village (Jennings)
World of Plenty (Paul Rotha)

1944

Children of the City (Budge Cooper)
Tunisian Victory (Boulting and Frank Capra)
Western Approaches (Pat Jackson)

1945

Burma Victory (Boulting)
A Diary for Timothy (Jennings)
The True Glory (Carol Reed and Garson Kanin)

Books on the Period

Aldgate, Anthony and Jeffrey Richards, *Britain Can Take It: The British Cinema in the Second World War*. Oxford: Basil Blackwell, 1986.

Aitken, Ian, ed., *The Documentary Film Movement: An Anthology*. Edinburgh: Edinburgh University Press, 1998.

Arts Enquiry, The, *The Factual Film*. London: Oxford University Press, 1947.

Chapman, James, *The British at War: Cinema, State and Propaganda, 1939–1945*. London: I. B. Tauris, 1998.

Coultass, Clive, *Images of Battle: British Film and the Second World War*. London: Associated University Presses, 1988.

Hardy, Forsyth, "The British Documentary Film," in *Twenty Years of British Film 1925–1945*, eds. Michael Balcon and others. London: Falcon, 1947, pp. 45–80.

Hodgkinson, Anthony W. and Rodney E. Sheratsky, *Humphrey Jennings: More than a Maker of Films*. Hanover, NH: University Press of New England, 1982.

Jennings, Mary-Lou, ed., *Humphrey Jennings: Film-Maker/Painter/Poet*. London: British Film Institute, 1982.

Lovell, Alan and Jim Hillier, *Studies in Documentary*. New York: Viking, 1972.

Manvell, Roger, *Films and the Second World War*. New York: Dell, 1974.

Powell, Dilys, *Films Since 1939*. London: Longmans, Green, 1947.

Rotha, Paul with Eric Knight, *World of Plenty: The Book of the Film*. London: Nicholson and Watson, 1945.

Sussex, Elizabeth, *The Rise and Fall of British Documentary: The Story of the Film Movement Founded by John Grierson*. Berkeley: University of California Press, 1975.

Swann, Paul, *The British Documentary Film Movement, 1926–1946*. Cambridge: Cambridge University Press, 1989.

Taylor, Philip M., ed., *Britain and the Cinema in the Second World War*. New York: St. Martin's Press, 1988.

Thorpe, Frances and Nicholas Pronay, *British Official Films in the Second World War: A Descriptive Catalogue*. Oxford: Clio, 1980.

Vaughan, Dai, *Portrait of an Invisible Man: The Working Life of Stewart McAllister, Film Editor*. London: British Film Institute, 1983.

Watt, Harry, *Don't Look at the Camera*. London: Paul Elek, 1974.

Winston, Brian, *Fires Were Started*. London: British Film Institute, 2000.

Chapter Eight
Expansion: Canada, 1939–1945

A t the outbreak of World War II, Canada was something of a sleeping giant. In certain ways it was also a geographical and cultural anomaly, which no orderly-minded nation planner would have perpetrated. Larger in area than the United States, with a sparse population stretched across a 200-mile-wide strip along its southern border, physically it represented a virtual extension of the United States up into the uninhabitable Arctic. Its prodigious breadth of forest and prairie, blocked at the western end by a fierce mountain range, took considerable conquering before the Atlantic was finally linked to the Pacific.

In addition to the formidable task of taming a wilderness, Canadians had always faced a struggle for national identity. At first it was the matter of establishing independence from Great Britain, greatly aided by the Balfour Declaration, which emerged from the Imperial Conference of 1926. It had declared the Dominions "autonomous communities . . . united by a common allegiance to the Crown, and freely associated as members of the British Commonwealth of Nations." More recently, the gravitational pull of its powerful neighbor to the south was smothering Canada's distinctiveness. Economically and culturally, as well as geographically, Canada had become something of an extension of the United States.

When war broke out in 1939 the film situation in Canada was considerably different from that in either Britain or the United States. In Canada there was no production of fiction feature films, and theatrical distribution and exhibition were even more dominated by the Americans than in Britain. In fact, there was a negligible amount of Canadian film production of any sort. Britain had a firmly established documentary movement. If the United States' documentary efforts lacked the coherence and overall effectiveness of the British, it had distinguished documentary filmmakers and films it could point to with pride. War and documentary arrived together in Canada at the end of the thirties.

A pioneer Government Motion Picture Bureau in Ottawa extended back to 1914. But it provided largely "scenic and travel pictures" lacking the social relevance of the documentary. By the 1930s it had fallen badly out of touch with current realities, and the filmmaking techniques and styles it employed were quite old-fashioned. Hollywood might occasionally make a nod to the romance of Canada in a musical (Jeanette Macdonald and Nelson Eddy in *Rose Marie*, 1936) or its epic scale in a spectacle (Cecil B. DeMille's *North West Mounted Police*, 1940). No image of productive, modern Canada appeared on the screens anywhere; no adequate acknowledgment was made of its role as a rising world leader with vast natural resources and agricultural and industrial potential. No sure sense of national identity was being given to the Canadian people through film (or through other media, for that matter). Culturally Canadians felt overshadowed by their southern neighbor, and they retained an inferiority complex about their former colonial status.

Founding of the National Film Board

By the mid-thirties representatives of the Canadian government in London had become interested in the success of British documentary—its dynamic presentation of government services, British people, and British problems. At about the same time, John Grierson was asked by the Film Committee of the Imperial Relations Trust, set up by the British government in 1937, to survey government film developments in Canada and other dominions. In 1938 Grierson was invited to Canada, where he investigated, reported on, and made recommendations to the Canadian government regarding its use of film.

In his report Grierson recommended the creation of a new federal agency. It would produce films that would contribute to a greater sense of relationship among the Canadian people and present an accurate picture of Canada to the rest of the world. The acceptance of his recommendations followed; legislation establishing a National Film Board was passed by the Canadian Parliament in May 1939 and the search for the new Film Commissioner began. Though a Canadian was intended and sought, no Canadian with adequate qualifications could be found. Grierson was chosen and accepted the offer in October 1939.

It is important to note that the Film Board was conceived in peacetime and for peacetime purposes. The legislation creating it decreed its principal mandate as that of helping "Canadians in all parts of Canada to understand the ways of living and the problems of Canadians in other parts." This was the same goal as that pursued at the Empire Marketing Board ten years earlier by Grierson and Stephen Tallents in showing one part of the empire to the rest. The Film Board's position as an autonomous government agency with its own budget and representation in Parliament came out of Grierson's frustrations with the limitations of sponsorship by the EMB and, especially, the General Post Office and made the NFB unique. The Board was also to concern itself with "distribution of Canadian films in other countries." The first six years of the National Film Board would, however, be focused to considerable extent on Canada's war effort—especially those films made for theatrical release.

Grierson began immediately to build the large and effective organization the National Film Board would become. In this he had the full support of Prime Minister Mackenzie King. Veteran ex-colleagues from Britain were brought over to assist. Stuart Legg, already in Ottawa making two films for the Canadian government, was joined by others including Raymond Spottiswoode, Stanley Hawes, Norman McLaren, and Evelyn Spice. Available documentary talent from other countries were hired as well: Irving Jacoby (screenwriter and producer) and Roger Barlow (cinematographer) among those from the United States; Joris Ivens and John Ferno from Holland; Boris Kaufman (Jean Vigo's cameraman) and Alexander Alexeieff (animator of the pinboard technique) from France. And hiring the young Canadians began, not unlike the hiring of young Britons in the earlier EMB and GPO days, except now in much larger numbers. Julian Roffman (who already had film experience), Ross McLean (who became Assistant Film Commissioner), Donald Fraser, James Beveridge, Budge Crawley, Tom Daly, Michael Spencer, Guy Glover, and Sydney Newman were among the early recruits.

The production of hundreds and hundreds of films commenced. The first year closed in October 1940 with some forty pictures either in distribution, in production, or in script preparation; by fiscal year 1943–1944 the annual rate of release had increased to two hundred. Two monthly series modeled on "The March of Time" were distributed in the theaters and subsequently released to nontheatrical audiences. It was a newsreel war not a documentary war, Grierson said, requiring the crude immediacy of reportage rather than the considered refinement of art.

Theatrical Series

The first series was "Canada Carries On," intended primarily to depict Canada's part in the war to its own people and to others. Produced by Stuart Legg, it was distributed by Columbia Pictures. The initial CCO release was *Atlantic Patrol* (April 1940). It was about the work of the Canadian navy in protecting the huge convoys that sailed from Halifax to Britain from German submarine attack. *Churchill's Island* (June 1941), about Britain at war, won an Academy Award.

The Canadian series demonstrated an uncanny knack for latching onto what was about to happen. *Warclouds in the Pacific* (November 1941), appearing ten days before the Japanese attack on Pearl Harbor, contained some borrowed "March of Time" footage. Louis de Rochemont tried to hold up its release to prevent it from scooping the MOT. *Zero Hour—The Story of the Invasion* (June 1944) was another scoop: the first account of the Allied invasion of Normandy to reach the screen. NFB personnel had assembled footage on D-Day preparations in Britain. Then they prepared more than a dozen different endings covering possible landing sites from Norway to the Mediterranean. When the invasion

Zero Hour, "Canada Carries On" series (Canada, 1944, Stuart Legg). Museum of Modern Art Film Stills Archive

occurred, the appropriate ending was added and the film was released in the United States and Canada within three days.

If "Canada Carries On" paid "The March of Time" the compliment of imitation, the second, even more ambitious series began to compete with MOT in the world market, including the United States. Entitled "The World in Action," it appeared two years after CCO had begun. Stanley Hawes took over "Canada Carries On" while "World in Action" became Stuart Legg's project. With some exceptions Legg wrote and directed every issue. United Artists distributed.

Technically this Canadian series advanced in some respects from its American counterpart. Words and images were cut together in complex and evocative connections. The music, by Louis Applebaum—who began a career as film composer at the Board, then alternated working in Hollywood (William Wellman's *The Story of G. I. Joe,* 1945) and Canada (Norman McLaren's *Around Is Around,* 1949)—was subtler and more sophisticated. The commentator, Lorne Greene, had a deeper, richer voice than Westbrook Van Voorhis; he would go on to play the father in the popular U.S. television series *Bonanza.*

The first of "The World in Action" series was *This Is Blitz* (January 1942). It used captured newsreel footage to reveal the devastation German aggression had caused; the second part dealt with Allied counterstrategy. Many of the issues concerned noncombative but important wartime topics. The WIA treatment of

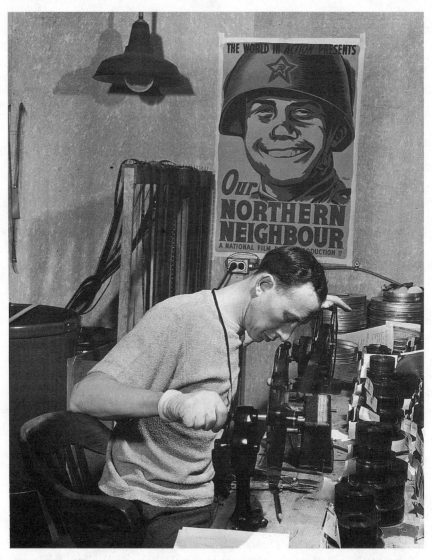

Stuart Legg, the producer of "The World in Action" monthly theatrical documentary series for the National Film Board of Canada, edits (1945, Canada, Stuart Legg). Canadian Government Photo Centre

economic/social/political subjects became one of its special distinctions. *Food—Weapon of Conquest* (March 1942), the second release, is one example. *Time* magazine called it "a blueprint of how to make an involved, dull, major aspect of World War II understandable and acceptable to moviegoers." *Inside Fighting Russia* (April 1942) comprised mostly footage obtained from the U.S.S.R. Since the Soviets tended to be secretive, this represented quite a coup. It came about, Grierson said, when he recognized that a Russian official in Canada had played one of the boys in the Soviet film *Road to Life* (1931), about homeless waifs during the Revolution, and talked him into making footage available to the NFB. *War for Men's Minds* (June 1943) concerned psychological warfare. (Grierson took secret delight in being called "the Goebbels of Canada," in reference to Nazi propaganda minister Josef Goebbels, though he thought Hitler the true genius of propaganda.) The most ambitious and intellectual of the WIA films, *War for Men's Minds* was also the first of the Canadian films to look ahead to peace.

The two series were distinctive in their departure from usual wartime propaganda emphases. There was very little hatred or violence in these films. "The World in Action" emphasis shifted from matters of immediate wartime preoccupations to those that would concern the postwar world. The international view and steady look ahead to peace were quite exceptional during wartime. The WIA particularly extended much beyond showing one part of Canada to the rest and in that respect surpassed the concurrent documentary work in Great Britain.

Examples of internationalism would be *Labour Front* (October 1943) and, especially, *Global Air Routes* (April 1944). Grierson felt satisfaction in turning the globe upside down, as he put it, in the NFB films: putting Canada at the center rather than the periphery of the world. *When Asia Speaks* (June 1944) was so accurate and farseeing in its analysis that it was still in active nontheatrical distribution long after the war. *Now—The Peace* (May 1945) dealt with the United Nations organization.

Nontheatrical Films

The great majority of those hundreds of films produced by the Film Board were for nontheatrical distribution rather than for the theaters, and were less likely to be war-related than the theatrical series. In fact, they dealt with a wide variety of subjects aimed at various audiences. These included intimate regional studies (for instance, on the life of a Quebec priest, or on Gran Manan Island), the building of the Alaska Highway, a pictorial exposition of the workings of credit unions, and animated charts on the meaning of unemployment insurance. There were also cultural shorts like the *Flight of the Dragon*, about the collection of Chinese art in the Royal Ontario Museum. *High Over the Borders* (written by Irving Jacoby and edited by John Ferno) concerned the facts and mysteries of bird migration in the Western Hemisphere. Gudrun Bjerring (later Parker) made a fifteen-minute film called *Before They Are Six*, intended particularly for mothers who ran a home and a lathe or a workbench in a wartime plant.

Canada's comprehensive system of 16mm nontheatrical distribution and exhibition was unequaled. It reported an annual audience larger than the national population. The films, in fact, grew out of the needs of the audiences to a remarkable degree; "audience response" was the key term, uniquely important in the growth of the NFB. A network of nontheatrical showings was created by the Board—preceding television, of course—with rural circuits, national trade union circuits, and industrial circuits being established. One typical circuit program was: *Food as It Might Be*, on the postwar future of farming and food marketing; *Getting Out the Coal*, on coal mining; *Trees for Tomorrow*, on forest conservation; *Mites and Monsters*, a natural history topic; and *News Roundup*, a report on the latest war developments. Later the circuits were supplemented by regional film libraries, volunteer projection services, and film councils doing the work locally with guidance and assistance from the Board.

Showings were held by the women's club or library, for example, or by the YMCA or at a grange meeting. Sixteen-millimeter prints were borrowed from regional libraries. Volunteer projection services provided trained projectionists and taught others to operate projectors. The film councils consisted of representatives from each of the local organizations using films. They would meet, once a month perhaps, to discuss and plan ways of improving the use of films. So, a kind of decentralized leadership emerged and a feedback process started. It was not just the government telling the Film Board what it wanted government films to be about and what kinds of information on those subjects were needed.

Summary

The salient observation to be made about the National Film Board is that the kind of organization Grierson was able to construct in Canada was an unrivaled information system, the largest and best-coordinated government film operation in the world. By 1945, the end of the war, it was producing 300 films a year (this in contrast to the 300 or so documentaries produced in Great Britain in the ten years before the war). Most of the Film Board releases reached an audience of roughly four million. It had a staff of about 700 in production and distribution. All of this was achieved by a nation with a population of only twelve million.

Looking back over the hundreds of films produced by the NFB during wartime, it must be admitted that they had little staying power. Almost none of them is distributed today, unlike a number of the British and American wartime documentaries and even some made in those countries in the 1930s readily available on video. This would not have mattered to Grierson at the time; the need for direct and rapid communication was the main consideration. The "5½ films a week," as Grierson characterized the Film Board output when it had reached full speed, were often skillfully made, usually timely in subject matter (rather than timeless), quickly produced, and designed to reach as wide an audience as the subject and purpose permitted. In artistic terms they had a roughness along with their urgency. Those films were valued by their audiences as well as by their producers for what they were—an almost television-like flow (before television) of information and coverage of important topics.

During the war a rift occurred between Grierson and his former British colleagues over the kinds of documentaries that needed to be made. Grierson thought the British documentaries too soft and "aestheticky." "Sure London can take it," he would say, in reference to the influential British documentary of that title, "but can she dish it out?" paraphrasing dialogue from one of his favorite gangster movies, *Little Caesar*. Grierson saw early British wartime propaganda as reflecting a country preparing to go down with quiet heroism into defeat. There is an anecdote about Grierson preventing the young Canadians from screening the print of *Listen to Britain* he had received so that they would not be distracted by its loveliness from the more vigorous style he wanted them to develop. Some of the British, for their part, found the Canadian films illustrated lectures lacking in artistic sophistication, which infuriated Grierson. They may have been at least as effective as the more polished British productions in reaching their intended audiences and achieving their purposes. In any case, it does seem inarguable that the Film Board played a part in giving Canada a sense of national identity and pride.

Perhaps, finally, the sheer establishment of the National Film Board—which went on to other kinds of achievements, including aesthetic excellence (to be dealt with in chapter eleven), while the documentary movements in Britain and America faltered—is the great legacy of the wartime documentary efforts in Canada. It stands as the largest and most impressive monument to Grierson's concepts and activities relating to the use of film by governments in communication with their citizens. It became a model for national film boards established in New Zealand, Australia, South Africa, India, and elsewhere. Grierson himself called the Film Board "a tidy operation, the tidiest [he] was involved with."

Films of the Period

1939

The Case of Charlie Gordon (Stuart Legg)

1940

Atlantic Patrol ("Canada Carries On" series, Legg)
Hot Ice (Irving Jacoby)
Letter from Camp Bordon (CCO, Raymond Spottiswoode)

1941

Canadian Landscape (F. R. Crawley)
Churchill's Island (CCO, Legg)
Peoples of Canada (CCO, Gordon Sparling)
Strategy of Metals (CCO, Stanley Hawes)
Warclouds in the Pacific (CCO, Legg)

1942

Action Stations! (Joris Ivens)
Food—Weapon of Conquest ("The World in Action" series, Legg)
Geopolitik—Hitler's Plan for Empire (WIA, Legg)
13th Platoon (Julian Roffman)
West Wind (Crawley)

1943

High Over the Borders (Jacoby)
The War for Men's Minds (WIA, Legg)

1944

Look to the North (James Beveridge)
When Asia Speaks (WIA, Legg)
Zero Hour—The Story of the Invasion (WIA, Legg)

1945

Food—Secret of the Peace (WIA, Legg)
Listen to the Prairies (Gudrun Bjerring [Parker])
Maps in Action (Evelyn Lambart)
Music in the Wind (Jean Palardy)
Now—The Peace (WIA, Legg)

Books on the Period

Backhouse, Charles, Canadian Government Motion Picture Bureau 1917–1941. Ottawa: Canadian Film Institute, 1974.
Beattie, Eleanor, A Handbook of Canadian Film. Toronto: Peter Martin Associates, 1973.
Beveridge, James, John Grierson: Film Master. New York: Macmillan, 1978.
Ellis, Jack C., John Grierson: A Guide to References and Resources. Boston: G. K. Hall, 1986.
Ellis, Jack C., John Grierson: Life, Contributions, Influence. Carbondale: University of Southern Illinois Press, 2000.
Evans, Gary, John Grierson and the National Film Board: The Politics of Wartime Propaganda. Toronto: University of Toronto Press, 1984.
Feldman, Seth and Joyce Nelson, eds., Canadian Film Reader. Toronto: Peter Martin Associates, 1977.

Grierson Project, McGill University, The John, *John Grierson and the NFB.* Toronto: ECW Press, 1984.

Hardy, Forsyth, *John Grierson: A Documentary Biography.* London: Faber and Faber, 1979.

James, C. Rodney, *Film as a National Art: NFB of Canada and the Film Board Idea.* New York: Arno Press, 1977.

Jones, D. B., *Movies and Memoranda: An Interpretive History of the National Film Board of Canada.* Ottawa: Canadian Film Institute and Deneau Publishers, 1981.

Manvell, Roger, *Film and the Second World War.* New York: Dell, 1974.

McInnes, Graham, ed. By Gene Walz, *One Man's Documentary: A Memoir of the Early Years of the National Film Board.* Manitoba: University of Manitoba Press, 2005.

McKay, Marjorie, *History of the National Film Board of Canada.* Montreal: National Film Board, 1964.

Nelson, Joyce, *The Colonized Eye: Rethinking the Grierson Legend.* Toronto: Between the Lines, 1988.

Chapter Nine

Expansion: United States, 1941–1945

In the United States the first two years of the 1940s were essentially an extension of the 1930s. The extreme hardships of the Depression were gradually alleviated as the country backed into war, supplying Great Britain in its fight against Germany through the Lend-Lease Act and other forms of aid, some of them covert.

At President Roosevelt's request, Prime Minister Winston Churchill agreed not to send official British wartime propaganda to the United States until the U.S. entered the war. Roosevelt was concerned that such a clear indication of his administration's pro-British and prowar stance would disturb the illusion of neutrality and provide American isolationists with evidence to use against him. Since no such agreement had been made with Canada, John Grierson, head of its National Film Board, saw to it that British documentaries reached the United States along with those of Canada. Britain's and Canada's early wartime documentaries may well have contributed to moving America from sympathy to action on behalf of Britain.

However, not until the Japanese attack on the U.S. naval base at Pearl Harbor on December 7, 1941, followed by Germany's declaration of war, did the United States join the widening world conflict. Entry into the war had as profound an effect on documentary film in the United States as it had had on America's allies, Britain and Canada.

The war brought English-language documentary together in ways and to a degree not true of any other period in its history. The peoples of Britain, Canada, and the United States viewed one another's films about the war. Film materials were exchanged—stock-shot library footage, combat footage, captured enemy footage—to be made into compilation films reporting wartime events and providing historical backgrounds. Films about each country were produced to orient troops and civilians as to their cultural differences as well as to their common ways and to the ways in which each nation depended on the other for survival. The joint production ventures near the end of the war of the "victory series" discussed in chapter seven, culminating with *The True Glory*, were the final and most complete examples of this collaboration.

The centripetal force exerted by war not only brought together documentaries and documentarians of the three countries, it pulled together documentary and fiction filmmakers within each country. Filmmakers of all sorts were working in common cause and sometimes on the same projects. Documentaries gained an unprecedented amount of theatrical screen time.

The degree and kind of wartime pulling together in each country were different, of course. Differences among the films of the three nations will be examined in the final section of this chapter. The sections up to that deal with the four major types of wartime films—training, indoctrination, records of battle, and social documentary—made in the United States.

Training

The military training films (and civilian instructional films pertaining to war industries, civil defense, conservation of materials needed for war, and the like) were not documentaries. But they are closely enough related as part of the general wartime film effort to warrant some attention. As mentioned in chapter 7 concerning British wartime documentary, hundreds of such "nuts and bolts" films were made, on every conceivable subject. A random sample of those in the U.S. might include the following: *Articles of War, Military Courtesy, Keep It Clean* (how and why to take care of a gun), *Resisting Enemy Interrogation, Clearing Enemy Mine Fields, Notes on Jungle Warfare,* and *Sex Hygiene*. In *Identification of the Japanese Zero* (1942) a young Ronald Reagan plays a flyer who mistakes a friend's P40 for a Japanese Zero and tries to shoot it down. In the end he gets a chance to down a real Zero. These training films were thought to be, and were tested to be, extremely effective pedagogically (see Hovland, Lumsdaine, and Sheffield, *Experiments on Mass Communication*, listed in Books on the Period). An anecdote about the use of film at Fort Leonard Wood, Missouri, where army engineers were being trained, illustrates this view. The second lieutenant who was to have instructed the platoon on how to construct a pontoon bridge failed to appear. The sergeant projected a film on the subject without the usual lecture and presentation of models and diagrams. The men were marched out to the river and put together a bridge without error in less time than it had taken other trainees who had had the benefit of full instruction.

Indoctrination

Rather than *indoctrination* or *propaganda*, the U.S. Armed Forces engaged in what it called *orientation*. Central to the massive effort directed toward converting more than nine million Americans from civilians into military personnel was the seven-part "Why We Fight" series.

Frank Capra, circa 1943, editing at the U.S. Army Signal Corps facility in Astoria, New York.

The production of this series and of other important information and education films was entrusted to Lieutenant Colonel Frank Capra. One of the most popular Hollywood filmmakers of the 1930s (*It Happened One Night, Mr. Deeds Goes to Town, Mr. Smith Goes to Washington*), Capra had no prior documentary experience. (The same could be said of virtually all the Hollywood filmmakers involved with wartime documentaries.) Capra was assisted by Major Anatole Litvak, and Captains Anthony Veiller and William Hornbeck—Hollywood veterans all; director, writer, and editor, respectively. Sergeant Richard Griffith (subsequently head of the film department of the Museum of Modern Art) did research. In addition to "Why We Fight," the Capra group made other large-scale films designed to orient American troops to the foreigners—allies and enemies—with whom they were about to come into contact. Examples are *Know Your Ally—Britain* (1943), the script by novelist Eric Knight (*Lassie Come Home, This Above All*), *Here Is Germany* (1945), and *Know Your Enemy—Japan* (1946).

"Why We Fight" was based on the assumption that servicemen would be more committed and able fighters if they knew about the events leading up to, and reasons for, American participation in the war. The spirit of isolationism— still strong in the United States right up to the Japanese attack on Pearl Harbor—

had to be counteracted. In this attempt "Why We Fight" presented a gigantic historical treatise from a particular "liberal" point of view—that is to say from the perspective of the New Deal Democratic administration, which became the predominant viewpoint in the country during the war. (The irony here is that Capra's personal politics were conservative Republican. But they rested on a kind of populism that united him with the common effort led by President Roosevelt.) History as the basis for organization was frequent in the American documentaries, from *The Plow That Broke the Plains* (1936) and *The River* (1937) on. It was not used in that way by wartime filmmakers in Great Britain or Canada.

"Why We Fight" is most impressive in the scale of its conception and the virtuosity of its execution. Almost entirely compiled (from existing footage including newsreels, Allied and captured enemy records of battle, bits from American fiction features, and Nazi propaganda films), through editing and commentary it presents a vast and coherent panorama.

The first three films—*Prelude to War* (1942), *The Nazis Strike* (1943), and *Divide and Conquer* (1943)—cover the period from 1918 to 1941. They document the increase in Japanese aggression in Asia, the growing menace of Hitler in Europe, and—above all—the changing American foreign policy and public opinion between the end of World War I and America's entry into World War II. *The Battle of Britain* (1943), *The Battle of Russia* (1943), and *The Battle of China* (1944) cover the efforts of America's allies, who were in the war before the U.S. entered it and continued to fight alongside American troops. *War Comes to America* (1945) offered a recapitulation and even more detailed examination of changes in American attitudes over the preceding two decades and of the conflicting impulses and ideologies that shaped them. Picking up and consolidating the themes of the first three films, it was made last but intended to be shown first.

The films, short features in length, were shown to all service personnel; viewing of all seven was compulsory before embarkation for overseas duty. Though designed solely for showing to military personnel, when their excellence and dramatic power were recognized by the War Department, some of these films were made available for civilian audiences through theatrical exhibition.

The chief artistic problem the makers of these films faced was one of giving structure to vast amounts of unstructured history. In this respect their work was like that of Shakespeare in his chronicle plays. Dramatic form was given to each of the films, with exposition, mounting action, climax, and denouement. They can be broken down into acts, in fact. *Divide and Conquer*, for example, has five acts, like classical tragedy. Act I contains exposition: Poland has been overrun by Germany; conquest of Britain is now its goal; German strategy is outlined; the theme of Hitler's lying treachery is sounded. The content of Act II is the successful German campaign against Denmark and Norway. Act III deals with the position of France, the Maginot line, and French weakness. Act IV comprises the German conquest of Holland and Belgium. Act V is the fall of France. The various participant countries are given character; they become characters, like dramatis personae. In this respect, rather than the Shakespearean histories this film bears a curious resemblance to *Hamlet*, with Germany as Claudius, the murderous villain, France as Hamlet, DeGaulle and French North Africa as Horatio, and England as Fortinbras. Here, as in *Hamlet*, things are not what they seem, with the villain protesting friendship and the tragic hero constricted by an incapacity for action.

A considerable variety of visual and audio resources are used in these compiled documentaries—very nearly the full range conceivable. Visuals in *The Nazis Strike*, for instance, include, in addition to newsreel footage, excerpts from the Nazi *Triumph of the Will*, *Hitlerjunge Quex*, and *Baptism of Fire*, bits of staged action (the victims of firing squads), still photos, drawings and maps, animated diagrams (the animation by Walt Disney Studio), newspaper headlines, and printed titles (Hitler's pronouncements). The sound track includes two narrators (Anthony Veiller for the factual, Walter Huston for the emotional), quoted dialogue (Churchill, and an impersonation of Hitler), music (by Dmitri Tiomkin, one of Hollywood's best), and sound effects.

Dramatic conflict is obtained by painstaking manipulation of combat footage. Editing conventions of matched action and screen direction are maintained. German attackers always move from right to left. A synthetic assemblage of diverse shots is edited into a cause-effect order: German bombers in formation, bombs dropping from planes, explosions in villages, rubble. The result is almost as if all of this footage had been shot for these films under Capra's or Litvak's direction.

Maps and animated diagrams give scope to the live-action sequences and clarify and relate random material to formalized patterns consistent with the actual movement involved. In *Divide and Conquer* the sequence of refugees on the roads being strafed by German fighter planes is especially striking; one reads into the actual what has just been seen in animated representation. In another instance from the same film, the animated arrows representing the panzer divisions thrust into an outlined Forest of Ardennes with speed and power. And the animation takes on symbolic and rhetorical meaning; in *Divide and Conquer*, yet again, swastika termites infest the base of a castle, and pythonlike arrows lock around the British Isles.

It must be admitted, however, that though "Why We Fight" may be greatly admired on technical and aesthetic grounds, there is some convincing evidence that it was not as effective indoctrination as hoped for and even thought to be. (See Hovland, Lumsdaine, and Sheffield, *Experiments on Mass Communication*, listed in Books on the Period.) The problem, the social scientists inferred from their testing, was with the historical approach. It seemed to have the desired effects only on those with the equivalent of some college education; it appeared to be too intellectual and over the heads of a majority of soldiers tested. As films, though, "Why We Fight" offers incontrovertible evidence of very great filmmaking skill and a remarkably full and varied use of film technique. It stands as a peak of achievement in the history of documentary and influenced subsequent historical compilation films, especially the many appearing on television, some of which will be discussed in chapter 12.

Records of Battle

As with the "Why We Fight" series, other of the most prestigious wartime documentaries were made for the armed forces by Hollywood veterans. Among them were John Ford, John Huston, and William Wyler.

John Ford's fiction features of the nineteen thirties gave him a status comparable to Capra's; he also emphasized American themes, though in his case usually historical (for example *Stagecoach, Young Mr. Lincoln, Drums Along the Mohawk*). He enlisted in the navy rather than the army. Much of *The Battle of Midway* (1942) Ford filmed himself with a 16mm handheld camera, and he was seriously wounded during the filming. The film won an Academy Award. It is early and unusual in using color; color would come into documentary for the first time during the war. (Eastman Kodak had introduced the first practicable 16mm color film for home movie use, Kodachrome, in 1935. Another Hollywood director, George Stevens, put together and released after the war 16mm color footage he had shot while serving in the Army Signal Corps in Europe.) Ford's *December 7th* (1943) is a largely recreated account of the Japanese attack on Pearl Harbor using miniatures, rear screen projection, process photography, and actors. (It was shot by Gregg Toland, cinematographer of *The Grapes of Wrath* and *Citizen Kane*.) Though the emotionalism of these two films may strike an audience today as excessive, they accurately reflect the feelings of many people at the time they were made.

John Huston (whose prewar success was *The Maltese Falcon*) made some of the finest and most personal of the wartime documentaries. His subsequent filmmaking seems to have gained considerably from that experience.

Report from the Aleutians (1943) was the first and least outstanding of Huston's three major documentaries. The problem with it is not so much of his making as of the situation the film is about. On the desolate Aleutian Islands extending west out of Alaska, American and Japanese forces feinted and parried. Bombing missions over Japanese-held Kiska Island comprised the principal U.S. military activity. The color filming (16mm Kodachrome) was done over a period of six months in the rain and almost constant fog of Adak. The commentary, written by Huston and spoken by his father, Walter, offers a sense that the dreary weather, the boredom, and the loneliness were as much the enemy as the Japanese.

Many think *The Battle of San Pietro* (1945) the finest American wartime documentary; perhaps it is among the most outstanding films yet made about men in battle. It is an engrossing account of a full week of savage fighting between American and German forces in Italy for the control of the Liri Valley. The

American troops on the attack in *The Battle of San Pietro*. Huston's original version, using the voices of dead men (recorded before battle) as narration over photographs of their bodies, was cut by the military authorities (U.S., 1944, John Huston). Museum of Modern Art Film Still Archive

taking of a small military objective becomes an indictment of modern warfare in general, with its incredible cost both in military and civilian casualties. This theme is further underscored as we see bodies of soldiers being buried beneath dog tag markers. After the battle, the people of San Pietro return to their devastated village and must somehow find the strength to rebuild their shattered lives. The weary Americans will move on to "more rivers, and more mountains, and more towns . . . more 'San Pietros,' greater or lesser—a thousand more." The commentary was written and read by Huston. *Let There Be Light* (1946), Huston's final wartime documentary, will be discussed later.

William Wyler (of *Wuthering Heights* and *The Little Foxes*) served in the Army Air Force. His *Memphis Belle* (1944) is, in a way, an answer to the British *Target for Tonight*. It is interesting that Hollywood director Wyler used candid color footage of a real raid (one of his cameramen was killed while filming) with voice-over narration, while documentarian Harry Watt had used simulated action (some of it shot in a studio), scripted dialogue, and directed performances. The "Memphis Belle" was a Boeing B17 "flying fortress" on its last bombing mission over Germany before its veteran crew was sent home. The world we

Memphis Belle (U.S., 1944, William Wyler). Museum of Modern Art Film Stills Archive

see and hear is that of the airmen—refracted images of sky and enemy fighters seen through Plexiglas, the drone of engines and excited voices over the intercom. The film seems to come very close to the reality of their experience.

The title of Wyler's *Thunderbolt* (1945, in color) is what the P47 fighter-bomber was called. The film deals with the activities of the Fifty-seventh Fighter Group in Italy destroying vital supply routes deep behind German lines. Much of it supports a statement made in the commentary that "The airman never sees the face of the people, but only the face of the country." The sequences on the ground suggest something of the prevailing fear and boredom. Between missions, these young men attempt to distract themselves through various forms of recreation but can't altogether overcome the nagging regret that they are not home finding jobs and getting married.

In addition to combat documentaries identified with particular Hollywood directors were those made collaboratively by film crews (sometimes including Hollywood talent) of the various armed services. A notable group of these reported on warfare in the Pacific.

The Battle for the Marianas (1944) concerns a joint army, navy, marine, and Coast Guard assault on Saipan, Tinian, and Guam, the major islands of the Mariana group. In *Attack! The Battle for New Britain* (1944) explanations of the strategy are accompanied by comments about life in the jungle. *To the Shores of Iwo Jima* (1945) is one of the fullest and most skillfully made accounts of a

Production still from the making of *Thunderbolt* **(U.S., 1945, William Wyler). Museum of Modern Art Film Stills Archive**

combined operation. *The Fleet That Came to Stay* (1945) documents the planning and staging of the Okinawa invasion as well as including much combat footage. *Fury in the Pacific* (1945) is unusual in the number and intensity of the shots of Japanese and Americans being killed in battle. Nine cameramen fell while filming. It was not released until after the war.

The *Fighting Lady* (1944) is about the final phase of the war in the Pacific (fought almost exclusively between American and Japanese forces). It is feature-length and in Technicolor. The title refers to an aircraft carrier, in this case the *Yorktown*. The action concerns defense against attacks of kamikaze pilots diving to their deaths, trying to take American warships with them. Directed by famed still photographer Edward Steichen, it was narrated by movie star Robert Taylor, both then in the navy. The film was produced by Louis de Rochemont, who had left "The March of Time" to become a producer at Twentieth Century-Fox, which distributed *The Fighting Lady* and, also, was then distributing "The March of Time."

Social Documentary

In 1940, before the United States' entry into the war, President Roosevelt appointed Nelson Rockefeller as Coordinator of Inter-American Affairs (CIAA).

The Fighting Lady, made by de Rochemont after leaving "The March of Time" (U.S., 1944, Louis de Rochemont). Museum of Modern Art Film Stills Archive

This new agency was occasioned largely by U.S. nervousness about the growing German presence in Latin America, through increased immigration and growth in trade. The conception of the CIAA was not unlike that of the earlier British Empire Marketing Board: government public relations working to increase economic and political interdependency and mutual support. CIAA films were intended to play an important role somewhat similar to that of the EMB films: to show aspects of life in the United States to the Latin American countries, and to show aspects of their life to American citizens.

One film about Latin America made for the CIAA was *The Bridge* (1944), directed by Willard Van Dyke and Ben Maddow. It is about the economics of South America and the importance of air transport in connecting its countries with one another and with North America. Another example would be *High Plain* (1943), directed by Jules Bucher, about the Indians of the Bolivian plateau. The latter is one of many films about Latin America produced for CIAA by Julien Bryan and intended for showing in the U.S.

Another cluster of films for the CIAA were produced by the Walt Disney Studio. They are clever and imaginative animated teaching and communication. *The Grain That Built a Hemisphere* (1943) is a historical survey of the importance of maize/corn in the nutrition and economies of the American continents. *Water—Friend or Enemy* (1944) offers basic education in the importance of uncontaminated water and methods for obtaining it. The Disney films were distributed widely in both Spanish- and English-language versions. (The Disney Studio also made instructional films for the armed forces. *Cold Front* and *Fog*, both 1943, part of a series produced for the Bureau of Aeronautics of the U.S. Navy, are two examples.)

Among the CIAA films, closest to a continuation of the prewar American social documentary were those in the "Ohio Town" series, produced by Julien Bryan in 1945. Made for showing in Latin America (in part to counteract Hollywood representations), films in this series were also circulated widely in this country and in Europe. Bryan selected Mt. Vernon, Ohio, as representative of small-town U.S.A. Four of the five films were built around a person and his or her work—a doctor, a factory craftsman, a county agricultural agent, an elementary schoolteacher—the fifth gives an overview of the town.

In 1942, following the United States' entry into the war, the Office of War Information (OWI) was set up. This agency was equivalent to the British Ministry of Information and the Canadian Wartime Information Board. News commentator Elmer Davis was named head of the OWI. The agency's function was to coordinate all government information released to the media and to develop its own means of informing the public. The Motion Picture Bureau of the OWI was headed by Robert Riskin, scriptwriter for some of Frank Capra's most successful features (*It Happened One Night, Mr. Deeds Goes to Town, Meet John Doe*). It established liaison with the Hollywood studios, primarily to insure that entertainment films did not contain material harmful to morale or to the U.S.'s relationships with its allies. The Motion Picture Bureau also produced its own films. Philip Dunne, another Hollywood scriptwriter (*Suez, The Rains Came, How Green Was My Valley*), was chief of production.

The purpose of the Domestic Branch of the Motion Picture Bureau was to make films for American civilian viewing, somewhat along the lines of the British Crown Film Unit or the Canadian National Film Board, presumably. The Overseas Branch was to make films for showing to allies, neutral countries, and countries that had been under Axis occupation. It is characteristic of Americans' suspiciousness about government information directed at them that the Domestic Branch never succeeded in getting a production program underway. The Overseas Branch, on the other hand, had a distinguished wartime record, its films made largely by documentary veterans. Though not as big or prestigious (or expensive) as the armed forces documentaries made by Hollywood directors, the OWI films, taken together, offer a broad and sensitive picture of diverse aspects of life in the United States. Here's a sampling.

The Autobiography of a Jeep (1943, Irving Lerner) is a jaunty tribute to that product of American wartime technology. Following a showing of it in liberated France the audience is said to have burst into shouts of "*Vive le jip! Vive le jip.*" *The Town* (1944, Josef von Sternberg) is about the contribution of many cultures to the United States as evidenced in the eclectic architecture, mixed population, and many religions of Madison, Indiana. *Pacific Northwest* (1944, Willard Van

Dyke) describes and interprets the Northwestern states, rarely settings for Hollywood entertainment (or other documentaries, for that matter). *Hymn of the Nations* (1944, Alexander Hammid), produced in honor of the liberation of Italy, is mostly a skillful and responsive film recording of Arturo Toscanini conducting the NBC Symphony Orchestra in Giuseppe Verdi's piece by that name.

In the final year of the war the following films were released by the OWI: *The Cummington Story* (1945, Helen Grayson and Larry Madison; score by Aaron Copland) is a moving reenactment of an actual experience of the tensions created and eventually overcome when war refugees are moved into a Connecticut town. *The Library of Congress* (1945, Alexander Hammid) presents many of the aspects—science, painting, music, literature—of this great institution as symbolic of Americans' regard for the non-materialistic things in life. *Tuesday in November* (1945, John Houseman; score by Virgil Thomson) is about the U.S. election system and election day in a small town. *Capital Story* (1945, Henwar Rodakiewicz) shows detective work of the U.S. Public Health Service in tracing a harmful ingredient in a shipbuilding process. *The Window Cleaner* (1945, Jules Bucher) offers a charming little sketch of life in the United States as seen from the point of view of a window washer on the Empire State Building. *A Better Tomorrow* (1945, Alexander Hammid) is a study of three progressive schools in the New York City system as representative of American public education.

Let There Be Light (1946, John Huston), though produced by the Army Pictorial Service, was intended mainly for civilian audiences. It serves as a painful and moving reflection on the mental and emotional casualties of war. What had been called "shell shock" in World War I became "battle fatigue" in World War II. (Later it would be called "post-traumatic stress disorder" and "Gulf War syndrome." Whatever its name, the symptoms are equally debilitating.) The film examines the rehabilitation of the psychosomatically disabled at Mason General Hospital in Brentwood, Long Island. The psychotherapy is observed with close attention to particular cases. A GI who lost his memory during a shell burst at Okinawa is hypnotized and begins to recall his terror and fear of battle. Another soldier, who stutters, is given sodium amytol. He begins to speak and then to shout, half sobbing, "I can TALK! Oh God, listen! God, I can talk." By the end of the film it is clear that the inabilities of these men to walk, to speak, or to remember are not symptoms of abnormality. Rather, "in the fulfillment of their duties as soldiers, [they] were forced beyond the limit of human endurance."

Let There Be Light was not released until almost forty years after it was completed. The army said they were concerned about invasion of privacy of the men shown. Huston said they were concerned about the human effects of war shown.

Comparisons: Great Britain, Canada, the United States

An unusual aspect of wartime documentary in the three countries was that the films were all government sponsored and related in one way or another to what was seen as needed in the national interest. Private sponsorship of nonfiction films virtually ceased during the war. Beyond that similarity, however, there were significant differences among the three countries, beginning with the context of documentary in each at the outbreak of war.

In Britain, before the war, documentary had become a thoroughly established enterprise. It was not large in terms of amounts of money, numbers of film-makers and films made, or total audience size, admittedly. But it had earned respect among opinion leaders and gained a central relationship to matters of public concern. The British entertainment film industry, on the other hand, rested more firmly on the distribution and exhibition of American films than on the production of British ones. As a result, it was the documentarians who obtained the choice assignments and made the finest of the British wartime documentaries. At the same time it must be acknowledged that the semidocu-mentaries—Britain's distinctive wartime contribution—came both from the government Crown Film Unit and from the commercial studios. In fact, early in the war two of the leaders of British documentary, Alberto Cavalcanti and Harry Watt, left the government unit for Ealing Studios, where they worked on docu-mentary-influenced fiction features.

In Canada, very little filmmaking of any sort had existed before the war. When the National Film Board was established, it became the main, almost the sole, producer of Canadian wartime films. Its staff—consisting of a few docu-mentary veterans from abroad and hundreds of Canadian tyros—made mainly documentary and related types of informational and instructional films.

In the United States, prewar documentary had been disorganized and lacking prestige compared to monolithic Hollywood with its proven success. As a result, it was the Hollywood filmmakers who got the big armed forces projects and made some of the most valuable and lasting of the wartime documentaries. (It seems curious that Hollywood filmmakers, experienced with storytelling, did not follow the semidocumentary line. Instead, they stuck to vigorous propaganda or unalloyed records of battle—moved fully over into documentary, in other words.) The American documentary veterans, for the most part, worked on smaller-scale projects for the Coordinator of Inter-American Affairs and the Of-fice of War Information. These were closer to a continuation of the peacetime documentary than were the other American wartime documentaries.

Let's conclude with a comparison of wartime nonfiction films produced in the United States, Canada, and Britain. Since the training films were generally alike, the comparison can be confined to the indoctrination films, records of battle, and social documentary.

As one might expect, the greatest differences among documentaries of the three nations are evident in their **indoctrination films**. In Britain the most im-portant of these took the forms of poetic shorts and semidocumentary features. One noteworthy characteristic of all these films is the lack of attention given to the violence and destructiveness of war, even less to vilification and hatred of the

One of 5,236 theaters that presented "The March of Time" to 12 million people every month during its heyday. From Raymond Fielding's book *The March of Time*

enemy. Instead, two themes are repeated, subtly and insistently. One is that Britain will survive; or, as put in the final words of "The British Grenadier" (aka "Rule Britannia"), which accompanies the conclusion of *Listen to Britain*, "England never, never will be slave." The other is that we British are all in this together, everyone is doing his or her job. The reason for the first of these two emphases is clear enough. Britain was facing German military might massed across a narrow channel and destruction rained down nightly from the skies. Survival was a matter of real and immediate, of general and personal, concern. The second emphasis relates to class divisions persisting in England. Many of the working class had come to feel that their sacrifices in earlier wars had benefited the already privileged more than themselves. This time all classes are shown working together for everyone's postwar world.

Canadian indoctrination films took the form of the two "March-of-Time"-like monthly theatrical shorts, "Canada Carries On" and "The World in Action." These offer information about and interpretation of aspects of the world at war, showing their meaning for Canadians and Canada's relationship to them. There are two emphases here as well. One is that we Canadians are doing our part (in a distinctive Canadian way). The other is that Canada is an important part of the world. These themes would seem to follow from Canada's uncertainty about its national character and its sense of geographical isolation, from its newness as a nation and lack of recognition as a world power. The divisive issue of differences between French-speaking Canada (which did not fully support the war effort) and English-speaking Canada (which did) was avoided. Canadians are Canadians are Canadians in these films, whatever their ethnic backgrounds.

In the United States the main form of indoctrination films was the large historical compilation (short feature in length). The "Why We Fight" series was the centerpiece. The emphases in these films are, first, that America's enemies (Germany, Japan, Italy) are unethical, sometimes even inhuman. (Audiences today are shocked by the racism, chauvinism, and incitement to hatred evident in these indoctrination films.) Second, it is in America's self-interest to join our allies in helping destroy these enemies. If we don't, eventually they will invade and conquer us. These thrusts seem a reaction against the earlier, majority attitudes of neutrality (the war seen as a foreign war, with neither side deserving American allegiance) and isolationism (the war seen as a long way off and the U.S. protected by two oceans).

British **records of battle** were mainly the large-scale feature-length "victory series," which chronicled successfully completed campaigns. The series began with *Desert Victory* (North Africa) and concluded with *The True Glory* (Europe).

Canadians made few "shot and shell" films, as Grierson called the accounts of combat. Strategy rather than tactics was the principal concern—the goals and progress of the war, the general problems that had to be resolved. Canadian films about warfare were mostly informational and analytical rather than descriptive and emotional; little battle action was shown.

The Americans made a large number of battle films and became especially accomplished with this kind of documentary. They are, of course, full of violence and the attitudes expressed are jingoistic and frequently racist (especially in regard to the Japanese). Americans were more distant from the war than were the British; more of them were involved in it than were the Canadians (where general conscription, a draft, was never adopted). So, there was felt to be a need for Americans to report back to Americans what war was really like. Also, it is possible that the Hollywood genre of war dramas served as inspiration for this form— the finest of the battle records were made by Hollywood directors.

Finally, there were continuations of the **social documentary**. British wartime documentaries frequently contain quite explicit references to what will be needed in the peace ahead, sometimes from what would seem a Labour party (that is, socialist) point of view. The work of Paul Rotha is noteworthy here, especially *World of Plenty*, about international food distribution, and *Land of Promise*, about postwar housing.

The Canadian films are exceptional in their selection of subjects having to do with peacetime needs and aspirations as well as with the wartime situation. Grierson said, "The aims of our society lie beyond war and in the love of peace. It would be a poor information service . . . which kept harping on war to the

Theatrical poster for *The Battle of Russia* of the "Why We Fight" series (U.S., 1943, Anatole Litvak). Academy of Motion Pictures Arts and Sciences

exclusion of everything, making our minds narrow and anemic." He would also say, from time to time, that everything that was built at the Film Board in wartime was built for peacetime as well.

The American wartime documentaries continued peacetime subjects and themes only for a special reason. Those films produced for the Coordinator of Inter-American Affairs were directed at improving U.S. relations with Latin American countries, and those for the Office of War Information were designed to present a favorable picture of American ways of life to neutral peoples and those who had been freed from occupation by the Axis powers. Admittedly what was shown was idealized, but the CIAA and OWI films reflect how a lot of Americans liked to think about themselves. These films were made not only to counteract enemy propaganda but also the pictures of American life offered by Hollywood movies, with their gangsters and millionaires, materialism and glamour.

By the end of the war, documentary in Britain, Canada, and the United States had reached a pinnacle. More money was being invested in documentary production, and more personnel were making more documentary films than ever before. Vastly larger audiences were seeing documentaries and related types of realist and educational films in theaters and in greatly increased nontheatrical showings. The effect of this wartime expansion on immediate postwar films will be the subject of the next chapter. In it the place documentary found for itself in the greatly enlarged nontheatrical film field will be considered.

Films of the Period

1943

The Autobiography of a Jeep (Irving Lerner)
The Battle of Britain ("Why We Fight" series, Anthony Veiller)
The Battle of Midway (John Ford)
Divide and Conquer ("Why We Fight" series, Frank Capra and Anatole Litvak)
High Plain (Jules Bucher)
The Nazis Strike ("Why We Fight" series, Capra and Litvak)
Prelude to War ("Why We Fight" series, Capra)
Report from the Aleutians (John Huston)
World at War (Samuel Spewack)

1944

Attack! The Battle for New Britain (War Department)
The Battle of China ("Why We Fight" series, Capra)
The Battle of Russia ("Why We Fight" series, Litvak)
The Bridge (Willard Van Dyke and Ben Maddow)
The Fighting Lady (Edward Steichen)
Hymn of the Nations (Alexander Hammid)

Memphis Belle (William Wyler)
The Negro Soldier (Capra and Stuart Heisler)
A Salute to France (Jean Renoir and Garson Kanin)
Steel Town (Van Dyke)
The Town (Josef von Sternberg)
Valley of the Tennessee (Hammid)
With the Marines at Tarawa (Marine Corps)

1945

El Agente agronomo (*The County Agent,* Julien Bryan)
The Battle of San Pietro (Huston)
A Better Tomorrow (Hammid)
Capital Story (Henwar Rodakiewicz)
The Cummington Story (Helen Grayson and Larry Madison)
Fury in the Pacific (Army, Navy, and Marine Corps*)*
The Library of Congress (Hammid)
Thunderbolt (Wyler)
To the Shores of Iwo Jima (Navy, Marine Corps, and Coast Guard)
Tuesday in November (John Houseman)
War Comes to America ("Why We Fight" series, Litvak)
The Window Cleaner (Bucher)

1946

Let There Be Light (Huston)

Books on the Period

Bohn, Thomas William, *An Historical and Descriptive Analysis of the "Why We Fight"
Series.* New York: Arno, 1977.
Capra, Frank, "Part III, The Great Struggle," in *The Name Above the Title.* New York:
Macmillan, 1971, pp. 325–367.
Culbert, David, ed., *Film and Propaganda in America: A Documentary History.* Westport,
CT: Greenwood, 1990.
Hovland, Carl I., Arthur A. Lumsdaine, and Fred D. Sheffield, *Experiments on Mass Com-
munication.* Princeton, NJ: Princeton University Press, 1949. Vol. 3 of *Studies in Social
Psychology in World War II.*
Look, ed., *Movie Lot to Beachhead.* Garden City, NY: Doubleday, Doran, 1945.
MacCann, Richard Dyer, *The People's Films: A Political History of U.S. Government Motion
Pictures.* New York: Hastings House, 1973.
Manvell, Roger, *Films and the Second World War.* New York: Dell, 1976.
Shale, Richard, *Donald Duck Joins Up: The Disney Studio During World War II.* Ann
Arbor, MI: UMI Research Press, 1982.
Short, K. R. M., ed., *Film and Radio Propaganda in World War II.* Knoxville: University
of Tennessee Press, 1983.

Chapter Ten

The Unfulfilled Promise: Postwar Documentary, 1945–1952

I f, during the war, documentary and fiction filmmakers drew closer together, as noted in the preceding chapters, it is also true that postwar documentary drew closer to the fiction film than it had been prior to the war. A prominent example is *Benjy* (1951), a short produced for the Orthopaedic Foundation of Los Angeles, with the cooperation of Paramount Pictures, directed by Fred Zinnemann and narrated by Henry Fonda. Though it used acted performances, studio lighting, and an opulent score to tell an authentic story of a crippled boy, it received the Academy Award for documentary. Mention has already been made of semidocumentary features produced by the Crown Film Unit after the war—*Children on Trial, Life in Her Hands, Out of True*, and *Four Men in Prison*. A British short, produced for the Central Office of Information (successor to the Ministry of Information), *David: Story of a Welshman* (1951), used an even fuller range of fictional techniques. In the United States, the three big documentaries of the immediate postwar years (and there were only three big ones) were features in length and narrative in structure. Two of them received theatrical distribution.

Robert Flaherty's *Louisiana Story* (1948) is about a Cajun family of father, mother, and young son, with a pet raccoon, who paddles his pirogue through the bayous. An oil-drilling rig enters this primeval wilderness to tap the riches beneath its surface. Two worlds come together, natural and technological, and a tentative affection develops between the boy and the drillers. Some find this the loveliest and most honest of the Flaherty films. It is, after all, called a story, thus disarming concerns about ethnographic accuracy.

Second, *The Quiet One* (1949) was made initially as a nontheatrical promotional film for the Wiltwyck School in upper New York State. It was scripted and edited by Helen Levitt, Janice Loeb, and Sidney Meyers. The narration was written by James Agee and is read by Gary Merrill. Meyers directed. This school

148

Ricky Leacock, who had been a combat cameraman in the Pacific during WWII, shooting *Louisiana Story* for Flaherty in 1946. Museum of Modern Art Film Stills Archive

offered a home and rehabilitation to emotionally disturbed adolescent boys, most of them African American, from the streets of Harlem. The film is about one such case, that of "Donald," his painful past, the nature of his treatment, and the hopes for his recovery. The principled and venturesome distribution team of Arthur Mayer and Sydney Burstyn acquired rights for theatrical distribution. (Mayer-Burstyn had distributed the first Italian neorealist films in the United States—*Open City, Paisan,* and *The Bicycle Thief.*) *The Quiet One* was blown up from 16mm to 35mm and played with some success among art theaters in large cities. It was also widely shown nontheatrically.

Third and finally, *All My Babies* (1952) began as an instructional film sponsored by the Georgia State Department of Health to demonstrate to midwives correct sanitary procedures to use in their deliveries. It was scripted and directed

Robert Flaherty wearing his Borsalino hat, near the end of his life. International Film Seminars

by George Stoney, himself a white southerner, who became sympathetically in-volved with the rural black people the film is about. Though it is a medical film and contains all the technical information required—some 118 points—it developed a length, a scope, and an emotional intensity that lift it into the realm of art. Its protagonist, Miss Mary, is not only a consummate midwife, she is a magnificent person commanding affection and respect. The "Aunt Jemima" stereotype she might seem to represent is exploded before our eyes. At first the official sponsors didn't quite know what to make of the film; they were impressed (and surprised) when it was selected for showing at the Edinburgh International Film Festival. Because Miss Mary's skill in delivering babies was carefully re-corded, the film was long afterward shown in medical schools. The warm and wonderful feelings it contains—for birth, for people, for life—surely did the stu-dent doctors no harm.

Semidocumentary developments in the commercial entertainment and non-theatrical fields proved to be somewhat of a deflection from the purposes and forms of documentary developed during the thirties. Grierson had been distrust-ful of the blandishments of narrative form and of box office returns as the main source for documentary financing. Efforts to hang onto the occasion provided

The challenge of merging synchronous sound with Flaherty's method was evident in *Louisiana Story*, his last film (U.S., 1948, Robert Flaherty). International Film Seminars

by World War II to have documentary-like films playing in the theaters petered out by the early fifties.

The war years had marked a high point of documentary achievement. More filmmakers had made more nonfiction films for larger audiences than ever before. Given this vastly increased activity, with films being used in all sorts of new

The Quiet One (U.S., 1949, Sidney Meyers). **Museum of Modern Art Film Stills Archive**

ways, it was assumed by most that the trend would continue onward and upward in the postwar years. Instead, what happened following wartime expansion was a severe cutback in the amount of money available for production, in the number of filmmakers employed, and in the quantity of films produced. Accompanying this contraction were losses in morale and leadership, and uncertainties about postwar purposes and subjects.

Personnel and Leadership

Two acute problems of the immediate postwar years were more people wanting to make documentaries than there were documentaries to be made and missing persons. Surfeit was accompanied by desertion.

In Britain some of the most talented of the documentary directors, such as Harry Watt and Pat Jackson, and principal producers, such as Alberto Cavalcanti and Ian Dalrymple, had moved from documentary units to commercial studios. Watt went on with an occasional success in the mixed mode (for example, *The Overlanders*, 1946, based on a harrowing wartime cattle drive across the Australian outback) as did Jackson (for example, *White Corridors*, 1951, drawing upon the drama of hospitals). Nothing of Cavalcanti's postwar production could be said to be documentary-like, and of Dalrymple's only *The Wooden Horse* (1950), about the escape of three British servicemen from a prisoner-of-war camp.

In the United States during the war not only had fiction film directors (among them John Huston, Anatole Litvak, William Wyler, and Garson Kanin) been responsible for most of the major wartime documentaries, they had also been in positions of administrative leadership (among them Frank Capra and John Ford). When the war ended these men returned to Hollywood. Some of them tended to make films more closely related to social problems and/or more realistic in style, perhaps as a result of their wartime experience. Ford's *They Were Expendable* (1945), Wyler's *The Best Years of Our Lives* (1946), Huston's *The Treasure of Sierra Madre* (1948), and Litvak's *The Snakepit* (1949) could be cited. But neither they nor their films were any longer directly connected to documentary.

In Canada the situation was different. The National Film Board, which had almost a monopoly on Canadian production, made no features. If there were no crossovers into fiction filmmaking, other sorts of difficulties arose. Canadian documentary was profoundly affected by Grierson's resignation from the Board and departure from Canada at the end of the war. The number of Film Board personnel was drastically reduced from the wartime high. As a result of this curtailment, some Canadian wartime filmmakers went into other fields; others moved to other countries.

Not only were there an insufficient number of jobs available, the postwar documentary makers were different from those of prewar years. The surfeit was made up mostly of young men who had received their training in filmmaking as a result of military service—"the R.A.F. types," Stuart Legg called them. The wartime recruits had been thoroughly trained technically but ideologically only to the extent that they shared the universal desire to defeat the enemy. They lacked a common core of values and aspirations for peacetime filmmaking of the sort that had existed in Britain—and in the United States as well, even if the political schisms discussed in chapter six are taken into account. Since the peacetime demand for films was much less great than it had been in wartime, competition for opportunities to make films led filmmakers to offer their services cheaply and with lowered professional standards.

Another more complicated difficulty surfaced in the postwar years. Partly because of lessons learned during the war, a kind of gap between the artist-filmmaker and the audiovisual educator widened and split the documentary impulse. Elaborate and sophisticated social-scientific testing of the effects of films on learning had been done on an unprecedented scale during the war. The results of this testing—for instance, that reported by Hovland, Lumsdaine, and Sheffield in *Experiments on Mass Communication*, discussed in chapter nine—seemed to define and limit what films could be expected to do in relation to audiences. They seemed surprisingly successful in teaching troops to assemble a pontoon bridge or clean and maintain the breech of a coastal gun—the so-called nuts-and-bolts films. Films used to teach desired attitudes, however—the so-called orientation films—seemed much less certain in their effect. For all its brilliance, *The Battle of Britain*, of the "Why We Fight" series, did not appear to do much to move American servicemen toward a greater sympathy and appreciation for their British allies. In the postwar years, while the 16mm nontheatrical field expanded, with educational and industrial applications drawn from the inspiration and models provided by wartime use of film, documentary-proper languished.

The power of documentary and its uniqueness lay exactly in its fusion of social purpose with artistic form. It is worth remembering that the young tyros of British documentary had been well educated in the liberal arts before Grierson drilled them in his social philosophy. After the war, especially in the United States, the social scientists (among educators) and the technicians (among industrial filmmakers) were predominant. Makers of classroom films worked from a formula: tell the audience what you are going to tell them; tell them; tell them what you have just told them. It left little room for imagination, wit, or beauty. Makers of industrial films offered gorgeous color and perfect exposures and left it to the sponsor to determine what would be said. Neither the educational nor the industrial filmmaker was likely to make emotionally or intellectually stimulating films.

This period saw the end of British documentary as a movement, at least as a Griersonian movement. The Crown Film Unit—successor to the Empire Marketing Board Film Unit (1930–1933) and the General Post Office Film Unit (1933–1940)—was terminated in 1952. The grounds were that it cost too much and that if films were needed by the government they could be made by private firms. Though this elimination of the central government documentary unit occurred while the Conservative party was in office, it had been prepared for during a Labour government, including years in which Grierson had been head of the Central Office of Information Films Division, of which Crown was a part.

In the United States, what collective leadership had existed on the political left or within the New Deal administration of Franklin Roosevelt had ended as war broke out. After the war Pare Lorentz, head of the short-lived U.S. Film Service, lapsed into semiretirement. Others were making industrially-sponsored films and a comfortable living. Willard Van Dyke, for example, in *American Frontier* (1953), produced for the American Petroleum Institute, retained some of the themes and style of his earlier work, but a prevailing blandness replaced the originality and conviction of *The City* and *Valley Town*. (See the Appendix for an additional account by George Stoney, one of the filmmakers of the time.)

In Canada, the National Film Board carried on after the war but defensively and without inspiration during the immediate postwar years. As Film Commissioner, Ross McLean, who had been assistant to Grierson from the early years on, patiently and determinedly warded off attacks on the Board from the political right and segments of the commercial film industry, which was beginning to expand after the war. The charges were that the Board was unjustifiably costly and extravagant, that it competed with private enterprise, that it harbored subversives, and that there was no need for it in peacetime. McLean's personality and background in Canadian civil service equipped him well for his tenure. If he lacked Grierson's imagination and aggressiveness, he probably fought the battle of attrition more skillfully and successfully than Grierson would have done.

In summary of documentary personnel and leadership in the immediate postwar years, 1945–1952, it can be said that in Britain, the United States, and, to a lesser extent, Canada, the veterans were dispersed and disorganized with no clear leadership or rallying point, scrambling for jobs in an overcrowded field. The younger documentarians, with only the war experience as background, had little commitment or sense of direction; they mostly made any kind of film they could, to the sponsor's specifications, or drifted into other fields.

Sponsorship

The established institutional sources that have supported documentary are government, industry, foundations and associations. During the war, governments were virtually the sole source of funding. The wartime Ministry of Information of the British **government** metamorphosed into the peacetime Central Office of Information. But the Labour party, following its resounding election victory at war's end, failed to back documentary as fully as expected. This profoundly dampened the spirits of the documentary people, most of whom were on the political left and Labour supporters. One reason for this neglect was thought to have been that Labour politicians were generally unimaginative in their thinking about government information services. When they considered them at all, it was in terms of pamphlets and speeches. (The Conservative politicians, on the other hand, who had been in power in the thirties, came largely from the upper classes. Having received educations that included the arts, and with some aristocratic attraction toward patronage of them, they were more open to the sponsorship of films.) Second, the postwar years were ones of rigorous austerity; funds were lacking for many forms of government activity, and film production could scarcely be regarded as essential.

In the United States, the Office of War Information was eliminated altogether and sustained government support for filmmaking existed only in the Department of Agriculture (with a long and honorable record of using films to communicate with farmers through the county agents scattered around the country), the armed forces (which, of course, had available an enormous stockpile of films of every conceivable sort), and the International Motion Picture Division of the Department of State (which used its films overseas only, for propaganda purposes).

Though the National Film Board of Canada was severely cut, it survived and adjusted to the more modest postwar needs of government and citizens. Financial support for it would gradually increase. By the mid-fifties it had moved into a new sort of eminence with shorts that won awards for documentary and animation at the major international festivals. The documentaries will be dealt with in chapter eleven.

Postwar **industrial** sponsorship in Britain was limited by the austerity of the economy. In Canada production of sponsored films outside the Film Board increased, led by Crawley Films, which had begun with contracts from the Board during the war. In the United States, industry became a big sponsor of films for the first time. In all three countries, however, businesses and industries were now justifying every bit of money spent on films in terms of increased sales and obvious good will. There existed virtually no industrial sponsorship of films in the general public interest, such as those sponsored by the oil and gas industries in Britain in the thirties. After the war company public relations officers, given the extensive use of films and the testing of their effectiveness during wartime, felt they knew very well what films should be like and could do. An increase in company profits rather than general public improvement was clearly the goal.

In Britain and in Canada, **foundations and associations** were less active sponsors of films than they were in the United States. There seem to have been fewer of them and they don't seem to have had as much money. But in the U.S. the large foundations and national associations were soon limited in what they would spend their money on by growing pressure from the political right. This postwar political reaction would come to be known as "McCarthyism." Senator Joseph McCarthy (Republican, Wisconsin) headed congressional committees and used whatever other power he could muster to ferret out suspected Communists and Communist sympathizers wherever he could find them. His work paralleled that of the House of Representatives Un-American Activities Committee, which was busy investigating Communist influence in the film and broadcasting industries. McCarthy's investigations were into subversive influence in the Department of State and the army. At the time of his death he was about to start on the large foundations, most notably the Ford Foundation, which were accused of sheltering "reds" and radicals. As a result of this political climate, the foundations restricted their grants to existing and widely accepted institutions and activities. They did not sponsor films that might prove "controversial" or might be made by filmmakers with a "past" (involvement with organizations and causes on the left). The national associations concerned with education and various health problems such as tuberculosis, cancer, or heart disease stuck to small, well-defined promotional films or informational films to be used as "audiovisual aids."

The overall result of these restrictions on sponsorship was that there just weren't as many big and important film statements being paid for as there had been in the thirties and first half of the forties, certainly nothing resembling *The City* or the "Why We Fight" series.

Subjects

Documentary can be thought of as a Depression baby that came of age during wartime. It seems to be true that it has thrived on crisis and disaster, criticism and attack. Following the war the great documentary causes of the thirties (unemployment and rural poverty, conservation of land and water, housing and urban planning) and early forties (the fight against fascism) were no longer relevant or popular. The situation in the immediate postwar era was greatly altered from that of prewar or wartime.

Internationalism

The first years of peace saw a great surge of international good intentions. The Axis powers—Germany, Italy, and Japan—had been defeated by the Allies—the British Empire, United States, Soviet Union, and China. A new United Nations organization had been established to sustain and extend this victory, to try to make one world out of this war-torn globe. In this spirit, documentarians saw that films were needed to interpret the meaning of the United Nations and its subsidiary organizations and to show aspects of their services to the world at large. Also needed were films confronting particular postwar problems and the concerns of war-ravaged and underdeveloped nations. For a brief period this international outlook prevailed.

The United Nations undertook some modest film production (through its Film Board) and distribution (through its Film Distribution Unit) from its beginnings, making and circulating films for and about the UN and its related agencies. Many of the films of the time were about the work of the United Nations Relief and Rehabilitation Administration (UNRRA). One of its films, *The Pale Horseman* (1946), written and produced by Irving Jacoby, was a grim and forceful survey of world devastation, famine, and the threat of pestilence. It took the stance that it was in U.S. self-interest to combat this menace, whether through UNRRA or other means. *Seeds of Destiny* (1946, David Miller), an Academy Award winner produced by the U.S. Army Signal Corps at the request of UNRRA, is similar in persuasive intent and compilation form.

Paralleling the UN-related production was that of the International Motion Picture Division of the United States Department of State (which would subsequently be absorbed into the United States Information Agency) working in conjunction with American economic aid abroad (what was called the Marshall Plan, conceived by General George C. Marshall, who had become Secretary of State). Though its films were shown abroad they were not seen in the United States. The Twentieth Century Fund, a private foundation particularly concerned with economic matters, sponsored *Round Trip: U.S. in World Trade* (1947). Made by Raymond Spottiswoode and Stuart Legg out of the World Today (a firm established in New York City by Grierson immediately after he left Canada), it, too, argued along lines of enlightened self-interest. Demonstrating that many of the products used every day come from overseas, the film claims that this does not represent a threat to the economy. On the contrary, American industry will be kept strong by matching these imports with exports.

Filmmakers also responded to increased curiosity about other parts of the world, which had been awakened by a global war. *The Russians Nobody Knows* (1946) was shot for "The March of Time" by Julien Bryan (who had earlier shot *Inside Nazi Germany* and footage on the fall of Warsaw at the outbreak of WWII). In the postwar film about Russia, emphasis is placed on UNRRA aid to the war-crippled Soviet economy.

In Britain there was a similar United Nations emphasis. As successor to his *World of Plenty* (1943), Paul Rotha made *The World Is Rich* (1947) for the Central Office of Information. Like the earlier film, it argues for more adequate international distribution of food and supports the work of the Food and Agriculture Organization (FAO). Rotha and Basil Wright made *World Without End* (1954) for UNESCO, showing how that organization helped solve food production and health problems in Mexico and Thailand, respectively.

Following the war Britain attempted to explain to its citizens (and the rest of the world) its changing conception of colonial stewardship. *Cyprus Is an Island* (1946, Ralph Keene) is a film with such a purpose. It is about deforestation and goatherds rather than the conflict between Greek and Turkish inhabitants that would erupt when Cypress achieved independence. *Daybreak in Udi* (1949, Terry Bishop), produced for the COI while Grierson was in charge of its Films Division, concerns the progress of community education in West Africa. It won an Academy Award.

In Canada during these early postwar years the National Film Board was struggling for its existence. One of the charges leveled against it was that it employed those with left-wing sympathies. In this climate, the internationalism that had characterized "The World in Action" series disappeared from the NFB films.

In fact, in the world as a whole the spirit of internationalism dwindled by 1948 with the outbreak of a "cold war" (as opposed to the hot one just ended) between the United States and the Soviet Union. Though it at first centered on occupied Berlin, the cold war subsequently changed political attitudes and military strategies throughout the world.

Other Postwar Subjects; New Types and Styles

With the cold war the sponsorship and distribution of films by and about the United Nations and its subsidiary organizations became very limited. Nor was it evident what other postwar causes documentary should advance. Looking at its earlier tradition was no help. Increased prosperity caused the subjects and rhetoric of the Depression to seem inapplicable, even old-fashioned. Growing conservatism and a cold war caused the main lines of liberal and antifascist criticism to be suspect. Sponsors and filmmakers alike were unwilling to risk making a "statement" at a time when political positions were being subjected to investigation. Consequently documentary subjects became essentially noncontroversial; certainly they were not socio/economic/political by and large, as earlier documentaries had been. In their own way, they were for virtue and against vice.

Kon Tiki, poster for a successful theatrical documentary during the 1950s. The film follows biologist Thor Heyerdahl's voyage from Peru to Tahiti on a raft, to prove his theory that South Americans were the original South Sea settlers (U.S., 1950, Thor Heyerdahl). Academy of Motion Picture Arts and Sciences

Daybreak in Udi (U.K., 1949, Terry Bishop). National Film Archive Stills Library

Another change of postwar documentary was that it had to exist within the nontheatrical film field to an even greater extent than formerly. The theaters lost interest in showing documentaries once the drama of war ended. On the other hand, the nontheatrical field became much larger as a result of the wartime stimulus. The documentaries that were made were geared to this field.

Grierson's discovery that more seats existed outside the theaters than within them was a valuable one. Still, major documentary achievements had reached large audiences in theaters with the possible social impact that allowed—*Night Mail, The River, Target for Tonight, Divide and Conquer*, for example. Now the nontheatrical field was the main means for documentary distribution-exhibition, and nontheatrical films were mainly used on behalf of industry or education. Documentaries had to be sponsored by businesses and industries for their particular goals, or be fitted into educational curriculums so that sufficient numbers of 16mm prints could be sold and rented to repay the cost of production.

As a result of industrial and educational requirements, as they were seen at the time, documentary seemed to lose its identity, its sure sense of function and form. In a way, the new subject emphases represented a retreat from the job of documentary as earlier understood. No longer significant as an approach to public information, or in the forefront of public policy—as Basil Wright had conceived it—documentary was now following or at least on the fringes of national concerns. Subjects dealt with for the first time, or with a new frequency, were the arts, mental health, public health, and race relations.

Films dealing with **the arts** first appeared in postwar Europe, especially in France and Belgium. Distributed widely abroad, they attracted considerable attention and started two new subgenres of the nonfiction film.

Some of these used art-related works as visual documents to portray times and places not otherwise available to filmmakers. In *Paris 1900* (France, 1947, Nicole Védres) photographs, early newsreels, drawings and paintings, newspaper front pages, and other artifacts were used for a historical essay. *1848* (France, 1948, Victoria Mercanton) takes its visual substance from engravings, etchings, and ink drawings of a contemporary Paris to revive that year out of a past century. *Images Médiévales* (France, 1950, William Novick) did the same with the Bibles created by fourteenth- and fifteenth-century monks, using scenes of court and country life in these illuminated manuscripts as a visual representation of the Middle Ages.

In a second kind of film, the arts themselves became the subject matter. Films were made about artworks, about their creators, and about the history of art. In France, Alain Resnais made *Van Gogh* (1948) and *Guernica* (1950), the latter about Pablo Picasso's great painting of the Spanish civil war. In Belgium, Henri Storck made *The World of Paul Delvaux* (1946) with the painter himself, and *Rubens* (1948) with art historian Paul Haesaerts. There were even two French films, by Roger Leenhardt, about the discoveries and inventions that led to the motion picture: *Animated Cartoons: The Toy That Grew Up* and *Biography of the Motion Picture Camera* (both 1946).

These films about the arts and those that used the arts to deal with other subjects became widely popular, perhaps owing to a general growth in art appreciation as prosperity and leisure increased. Sometimes they were shown as shorts in the "art theaters" specializing in European or otherwise non-current Hollywood feature films and in the film societies developing during these years. They were also shown in schools, libraries, and museums.

American, British and, to a lesser extent, Canadian documentary filmmakers turned to these forms. Many documentarians had been trained in or were especially sympathetic to the arts. Even Robert Flaherty shot material for a study of *Guernica* a year before Resnais's film mentioned above and became involved in the promotion and distribution of *The Titan—Story of Michelangelo* (a revised version released in 1950 of a film made in Italy by the Swiss director Curt Oertel between 1938 and 1940). The latter is a feature-length biography of Michelangelo using only contemporary architecture, interior settings, and artworks as its visual material. This sort of compilation would become common in documentaries made for television, to be discussed in chapter twelve.

That this impulse toward the arts was a documentary impulse was acknowledged by Englishman John Read, who called his films about artists "documentaries." In his *Henry Moore* (1951), for example, we see and learn about the artist's way of living and working, get a sense of the man and his approach to art, examine him at work creating, and view some of his created works. Willard Van Dyke, veteran American documentarian who had been a student of Edward Weston's, made a similar film about Weston entitled *The Photographer* (1948). Read's *Artists Must Live* (1953) explores the relationship between the artist and his or her patron.

More akin in subject and style to earlier documentary forms than those concerning arts and artists were documentaries about **mental health**. A profound difference between them and earlier documentaries, however, was that the mental health documentaries dealt with men and women, adults and children, in relation to themselves—their individual, interior lives—rather than with their relationships to society and to social problems. *The Quiet One* (U.S., 1948, Sidney Meyers), discussed at the outset of this chapter, is an outstanding example. If this film had been made in the thirties, it would have centered on the social, economic, and political causes for the unhappy lives we see. Here, the Harlem ghetto and broken families serve merely as background for the disturbances in Donald's psyche. In *Out of True* (U.K., 1950, Phil Leacock) a middle-class woman has a severe emotional breakdown and is helped back toward recovery by modern psychiatry.

But it was in Canada, at the National Film Board, that the most important pioneering work was done. The "Mental Mechanisms" series was made for the mental health division of the Department of National Health and Welfare. Directed by Robert Anderson, it made original progress in ways of presenting emotional disorders for study and understanding and provided models for subsequent films on mental health. On a case-by-case basis, Anderson dealt with various psychological malfunctions. *The Feeling of Rejection* (1947), *The Feeling of Hostility* (1948), *Overdependency* (1949), and *Feelings of Depression* (1950) were among them.

Documentaries on matters of **general public health** became much more plentiful and effective than before. The most skilled and dedicated practitioner in this field was George Stoney, whose *All My Babies* (U.S., 1952), dealing with midwives and their work in rural Georgia, was discussed at the beginning of this chapter. Another film with which Stoney was involved, *Feeling All Right* (1949, his preliminary script; direction by Fred Lasse, cinematography by Gordon Weisenborn), dealt with the detection and treatment of syphilis in a semidocumentary narrative form. Sponsored by the Mississippi State Board of Health, it was set among the black population of Washington County. Among the many later noteworthy Stoney films about health problems is *Still Going Places* (1956, made for health professionals; the lay version entitled *The Proud Years*), about the care and treatment of the aged. In Great Britain, *The Undefeated* (1950, Paul Dickson), which won an Academy Award, was about the therapy administered to permanently disabled World War II veterans. It centered on a patient who had lost his speech and the use of both legs at the battle of Arnhem.

Films about **race relations** were much in evidence in the United States. This subject was dealt with using a number of styles and techniques in addition to documentary. In a theatrical short, *The House I Live In* (1945, produced by RKO Radio Pictures), Frank Sinatra sings the song of the title and speaks against anti-Semitism. A cluster of animated race-relations films began with the very popular *Brotherhood of Man* (1946), sponsored by the UAW-CIO. It was an early effort of United Productions of America (UPA), the talented group that broke away from the Disney Studio and went on to create Mr. Magoo and Gerald McBoing Boing. It was followed by Philip Stapp's *Boundary Lines* (1947) and *Picture in Your Mind* (1949) from Julien Bryan's International Film Foundation. Then there were dramatizations. *The High Wall* (1952) presented a conflict among teenagers of different ethnic and class backgrounds and parental prejudices. Though such efforts deserve respect, it can't be said with any certainty that the "brotherhood films," as the nontheatrical shorts were called, contributed much to greater racial understanding and tolerance.

Approaches and Techniques

There are other noticeable differences between the documentaries of 1945 to 1952 and those that preceded them that apply more generally. The later films are aimed more clearly at nontheatrical application and more specialized audiences. Mostly they are educational, since even industrially sponsored films were generally designed to be shown in classrooms. Films for adult education and discussion were also made—for parents with small children, say, or labor or management groups, or a cultural elite with one sort of interest or another. They were mainly films of reassurance rather than criticism or attack; they rarely dealt with social/economic/political issues. At the same time, they seem to have been intended to serve the community rather than to persuade or indoctrinate and to meet the needs of audiences for information about and understanding of certain subjects. This is especially true of the work of the National Film Board of Canada.

As for their formal aspects, the postwar films are freer and more varied in their techniques than were the earlier documentaries. More nonactuality was employed—fictional and dramatic elements—and structurally they tended to be organized as narrative or drama. There was an increased use of actors and performance and more location sound, especially synchronous ("sync") sound. The latter was made possible by the introduction of magnetic tape, which made recording outside the studio much more practicable than it had been with the optical system. The narrative structures and sync dialogue coincided with the tendency of these postwar documentaries to center more on individuals than had the films of the thirties. In the postwar years even large-scale problems—race relations, mental health—were dealt with in terms of how they affected individuals. In this respect the postwar documentaries not only resemble the British wartime semidocumentaries, they look ahead to the kind of documentary called cinéma vérité and direct cinema, to be dealt with in chapter fourteen.

Final Observations

The years treated in this chapter fall between the end of World War II, with the prominence documentary achieved, and the beginning of a United States blanketed by television. Between 1945 and 1952 documentaries were mostly industrially sponsored or classroom films.

Generally, the industrially sponsored documentaries were undistinguished and limited in scope. The oil industry provided the major exceptions. This may have been because it had more money than other industries or because it had more need for improved public relations. In either case, it sponsored some noteworthy films during these years. In Britain the Petroleum Films Bureau sponsored *Forward a Century* (1951, J. B. Napier-Bell), a large-scale historical survey of technological and social advance. The film unit of British Shell Oil continued its production of brilliant informational and instructional shorts. A little later, in Australia, Shell sponsored *The Back of Beyond* (1954, John Heyer), an appealing semidocumentary feature about a mailman whose route takes him into the far reaches of that vast subcontinent. In the United States, Standard Oil of New Jersey sponsored Flaherty's *Louisiana Story* (1948), discussed earlier in this chapter. However, later public relations officers must have doubted the wisdom of those investments because sponsored films of this sort did not continue.

Among classroom films, increased ambition and improving artistry were in evidence occasionally. Two examples, about city planning, were *The Baltimore Plan* and *The Living City*. Both were sponsored by the Twentieth Century Fund, directed by John Barnes, and released by Encyclopedia Britannica Films in 1953. The latter was nominated for an Academy Award. But such "prestige pictures didn't pay the rent," as they said at EBF at the time, unlike those fitting more neatly into K–12 curriculums, so they remained exceptions.

Documentary in Canada experienced some of the same doldrums between the end of the war and the arrival of television as a new source for sponsorship and audiences. The National Film Board, reduced in budget and personnel, was having to tailor its films to clearly identifiable informational and educational needs and nontheatrical distribution. But within that setting, in the late 1940s and early 1950s there developed an extraordinary collective of creative talent identified as Unit B, which produced some brilliant and original work that will be the subject of the next chapter.

Films of the Period

1946

Cyprus Is an Island (U.K., Ralph Keene)
The Pale Horseman (U.S., Irving Jacoby)
Seeds of Destiny (U.S., David Miller)

1947

The Feeling of Rejection (Canada, Robert Anderson)
First Steps (U.S., Leo Seltzer)
Journey into Medicine (U.S., Willard Van Dyke and Jacoby)
Muscle Beach (U.S., Joseph Strick and Irving Lerner)
The Roosevelt Story (U.S., Julian Roffman and Ben Kerner)
The World Is Rich (U.K., Paul Rotha)

1948

Louisiana Story (U.S., Robert Flaherty)
Make Way for Youth (U.S., Robert Disraeli)
The Photographer (U.S.,Van Dyke)

1949

Creation According to Genesis (U.S., Paul Burnford)
Daybreak in Udi (U.K., Terry Bishop)
Feeling All Right (U.S., Fred Lasse)
Nomads of the Jungle (U.S., Victor Jurgens, "The Earth and Its Peoples" series)
One God—The Ways We Worship Him (U.S., Nicholas Farkas)
The Quiet One (U.S., Sidney Meyers)
A Time for Bach (U.S., Paul Falkenberg)
Waverly Steps (U.K., John Eldridge)

1950

The Titan—Story of Michelangelo (Switzerland, Curt Oertel)
The Undefeated (U.K., Paul Dickson)

1951

Angry Boy (U.S., Alexander Hammid and Jacoby)
Benjy (U.S., Fred Zinnemann)
Forward a Century (U.K., J. B. Napier-Bell)
Steps of Age (U.S., Ben Maddow)
Waters of Time (U.K., Basil Wright)

1952

All My Babies (U.S., George Stoney)
Notes on the Port of St. Francis (U.S., Frank Stauffacher)

Books on the Period

Beattie, Eleanor, *A Handbook of Canadian Film*. Toronto: Peter Martin Associates, 1973.
Evans, Gary, *In the National Interest: A Chronicle of the National Film Board of Canada from 1949 to 1989*. Toronto: University of Toronto Press, 1991.

Feldman, Seth and Joyce Nelson, eds., *Canadian Film Reader*. Toronto: Peter Martin Associates, 1977.

Film Council of America, *Sixty Years of 16mm Film, 1923–1983*. Evanston, IL: Film Council of America, 1954.

Jones, D. B., *Movies and Memoranda: An Interpretive History of the National Film Board of Canada*. Ottawa: Canadian Film Institute and Deneau Publishers, 1981.

Starr, Cecile, ed., *Ideas on Film: A Handbook for the 16mm. User*. New York: Funk & Wagnalls, 1951.

Waldron, Gloria, *The Information Film: A Report of the Public Library Inquiry*. New York: Columbia University Press, 1949.

Chapter Eleven

In Pursuit of Excellence: National Film Board of Canada's Unit B, 1948–1964

Though maintaining its level of informed subject matter and technical competence, production at the immediate postwar National Film Board was confined mainly to the pedantic and pedestrian short films intended to meet specific informational and educational needs. (Best and most inventive of these were in the "Mental Mechanisms" series mentioned in the preceding chapter.) It had inherited from its beginnings in World War II a system of twelve specialized production units, each making one kind of film.

By 1948 this structure, which had been established by the first film commissioner, John Grierson, was thought to have become somewhat unwieldy, and the twelve units were consolidated into four larger, more comprehensive ones—Units A, B, C, D—reporting to an overall director of production. In 1951 Tom Daly, one of the earliest recruits to the Film Board, who had gained his experience working as Stuart Legg's assistant and researcher on "The World in Action" series discussed in chapter eight, was appointed executive producer of Unit B. This unit made sponsored, scientific, cultural, and animated films.

It was following the release of the much-praised *Neighbours* (1952) that Unit B absorbed the Animation Unit, headed by the creator of that film, its universally recognized experimental genius, Norman McLaren. The seminal film that began Unit B's move into the spotlight of widespread praise and awards, eventually reaching large audiences worldwide, was another animated film: *The Romance of Transportation in Canada* (1953). Curiously, this was a modest little (11-minute) film intended for classroom use. *The Romance of Transportation* broke out of the standard requirements of the educational film, however, sketching the history of Canadian transportation from snowshoes to jet planes with an appealing lightness and deftness, including spoofs of Hollywood cartoon clichés. Widely popular, it was nominated for an Oscar and won several international awards.

But even more important, *The Romance of Transportation in Canada* brought together for the first time some of Unit B's key personnel—Colin Low (direction

John Grierson retired from the National Film Board of Canada in 1945.

and animation), Wolf Koenig and Robert Verrall (animation), Eldon Rathburn (music) and, of course, Tom Daly (production)—who would form the creative core of Unit B. (Low, Verrall, and Koenig had been trained by McLaren.) In terms of live-action documentary the two breakthrough films came the next year: *Corral* and *Paul Tomkowicz: Street-railway Switchman*. These were part of a "Faces of Canada" series of short films designed to fulfill a Griersonian mandate for the earlier Board of interpreting the lives of one group of people for people in other parts of the country.

Corral, directed by Colin Low, was filmed on the southwestern Alberta ranch where he had grown up. (Camera was by Koenig; music by Rathburn; editing and production by Daly, who produced all of the films to be discussed.) The subject is a ranch hand working with a half-broken horse in a corral. There is a pairing of man and horse—a pas de deux, cutting back and forth between movements of man's feet and horse's front hoofs; a handheld moving camera in medium close-ups predominates in the roping sequence. Finally the man mounts and rides off in long shot, horse and rider running out into the surrounding countryside with foothills in the background. Lyrical and wordless, the sound track consists solely of a guitar accompanying the images with variations on several western ballads.

Corral (Canada, 1953, Colin Low and Wolf Koenig). National Film Board of Canada

The other of the celebrated first two films, *Paul Tomkowicz: Street-railway Switchman,* was directed and edited by Roman Kroiter—his first Film Board film—and shot in his hometown of Winnipeg. It follows its subject on his night shift along the streetcar tracks in the bitter cold of a winter night, accompanied by his narration (actually an actor redoing material from taped interviews that hadn't recorded satisfactorily). There is the sympathetic attention to this single unexceptional person that one would come to expect from Unit B films. Beyond that, what seems most extraordinary is the concreteness of its detail: from the specificity of the title, through the images of harsh lights in the blackness of the night, the snow and ice, Tomkowicz's visible breath, to the personality that comes through in the narration—things he thinks worth mentioning, words used, his Polish accent.

Following those two films, and others of distinction that came out of Unit B in its ascendant years, were several even more exceptional productions, innovative in conception and remarkable in technical achievement and aesthetic quality. Most celebrated were *City of Gold* (1957), *Universe* (1960), and *Lonely Boy* (1961).

In *City of Gold* the main story concerns the Klondike gold rush of 1898, recorded in contemporary still photographs. The brief live-action sequences that frame the main story show Dawson City in the mid-1950s. On the Yukon River,

A rare example of mythmaking in Canadian documentary, *City of Gold* created a para-
dox of living people and dead objects in a way that inspired the future work of Ken
Burns (Canada, 1957, Colin Low and Wolf Koenig). National Film Board of Canada

not far from the Arctic Circle, this was the jumping-off point for the journey
north and the climb over Chilkoot Pass to the goldfields. It was also the hometown of Pierre Berton, a well-known journalist, who wrote and reads the narration. Berton's remembered childhood is from the 1920s.

City of Gold is half documentary, of life in Dawson City in the summer of
1898, and half "art film," of the motion picture camera moving over still art
objects—photographs of this "American town [i.e., most of its population at the
time were U.S. citizens] on Canadian soil"; Independence Day and Dominion
Day were celebrated together. The miners fancied that "they were going to become rich beyond the wildest dreams of avarice." Though that didn't happen,
they were all heroes and had done things they didn't know they were even capable of.

The music used throughout is of the earlier time and place; it becomes part
of the document. The intimate perspective of the narrator warms and gives life
to the images. The immobile subjects seem so completely "real" (except for lack
of movement) that we forget we are watching photos and expect the people to
move at any moment. To achieve this sense of liveness, the camera travels stead-

Universe was intended as a classroom film on astronomy to present a picture of the universe as it might appear to a space traveler (Canada, 1960, Colin Low and Roman Kroiter). This is a production still with Colin Low and models. National Film Board of Canada

ily and carefully over the photos as if it were actually at the scene. Direction is by Wolf Koenig and Colin Low, with music again by Eldon Rathburn and editing by Tom Daly.

Transitions from the present-day live action into the aged photos and out again are quite remarkable, especially in that they are almost imperceptible. For example, at the conclusion of the film we are brought back to present-day Dawson City by gradual degrees. First we are on photographs; then we are on a still life scene in which we detect a tiny particle of matter dangling in a cobweb; then we have a still landscape with off-camera voices of children at play; and finally we are in the midst of a ball diamond with all the usual shouting accompanying the game. This is the first time in the film that location sound is introduced. It appropriately breaks the spell of reminiscence and returns us to the mid-twentieth century.

The directorial pair of Roman Kroiter and Colin Low did the strikingly different and equally, in many ways more, original and inventive *Universe* (1960). Again framed by live-action sequences, in an observatory near Toronto, the film moves along an extraordinary probe into the solar system, in which the filmic material consists largely of three-dimensional models of the moon and most of the planets. A second probe takes us beyond the solar system into our galaxy. A third and final probe asks the audience to imagine being able to "move with the freedom of a god . . . so that a million years pass in a second." We would come to "an endless sea of night" dotted with islands of stars—galaxies—so immense "that they have been observed slipping through one another like phantoms. . . . [W]hat civilizations have risen, looked into the night, seen what we see, asked the questions that we ask . . . ?" (Jones, *The Best Butler in the Business*, 75)

Stanley Jackson, who had worked on the narration for *City of Gold* with Berton, wrote the commentary. Editing was done by Daly, music by Rathburn.

The animation consists of astonishing 3D constructions in credible and scary movement. (During the production of *2001: A Space Odyssey*, Stanley Kubrick bought several copies of *Universe* for his technicians to study.) The music is very dramatic, like that for a fiction feature, and "atmospheric," recalling Gustav Holst's *The Planets*.

An extraordinary amount of technical detail is presented simply and clearly. The commentary is read in a friendly, casual, unscientific way. It is marvelous science teaching and yet remains beautiful and magical, preserving the mystery. Even with all the things we know, the fact of the universe is still incomprehensible.

As it happened, the Soviet Union launched *Sputnik*, putting the first man into space, just as *Universe* was being completed. It became one of the most celebrated Film Board productions, won twenty-three awards worldwide, and sold a record number of 16mm prints at home and abroad.

Lonely Boy (1961), directed by Wolf Koenig and Roman Kroiter, took full advantage of the newly available technology that led to the technique called direct cinema (to be discussed in chapter fourteen). Its subject is Paul Anka, Ottawa-born pop singer of the time, and its title comes from the lyrics of one of his songs used to open and close the film: "I'm just a lonely boy, lonely and blue . . ."

It follows Anka on engagements around the New York City area—at the Steel Pier in Atlantic City, Copacabana nightclub in Manhattan, Freedomland amusement park in the Bronx—in performances and behind the scenes. It also devotes considerable attention to the adulation of his teenage female fans. In short, it offers what might be considered an anthropological record of the sort of social phenomenon that began with Frank Sinatra and the bobby-soxers of an earlier generation and continued afterward with Elvis Presley, the Beatles, Mick Jagger, and onward.

Because Anka was then a popular and appealing star, the filmmakers' view of him may be more ambivalent than it might appear to viewers today. Since he no longer has that star aura, it is perhaps easy to see the film as a put-down or send-up of the kind of artistry involved in Anka's musical compositions and performance style and, especially, of the girls' near-hysterical reactions. And there is that. On the other hand, there seems to be some evidence that the film-

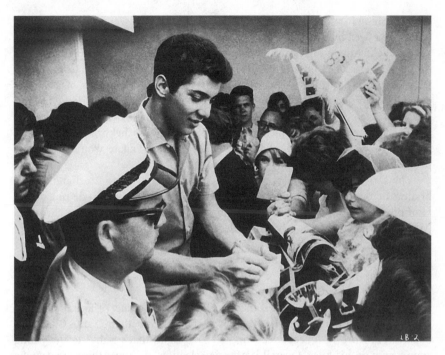

Paul Anka, the teen idol in *Lonely Boy* (Canada, 1962, Roman Kroiter and Wolf Koenig). National Film Board of Canada

makers may respect Anka's thoroughgoing professionalism (like their own), echoing his manager's and his statements that he always knows what he is doing, is in control.

In any case, some of the most attractive moments in the film are ones that would have been outtakes for other filmmakers, revealing the manipulation necessarily involved in this sort of filmmaking, or, another way of thinking about the matter, introducing the reflexivity that would later become obligatory for some documentarians. The inclusion of these moments adds to the ambiguity. There's the scene when Paul, rushing into his dressing room to change clothes, is surprised and startled that the crew is there waiting to start filming. (He had forgotten about them.) And there is the much commented upon incident when Anka spontaneously kisses the owner of the Copacabana on the cheek and the filmmakers, who evidently weren't quite ready, ask him to repeat the action so they can capture it.

Ironically Anka appears actually to *be* a lonely boy—though he no doubt would have denied it. Surrounded by people—his retinue, his fans—the life he apparently lives appears strained and empty: ambition and drive don't seem to bring much satisfaction or contentment huts, instead, an edgy stimulation that keeps pushing him on. Whether success is its own reward seems to be one of the questions raised by the film.

Paralleling these high-profile separate works was the "Candid Eye" series of thirteen 24- to 28-minute films made for Canadian Broadcasting Corporation television, even earlier than *Lonely Boy,* in exploring the possibilities of the direct cinema technique. The series began with *The Days Before Christmas* (1958), which marked Terence Macartney-Filgate's Film Board debut, as codirector (along with regulars Stanley Jackson and Wolf Koenig; Michel Brault and Roman Kroiter were also members of the crew). Macartney-Filgate would become a principal creative force in the "Candid Eye" series.

The Days Before Christmas is both a city symphony of Montreal and a celebration of the holiday. Disparate images are cut together in a style not unlike Humphrey Jennings's in *Listen to Britain.* Some of the sound is synchronous with the images; some not, but recorded on location and cleverly overlaid over non-sync footage. Montreal is presented as big, cosmopolitan, wintry: a melting pot, with cold, dirty winters, but also a sweet place where people live. Certainly it is different from other parts of Canada, but the filmmakers' view of it is accepting and even-handed.

As for Christmas, there are some lovely images, especially of faces, and most especially of children's faces, but there is also an unempathetic Santa Claus in a department store who keeps repeating "That's right, that's right" to the young supplicants on his knee. Overall it offers a selection of simple things that make Christmas wonderful.

On *Blood and Fire* (1958) Macartney-Filgate was sole director. The title comes from the motto of the Salvation Army. The film surveys the activities of one unit: its band, in rehearsal and then in uniform on parade; Army members preaching on the street (with some marvelous vignettes of individuals' responses) and distributing its paper, the *War Cry*; a meal provided at the hostel and the religious service following, including the conversion of two men who move down front to be individually comforted and counseled by two Army members. The film ends with a classy parade of the disciplined band and women marchers swinging and tapping tambourines in rhythm (with no spectators on the sidewalks watching them, however).

Here the drama is psychological or spiritual, difficult for a visual medium— especially this nondirected, nonacted, spontaneous sort of filmmaking. The sincerity of this film (that is to say, of its makers) and the decency of the Army members shown are astonishing. The courage and confidence of the Army people—in their lives, in what they are doing—are clearly evident without special emphasis. *Blood and Fire* is intriguing, moving, and powerful in a quiet way.

In contrast, *The Back-breaking Leaf* (1959) concerns ideal subject matter for this kind of filmmaking: physical work. About tobacco harvesting in southern Ontario, even the title—through hyperbole—tries to suggest what the film shows with great force. Macartney-Filgate was again director (and also cocinematogra-

Very Nice, Very Nice was a film montage, without commentary—a first film by its maker that was nominated for an Oscar (Canada, 1961, Arthur Lipsett). National Film Board of Canada

pher). As with all the other "Candid Eye" series the sympathy and warmth with which people and their activities are presented is singularly engaging.

On the other hand, the last film of exceptional quality out of Unit B is markedly cynical. *Very Nice, Very Nice* (1961) is a seven-minute idiosyncratic work of one filmmaker, Arthur Lipsett, a member of the characteristically experimental Animation Unit. He made it solely from snippets of film and audiotape (including Unit B productions), outtakes culled from racks and bins in cutting rooms around the NFB. It makes little sense, in the *usual* sense of that phrase, but this cacophony of sights and sounds is perhaps intended to mimic and satirize the informational overload of modern media life. Lipsett presents a bleak view of rampant commercialism and also seems preoccupied with bits of evidence suggesting that we may be mindlessly moving toward nuclear annihilation. *Very Nice, Very Nice* would become a model, or forerunner at least, for other avantgarde filmmakers playing in similar ways with "found" material and, curiously, for subsequent television commercials employing comparable sorts of disjunctive assemblage.

In thinking about the main thrusts of Unit B in general, there is the emphasis on the increasingly sophisticated technology available and the greater ease and control with which its members learned to move about in—to record and reveal aspects of—the real world. In addition, there are two aspects of the work that differ notably from the Griersonian documentary with which the Film Board began.

First is the emphasis on individuals characteristic of most of these films. Grierson dealt with broad social issues and problems, and with people in groups according to occupation, nationality, age (schoolchildren), gender (housewives), and so on. Asked once whether a derelict lying drunk in the gutter didn't deserve as much attention as larger matters, Grierson replied that that man and his personal problems didn't interest him very much. The Unit B filmmakers tended to focus on an individual, as fiction filmmakers do—a cowboy, a streetcar switchman, a pop singer. Even the Klondike gold rush is evoked through the recollection of someone who grew up in that territory, and the exploration of the solar system returns repeatedly to a lonely astronomer observing it. The "Candid Eye" series was more Griersonian in this respect: Christmas shoppers, Salvation Army members, tobacco harvesters.

The other difference from Grierson's documentary was Unit B's striving for artistic excellence—their "attitude toward the craft," as veteran Stanley Jackson put it—and for recognition of it by awards and praise from reviewers. (Eight Unit B films received Academy Award nominations—an understandable source of pride, especially coming from its dominant neighbor, and HOLLYWOOD at that!) This orientation Grierson would not have encouraged. On a trip to India near the end of his life he attacked its Films Division's "attempts to gain renown by competing for awards in all sorts of festivals . . . . They are using public money for self-indulgence," he charged. Instead, "The Films Division should be more reflective of the overwhelming story of India, its new economic and social programs, the new life for the people." In short, he thought the chief responsibility of government filmmakers was to the citizens of the nation rather than to aesthetic ideals.

At the NFB in the fall of 1963 an underground swell of resentment regarding the unit system and, especially, of the power of the executive producers in each unit surfaced in December in a memo based on interviews with the filmmakers themselves: "A Summary of Staff Opinion on the Structure and Organization of the English Production Branch." As an alternative to the unit system, a pool system was proposed in which filmmakers could choose among projects and producers. Creative independence would thus be distributed equally among all filmmakers, it was argued.

Two months later—in a memo from the director of English production to all of its producers, directors, editors, and writers—the establishment of a pool system was announced, incorporating most of the filmmakers' recommendations. Thus ended Unit B, though its body of work remains as an extraordinary legacy and challenge for emulation. And in some ways the new system was an attempt to institutionalize the authority of filmmaking over administration that had been at the core of Unit B's success. In any case, after some initial uncertainties, the new system allowed for future creative achievement at the Board as distinctive and fine as that of Unit B, for example, the work of Donald Brittain and of Michael Rubbo, to be dealt with in chapter fifteen.

Films of the Period

1954

Corral (Colin Low)
Paul Tomkowicz: Street-railway Switchman (Roman Kroiter)

1957

City of Gold (Wolf Koenig and Low)

1958

Blood and Fire (Terence Macartney-Filgate)
The Days Before Christmas (Macartney-Filgate, Stanley Jackson, Koenig)

1959

The Back-breaking Leaf (Macartney-Filgate)

1960

Universe (Kroitor and Low)

1961

Circle of the Sun (Low)
Lonely Boy (Koenig and Kroitor)
Very Nice, Very Nice (Arthur Lipsett)

Books on the Period

Beattie, Eleanor, *A Handbook of Canadian Film*. Toronto: Peter Martin Associates, 1973.
Evans, Gary, *In the National Interest: A Chronicle of the National Film Board of Canada from 1949 to 1989*. Toronto: University of Toronto Press, 1991.
Feldman, Seth and Joyce Nelson, eds., *Canadian Film Reader*. Toronto: Peter Martin Associates, 1977.
James, C. Rodney, *Film as a National Art: NFB of Canada and the Film Board Idea*. New York: Arno Press, 1977.

Jones, D. B., *The Best Butler in the Business: Tom Daly of the National Film Board of Canada*. Toronto: University of Toronto Press, 1996.

Jones, D. B., *Movies and Memoranda: An Interpretive History of the National Film Board of Canada*. Ottawa: Canadian Film Institute, 1981.

Kolomeychuk, Terry, ed., *Donald Brittain: Never the Ordinary Way*. Winnipeg: National Film Board of Canada, 1991.

Chapter Twelve

A New Channel: Documentary for Television, the "Golden Years," 1951–1971

English-language documentary films began as a regular part of theatrical film exhibition, from *Nanook of the North* in 1922 on. At the time of *Nanook* and before, the only way to see a movie was in a movie theater. The 35mm film stock standard for theatrical showings had a base of cellulose nitrate, which was highly flammable. It had to be projected from booths constructed in conformance with local ordinances. Exceptions, like the projection vans used by the Soviets and later by the British, were few.

In 1923, at the urging of educators, Eastman Kodak Company made available a film 16mm in width, with a cellulose acetate base. Because it was nonflammable (it was called "safety stock") and the narrower width made lighter equipment possible, portable 16mm projectors could be set up in schoolrooms, church basements, union halls—anywhere, in fact.

With 16mm projectors manufactured and sold and prints of films available for rental and purchase, the nontheatrical field became a recognizable entity by the late 1930s. World War II caused an explosion in the use of films as means of informing and educating. Following the war the nontheatrical field, with industrially sponsored and classroom films predominating, expanded enormously compared to prewar. But, as discussed in chapter ten, the expansion of the nontheatrical field did not at first work to the advantage of documentary. It didn't fit comfortably into the rather narrow requirements of industrial sales and promotion or of formal education. Nor did documentary have the access to theaters it had had during wartime.

As documentary was slipping into the background, losing financial support and audiences as well as earlier subject matters and purposes, a new channel for distribution and exhibition was opening up. This new channel would provide a

179

substantial and sustained basis of support. Thanks to television, more documentaries and related types of public information programs were shown to larger audiences than at any other time in history.

Historical Background

Telecasting had begun on an experimental and very limited basis in both Great Britain and the United States before the war—Britain being ahead of the U.S.— but military requirements of wartime had stopped further development. After the war, regular television broadcasting began in Great Britain, then in the United States, then in Canada. Let's discuss briefly the arrival of television in Britain and Canada before turning to and concentrating on commercial network television in the United States, as this chapter will mostly do.

In 1946 the British Broadcasting Corporation began regular telecasting. A Documentary Department was established in 1953, with documentary veteran Paul Rotha head of it until 1955. The BBC's first major documentary series was *Special Inquiry*, which ran from 1952 to 1957. Norman Swallow was its producer. But as a quasi-governmental organization supported by a tax on television sets, the BBC did not attract anything like the audience that would develop when commercial broadcasting was permitted to operate alongside BBC-TV from 1955 on. The Independent Television Authority (ITA, initially; later called Independent Television, ITV) ran programs produced by a number of commercial companies. Documentaries were included. For example, from Granada Television came *World in Action*, a public affairs and documentary series the title for which was borrowed from the wartime National Film Board of Canada. Thames Television subsequently produced the outstanding twenty-six-part documentary series about World War II, entitled *The World at War*. Scottish Television produced John Grierson's weekly television program devoted to documentary and experimental shorts, *This Wonderful World* (later changing its title to *John Grierson Presents*), from 1957 to 1968.

The situation in Canada was anomalous. Though the Canadian Broadcasting Corporation (a government-related system) did not begin telecasting until 1952, most of Canada's population lived close enough to its southern border to receive U.S. television directly or via community antenna. Canada's bilingual culture was acknowledged by the CBC, with a French-language as well as an English-language network. Curiously, the National Film Board continued to work separately from CBC-TV, with little exchange between the two organizations of produced materials or means of distribution.

In the United States, 1946 was the year television was removed from the wartime freeze. In 1948 big-time TV was born. A network out of New York linked the major cities; the most popular shows were Milton Berle's *Texaco Star Theatre* comedy and Ed Sullivan's *Toast of the Town* variety show. By 1950 one hundred stations telecast to four million sets. In 1951 coaxial cable and microwave relay connected the country coast to coast. (Not altogether coincidentally, that was also the year "The March of Time" ended.)

In the 1951–1952 season Edward R. Murrow and Fred W. Friendly's *See It Now* (out of their radio series *Hear It Now*) appeared. The 1952–1953 season contained *I Love Lucy* and *Victory at Sea* (supervised by historian Henry Salomon, Jr., and edited by Isaac Kleinerman). The situation comedy about a married couple (starring a married couple) and the twenty-six half-hour films about U.S. naval warfare in World War II (compiled from over six million feet of combat footage) are among the most successful and seminal television programs ever aired.

While dramatic and other entertainment programs shown on television came from outside producing agencies, production of documentaries was carried on primarily by the networks and local stations themselves. Both the National Broadcasting Company (NBC) and the Columbia Broadcasting System (CBS) established units for that purpose, with personnel initially drawn from the ranks of the nontheatrical documentarians. American Broadcasting Company (ABC) documentary production was later and weaker, with a news emphasis. The main function of these units was the creation of special programs, frequently nonsponsored, presented as prestige or public service features.

In 1953 what is now the Public Broadcasting Service (PBS) began as National Educational Television (NET). This noncommercial network, supported by funds from the federal government, initiated and distributed substantial quantities of documentaries and public affairs materials. Its budgets tended to be smaller than those of the commercial networks, but it made up for this by purchasing independently produced documentaries and importing many significant documentary programs and series from abroad, principally from Britain.

The number of documentaries shown on commercial and public television during the peak years of network documentary from the fifties into the early seventies was very large indeed. What follows is a selective sketch of those series that were the longest running, contained some of the most memorable programs, and established forms and contents most prevalent among documentaries made for television.

Documentary Series

See It Now was the first regular documentary series. A sort of news magazine of feature stories in "The March of Time" tradition, it had a much quieter and more intimate tone suitable to the living room. Murrow and Friendly produced it for CBS; Murrow was the onscreen host and commentator. At first *See It Now*, like "The March of Time" and the present-day *60 Minutes*, presented several different stories in each half-hour program. In 1953 that format changed to include only one story a week. Among the *See It Now* programs best remembered are "Christmas in Korea" (1953), made during the Korean War, the several programs dealing with McCarthyism, including one in 1954 in which Senator Mc-Carthy was given a program for reply (consistent with an American broadcasting dictum called "the Fairness Doctrine"), and a visit with nuclear physicist J. Robert Oppenheimer (1955).

Like "The March of Time," too, See It Now contained consistent structural and stylistic characteristics—its format—which will be touched upon in a later section. A look at two programs may serve to give some sense of its distinctiveness.

"Argument in Indianapolis" (1953) presents opposing factions in that city when the American Civil Liberties Union, attempting to form a local chapter, is opposed by the American Legion post. One of the extraordinary things about this program is its balance in handling a controversial subject, necessary, no doubt, for it to be telecast at all. Depending on your sympathies, the Legion members become fascist monsters or upholders of true Americanism; the ACLU group, pleasant, sensitive intellectuals or dangerous radicals and subversives. At any rate, the faces, speech, and manner of the protagonists are caught more or less candidly. A remarkable study is offered of diverse ideologies and personalities that exist in uneasy relationship to one another within this republic.

"Segregation in Schools" (1954) was made the week following the Supreme Court decision that declared that separate education for blacks and whites was neither equal nor constitutional. It reports on reactions to the decision in two southern towns—Natchitoches, Louisiana, and Gastonia, North Carolina. What today seems a curious stiffness and formality—on the part of both black and white interviewees, with stand-up microphones visible and some statements read or rehearsed—may have to do with extremely strong feelings being controlled as well as a less flexible technology than is presently available. When feeling does break through—actual expressed emotion of an older black woman, a black high school youth, an elderly white woman, and a black male teacher—it is moving and becomes real in a way that helps us to understand more fully what is involved than do the prepared statements.

In 1955 Alcoa (Aluminum Company of America) withdrew its sponsorship of See It Now. The program then changed from regularly scheduled weekly half hours to hour-long programs that appeared at intervals—"specials," in effect. Media critic Gilbert Seldes quipped that it had become See It Now and Then. In 1958 See It Now was terminated, to be followed by CBS Reports.

CBS Reports developed its own excellence. "The Population Explosion" (1959), while attempting to cover the problem generally, used India as its example. Spokespersons offering various solutions to overpopulation were presented. "Lippmann on Leadership" (1960) allowed the newspaper columnist and political philosopher to express his views. Murrow's last program for the series, "Harvest of Shame" (1960), was about the exploitation and hardships suffered by migrant agricultural workers. It was aired on Thanksgiving Day. Murrow left CBS to become director of the United States Information Agency. Subsequent

Edward R. Murrow as seen on a television screen

"Harvest of Shame" showed to critical outcry on Thanksgiving Day as part of the *CBS Reports* series (U.S., 1960, David Lowe). J. Fred MacDonald

A shot from a television screen of "The Selling of the Pentagon" (U.S., 1971, Peter Davis)

CBS Reports included "Biography of a Bookie Joint" (1961), a neat job of investigative reporting by Jay McMullen, "Hunger in America" (Martin Carr and Peter Davis, 1968), which is credited with facilitating the introduction of the federal food stamps program, and "The Selling of the Pentagon" (1971, Peter Davis), a critical examination of the military's extensive public relations activities.

NBC's response to *See It Now* was the quite different *Project XX* series, which began in 1954. It grew out of the success of *Victory at Sea,* and its production unit included many of the same personnel. Rather than a weekly series, however, *Project XX* offered occasional hour-long specials. Like *Victory at Sea* its programs were compilation films whose origins could be traced back to the "Why We Fight" series, which in turn could be traced back to "The March of Time." *Project XX*'s programs were devoted to recreating aspects of the history of the century (hence *XX*) using existing footage—newsreel, documentary, and feature—and occasional reenactments. Among those that attracted most attention were "Nightmare in Red" (1955), which chronicled the rise of Soviet communism, "The Twisted Cross" (1956), which did the same for German nazism, and "The Real West" (1961). The latter, produced and directed by Donald Hyatt, used paintings and photographs—that is, still visual material—music and words of the era to capture the spirit of a particular time and place. (It was a forerunner of the subsequent Ken Burns historical series.) The commentary, written by Phil

"The Battle of Newburgh," NBC *White Paper* series (U.S., 1962, Arthur Zegart). J. Fred MacDonald

Reisman, Jr., and spoken by Gary Cooper, took on a period flavor as well. Regarding the great cattle drives from Texas to the railhead towns of Kansas and Missouri: "The longhorns were as treacherous as the backlash of a bullwhip. Later, the breed was white-faced and dimple-kneed, but spookier than a wing-busted bird in cat country."

The NBC series comparable to CBS's *See It Now* and *CBS Reports* was *White Paper*, begun in 1960, with Irving Gitlin as executive producer. For the most part it stuck even closer to current or recent headlines. "The U-2 Affair" (1960) dealt with an incident that exposed U.S. aerial spying on the Soviet Union. Other programs also announced the currency of their topics in their titles: "Angola: Journey to a War" (1961), "The Death of Stalin" (1963), "Cuba: Bay of Pigs" (1964). A domestic local situation that had become national news was examined in "The Battle of Newburgh" (1962). At issue was the controversy that developed over the decision by the city manager of this New York town to rid the community of "welfare chiselers."

The Twentieth Century weekly series, which began on CBS in 1957, was sponsored by the Prudential Insurance Company and produced by Burton Benjamin and Isaac Kleinerman. Its programs were mostly half hour, though a few were hour-long. Many of these were historical compilations, such as "Trial at Nuremberg" (1958), "Paris in the Twenties" (1960), and "The Western Hero" (1963). The format of "From Kaiser to Fuehrer" (1959) is typical. Host Walter Cronkite introduces the program then retreats offscreen to voice-over commentary. It owes a debt to *The Fall of the Romanov Dynasty* and "Why We Fight," of course. Clips from German films of the twenties are its main visual content. In addition to newsreels, extensive use is made of *Berlin: Symphony of a Great City* and *Variety*, a fictional feature. The cutting pace is rapid and the editing skillful; a full orchestral score contributes to continuity and dramatic effect.

Other *Twentieth Century* programs were on contemporary subjects and used freshly shot material and interviews: "Ireland: The Tear and the Smile" (1961), "The Burma Surgeon Today" (1961), and "So That Men Are Free" (1962). Willard Van Dyke directed the last (and a number of other *Twentieth Century* films including "Ireland," above, and "Sweden" (1961). In 1966 *The Twentieth Century* became *The Twenty-First Century* before its final season of 1970–1971. The new title was intended to suggest a shift in emphasis to scientific development and the future.

ABC-TV distinguished itself with *Close-Up!*, a series using cinéma vérité—more precisely, the American version of it called direct cinema. This new technique, made possible by new technology, is the subject of chapter fourteen. The idea for the series came from *Primary* and *On the Pole* (both 1960), films produced by Robert Drew Associates (which included, along with Drew, Richard Leacock, D. A. Pennebaker, Terence Macartney-Filgate, Albert and David Maysles, Hope Ryden, Gregory Shuker, among others) for Time-Life Broadcast. Not all the Drew Associates were on every film, of course, but there were many of them. These undirected sync-sound essays were of the Wisconsin presidential Democratic primary contest between Hubert Humphrey and John F. Kennedy, and of the Indianapolis automobile race, following driver Eddie Sachs. They were shown on four local stations owned by Time, Inc. ABC was sufficiently impressed to hire Drew Associates to produce five one-hour documentaries for the *Close-Up!* series: "Yanki No!" (1960), "X-Pilot" (1960), "The Children Were Watching" (1960), "Kenya" (1961), and "Adventures on the New Frontier" (1961). The first had to do with anti-Americanism in Latin America. The subject of the second is the final test flight of a new airplane and the personality of the test pilot. The third was shot in New Orleans during one week of a school integration crisis. It presents the attitudes of white segregationists and their effects on a black family whose daughter is supposed to be one of the first to attend a previously all-white school. Finally "Adventures on the New Frontier" presents "a day in the life of" John F. Kennedy in the White House.

Drew Associates did not continue on *Close-Up!* but the executive producer of that series, John Secondari, appeared to have learned from them and produced valuable programs using direct cinema technique with his own personnel. Nicholas Webster was one of these, who produced and directed "Walk in My Shoes"

"Walk in My Shoes," *Close-Up!* series (U.S., 1961, Nicholas Webster). J. Fred Mac-Donald

(1961). It presents the anger, resentment, and feelings of frustration of black Americans largely from their point of view and in interview situations of one sort or another. Webster's "Meet Comrade Student" (1962) examines Soviet education after the launching of *Sputnik*, which had caused Americans to feel left behind in scientific knowledge and training.

During this same period young producer David L. Wolper was pioneering a different type of television documentary. Like Robert Drew, but unlike most of the others then producing television documentaries, Wolper did not work for any of the three networks. Yet he wanted to sell his shows to the networks. In 1957, when a representative from Artkino, the official U.S. film distributor for the U.S.S.R., mentioned to him that he had footage of the Soviet space missions to sell, Wolper conceived the idea of creating a documentary on the rockets and the then-hot space race, and selling it to the networks as a completed project. Financing it himself, he enlisted the help of friends Jack Haley, Jr., and Mel Stuart to locate footage, shoot interviews, and create *The Race for Space* (1958).

At that point Wolper was not a documentarian but a man who had decided to be in the entertainment business. His experience in film had mainly been selling old Hollywood movies to individual television stations. This background paid off handily with *The Race for Space*, since in these years the networks refused

David L. Wolper. The Wolper Organization

to broadcast any documentary that was not made by their own in-house production units. Worries about the Fairness Doctrine and sponsor accountability made
network executives loath to buy from outsiders. Wolper was able to convince
individual stations, both independents and network affiliates, to buy and air *The
Race for Space*. It ran on various stations for one week in April 1960 and proved
to be a huge critical and financial success. It was even nominated for an Academy
Award, the first made-for-television documentary to be so recognized. The
Wolper empire and a substantial American television syndication business was
born.

Over the next forty years Wolper and his teams were responsible for fifty-
eight television documentary specials and twenty documentary series consisting
of 347 episodes—a prodigious output. (He is perhaps best known, though, for
his fictional miniseries—fourteen of them at 108 hours, including *Roots* and *The
Thorn Birds*.) He also produced twenty theatrical motion pictures, many of them
successful documentaries. The various Wolper companies provided hands-on
training grounds for at least two generations of documentarians, and he has won
Oscars, Peabodys, and Lifetime Achievement Awards galore.

Documentary history has tended to pass over the importance of David
Wolper's work for a number of reasons. He always asserted that he was in the
business to make money, and at this he was more successful than any other
documentarian in history. He didn't claim that his films could change the world,
yet many of them deal compassionately with serious social and political issues.
He was located on the West Coast, in Hollywood, and in later years had offices
on the Warner Brothers lot rather than in New York City, the traditional center

of documentary production. He has said that he didn't know his films were not supposed to be entertaining in addition to being informative, and admits to being a passionate and very adept salesman—a trait he shares with the most effective documentarians from Robert Flaherty and John Grierson to Ken Burns and Michael Moore. All of these men could sell their ideas to funders, their films to distributors, and themselves to the public.

By contrast Frederick Wiseman, one of the most skilled and talented makers of direct cinema, produced for public television. *High School* (1968), *Law and Order* (1969), *Hospital* (1970), and *Basic Training* (1971) were supported in varying proportions by the Public Broadcasting Service, WNET Channel 13 in New York City, and income from nontheatrical rentals of his films. After *Basic Training* Wiseman contracted with WNET to do one documentary each year to play on the PBS network. His subjects have been various American institutions, the titles generally making clear which one. Wiseman's films will be discussed in chapter fifteen.

Among the television documentary news magazines the biggest success story to date, of course, is CBS's *60 Minutes*, produced by Don Hewitt, which began in 1968. It brought documentary-like content and production methods into commercial television just as "The March of Time" earlier had introduced its own kind of nonfiction forms and subjects into movie theaters. Like "The March of Time," *60 Minutes* developed a format that fit the medium within which it was received. In this case, since the medium was television, its origins are directly traceable to *See It Now* and *CBS Reports*. In *60 Minutes* the American journalistic term "news story" is taken quite literally. The several stories of each program —some light, some serious—use a combination of aggressive investigative reporting, personable on-the-air reporters (Mike Wallace, Morley Safer, Harry Reasoner, Diane Sawyer), and tight narrative structures. The program was successful not only in comparison with other television news, public affairs, and documentary series, but reached the Top Ten among television shows generally in terms of numbers of viewers attracted and amount of money earned. The success of *60 Minutes* was also awarded the compliment of imitation, and the magazine format made up of short segments gradually replaced traditional documentary forms on television.

Special Characteristics of Television Documentary

Many of the new elements common to documentaries made for television can be traced to the new technological characteristics of this electronic means of distribution-exhibition, and to the new relationship with the audience sitting—as individuals or members of small family groups—at home. Television emerged from the earlier forms of radio broadcasting and retained practices common to it.

In regard to the content of documentaries made for television, three major types predominated throughout the 1950s and 1960s, and they correspond to emphases of the documentary series and specials discussed above. First is the documentary based on a newsworthy subject, something that is of current, widespread interest. This is television's major contribution to the evolution of documentary subjects and forms, a genre in which it has been uniquely effective. *See It Now* and *CBS Reports* offered noteworthy examples; among them "Annie Lee Moss Before the McCarthy Committee" (1954) and "Protective Tariff vs. Free Trade" (1957) in the former; "The Business of Health: Medicine, Money and Politics" (1961) and "Storm Over the Supreme Court" (1963) in the latter. Second are the historical and often nostalgic subjects of the compilation series and programs—*Project XX* ("The Innocent Years," 1957; "The Story of Will Rogers," 1961) and much of *The Twentieth Century* ("The Olympics," 1959; "Turn of the Century," 1960). Lastly there is what could be called "human interest," the curiosity we all have about others, their personalities, and their problems. This sort of content is most manifest in the use of direct cinema, in the early *Close-Up!* ("The Miner's Lament," 1963; "A Vanishing Breed: Portrait of a Country Editor," 1963) and in the Frederick Wiseman features (*Hospital*, 1970, and *Basic Training*, 1971, for example).

The range of subjects of television documentaries may be wider as well as different from that of earlier documentaries. A kind of "entertainment documentary" emerged—the nostalgia and human interest categories—in which the issues no longer were of national concern or even social significance. Lyman Bryson observed, in his essay "Popular Art" (in *The Communication of Ideas*, 1948), that the function of the mass media, the experience they offer, is more like that of gossip than like that of traditional art forms. Certainly television offers materials as diverse as those of a neighbor talking to us over the back fence—in our electronic global village, a concept another media scholar, Marshall McLuhan, suggested (in *Understanding Media*, 1964). Scandalous secrets are revealed (daytime dramas), amusing anecdotes told (situation comedies), conundrums posed (game shows), local events recounted (news), and the like. This gossipy quality reached its apex—or nadir—in the reality programming of the twenty-first century.

Another McLuhan concept was that television is a "cool" medium. Its lack of technological refinement of image and sound means the viewer has to complete the message rather than having it beamed at him with the visual and emotional intensity of movies or the auditory fidelity and richness of radio. To some, the content of television documentaries seemed less compelling, slower paced, more redundant—than that of films made to be shown in theaters. In this view *The City* or *Listen to Britain* would be regarded as "hotter" than *See It Now* or Mike Wallace interviewing on *60 Minutes*.

At the same time, television documentary tended to maintain a small-scale intimacy. In *The Twentieth Century*, for example, a program on "Gandhi" (1959) is as much about the man as about the magnitude of his accomplishments; it seems quite unlike *The River* or films of the "Why We Fight" series. Television documentaries often centered not only on individuals but on values (ethical, spiritual, psychological) rather than on material concerns (work, housing, poverty), as did earlier documentaries. (Perhaps this difference was due as much to changed postwar preoccupations as to the influence of television; but whatever the cause, the difference is evident.)

Frequently in the television documentary the commentator was the star and appeared on camera. In earlier documentaries the commentator was usually anonymous and unobtrusive; his voice was heard over the images, and he never appeared onscreen. At most he added a bit of emotional color. The few exceptions that occurred seemed awkward at the time. In one of the "brotherhood films," mentioned in chapter ten, Frank Sinatra talked and sang directly to the audience. You might have felt embarrassed somehow (for him, or for yourself), knowing that he was not really in the theater, as he was pretending to be, but out in Hollywood several months ago. Television created the illusion, and stressed it, that all of it was "live," though of course most of it was not. We knew that the images and sounds were constantly there in the TV set, just as electricity was in the wires and water in the pipes, ready to be turned on at any time. The celebrity commentators—Ed Murrow, Walter Cronkite, Charles Kuralt, Chet Huntley, Dan Rather, et al.—fed into and emphasized the quality of liveness. The audience tuned in to see what Ed was offering on a Friday night. He talked directly to us from the control room, his reporters available to come in over the monitors as he called on them. (Actually, given the technology available at the time, they were filmed beforehand with the film flown to New York City, processed in the lab, and edited before being aired.) The scenes in *See It Now* were shot more as if they were being captured live and undirected than they were in earlier documentaries.

And perhaps out of courteous respect for us (the audience), the commentator's own point of view in what was said and in what was chosen to be shown was generally withheld, or balanced—or maybe just ambivalent, and therefore ambiguous. Exceptions to this rule sometimes created a furor. "Harvest of Shame" (*CBS Reports*, 1960, David Lowe) drew outraged protests from the agriculture industry. "The Selling of the Pentagon" (CBS Special, 1971, Peter Davis) provoked a congressional committee to investigate the fairness of its presentation and threaten to subpoena the president of CBS, Frank Stanton, to force him to turn over outtakes (footage not used), sound recordings, and production notes from the program. "Sixteen in Webster Groves" (CBS Special, 1966, Arthur Barron) is an exceptional case. In a sequel, "Webster Groves Revisited," parents and other residents of this posh suburb of St. Louis were permitted to offer a counterview to the one presented by the teenagers in the first program.

In documentaries made for television there was an increased use of sync sound, especially talk; interviews were used much more extensively than they

Star reporters of the *60 Minutes* series, left to right: Ed Bradley, Mike Wallace, Morley Safer, Diane Sawyer, and Harry Reasoner (U.S., 1988, CBS News).

had been prior to television. The sound track carried at least as much content as the visual track, and the visuals tended to be less rich and interesting than in nontelevision documentaries. In the early days of television, a former radio executive made the egregious blunder at a sales meeting of proudly announcing that more people were listening to television than ever before. As a result of this balance between words and images, the *auteurs* ("authors") of television were usually the producers, writers, and commentators rather than the directors, as was more often the case in films made for theatrical exhibition. A redundancy developed in the documentary made for television that permitted the viewer-listener to go to the refrigerator for a beer and still follow what was going on, or vacuum the living room carpet while keeping an eye on the tube without missing much.

As already noted, television documentaries tended to appear in the context of a series. Before television this was true only in exceptional instances such as "The March of Time" or "Why We Fight." Television documentaries also had to fit into quite precise airtimes, down to the second, allowing pauses for and building structures to accommodate the commercial breaks. The running times of the earlier documentaries varied considerably and were determined, to considerable extent at least, by the form and content of each film: *The Spanish Earth* runs fifty-five minutes; *And So They Live*, twenty-four; *London Can Take It*, nine; *Fires Were Started*, seventy-two; and so on. The fixed times of television resulted in some strains, with insufficient time available to deal adequately with a subject, or padding required to fill out the half hour or hour even though less time would have been sufficient. In the series context and in the daily flow of television programming, it may have been difficult for particular documentaries to offer the kind of aesthetic experience or to achieve the social impact on those they did reach (though they reached many more people instantly) to the extent that some documentaries shown in theaters and to nontheatrical audiences may have done. Lyman Bryson, again, doubted that the mass media could do very much about educating people soundly or altering their opinions on the subjects with which they dealt. He thought the significance of the media in relation to their effects on social attitudes and behavior was essentially to call public attention to matters that seemed important to the producers of media. Television became virtually *the* mass medium, certainly as far as documentary was concerned. It was the best qualified of any medium of art and communication yet devised to quickly call large numbers of people's attention to various subjects. It established its ability to do that—and sometimes did it superbly. In the following chapters documentaries will be dealt with individually without consideration of the channel in which they were distributed-exhibited.

Films of the Period

1952–53

Victory at Sea series (Henry Salomon and Isaac Kleinerman)

1953

"Argument in Indianapolis" (*See It Now* series, Edward R. Murrow and Fred W. Friendly)
"Christmas in Korea" (same as above)

1954

"Edward R. Murrow Talks on Senator McCarthy" (same as above)
"Segregation in Schools" (same as above)

1955

"Nightmare in Red" (*Project XX* series, Salomon and Kleinerman)

1956

"Out of Darkness" (*The Search* series, Albert Wasserman)
"The Twisted Cross" (*Project XX,* Salomon and Kleinerman)

1957

"The Innocent Years" (*Project XX*, Salomon)

1958

"From Kaiser to Fuehrer" (*The Twentieth Century* series, Burton Benjamin and Kleinerman)

"The Population Explosion" (*CBS Reports* series, Av Westin)

1960

"The Children Were Watching" (*Close-Up!* series, Robert Drew Associates, Richard Leacock)

"Harvest of Shame" (*CBS Reports*, Murrow, Friendly, and David Lowe)

"Paris in the Twenties" (*The Twentieth Century*, Benjamin and Kleinerman)

"The U-2 Affair" (*White Paper* series, Wasserman)

"Yanki No!" (*Close-Up!*, Robert Drew Associates, Leacock, Albert Maysles, and D. A. Pennebaker)

1961

"Angola: Journey to a War" (*White Paper*, Wasserman)

"Biography of a Bookie Joint" (*CBS Reports*, Jay McMullen)

"The Business of Health: Medicine, Money and Politics" (*CBS Reports*, Stephen Fleischman)

"Ireland: The Tear and the Smile" (*The Twentieth Century*, Benjamin and Kleinerman)

"New York in the Twenties" (same as above)

"The Real West" (*Project XX*, Donald B. Hyatt)

"Vincent Van Gogh: A Self-Portrait" (NBC-TV Special, Ray Garner)

"Walk in My Shoes" (*Close-Up!*, Nicholas Webster)

1962

"The Battle of Newburgh" (*White Paper*, Wasserman)

"Meet Comrade Student" (*Close-Up!*, Webster)

"Shakespeare: Soul of an Age" (NBC-TV Special, Guy Blanchard)

"So That Men Are Free" (*The Twentieth Century*, Willard Van Dyke)

1963

"The Business of Gambling" (*White Paper*, Arthur Zegart)

"Crisis Behind a Presidential Commitment" (For ABC-TV, Robert Drew Associates, Hope Ryden, Gregory Shuker)

"The Death of Stalin" (*White Paper*, Len Giovannitti)

"Greece: The Golden Age" (*White Paper*, Lou Hazam)

"The Miner's Lament" (*Close-Up!*, William Weston)

"The Plots Against Hitler" (*The Twentieth Century*, Benjamin and Kleinerman)

"That War in Korea" (*Project XX*, Hyatt)
"A Vanishing Breed: Portrait of a Country Editor" (*Close-Up!*, Sam Rosenberg)
"The Vatican" (*Close-Up!*, John Secondari)

1964

"Cuba: Bay of Pigs" (*White Paper*, Fred Freed)
"Cuba: The Missile Crisis" (same as above)
"Orient Express" (NBC-TV Special, Thomas Priestly)

1966

"Sixteen in Webster Groves" (CBS-TV Special, Arthur Barron)

1967

"Morley Safer's Vietnam" (CBS-TV Special, Morely Safer)

1971

"The Selling of the Pentagon" (CBS-TV Special, Peter Davis)

Books on the Period

Bluem, A. William, *Documentary in American Television*. New York: Hastings House, 1965.

Curtin, Michael, *Redeeming the Wasteland: Television Documentary and Cold War Politics*. New Brunswick, NJ: Rutgers University Press, 1995.

Friendly, Fred W., *Due to Circumstances Beyond Our Control. . . .* New York: Random House, 1967.

Hammond, Charles Montgomery, Jr., *The Image Decade: Television Documentary 1965–1975*. New York: Hastings House, 1981.

Kendrick, Alexander, *Prime Time: The Life of Edward R. Murrow*. Boston: Little Brown, 1969.

Kilborn, Richard and John Izod, *An Introduction to Television Documentary: Confronting Reality*. Manchester, UK: Manchester University Press, 1997.

Madsen, Axel, *60 Minutes: The Power & the Politics of America's Most Popular TV News Show*. New York: Dodd, Mead, 1984.

Murrow, Edward R. and Fred W. Friendly, *See It Now*. New York: Simon and Schuster, 1955.

Sperber, A. M., *Murrow: His Life and Times*. New York: Freundlich Books, 1986.

Swallow, Norman, *Factual Television*. New York: Hastings House, 1966.

Wolper, David L., *Producer*. New York: Scribner, 2003.

Chapter Thirteen

British Free Cinema and Social-Realist Features, 1956–1963

In the late forties and early fifties documentary in Britain had run down, as it had in the United States and, to a lesser extent, in Canada, following the wartime boom. Grierson and his old boys were locked into former subjects and purposes that no longer seemed as relevant to the needs of the society as they once had—not as urgent anyway, and certainly not as exciting. In part they were suffering from their success. British documentary films of the thirties could be seen as having pointed to the need for a more collectivized, socialized state. Now that state had arrived.

Following the Labour party's enormous postwar victory at the polls, it remained in office from 1945 to 1951. When the Conservative party returned to power, it did little to reverse the social and economic changes effected by Labour. But beginning in the mid-fifties a sort of cultural revolution commenced, which affected British life generally and became manifest in film as well. With the advent of commercial television and a vitality in the political left that extended into the arts, new popular values ("vulgar" they were thought to be in some quarters) came to the fore.

Expressing these new values was a group of novelists, playwrights, and political essayists who were dubbed the Angry Young Men. What they were angry about was the conformity, the ugliness, the lack of individuality present in what was being called a welfare state—the very sort of state that Labour and the earlier documentary films seemed to be seeking. Further, the Angry Young Men protested that even within this welfare state the class system persisted, with the upper classes controlling government, business, education, and the media. They believed that these upper-class people through these institutions—"the Establishment"—were responsible for the flattening of the working class, for keeping the common people not only helpless but listless. Part of this agitation among young intellectuals and artists—the initial public evidence of it, as a matter of fact—occurred in the documentary film. It took the form of a short-lived and slight but highly influential movement called Free Cinema. This was the first substantial reaction against the Griersonian main line since its beginnings back in 1929.

Critical Background

The roots of Free Cinema lay in a critical position espoused by a group of young people at Oxford University in the late forties. What they started as *Film Society Magazine* in 1947 quickly became *Sequence*. Persons associated with *Sequence* would become extremely important in the British film scene. Penelope Houston became longtime editor of *Sight and Sound*, the prestigious international film journal published by the British Film Institute. Gavin Lambert was her assistant editor, then screenwriter and author of a noteworthy collection of short stories (*The Slide Area*) and a novel (*Inside Daisy Clover*) about Hollywood. Tony Richardson, Karel Reisz (the only member of the group not from Oxford; he was Cambridge, from which a high proportion of the Grierson alumni had come), and Lindsay Anderson were three others. All three would become filmmakers of considerable distinction.

The editorial emphases of *Sequence* were clear-cut and contentious; it was strongly against some things, strongly for others. The British entertainment film industry was denigrated for being dominated by the Americans and failing to produce films having a national character. British documentary was scorned for its didacticism, dullness, and collective (as opposed to personal) creation. Certain new European films and filmmakers were lauded, for instance, *Farrebique* (France, 1946, Georges Rouquier), *People in the City* (Sweden, 1947, Arne Sucksdorff), and *Blood of the Beasts* (France, 1949, Georges Franju). A poetic cinema in Britain was called for that would also provide a national expression—a poetry of reality and of the common person. (This poetry was not to be confused with the poetry of ships, machinery, and trains prevalent in the Grierson documentaries, presumably.)

Lindsay Anderson was the leader of this group. Like Grierson before him, Anderson was the articulate spokesman and the first to begin making films. Also like Grierson, Anderson searched for precedents for the sorts of films he wanted to be made. He wrote seminal reevaluations of the work of Jean Vigo, John Ford, and Humphrey Jennings, finding in their films evidence of the poetic and of the expression of their respective cultures. When *Sequence* ceased publication in 1952 (Anderson and Reisz edited the last issue), the former *Sequence* people made and wrote about Free Cinema. They were vigorous polemicists, as the Griersonians had been.

Free Cinema Films

Anderson, in addition to his work on *Sequence*, had been making sponsored shorts since 1948. His first significant documentaries were released in 1954.

Thursday's Children, codirected with Guy Brenton, celebrated the pupils and the loving, skillful teaching being done at the Royal School for Deaf and Dumb Children in Margate, England. *O Dreamland* (1953) castigated the dull and synthetic pleasures being offered the bemused masses at a seaside amusement park. Anderson himself described it as "a horrid little film." The cameramen on these two films would become principal technicians of the Free Cinema films: Walter Lassally (who subsequently became one of the world's great cinematographers) and John Fletcher (who would concentrate on sound and editing), respectively.

In 1955 Karel Reisz and Tony Richardson made *Momma Don't Allow*, about a lively London jazz club patronized by working-class teenagers. A year later Lorenza Mazetti made *Together*, which deals with the emotionally impoverished lives led by two deaf-mute dockworkers in London's East End. *Together* along with *Momma Don't Allow* and *O Dreamland* comprised the first program shown under the Free Cinema banner in February 1956 at the National Film Theatre of the British Film Institute.

Of the subsequent Free Cinema films—there were only a dozen or so altogether—*Nice Time* (1957) was made by a couple of Swiss aliens, Alain Tanner and Claude Goretta, who would return home to become fiction filmmakers. It is about the people in Piccadilly Circus in London's West End (comparable to Times Square in New York City) on a Saturday night. Lonely and disconsolate by and large, they are shown seeking pleasure and diversion among the movie theaters, the refreshment stands, the prostitutes, and the milling crowds of others like themselves.

Every Day Except Christmas (1957), by Lindsay Anderson, is about the Covent Garden produce market (which no longer exists). It is an observation of the workers and their culture—the look, the feel, and the activities of the place—from early evening, as the trucks come in from the country with vegetables, fruits, and flowers, until closing the following morning. *We Are the Lambeth Boys* (1959), is about teddy boys—kids from a tough part of London—at a social center and on an outing to a cricket match at a posh suburban private school. It is a sympathetic and respectful view of these young people whom the popular press were presenting as gangs of dangerous delinquents.

What did these filmmakers mean by Free Cinema? Essentially independent: free from serving the sponsor's purposes (as in traditional British documentary); free from pandering to the demands of the box office (as in entertainment features). "Implicit in our attitude," they wrote in their program note for the first showing, "is a belief in freedom, in the importance of people and in the significance of the everyday."

Gavin Lambert, in an article in *Sight and Sound* (Spring 1956), wrote of the three films shown at that first Free Cinema program. Likening their spirit to that of D. H. Lawrence's writings, he noted that they "sprang from non-conformism, from impatience with convention, sadness about urban life." Like Lawrence's

Momma Don't Allow (U.K., 1955, Karel Reisz and Tony Richardson). Museum of Modern Art Film Stills Archive

The Covent Garden Market in *Every Day Except Christmas* (U.K., 1957, Lindsay Anderson). Museum of Modern Art Film Stills Archive

work, too, they represented "a desire to regain contact with a more vital, individual force." Lambert continued:

> In the broadest sense, they are films of protest; they are not conceived in sweeping terms . . . but the camera-eye they turn on society . . . is disenchanted, and occasionally ferocious and bitter. . . . If compassion is explicit in Lorenza Mazetti's film [*Together*], implicit in Lindsay Anderson's [*O Dreamland*], it is the most rigorous, difficult and austere kind of compassion: not for the moment or the particular situation, but a kind of permanent temperamental heartache for the world and the people apparently lost in it.
>
> No doubt of it, this is the world in which we live. In seizing upon these aspects—the anonymity of urban life, the aimless lonely figures swallowed up in the greater loneliness of the crowd, the pleasures hideous and mechanical or imaginatively aspiring—the film-makers compel above all the shock of recognition.

A collusion apparent here between critic and creator is reminiscent of the Grierson documentary people who wrote about their own films in *Documentary News Letter*, which they had established. Anderson, in his seminal essay "Stand Up! Stand Up!," also published in *Sight and Sound* (Autumn 1956), demanded that film criticism be socially committed. Commitment, individuality, and poetry were key terms in the rhetoric of Free Cinema.

We Are the Lambeth Boys (U.K., 1959, Karel Reisz). **Museum of Modern Art Film Stills Archive**

The Free Cinema films continued to feature workers and the working class, as had the documentaries of the thirties. But rather than their work, Free Cinema was concerned with how the workers spent their leisure time. The films address the values of the people, their pleasures or lack of them. Rather than material progress and improvements, they concern matters of social psychology and of the spirit. The one Free Cinema film dealing with workers working, *Every Day Except Christmas*, shows what the people working in Covent Garden are like more than what they do and how they do it.

As for purpose and approach, the Free Cinema films are nondidactic, aesthetic rather than informative; they appeal to emotion more than to reason. The sluggish, unimaginative, and flaccid are censured (*O Dreamland, Nice Time*); the lively, vigorous, and idiosyncratic are extolled (*Momma Don't Allow, Every Day Except Christmas, We Are the Lambeth Boys*). They have in common a vaguely anarchic, nihilistic, iconoclastic air. What they seem to be calling for is a total reordering of society—they are consistently anti-Establishment—rather than trying to make the existing system work better. They are implicitly revolutionary rather than actively evolutionary, as Grierson saw his position to be. (He observed of them that they seemed strangely French.) If English precedents are required, they can be found in the writings of D. H. Lawrence, as Gavin Lambert suggested, and also in those of George Orwell.

The formal aspects of the Free Cinema films, especially their structural organizations, are closer to the work of Humphrey Jennings, much admired by Anderson, than they are to the documentaries more directly in the Grierson main line. The Free Cinema films are impressionistic. Though they employ a loose chronology, they follow feeling more than logic. Neither narrative continuity nor a topical outline will altogether account for the selection and ordering of their parts. Commentary is eschewed for the most part. (There is some in *Every Day* and *Lambeth*, but none in the other four examples cited.) Instead, the filmmakers' points are made through their choice and arrangement of sights and sounds. Juxtaposition of symbolic contrasts and counterpoint of the visible and audible abound. Considerable irony and wry humor result.

The production techniques and technology used grow out of the subjects and purposes of Free Cinema. The filmmakers confined themselves to what could be seen and heard on the location. The sights and sounds used are those that could be captured without direction (though bits of invented performance are inserted into *Momma Don't Allow*, as in *Rien que les heures* and *Berlin* much earlier). Quite a lot of Free Cinema is candid—the subjects are unaware they are being filmed—hence the preponderance of places where people gather publicly: amusement park, dance hall, Piccadilly Circus, social center, Covent Garden. In the early examples cited the camera was handheld, the images grainy and underexposed. Location sound, including the inferior quality of a public address system, constitutes the sound track. Between 1954 and 1959 there is increasing technical/technological refinement, from non-sync sound (a so-called "wild track" being recorded and edited to the footage available), to simulated sync, to sync. The camerawork goes from candid to increasing awareness on the part of the subjects that a camera is present to steadier and more carefully composed images. In adjectival terms you might say that the visual-aural style progresses from ugly to casual. But throughout, the roughness of the impressionistic form and nondirected "grab" shooting are in contrast to the Grierson documentary.

The main reason Free Cinema ended seems to have been economic. Free cinema indeed, snorted Grierson, in the most expensive artistic medium yet devised by man! If the films were free from the sponsor (and those who could afford to sponsor films were not likely to pay for the dissent offered by Free Cinema), if their forms and contents did not need to be shaped for the box office (and the public was not much interested in poetry or commitment), how were the films funded? *O Dreamland* cost a few hundred pounds and was paid for by Anderson himself. The other three of the first four films received grants from the British Film Institute Experimental Film Production Fund. The last two listed were sponsored by the Ford Motor Company, evidently with a sense of noblesse oblige similar to that which Grierson cultivated among big oil and gas companies in the thirties. But apparently no more industrial sponsorship was available after *Every Day* and *Lambeth Boys*.

As for the arguments between the Free Cinema newcomers and the old-line documentarians, the former were just as much propagandists as the latter, despite their attacks on earlier documentaries as attempting to manipulate viewer opinion. Merely the ends were different—New Left vs Old Left—as well as the techniques and styles used to advance those ends. If Grierson was correct in anticipating that Free Cinema would cease for lack of economic base, he also foresaw that it would metamorphose into something else. It filtered into the fiction feature film in conjunction with the work of other Angry Young Men and Women of theater and literature.

Political and Cultural Context

The year 1956 was a crucial one in the political and cultural life of Britain. It was the year of one of the last gasps of imperial arrogance in the foolish and failed invasion of Suez. As a result of that debacle the whole governmental system was discredited. To many on the left, the Labour party, which worked within the system, seemed as culpable as the ruling Conservatives. Nineteen fifty-six was also the year of the Khrushchev attack on the cult of personality under Stalin, and of the Soviet invasion of Hungary, which caused many Marxist intellectuals finally to become disillusioned with Stalinist communism.

Partially in reaction to these events, a politically sophisticated younger generation of dissidents arose around the universities—particularly Oxford, which most of the Free Cinema group attended. The label New Left was attached to them, and their publication was entitled *New Left Review* (originally *Universities and Left Review*). The New Left wanted to go beyond the old-line socialists, with their basis in dialectical materialism, trade unionism, nationalization of industry, and social welfare. They were concerned more with theory and a fundamental restructuring of society that would affect the total quality of people's lives. As an intellectual movement that also encompassed the arts, the New Left in Britain was more like the continental Left.

The creators in various media who arose out of this spirit of the time, many of them with a working-class background, attacked the Establishment and the rigidities and inequities of the class system. In 1956 John Osborne's play *Look Back in Anger*, directed by Tony Richardson, opened. (Both Richardson and Anderson directed more plays than films for the simple reason that financing for theater was more readily available.) At about the same time Joan Littlewood's Theatre Workshop started. Playwrights such as Arnold Wesker and Shelagh Delaney soon joined Osborne to create an outpouring of plays set among the lower classes that were articulate and sometimes strident in their social criticism. Novels of a similar tone began to appear as well, with John Braine's *Room at the Top* in 1957 followed by Alan Sillitoe's *Saturday Night and Sunday Morning*, Stan Barstow's *A Kind of Loving*, and David Storey's *This Sporting Life* among them.

Though Free Cinema had in fact appeared slightly before the explosions in the other arts, it wasn't until it connected with the new drama and literature that its kind of expression moved over into the feature film and became economically viable. The Free Cinema movement as such virtually ceased with *We Are the Lambeth Boys* in 1959. Nonetheless, the attitudes and some of the rough-hewn style of Free Cinema carried over into the new social-realist features that began just as the Free Cinema shorts ended.

Social-Realist Features

Room at the Top (1958), much more conventional than Free Cinema in both content and form, launched the new phase. Set in an industrial northern town, it deals with the compulsions and confusions of a cynical young arriviste determined to climb up out of his slum origins. Its romantic conflict is class-based. *Look Back in Anger* (1959) put some of the same matters, and others, in a clearer and less ambiguous way. Through the Jimmy Porter character's brilliant and paranoiac monologues, we could begin to understand what the anger was all about. At least it was clear what he was trying to tear down (the Establishment, personified by his wife's parents) and what he was trying to preserve (the working-class virtues, represented by his friend Ma Tanner).

Those two films, double-billed in the United States, began the social-realist cycle that dealt with various aspects of working-class character and problems. As a body the films tended to be set in the industrial regions north of London. Thus they contrasted with British entertainment films made up to that time, which, according to the Free Cinema group at least, had reflected almost exclusively the outlook of metropolitan southern English culture and the middle and upper classes. Here were efforts to include "the rich diversity of tradition and personality which is the whole of Britain" called for in one of Free Cinema's manifestos.

Of the Free Cinema trio of Anderson, Reisz, and Richardson, it was Richardson who first entered the feature field with *Look Back in Anger*. Those three were joined by John Schlesinger, an Oxford classmate of Richardson's. Together they constituted the main directorial talent of the social-realist features of the early sixties. New in content—in their concern with working-class characters and criticism of the Establishment—these films were essentially conventional in fiction film narrative technique. All of them were based on the writings of the so-called Angry Young Men (or Women, as the case might be). Richardson went on to direct three more of those features in rapid succession. *The Entertainer* (1960), from another Osborne play and script, was seen as offering evidence of collapse within English society. *A Taste of Honey* (1961) was from a play by Shelagh Delaney, who worked on the screenplay as well. The distinctive location cinematography in Lancashire was by Walter Lassally, who became as prominent a figure in the social-realist features as he had been in the Free Cinema shorts. *The Loneliness of the Long Distance Runner* (1962)—from a story by Alan Sillitoe, who also wrote the script—portrays the life, frustrated ambitions, and resentments of a lower-class youth who wanders into crime and is sent to prison. The causes of his problems are portrayed as societal; sympathy as well as understanding is offered for his form of rebellion.

Karel Reisz directed only one of the social-realist features (Richardson produced it), but his *Saturday Night and Sunday Morning* (1960) is in many ways the most exemplary of their tendencies as a whole. The documentary intention dominates. Served equally well by a story that grows out of the situation (rather than being imposed on it) and by convincingly natural performances, the film flies in the face of accepted demands of both box office and dramatic convention. From Sillitoe's popular novel (and he again did the script), it focuses on a working-class rebel. Though hostile to the system, the young lathe operator finally lacks the resources—the imagination and understanding—to break free from it. Proudly indigenous as the film is, one doesn't have to know England to sense that the rows of identically drab houses, the father glued to the telly, the job without meaning, and the inadequate release of a Saturday night's drunk and tumble in the hay must be how it was for a large segment of the population (as it was elsewhere). If an epilogue were to be added to it, it could borrow from Dylan Thomas, as did the Free Cinema filmmakers for their first program: "This is the world. Have faith."

Lindsay Anderson, acknowledged leader and spokesman of the Free Cinema group, was last to arrive at features. Curiously, his first, *This Sporting Life* (1963), if it marked a high point in the social-realist cycle, also indicated a turning away from the sources that had given that demimovement its character and strength. From a novel and script adaptation by David Storey, it has the requisite general characteristics of northern industrial town and working-class background. Where it departs from the other films is in its concentration on the tortured love affair between the miner turned professional rugby player and his widowed landlady, and in its flashback sequences of surrealist exaggeration. At the time of its release Anderson was complimented by British reviewers for having broken out of the confines of the social-realist films—with their air of objectivity and use of the representative to make their criticism stick—into richer areas of individual feeling, the traditional concerns of great art. Perhaps what was by then being referred to as the "kitchen sink" school of filmmaking was limited in certain important ways and had run its course. Whatever the reasons, *This Sporting Life* along with *Billy Liar* (directed by John Schlesinger in the same year) proved to be the last films directly connected to the line that had begun with *Room at the Top*.

The documentary influence has contributed to some of the most interesting and distinctive cycles of British fiction production: wartime semidocumentaries, postwar Ealing comedies, and social-realist features. It might be argued that the quiet genius of British cinema has always pointed most surely in the direction of realism and what John Grierson called the documentary idea. For a while in the nineteen sixties, as the young men of Free Cinema came together with the young men and women of theater and literature who had been tackling similar themes, the veracity of documentary detail was warmed and strengthened by the addition of story and character. Perhaps those who made the social-realist features between 1958 and 1963 got some of the older documentarians' preoccupations and methods more widely and effectively before a larger public.

At the time Free Cinema ended and metamorphosed into the social-realist fiction features, another development began that would move documentary closer to the dividing line between art and life it has always tried to cross. Called *cinéma vérité* in France and direct cinema in America, this development is the subject of chapter fourteen.

Films of the Period

1953

O Dreamland (Lindsay Anderson)

1955

Momma Don't Allow (Karel Reisz and Tony Richardson)

1956

Together (Lorenza Mazetti)

1957

Every Day Except Christmas (Anderson)
Nice Time (Alain Tanner and Claude Goretta)

1958

Room at the Top (Jack Clayton)

1959

Look Back in Anger (Richardson)
We Are the Lambeth Boys (Reisz)

1960

The Entertainer (Richardson)
Saturday Night and Sunday Morning (Reisz)

1961

A Taste of Honey (Richardson)

1962

A Kind of Loving (John Schlesinger)
The Loneliness of the Long Distance Runner (Richardson)

1963

Billy Liar (Schlesinger)
The Leather Boys (Sidney Furie)
This Sporting Life (Anderson)

Books on the Period

Gaston, Georg, *Karel Reisz*. Boston: Twayne, 1981.
Lovell, Alan and Jim Hillier, *Studies in Documentary*. New York: Viking, 1972.
Orbanz, Eva, *Journey to a Legend and Back: The British Realistic Film*. Berlin: Verlag Volker Spiess, 1977.
Silet, Charles L. P., *Lindsay Anderson: A Guide to References and Resources*. Boston: G. K. Hall, 1978.
Sussex, Elizabeth, *Lindsay Anderson*. New York: Frederick A. Praeger, 1970.

Chapter Fourteen

Direct Cinema and Cinéma Vérité, 1960–1970

I n the late 1950s major breakthroughs began to occur in the technology available to filmmakers. These occasioned what can be thought of either as something totally new under the artistic sun or merely as new ways of doing old things. What they permitted was the synchronous recording of sight and sound outside the confines of soundstages and studio back lots. Virtually anything that could be seen and heard could now be captured on sound film almost anywhere.

These new technical possibilities did not dictate the uses to which they would be put, however. One of those uses was that of the Americans who called what they were doing direct cinema. Another was that of Frenchman Jean Rouch, who coined the term *cinéma vérité* (film truth) to apply to his own work. These two contrasting practices and theories will be dealt with in a later section of this chapter.

Historical Background

Documentarians have always sought technological additions that would permit them to film more easily under difficult conditions and to convey more of the observed actuality to their audiences. The initial division between the creative impulses that led to documentary and those that led to fiction was caused at least partly by equipment. The first films made by the Edison Company in the 1890s were shot with the Kinetograph. This electrically powered camera was so large and heavy it was confined to a studio built to house it. Edison technicians recorded vaudeville and circus acts, and bits of stage plays performed in the Black Maria, as that studio was called, thus inaugurating the theatrical/fictional mode of filmmaking. Louis Lumière, on the other hand, designed a lightweight, hand-cranked camera, the Cinématographe, which permitted him to record life on the streets, thus establishing the documentary mode.

By the 1920s, when documentary proper began to evolve, the cameras used were portable but still cumbersome, requiring tripods. The comparatively insensitive film—all of it black and white—needed lots of light. No sound was available until after 1927, except that provided in the theaters by pianos, organs, or pit orchestra as films were being exhibited. Flaherty's descriptive sort of documentary, which showed the surroundings, physical appearances, and outdoor activities of unfamiliar peoples, was ideal for the limitations of that technology. Yet, though Flaherty's locations were far from the studios, he used studio methods of directed action repeated for change of camera position and lens. His shots were edited together to match the action in the usual long shot-medium shot-close-up sequence.

In the 1930s, with the optical sound track added, the production equipment became so bulky that synchronous recording of sight and sound on location was difficult to impossible. It was like Edison's camera all over again, and fiction filmmakers retreated into the studio. The standard documentary sound-film method became that of shooting silent, subsequently adding to the edited footage spoken words plus music plus sound effects. To have documentary "talkies," a voice-over commentary was obligatory. Though an artificial element, commentary did permit the addition of information and interpretation to visual surfaces and some analysis of complex contemporary issues—the Grierson and Lorentz kind of documentary, in short.

Black-and-white images accompanied by post-synchronized sound remained the visual-auditory representation available to documentary makers throughout the thirties and forties. The so-called classic documentaries—*Song of Ceylon, The Plow That Broke the Plains, Night Mail,* the "Why We Fight" series, and the rest—were all made within those limitations. Filmmakers kept trying to come closer to capturing the sound with the natural scene. This goal and the development of equipment to reach it were not confined to those with documentary interests (though they would win the race). Notable efforts occurred in realistic fiction filmmaking as well.

The Italian neorealists, especially Roberto Rossellini, made remarkable strides in adding audible reality to their images. Their sound was still post-synchronized, however; the dialogue was all dubbed. Jean Renoir was another fiction filmmaker who disliked the confinement of the studio and the rigidity of the large and heavy Mitchell BNC (Blimped Noiseless Camera) standard in studio shooting. In an amusing interview, Renoir likened the 35mm studio camera to a great metal idol to which humans are offered up sacrificially. Everything was done for the convenience of the camera. Actors had to move to chalk marks on the floor to be in focus, to turn their faces a certain way to catch the light. Renoir wanted, instead, the machine (camera) to be subservient to people (actors)—to follow them around, to attend to them (*Movie,* April 1963).

Early efforts to achieve such a technology/technique were made by Morris Engle, a former still photographer. In three independent fiction features shot in

New York City—*The Little Fugitive* (1953), *Lovers and Lollipops* (1955), and *Weddings and Babies* (1958)—Engle moved toward an increasing flexibility of equipment. The last film was the first 35mm fiction feature to be made with a portable camera with synchronous sound attachment.

Obviously the lighter equipment of 16mm offered documentarians advantages over 35mm. Eastman Kodak had manufactured silent 16mm film since 1923. If desired, films shot on 16mm could be "blown up" to 35mm for theatrical exhibition. Lionel Rogosin made *On the Bowery* in 1956 and *Come Back, Africa* in 1958 in this way, with some remarkable sync-sound actuality set within semidocumentary narratives. In 1960 John Cassavetes, in *Shadows*, allowed actors to improvise while their actions and words were recorded on portable 16mm equipment.

New Technology and First Films

From that point on the key equipment that made direct cinema/cinéma vérité possible began to appear. As for the visual aspect, by substituting plastic for metal moving parts, 16mm shoulder-mounted cameras became even more lightweight and noiseless, no longer requiring blimps (i.e., casing containing acoustic insulation). The French Eclair NPR (Noiseless Portable Reflex), developed by André Coutant in 1961, and the German Arriflex SR (Silent Reflex) are cameras of this sort in subsequent standard use. Cameras with reflex viewing (looking through the lens while shooting) plus zoom lenses permitted cinematographers to alter the field of view—from close-up to long shot, for example—without having to stop to change lenses or to focus. The French Angenieux 12 to 120mm zoom lens was commonly used. Increasingly "fast" film stock (that is, with emulsion very sensitive to light, thus needing little light) permitted shooting without adding illumination to that available, first in black-and-white and then in color. Eastman Kodak 16mm color negative was in widespread use from the mid-1970s on, replacing the reversal processes (Kodachrome and Ektachrome) because of its superior qualities. Added to faster film stock was a laboratory "intensification process," which could push the sensitivity of a film to over 1000 ASA (an acronym for American Standards Association; the higher the number the faster the film; standard color negative had an ASA of 100).

As for sound, ¼-inch magnetic tape recorders were developed, which could be synchronized with cameras through use of an inaudible sixty-cycle pulse. The Nagra, developed by Swiss engineer Stefan Kudelski in 1958, became the tape recorder of this type in most common use. When crystal synchronization was added, there was no longer even the need for a cable between camera and recorder. Around 1960 vacuum tubes, which consumed a lot of energy, were replaced by transistors, and the weight of sound recorders was reduced from 200 pounds to 20 pounds. This new technology permitted recording action taking place in front of the camera and microphone without altering or interrupting it.

Les Raquetteurs/The Snowshoers (Canada, 1958, Michel Brault and Gilles Groulx). National Film Board of Canada

The first successful films using it were made between 1958 and 1961 in Canada, the United States, and France.

In 1958 at the National Film Board two young French Canadians, Michel Brault and Giles Groulx, using film left over from another project, shot more or less secretly *Les Raquetteurs* (*The Snowshoers*). The event with which the film is ostensibly concerned—snowshoe races in Sherbrooke, Quebec—seems mainly to be the occasion for a parade and a party. The film records these activities but concentrates on the people and their relations with one another. The filmmakers must have entered into the sociability and evidently were fully accepted by the townsfolk.

Les Raquetteurs raised some hackles in official Canada, however. Concern was expressed about the nonofficial way in which it was produced. More serious was the question about the motivation of the filmmakers. Though they appear to be in affectionate if amused sympathy with their subjects, some French Canadians were made uneasy by the unprettified view of robust conviviality presented. Such a portrayal, it was alleged, helped perpetuate the false stereotype of the crude and dull-witted "Canucks."

In 1960, in the United States, *Primary*, already mentioned in chapter 12, was produced by Drew Associates, Robert Drew being executive producer. Most of

Producer Robert Drew (left) and cameraman during the filming of *Primary* (U.S., 1960, Drew Associates). Drew Associates

the shooting was done by D. A. Pennebaker, Albert Maysles, Terence Macartney-Filgate, and Richard Leacock. Drew and Pennebaker recorded the sound. All of the crew worked on the editing; 18,000 feet (seven and one-half hours) of film was cut down to 2,000 (fifty minutes).

The film deals with the 1960 Wisconsin Democratic primary election contest between senators Hubert Humphrey and John F. Kennedy. Not only does it follow each candidate through his public appearances and activities, intercutting between the two men, as television news might do, it also enters into the more private times when the candidates are in their hotel rooms or in an automobile riding to the next engagement. Of the many remarkable moments the film contains, perhaps the most often mentioned is a seemingly uninterrupted shot with synchronous sound that follows Kennedy from outside a building into it, down a long corridor, up some stairs, out onto a stage, ending with a view of the wildly applauding audience. Maysles shot it. The novelty at the time was breathtaking. Another startling innovation—little remarked on—was the absence of interviews, no people talking to the camera—unprecedented for that sort of subject. We get a full enough account of persons and events just by observing.

One could say that French cinéma vérité began in 1959 at a Robert Flaherty Seminar—an annual event started by Flaherty's widow, Frances, and brother, David. On that occasion ethnographer-filmmaker Jean Rouch saw *Les Raquetteurs* and met Michel Brault, who would become principal cameraman for

Jean Rouch (left) and Edgar Morin in the conclusion of *Chronicle of a Summer* (France, 1961). Museum of Modern Art Film Stills Archive

Chronicle of a Summer (1961), directed by Rouch in collaboration with sociologist Edgar Morin. *Chronicle* was first shown in the United States at another Flaherty Seminar, in 1963, along with Drew Associates' *The Chair* and Albert and David Maysles's *Showman* (both 1962). (Curiously, Robert Drew, working his way toward film, had earlier crashed a Flaherty Seminar looking for Ricky Leacock to help him execute his ideas.)

Chronicle of a Summer broke from the Griersonian/Anglo-Saxon tradition in ways even more basic than did *Les Raquetteurs* or *Primary*. Its subject matter consists of a sampling of individual opinions, attitudes, and values of Parisians in the summer of 1960. What the film offers is a chance to understand something of the interviewees and of their culture, of their positions within it, and their feelings about it.

The filmmakers' purpose and approach seem, like Flaherty's, to be that of discovery and revelation. These natives played at least as large a part in the creation of the film as did Nanook or Moana. They are sophisticated (at least modern urban) and articulate, however. Their concerns, as well as those of the filmmakers, are about their feelings rather than about the work they do and how they do it. (In this respect *Primary* is more Griersonian: It is about people

John F. Kennedy on the campaign trail caught in a famous shot by cameraman Al Maysles in *Primary* (U.S., 1960, Drew Associates). Drew Associates

working—what they do rather than what they think and feel.) In fact, work is viewed negatively—one has to be dishonest to make a living, one tries to earn enough money to be oneself; work is boring, repetitive, mechanical—and we see very little of it, only hear about it, for the most part.

Like Flaherty's films the overall structure of *Chronicle* is a loose chronological narrative, as the title implies. It also resembles, however, an anthology of essays and short stories. Through it we get to know more about Parisians—Marceline, who survived a Nazi concentration camp; Angelo, a Renault factory worker; Marilou, an emotionally troubled Italian working in Paris; or Landry, a black African student—than we do about Humphrey or Kennedy in *Primary*. We are told by the filmmakers that part one of the film is intended to deal with the "interior," personal lives of the subjects; part two is about the "exterior," more general world around them as they see it. (The Algerian war was still being waged.) Narrative links among the sequences are made through groupings of persons and topics of conversation; and there are some startling contrasts—a cut from newspaper headlines about the murder of whites in the Belgian Congo to a shot of a young woman waterskiing off Saint-Tropez. The approach is persistently reflexive: The people on camera and we in the audience are continually reminded that a film is being made, that we are watching a film. The penultimate scene is of the persons the film is about discussing themselves as they have appeared in the film they and we have just seen.

Here the new sync-sound technology is used primarily for discussion and interview. There is even a soliloquy as Marceline, strolling by herself in the Place de la Concorde and Les Halles market, recalls painful episodes from her past. Angelo, the Renault worker, gives a kind of improvised performance for the camera, pointedly ignoring its presence. He pretends to wake in the morning, to get ready for work, to go off to work, to work, and later to return home—all this so that his actions might be recorded on film, as Nanook's were.

Throughout the film the cinematography of Michel Brault, Raoul Coutard, and A. Vignier, though different from Flaherty's in its spontaneity, is equal to his in skill and certainty. The filmmakers' ability to move smoothly and seemingly effortlessly with their subjects is astonishing. Unlike Flaherty, however, the two directors are frequently on screen, engaged in conversation with their subjects. This is a film being made by Rouch and Morin, they seem to be telling us, and here we are so you can see how we are going about it.

The final scene is of Rouch and Morin talking to each other about their expectations in regard to the film and about their subjects' reactions to it. As they leave the Musée de l'Homme, where the screening has just taken place, Morin expresses disappointment that not all the participants liked the persons and scenes he liked. The final words on the sound track are those of Rouch saying to Morin, "We're in for trouble," as the two separate.

Direct Cinema vs Cinéma Vérité

The American use of the new equipment, largely with an approach called direct cinema, was pioneered by Drew Associates in the *Close-Up!* series on ABC-TV discussed in chapter twelve. Its tenets were articulated most forcefully by Robert Drew and, especially, by Richard ("Ricky") Leacock. The Drew-Leacock approach falls within the reportage tradition, stemming from Drew's "picture story" background in photo-journalism and Leacock's experience as a documentary cinematographer.

Their technique assumed the possibility of an objective observer. While acknowledging that subjectivity occurs in selecting persons and situations and aspects of them, once those choices are made the filmmakers do not direct or participate in, or even influence (they contended), the scene in any way. They felt that the presence of the camera was soon taken for granted by the subjects— ignored mostly, sometimes forgotten altogether. In their approach, the relationship between filmmakers and subject persons had to be relaxed and trusting in order for the filmmaking to fit into the ongoing action without affecting it. Leacock was particularly adept at winning confidence from the people he was shooting; a warm and engaging person, he could be casual and unassuming with his camera and the people in front of it.

In the course of their work Drew Associates discovered that their method functioned best if something important was happening to their subjects—if they were involved in an activity demanding their full attention and evoking a certain unalterable behavior. This was the case in *Primary*. Humphrey and Kennedy were much more concerned with winning an election than with how they would appear on screen. They were attempting to charm and influence people in order to obtain their votes, and public appearance was a normal part of their lives, which the presence of a camera and microphone would scarcely alter. *Mooney vs. Fowle* (1961, aka *Football*) builds up to the climaxes with a high school football game in Miami, Florida, between two rival teams. It concentrates on the players, coaches, immediate families—those most completely preoccupied with this contest. *The Chair* (1962) centers on the efforts of a Chicago attorney, Donald Page Moore, to obtain a stay of execution for his client, Paul Crump, five days before it is scheduled to take place. *Jane* (1962) concerns Jane Fonda in the production of a play, from the rehearsal period through the negative reviews following its Broadway opening and the decision to close it.

As these examples suggest, Drew Associates also discovered that their method worked best if the situation they chose had its own drama (with a beginning, middle, and end), which would come to a climax within a limited time. This conforms to certain characteristics noted by Aristotle as common to Greek drama. Stephen Mamber, in an analysis of the films of Drew Associates (*Cinema Verite in America*), identified this as the "crisis structure." When such a situation did not exist the films lacked point and force, Mamber felt. He gives as examples *Showman* (1962), about movie mogul Joseph Levine, and *Nehru* (1962), about the then prime minister of India. Though these are interesting and significant figures, the days shown are cluttered and formless—nothing very dramatic happens, and we don't really gain much in our understanding of either man or of why he behaves as he does.

Nowadays the term cinéma vérité is frequently used generically for nondirected filmmaking (and in the United States usually without the French accents, as in the title of Mamber's book), but originally it was applied exclusively to the Rouch/French approach, to distinguish it from the Drew-Leacock/American direct cinema. The differences between the two approaches are clear and significant and worth discusssing.

The term *cinéma vérité* was first applied by Jean Rouch to *Chronicle of a Summer*. It refers back to the Russian equivalent, *kino pravda*, used by Soviet filmmaker Dziga Vertov forty years earlier. Rouch subsequently said on numerous occasions that what he was attempting was to combine Vertov's theory and Flaherty's method.

Rouch denied that the filmmaker can achieve objectivity or that the camera can be unobtrusive. Since it is, finally, the filmmaker rather than the subject who is making the film, Rouch felt that he or she must have a strong attitude toward the subjects and must plan what to draw from them. In Rouch's films (and those of others following this approach) the subjects are not necessarily occupied with something more important to them than the camera and microphone. Virtually everything we see and hear in *Chronicle* is occasioned by the making of the film. Rouch argues, and many instances can be seen in his films and those of others (Chris Marker's *Le Joli Mai* [*The Lovely May*, 1963], or Michel Brault and Pierre Perrault's *Pour la suite du monde* [English title *Moontrap*, 1963], or the Maysles's *Grey Gardens* [1975], for example), that the camera acts as a stimulant. It causes people to think about themselves as they may not be used to doing and to express their feelings in ways they ordinarily would not. Perhaps there is an appropriateness in this approach coming out of a Catholic culture; there is a strong element of the confessional in Rouch's films. It also bears some relationship to psychodrama and to group psychotherapy.

In 1963 in Lyons, France, a memorable meeting devoted to cinéma vérité and direct cinema was sponsored by Radio Television Française (the French national broadcasting system). In *What Is Cinéma Vérité?* (see Books on the Period), Issari and Paul offer an account of the most important aspects of this event, and much of what follows is drawn from it. Two of those present had contributed importantly to the technology that made the technique possible: André Coutant (Eclair camera) and Stefan Kudelski (Nagra tape recorder). While Coutant was displaying his camera he withdrew a fountain pen from his pocket and said, "The camera is still not as simple to use as this, but we're working on it." Filmmaker attendees included Jean Rouch, Mario Ruspoli, and Edgar Morin from France; Robert Drew, Richard Leacock, Albert and David Maysles from the United States; Michel Brault from Canada. The greatest excitement was generated by a lively ongoing debate between Rouch and Leacock.

Both of them were hoping to find "the reality of life," "the truth in people" hidden under the superficial conventions of daily living. Rouch sought to pierce the observable surface to reach this underlying truth by means of discussion, interview, and a fictional sort of improvisation. Leacock thought he could capture this same obscured reality by photographing people without intruding; that subjects would reveal what they really felt and were like when unself-consciously relaxed or deeply involved in some activity. Rouch attempted to unmask truth through a process of deliberately encouraged self-revelation. Leacock tried to expose this reality through capturing unguarded moments of self-revelation in the movement of actual life. Rouch wanted to explain the *raison d'être* of life, whereas Leacock wanted to let life reveal itself.

During the arguments animosity developed and the two positions remained essentially unresolved; perhaps they are not resolvable. Leacock claimed that Rouch prevented people from being themselves, that he forced meanings from them according to a pattern he had arbitrarily set. Rouch faulted Leacock for being too uncritical, for accepting whatever came along as part of "the American way of life." It could be said with equal justice that Rouch's view seems especially "French." That is to say, as Issari and Paul in fact do, "Their sharp exchanges of opinion at the Lyons conference may be explained by their different national and cultural backgrounds. The individual style of each is a reflection not only of his personality—and cinéma vérité [and direct cinema] probably reflects the personality of its author more faithfully than any other style of film making—but also the society of which he is a part" (p. 172). Rouch and Leacock, however, did eventually become close, so much so that when Rouch died in 2004 at the age of eighty-seven, Leacock was occupying Rouch's Paris apartment.

Effects on Documentary Subjects and Styles

It seems quite appropriate that Ricky Leacock would be one of the pioneers of direct cinema/cinéma vérité. A scene in Flaherty's *Louisiana Story* (1948), on which he was cinematographer, made a profound impression on him early in his career and served as a foreshadowing of what was to come. The scene is the one in which the father tells a story about a man who had his jaw bitten off by an alligator.

According to the recollections of some of those involved, this occurred while the crew was setting up to shoot a scripted scene. Camera and recorder were turned on merely for testing, but Flaherty let them run to preserve the telling of the story. He was so taken with the results that he included it in the film, though its nondirected verisimilitude is quite different in style from the rest. This was truly the thing itself, for its own sake, which is what Frances Flaherty said her husband was after. Leacock became committed to trying to arrive at portable synchronous sound equipment that would permit the recording of actuality in this way generally—without script, without direction, with scarcely any editing.

The technology that did evolve has pulled documentary filmmakers back to Flaherty—Rouch and cinéma vérité as much as Leacock and direct cinema. It permits continuous takes even longer than those characteristic of Flaherty. Reflex viewing through a zoom lens requires no pauses for lens changes or refocusing. A camera loaded with four hundred feet of 16mm film can simply be kept running for ten minutes. Of course, the act of cutting the 18,000 feet of film that passed through the cameras for *Primary* down to the 2,000 feet that appear in the final version suggests that a highly selective point of view is operating. Still, sync sound prevents the breaking up and manipulation of shots as freely as is possible with footage shot silent and sound added later. Within scenes the film-maker is bound closely to the real time and real space of the events. With film, it is difficult to cut into a continuous sound track without the cut being noticeable; sound locks images into place.

This technique not only permits but encourages coming in close, in selecting and concentrating on individuals (like Flaherty, unlike Grierson). In the National Film Board film about Paul Anka discussed in chapter eleven, *Lonely Boy*, there

Frederick Wiseman editing film on a flatbed eight-plate Steenbeck machine. Zipporah Films

is a scene in which Anka is singing before a huge audience at Freedomland amusement park in the Bronx. The camera panning a crowd of teenage girls screaming in adulation catches one face that seems to be dissolving in emotion. Just after the camera passes her it stops, pans back, zooms in, and refocuses on a close-up. You can almost hear the cameraman saying to himself as this image registers on his consciousness, "Wow, look at that!" In *Welfare* (1975), a subject that would have been treated by earlier documentarians with attention to institutions and processes, Wiseman instead attends to individuals and their relationships in a particular New York City office—those applying for financial aid and those dispensing it.

Some of the human complexity of persons being zoomed in on can now be suggested. They can tell us what they think and feel as well as show us what they do. Now we have a seeing and hearing machine that could film Nanook straight through while he is catching a seal, with Nanook's shouts to his family coming to join him and the thumping and bumping on the ice accompanying the images. Even more important, this new technology/technique permitted the filming of a sophisticated, urban Nanook in some psychological depth. In *The Chair*, for instance, there is a moving scene in which the attorney breaks into tears and expresses his incredulity after he receives a phone call from a stranger offering support for him in his efforts to save his client's life.

An even greater innovation is the way in which the action is determined and who determines it. In *Nanook* (and virtually all documentaries dealing with

Paul Crump faces execution in a shot by Ricky Leacock in *The Chair* (U.S., 1962, Drew Associates). Drew Associates

individuals up through the 1950s), Flaherty observed what Nanook did. Subsequently—days, weeks, months later—he had him redo it for the camera. Flaherty might ask Nanook to do it a slightly different way, to do it again for another take, or for a shot from a different camera distance and angle. These shots would then be cut together to create an illusion of continuous action. In short, though Flaherty did not use written scripts, he "scripted" in his mind and "directed" *Nanook* according to that "script" in a way not fundamentally different from the creation of fiction films. In *The Chair*, Donald Page Moore was essentially "directing" himself in action that could not have been scripted or even anticipated. No one had ever phoned him in that way before; neither he nor the filmmakers knew how he would react to the call.

Some people today think documentaries made before 1960 should not be called documentaries at all, that they are patently fabricated and false. A counterproposition might be that the predominance of the cinéma vérité/direct style (cv/direct) has brought losses as well as gains to what is called documentary. While it does seem possible to say that if cinéma vérité (and related forms) is not necessarily the cinema of truth, it does keep one from lying so much. But lying in this context may merely mean being as selective or as subjective as filmmakers or any creators may need to be. Cv/direct is less efficient or effective for some subjects and purposes than other techniques. It is not as good for propaganda or poetry, for example, which require forms that are carefully controlled and fully shaped. *Night Mail* and *O Dreamland, The Quiet One* and *City of Gold*, have a clarity and force in representing their makers' points of view and conveying them with heightened feeling. In Frederick Wiseman's films—which have become increasingly long, well over two hours in every instance—the accumulation of detail, rather than steadily adding to what we know about the subject, at some point may return the viewer to the uncertainties and confusions of life itself. On occasion Wiseman may even get an audience response opposite from the one he had hoped for and expected—what sociologists would call a boomerang effect.

Less shaping, less personal statement may mean less art—in the traditional sense, certainly. On the other hand, the cv/direct pull toward individuals, toward continuous recording of their words and actions, is a pull toward narrative— toward telling the sorts of stories that are true, the kinds of stories Flaherty tried to tell. Cv/direct is closer to narrative forms, in any case, than to the descriptive, expository, argumentative, or poetic forms that documentary earlier concentrated on and developed in unique ways.

The technological bias of zoom lens and directional microphone that pulls cv/direct in on the individual has made it an attractive technique for television. Notable successes of early television included intimate realistic dramas about ordinary lives (*Marty, Bachelor's Party, A Catered Affair*), game shows (*You Bet Your Life, What's My Line?*), and talk shows (*Tonight*, which began with Steve Allen and became a smash hit with Jack Paar and later Johnny Carson and Jay Leno) in which real people played themselves. If television is the cool medium Marshall McLuhan thought it to be, with its message completed by the viewer-listener, if it favors personalities and gossip, as Lyman Bryson suggested, these characteristics are shared by cv/direct. Perhaps it is no accident that cv/direct arrived after television and that its first substantial successes, Drew Associates' in the *Close-Up!* series, were designed for exhibition on what was then "the tube." The rough-edged sights and sounds of cv/direct may be better suited for television than the refinements of theater projection. (It is interesting that at about the same time cv/direct was developing, and in response to the competition of television, wide screens and stereophonic sound offered a theatrical equivalent of life more fully caught, of less editing, and resultant ambiguity. For all its formal polish and care in the making, Michelangelo Antonioni's *L'Avventura* [1960] resembles cv/direct in the looseness and irregularity of its narrative structure.)

As has already been suggested, with the arrival of cv/direct the sharp distinctions between documentary and fiction (on which the first part of this book are based) have blurred. Offering a close relationship to life as it is being lived, the cv/direct films are preponderantly, almost automatically, narrative in form. They show something happening, followed by something else that happens, followed by yet another thing, and so on. People in cv/direct are presented acting and reacting to one another in ways analogous to the behavior of characters in fiction and drama. *Eddie* (1961, Robert Drew, Richard Leacock, Albert Maysles, D. A. Pennebaker [the original version entitled *On the Pole*]) is about a race-car driver before, during, and after a race (which he did not win). So is the fiction feature *Red Line 7000* (1966, Howard Hawks). *David* (1961, Drew, Gregory Shuker, Pennebaker, William Ray) is about an attractive jazz musician who has sequestered himself in Synanon, a sanatorium on the beach in Venice, California, in an effort to rid himself of his addiction to drugs. *The Man With the Golden Arm* (1956, Otto Preminger, from a novel by Nelson Algren) is about a similar topic and person. Also, cv/direct films suggested techniques and styles used by John Cassavetes in *Faces* (1968), Jean-Luc Godard in *Tout va bien* (1972), and fiction films coming from the third world (*Blood of the Condor*, Bolivia, 1969, Jorge Sanjines; *The Jackal of Nahueltero*, Chile, 1969, Miguel Littin) and innumerable subsequent filmmakers.

Aesthetic and Ethical Considerations

Aesthetically, one of the central issues of direct cinema and cinéma vérité is the one just raised. In their narrative structures, the forms of these films are analogous to those of fiction. The stories they are telling may be truer (or may not be, for that matter), but they are in many ways stories all the same. A second crucial matter is the extent to which cv/direct filmmakers can express a personal point of view through this increased amount of uncontrolled actuality. Ethically, the central questions involve the honesty and responsibility of the filmmakers toward their subject persons and their audiences. These matters of form and authorial point of view, of art in relation to reality, of fact in relation to fiction, present intriguing perplexities.

The musical *Gold Diggers of 1933* (1933, Mervyn LeRoy) seemed a known and classifiable aesthetic-ethical object when it was released. But what are we to make of *Gimme Shelter* (1971, Albert and David Maysles, Charlotte Zwerin), a record of an ill-fated rock music concert by the Rolling Stones at Altamont, California, in which a real murder becomes the climax of a film which is, at the same time, used as courtroom evidence? Or, consider attaching camera and sound recorder onto a real family and filming the course of their relationships with one another over weeks or months. With this new artistic possibility a whole new set of ethical problems were raised. In *A Married Couple* (1969), Allan King made such a record of two friends of his. He chose them at least partly because he sensed their marriage was breaking up.

The best-known instance of this sort was the twelve-hour series *An American Family*, produced by public television veteran Craig Gilbert, camera by Alan and sound by Susan Raymond, and aired on PBS in the spring of 1973. It raised a lot of questions and caused considerable controversy along ethical lines. Did the Loud family of husband, wife, and five teenage children living in Santa Barbara,

The Louds of Santa Barbara, California, the subjects of *An American Family* (U.S., 1973, Craig Gilbert and Alan and Susan Raymond). Museum of Modern Art Film Stills Archive

California, behave differently than they would have if the camera and mike had not been there? Were they performing for it? Did the filming exacerbate, perhaps even cause, the strains and ruptures we witness? Did the filmmakers distort, through selection and arrangement, what actually occurred? What is "true" in it; what is "story"?

Along with these ethical considerations is an odd aesthetic aspect. At the time *An American Family* was being aired, members of a college documentary class watching it complained that the big scene—when Pat Loud announces to husband Bill that she has decided on a divorce—was not done well. What they meant was that it was not sufficiently dramatic; i.e., the Louds didn't give good performances, they were too casual, and the episode did not build to a climax. This is rather startling, when you think of it: viewing life as art. As art it was expected to follow the conventions of dramaturgy and performance one would find on *Days of Our Lives* and other afternoon serials.

The cv/direct technology/technique seems to offer an ultimate possibility of show-and-tell—of telling a real story as it is happening rather than sitting back and creating it out of remembered experience and imagination. At the same time, it seems that cv/direct is closer to life than to art, that it can seem unselected, formless, dull—a mere record. "At such a point," Louis Marcorelles observed (in an article in *Image et Son*, April 1965), "cinema has disappeared." Even at its best cv/direct does not offer an aesthetic experience culminating in a final act as in Shakespeare's *Hamlet*, with all the threads tied together, or Beethoven's *Ninth Symphony*, with its transcendental final movement. And what about the people whose lives have been invaded and used as material for the creation of this lifelike art object? Can we in fact trust the filmmakers' representation of them?

If the cv/direct filmmaker-artist is able to work directly from ongoing life, he or she shapes and refines the presentation of real people and events. Through selection and arrangement "characters" and "actions" are "created." This creation may be different from that in the traditional arts, but it is still creation of a sort. It could be the "writing with the camera" French filmmaker-critic Alexandre Astruc called for with his phrase *caméra-stylo* (camera-pen). What Astruc sought was the possibility of creating the fiction of a film in its making rather than merely supplying images and sounds for a fully realized and prefixed conception. If we aren't yet able to write with the camera in this way, it does seem a potential that cinéma vérité/direct has built within it. Eventually mightn't little distinction be made between documentary and fictional/dramatic forms? In documentary, if not in fiction, it is presently possible to create films as we go—with some of the freedom of action painting and jazz improvisation—without detailed scripts and resultant rigidities of preproduction planning. Perhaps this is full circle to Flaherty. "Non-preconception" isn't so much an issue as the possibility of recording and shaping actuality to fit a personal vision, as Flaherty in fact did. The technology that has become available simply brings film closer to life as it is being lived.

Films of the Period

1958

Les Raquetteurs (*The Snowshoers*, Canada, Michel Brault and Gilles Groulx)

1960

On the Pole (U.S., Robert Drew, Richard Leacock, D. A. Pennebaker, William Ray, Abbot Mills, Albert Maysles)
Primary (U.S., Drew, Leacock, Pennebaker, Terence Macartney-Filgate, Maysles)

1961

Football/Mooney vs. Fowle (U.S., Drew Associates, James Lipscomb)

1962

The Chair (U.S., Drew Associates, Gregory Shuker, Leacock, Pennebaker)
Lonely Boy (Canada, Roman Kroiter and Wolf Koenig)

1963

Happy Mother's Day (U.S., Leacock and Joyce Chopra)
Pour la suite du monde/Moontrap (Canada, Brault and Pierre Perrault)
A Stravinsky Portrait (U.S., Leacock)

1966

Don't Look Back (U.S., Pennebaker)
A Time for Burning (U.S., William Jersey)

1967

The Anderson Platoon (France, Pierre Schoendorffer)
Portrait of Jason (U.S., Shirley Clarke)
Warrendale (Canada, Allan King)

1968

Birth and Death (U.S., Arthur Barron and Gene Marner)
The Endless Summer (U.S., Bruce Brown)
Monterey Pop (U.S., D. A. Pennebaker)

1969

Salesman (U.S., Albert and David Maysles, and Charlotte Zwerin)

1970

A Married Couple (Canada, King)

Books on the Period

Issari, M. Ali and Doris A. Paul, What Is Cinéma Vérité? Metuchen, NJ: Scarecrow, 1979.
Levin, G. Roy, Documentary Explorations. Garden City, NY: Doubleday, 1971.

Mamber, Stephen, *Cinema Verite in America: Studies in Uncontrolled Documentary*. Cambridge, MA: MIT Press, 1974.

Marcorelles, Louis, *Living Cinema*. London: George Allen and Unwin, 1973.

O'Connell, P. J., *Robert Drew and the Development of Cinema Verite in America*. Carbondale: Southern Illinois University Press, 1992.

Rosenthal, Alan, *The New Documentary in Action: A Casebook in Film Making*. Berkeley: University of California Press, 1972.

Ruoff, Jeffrey. *An American Family: A Televised Life*, "Visible Evidence" series, vol. 11. Minneapolis: University of Minnesota Press, 2002.

Chapter Fifteen

English-Language Documentary in the 1970s: Power of the People

The documentary impulse has always been linked closely to its social and intellectual environment. In the 1920s Flaherty's films were set within the beginnings of anthropology and interest in comparative cultures. Vertov and the Soviet filmmakers attempted to meet the needs of a new state, the first communist society. The continental realists were part of the avant-garde, experimenting with artistic means for expressing concepts coming from the physical and psychological sciences.

Documentaries in the 1930s were connected with economic and political upheavals and innovations. Totalitarian regimes employed them to gain the allegiance of their peoples. In Britain and the United States they were used to try to strengthen democratic societies in the face of ailing economies at home and imperialist aggression abroad.

The 1940s were the years of World War II and its aftermath. During the first half of that decade documentaries were used in unprecedented numbers by the English-speaking countries in their fight against the Axis powers. In the second half of the decade, the United States, and to some extent Britain and Canada, employed documentary in the cold war against communism.

The 1950s, in the United States at least, were marked by conservatism and complacency; and, as it would subsequently appear, hidden uncertainties. It was not a significant or innovative decade for documentary except as new types of subjects and forms compatible with distribution nontheatrically and over television were explored. The 1960s saw the beginnings of direct cinema and cinéma vérité.

For documentary, the transition from the 1960s into the 1970s was a vital era, a time of fruition and fullness. It was the peak of independent 16mm-movie funding and production, distribution, and exhibition. The nontheatrical 16mm marketplace—schools, libraries, colleges and universities, film societies, art theaters, even prisons, and later airlines—was substantial in the United States. It provided a financial base that allowed considerable creative development for independent filmmakers working outside traditional Hollywood and New York film and television establishments. The early seventies was also a time to pass the nonfiction baton. A new generation of documentary filmmakers, those who had not lived through the experiences of world depression and WWII, began to come into their own. The 16mm educational and nontheatrical market base, the emergence of degreed film programs, the political and social upheavals of the 1960s, and a variety of personal factors combined to make documentary filmmaking a leading means of creative expression for more people than ever before. But first a look at what some veteran filmmakers were doing.

Veteran Filmmakers

Four major figures were among the sturdiest and most influential documentary makers in North America as the 1960s turned into the 1970s. Two of these worked in Canada—Donald Brittain and Michael Rubbo—and two in the United States—Emile de Antonio and Frederick Wiseman. All four had entered filmmaking following other careers.

Donald Brittain worked as a journalist until he joined the National Film Board in 1954 as a writer. He scripted most of his own films (as well as those of many of his colleagues); frequently he collaborated on their direction. Brittain's "writing" is really his matching of words and images; the creative process for him existed centrally in editing. In this respect he might make one think of Stuart Legg's work on "The World in Action" series in the early days of the Film Board. Or, perhaps even more, of Frenchman Chris Marker of Le Joli Mai, etc. Both Brittain and Marker had an insatiable and uninhibited curiosity about people and a wry sense of humor. Brittain's approach was characteristically oblique and understated, yet he involves us with his subjects in a way that makes them stick firmly in our memories.

Ladies and Gentlemen, Mr. Leonard Cohen (1966, with Don Owen) is an affectionate, nonadulatory portrait of the then young Canadian poet, who is allowed to participate fully in the presentation. Lest we take him too seriously, Cohen himself offers an injunction for us at the end of the film, written on a steamy glass while he is bathing: caveat emptor: let the buyer beware. Memorandum (1966, with John Spotton) is an account of a reunion of Jewish survivors of Nazi concentration camps twenty years after their liberation. It centers especially on a Canadian father making the pilgrimage with his teenage son. This subject seems scarcely open to the whimsical, irreverent approach characteristic of Brittain, yet he manages to root his observation in the mundane and to make very real the banality of horror. Memorandum is an important film on the Holocaust, comparable in its force but quite different in its manner from Alain Resnais's Night and Fog. Another significant Brittain film was the Academy Award-nomi-

Emile de Antonio. Museum of Modern Art Film Stills Archive

nated feature *Volcano: An Inquiry into the Life and Death of Malcolm Lowry* (1976), an impressionistic rumination on the life and work of the self-destructive author who was thought by some to be one of the literary geniuses of the twentieth century, but who wrote only one major book: *Under the Volcano*. Brittain died in 1989, a much-honored figure who had made over 100 films in his fifty-year career at the NFBC.

Emile de Antonio came to film after careers as a philosophy professor, longshoreman, and art promoter. His documentaries, all feature-length, received some theatrical distribution. Consistently he advanced a left-wing political view, frequently using compilation—"radical scavenging," he called it—and avoiding the documentary mainstream of cinema vérité/direct as well as the standard voice-over narration. His documentary technique consisted in large part of obtaining footage from television networks, sometimes surreptitiously (that is, illegally) and excerpting and editing it to make damning critiques of aspects of American politics and culture. He labeled his work "the theater of fact."

De Antonio's first success was *Point of Order* (1963), which enjoyed an extensive theatrical run. It was made from 16mm kinescopes of the televised 1954 Army-McCarthy hearings. The title comes from an oft-repeated interruption of the proceedings by Senator Joseph McCarthy—"Point of order, Mr. Chair-

Counsel for the U.S. Army, Joseph Welch, as he appeals to the 1954 Army-McCarthy hearing panel in *Point of Order* (U.S., 1964, Emile de Antonio). Museum of Modern Art Film Stills Archive

man"—and the film allows the senator to discredit himself and his methods without voice-over commentary or manipulation of the footage other than reducing 188 hours to 97 minutes.

In the Year of the Pig (1968), perhaps de Antonio's best and most influential film, is a compilation about the history of the Vietnam War. It employs a mix of news footage, political propaganda, antiwar speeches, and other sorts of evidence and argument including the famous photograph of a young U.S. soldier with *Make War, Not Love* scrawled on his helmet. It is highly critical of United States involvement. *Millhouse: A White Comedy* (1971) is a witty and savage attack on Richard Milhous Nixon, made the year before he was elected president. The sardonic misspelling of Nixon's middle name suggests the satirical intention. In this case, added to newsreel and television footage are interviews with various political commentators. Less than a year after its release the Watergate scandal broke.

De Antonio's relationship with younger radicals was considerable. Perhaps the most potent example of this is *Weather Underground* (1975, with Mary Lampson, shot by Haskell Wexler). In this remarkable document we see, from rear view or through gauze, most of the core group of the then fugitive Weather

Underground—Cathy Wilkerson, Kathy Boudin, Bernardine Dohrn, Jeff Jones, and Bill Ayers. These people had been responsible for five and one half years of bombing at the Pentagon, the State Department, the U.S. Capitol, and twenty-two other targets. As they sit beneath a homemade quilt emblazoned with the motto *The Future Will Be What We the People Struggle to Make It*, they elucidate their philosophy for the camera, leaving us an indelible record from the most strident of the "New Left" of the 1960s and 1970s.

De Antonio died at the end of 1989. His final project was a self-reflexive biographical eulogy. *Mr. Hoover and I*, released after his death, is fraught with the formalism of jump cuts and John Cage music. Like all of his work, it retains the mark of a dedicated "Old Leftist" radical and artistic modernist.

Michael Rubbo, an Australian painter and photographer with an education and interest in anthropology, joined the National Film Board in 1965 after studying film at Stanford University. His best-known work is *Sad Song of Yellow Skin* (1970).

Sad Song was shot in Vietnam in 1969. Rather than military action, then at its peak, we see life on the streets of Saigon: the shoeshine kids ("dust of the streets"); three idealistic young American journalists trying to help them; the opium lady, who died in the tomb she lived in while the film was being shot; and a little monk in saffron-colored robes who takes a symbolic walk each day from "Saigon" to "Hanoi" and back. In talking about his work on this and other films, Rubbo said, "[T]hese days I even make a virtue of being unprepared." He then advanced a position that sounds rather like Frances Flaherty talking about her husband's "non-preconception" and finding his story by living with his subjects. Rubbo explained, "You go out with vague ideas about what you want and then just let things happen, trusting in your good instincts. I know it sounds dangerous, but life will inevitably serve up much better stories than you could ever think up beforehand. The trick is to get involved, to get in."

Another widely discussed and characteristic Rubbo film is *Waiting for Fidel* (1974), which came about in a curious way. A Canadian multimillionaire owner of radio and television stations, Geoff Stirling, had arranged an interview with the president of Cuba. He invited along his old friend Joey Smallwood, ex-premier of Newfoundland, and a Film Board crew headed by Rubbo. When Castro failed to appear, Rubbo began recording the ongoing dialectic between capitalist Stirling and socialist Smallwood about what they were seeing in communist Cuba. The making of the film itself became part of the argument. Stirling was furious about what he regarded as the waste and non-professionalism of shooting a nonevent. Following one of those confrontations Rubbo asked his cameraman, Doug Kieffer, if he appeared in the shot. "Are you in the shot," was the reply, "my God, you are all over the shot!" The film figured in the debates about a filmmaker's presence in his/her films, as discussed below. In subsequent years Rubbo returned to Australia to a teaching career and a renewed interest in painting.

Waiting for Fidel, left to right: Geoff Stirling, Joey Smallwood, and Michael Rubbo (Canada, 1974, Michael Rubbo). National Film Board of Canada

Frederick Wiseman, formerly a lawyer, began filmmaking as producer of *The Cool World* (1964), a fictional feature directed by Shirley Clarke. Shot in Harlem and using many nonprofessional actors, the film has some semidocumentary characteristics. Wiseman's first direct cinema documentary was *The Titicut Follies* (1967), codirected with John Marshall (subsequently a very important figure in visual anthropology documentary whose credit was later removed from the film after editing disputes). It is an examination of the Bridgewater State Hospital for the criminally insane in Massachusetts. The title refers to an annual variety show performed by inmates and employees. The film offers an unflinching look at the day-to-day situation within the institution. Without doing more than showing the treatment the inmates receive and the attitudes and behavior of all involved, the hopelessness of the combined care and incarceration meted out becomes evident. The film became the subject of litigation, and the Supreme Court of Massachusetts banned its showing within the state; subsequently the film became a cause célèbre in the documentary world.

As examples of Wiseman's more than forty subsequent films, two from this period have been chosen for discussion. They are not typical but instead more innovative and ambiguous than the detailed and sustained observation (in films of increasing length, some over three hours) of most of his later work. *Law and Order* (1969), about the Kansas City Police Department, is the first.

Law and Order (U.S., 1969, Frederick Wiseman). Photo by Oliver Kool, 1969. Zipporah Films

After *The Titicut Follies* (and *High School,* 1968) one might have expected Wiseman to continue with what could be seen as his exposé of public institutions. Given prevalent feelings about police at the time, the height of the Vietnam protest, it seemed quite likely that he would find brutality, corruption, incompetence, and stupidity. However, he did not present such a picture. Some violence, insensitivity, and perhaps racial prejudice are evident in the film, but only as part of a whole that is equivocal—no doubt reflecting Wiseman's own ambivalence about what he found. In fact, the evidence offered in *Law and Order* could have served to counter the widespread prejudices of the time, though that may not have been Wiseman's intention.

Another example of Wiseman's work, which is dissimilar in other ways from the bulk of his films, is *Model* (1981), about the business of fashion modeling headquartered in New York City. Throughout, it alternates between fashion modeling (concentrating on a single agency) and life on the streets of Manhattan. The model business is based on glitz and illusion; real life is nitty-gritty and diverse. One intriguing sequence shows passersby watching a commercial being shot on a residential street. Elderly women, construction workers, derelicts, young businessmen, and dogs regard somewhat indifferently the sexy model, the high-tech equipment, and the Hollywood mannerisms of the crew. Another extended sequence concerns the production of a hosiery commercial that involves interminable takes (up to fifty-five on one shot). The sequence concludes with the thirty-second result of all this professional skill, perfectionism, and grueling work.

The myriad of detail offered by the film (it runs 125 minutes) can be read in at least two ways, probably many more. One is that *Model* is essentially a not uncritical celebration of a bizarre, fascinating, glamorous, and crazy institution in the Big Apple of our society. The other is as an exposé of exploitative, manipulative, frivolous, and greedy people working at a profession that is the epitome of consumerism gone berserk. But the final sequence seems to confirm the first view. It is of the fashion buyers' show, which resembles, and is shot and edited like, a musical. Beautiful young women in high-style gowns pirouette down a runway to show tunes ("Strike Up the Band" among them). Unusual camera angles and dynamic cutting complete the choreographic effect. It ends with dancing and applause. The fact that the intent of the film can be debated—exposé or celebration?—may suggest that the many snippets we are offered form a mosaic of, or a metaphor for, aspects of our culture, which, of course, is open to as many interpretations as there are cultural observers.

In England, a cinéma vérité counterpart to Wiseman is American-born television documentarian **Roger Graef**, who has been producing and directing programs for various British channels since before 1970. Like Wiseman he is a proponent of filming without interference, has received most of his funding from broadcast television, and is interested in the everyday workings of institutions. The name of Graef's production company, Films of Record, sums up his own goals for documentary as unadulterated looks at reality. His earliest major series was *The Space Between Words* (1972) for BBC, which explores the processes of communication within various organizations. Graef's films in the 1970s, mostly for Granada Television, are examinations of powerful institutions such as British Steel, Occidental Petroleum, the British Communist party, and the European Commission.

His most highly acclaimed series is *Police* (1981), about the Thames Valley Police force, shown on BBC between January and March of 1982. It foreshadowed Graef's continuing interest in the workings of law enforcement and the institutions of criminality. One episode, "An Allegation of Rape," contains interrogation of a rape victim—shot over her shoulder, never revealing her identity—by three male police officers. Their apparently insensitive treatment of the victim led to public outcry and ultimately to a change in the laws regarding police procedure in rape cases. *Police* was second only to the American nighttime soap opera *Dallas* in audience ratings during the three months it aired, and it has been cast by some as the progenitor for the highly successful Malcolm Barbour and John Langely Fox television series *COPS*, although *COPS* did not premiere until March 1989.

New Directions in Vérité

Another predecessor of *COPS* was *Police Tapes* (1976), made by Alan and Susan Raymond. Like Wiseman's *Law and Order*, it focuses on one police station, this time in the South Bronx. Perhaps best known for their intimate involvement (camera, sound, directing) in the groundbreaking U.S. public television series *An American Family*, the Raymonds have made numerous significant films in the last thirty years. For *Police Tapes* they rode in patrol cars, Alan shooting video and Susan taking sound. Recording what they saw and heard, they also talked with the police about their work. What resulted is a chilling view of criminal activity in the city, and of public servants trying to do an impossible job. *Police Tapes* was also the direct predecessor of the hit ABC television series *Hill Street Blues*. The first episode of *Hill Street Blues* is an almost scene-for-scene reproduction of the Raymonds' vérité style, particularly in its use of naturally overlapping dialogue. *Blues* producer Steven Bochco has been quoted as saying, "We really stole the style of *Hill Street Blues* from something called *The Police Tapes*. . . . It was one of the most arresting things I'd ever seen in my life. We said, 'This is the feeling we want. We want to create something that gives the illusion of a random event.'"

Cinéma vérité methods continued to evolve in ever more complicated intertwinings of reality and fiction. The generation of filmmakers who matured in the 1970s strengthened a trend toward blurring the conventional distinctions between documentary, experimental, and fictional films that had existed at least as far back as Vertov's "Kino-Pravda." In some cases this took the form of the "staged vérité documentary." Controversy about directing documentary participants to engage in activities outside their normal routines has raged from the work of Robert Flaherty onward. There is also the ongoing ethical question of how far a filmmaker should go in exposing the personal lives of her/his subjects. What was different from straightforward documentary for a certain segment of 1970s filmmakers was their intention to confuse the audience about the veracity of the work.

An early and influential example is *David Holzman's Diary* (1968). It concerns a young man who begins filming his apartment, his girlfriend, the people in his neighborhood, and every aspect of his life with his portable sync-sound camera rig. Initially the film appears to be a direct-cinema documentary about such a situation. David Holzman is inspired by his conviction that the motion picture camera is capable of recording and representing "truth." But his obsession with trying to capture everything as it really exists, rather than leading him closer to reality, removes him from it. As the film progresses the Eclair camera and Nagra tape recorder replace Holzman as protagonist. Further, when the credits appear at the end we discover that we have been subjected to a hoax. L. M. "Kit" Carson plays Holzman (and also wrote much of the dialogue); James McBride directed; cinematography is by Michael Wadleigh. In short, this is a fictional film about documentary filmmaking—about reality and illusion.

David Holzman's Diary, a classic of staged cinéma vérité (U.S., 1968, Jim McBride). Museum of Modern Art Film Stills Archive

. . . *No Lies* (1973, Mitchell Block), shot in cinéma-vérité style, is a staged film about rape. Appearing to be a documentary, it plays upon our expectations until we discover at the end that what we wish had not happened in fact has not happened. Another filmmaker who worked in a similar vein is Michelle Citron. Her two best-known films, *Daughter Rite* (1978) and *What You Take for Granted* (1983), experiment with the traditional modes in the process of exploring issues of central concern to women. *Daughter Rite* is about the position of women in the nuclear family. It concentrates on the relationship between two daughters and their mother and between one another. *What You Take for Granted* addresses the situation of women in jobs thought of at the time as traditionally "man's work." Both of Citron's films are acted, but the roles and the dialogue are drawn from extensive research and interviews, as is the case with . . . *No Lies. Daughter Rite* and . . . *No Lies* look like cinéma vérité, complete with rack focusing, panning back and forth between people in conversation, not having the camera where the action is, and so forth. *What You Take for Granted* employs a more didactic documentary style with talking head shots. While the three films are visually coded to be seen as documentaries, all are done with actors.

Barry Spinello's body of work is intriguing in its boundary crossing. He started as an abstract experimental filmmaker, drawing directly on film stock,

. . . *No Lies,* with Shelby Leverington, plays upon documentary expectations (U.S., 1973, Mitchell W. Block). DCL © 2005, all rights reserved

but then won an Academy Award for his fictional short *A Day in the Life of Bonny Consulo* in 1975. The melding of staged documentary, actuality shooting, and pure fiction continued in *Rushes* (1979), in which Neil (Spinello) turns to the camera and says, "Film everything for the next twenty-four hours, 'cause I've come to a strong, positive decision—namely, to commit suicide." We then see what appear to be the last twenty-four hours of Neil's life. We see him direct the film from inside the film and only learn that it is a total fiction as the final credits roll. *Rushes,* like *David Holzman's Diary* and . . . *No Lies,* also uses the technique of self-reflexivity in which a genuine filmmaker appears as part of the production as the filmmaker but is, in fact, also acting. The staged documentary would be pushed much further in the 1980s.

A documentarian who began in the 1970s and became one of the avant-garde of self-reflexive cinema in the 1980s and 1990s and beyond is Nick Broomfield, though his route to self-interjection on camera is different from that taken by filmmakers discussed above. Unlike them, Broomfield's subjects have no relationship with the filmmaker prior to making the documentary. Nor is his work scripted and acted. A London-born graduate of Britain's National Film School, Broomfield started making films in England in 1971. It was when he teamed up with codirector Joan Churchill on a succession of films that his work solidified. Their most well-known early work together, *Soldier Girls* (1980), is a feature-length documentary in the vérité style that follows three female U.S. Army re-

The staged documentary becomes ever more disturbing with Barry Spinello in *Rushes* (U.S., 1979, Barry Spinello). DCL © 2005, all rights reserved

cruits through the rigors of basic training. It focuses intimately on the women soldiers, a subject never tackled before. Like Wiseman's films it employs no narration, no subtitles, and no interviews. Unlike his *Basic Training*, however, Churchill's and Broomfield's film centers on the personal more than on the institution of the army. It is a fully realized work in the tradition of following an

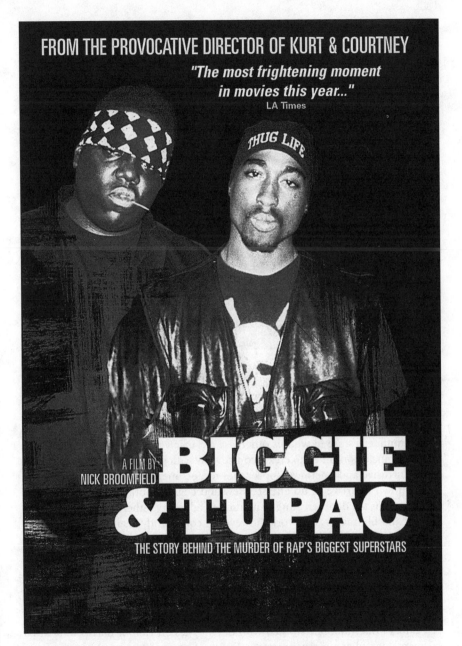

A poster for *Biggie and Tupac* (U.K., 2000, Nick Broomfield).

Privates Joanna Johnson, Jackie Hall, and Carla Tuten in *Soldier Girls* (U.S., 1980, Joan Churchill and Nick Broomfield).

emotional story line from an observational point of view. Toward the end of the film the subjects acknowledge the presence of the filmmakers in an onscreen hug, a unique gesture in what is otherwise a classic vérité approach.

Broomfield continued to create controversy with what some critics character- ize as intrusive and unethical approaches to documentary. For example, he has been known to arrive to do an interview and begin shooting as an unprepared subject opens the door, creating a situation of adversity rather than trust between subject and filmmaker. His work, however, is consistently challenging and richly layered, always underpinned by a commitment to story.

Joan Churchill, the cinematographer on *Soldier Girls*, has had a lifelong pas- sion for filming observational documentaries, which she has described as "A subjective camera style that throws the viewer into an intimate, firsthand experi- ence with participants doing what they would have been doing if the camera wasn't there." Part of a documentary-making family, Churchill is steeped in vé- rité camera tradition. She worked with the Maysles on *Gimme Shelter* and was a cocinematographer on *An American Family*. She and Broomfield hooked up, both professionally and personally, while she was teaching at the National Film School. Her collaborations as both cameraperson and director have continued with many and various filmmakers for over thirty years.

Nana, Mom, and Me (U.S., 1974, Amalie R. Rothschild). Amalie R. Rothschild

By leaving in the onscreen good-bye hug of the recruit rejected by the army, Churchill and Broomfield helped to move the classic direct cinema style in the direction of reflexivity. After the two parted ways, Broomfield's films began to include more and more interaction between subject and filmmaker, challenging the objectivity of the filmmaker. Critical controversy raised by his insertion of self into the films reached a boiling point when Broomfield is seen onscreen handing money for interview time to his leading subject in *Heidi Fleiss: Hollywood Madame* (1995). In part his work seeks to confront on deeper and deeper levels the dilemma of how the presence of a film crew can alter subjects' behavior in vérité films. On the other hand, Broomfield became the "star" of his own later documentaries, with his presence as agent provocateur creating serious tensions with the films' ostensible subjects.

An important part of 1970s feminist documentary making, perhaps arising from the consciousness-raising techniques of feminism, dealt with self-reflexivity. Documentaries made primarily by women, notwithstanding the work of Leni Riefenstahl in the 1930s or Esfir Shub in the 1920s, were few and far between prior to the 1970s. In the later decade women found an unprecedented and distinct voice in North American documentary on personal, political, and professional levels.

Nana, Mom, and Me, made by Amalie Rothschild in 1974, confronts some of the same issues of relationships between mothers and daughters as Citron's *Daughter Rite*. Rothschild's work is not acted by performers, however, but rather captures unscripted interaction among three real generations of women—

Antonia Brico in *Antonia: Portrait of a Woman* (U.S., 1974, Judy Collins and Jill God-milow). **National Film Archive Film Stills Library**

Rothschild, her mother, and her mother's mother. Canadians Claudia Weill and Joyce Chopra's *Joyce at 34* (1972) explores the conflicts Chopra faces as she juggles career, husband, and the prospect of a new baby. Both women later pursued careers in which they directed successful mainstream Hollywood fiction feature films. *Antonia: Portrait of a Woman* (1974), by filmmaker Jill Godmilow and singer/songwriter Judy Collins, profiles the fascinating career of symphony conductor Antonia Brico and her fight to be able to use her great skill in an almost entirely male profession. The film, in which we hear the voice of Godmilow and see Collins interviewing Brico, explores the career and artistic ambitions not only of the subject but also of the filmmakers.

Social and Political Emphases

Vietnam

The monumental event affecting American society in those years, and the rallying point for much of the social unrest, was the war in Vietnam. Documentary filmmakers were very much a part of articulating opinion about the war, particu-

Letters From Vietnam, **photographed by Abbot Mills (U.S., 1965, Drew Associates).**
Drew Associates

larly for those who opposed it. The repercussions of the war, both direct and indirect, became central topics for some of the best nonfiction work of the 1970s.

The 16mm technology available by the late 1960s had become relatively easy to use, portable, and inexpensive; and film stock prices were low compared with earlier eras. Raised on post-WWII audiovisual media, both at home and in the classroom, hundreds of American baby boomers became infatuated with the power of film as a way to communicate personally. Attending film school in college slowly became a legitimate alternative to studying creative writing, theater, or other subjects in the arts. Filmmaking, especially documentary filmmaking, became accessible to a generation of affluent young Americans, and it evolved into a principal medium through which antiwar and "youth movement" values were promulgated. Hundreds of 16mm films that criticized the status quo of U.S. military and social policies were made and shown.

Letters from Vietnam (1965) is not an antiwar film by intent, but it becomes a questioning of U.S. involvement, even at that early date. Made by Robert Drew Associates, with Gregory Shuker as "correspondent" and Abbot Mills as cameraman, it was shown on ABC television. The film follows a young helicopter pilot as he flies missions over enemy territory; this was the first instance of synchronous sound film being shot in a helicopter. We learn his story through the device of the audiotape letters he sends to his girl back home and come to feel his discomfort as he visits a Vietnamese orphanage and meets some of the child victims of the war.

The Anderson Platoon (1969) is actually a French television production, but with an English narration it was widely seen in the United States. French documentarian Pierre Schoendorffer had served as a combat soldier in Vietnam in the 1950s, during the French colonial occupation. In the fall of 1966 he returned with a cameraman and spent six weeks with an American infantry platoon, a racially integrated combat unit led by an African-American West Pointer, Lieutenant Joseph B. Anderson. The film follows the infantrymen as they eat, sleep, fight, and die. According to Robert J. McNamara, then U.S. Secretary of Defense, "*The Anderson Platoon* doesn't tell you, it shows you, and this remarkable film resonates deeply."

Interviews with My Lai Veterans (1970) won an Academy Award for Best Documentary Short for filmmaker Joseph Strick (best known for his ambitious fiction film adaptations of *Tropic of Cancer* and *Ulysses*). It is a deep indictment of a highly publicized and controversial decimation of a whole Vietnamese village. With interviews of five veterans of this encounter, shot by Haskell Wexler, the chaos of warfare is revealed. Peter Davis's *Hearts and Minds* (1974) presents a detailed, compiled history of Vietnam going back to the French conflict following WWII and ending with a critical appraisal of the grievous hurt done to all sides by these wars. *The War at Home* (1979, Glenn Silber and Barry Brown) is about the increasingly violent student protests against the war as manifested at the University of Wisconsin, Madison.

Newsreel Collective

Like the Film and Photo League, which began in 1930, Newsreel Collective started in New York in 1967 then spread to other cities—Boston, Chicago, San Francisco, and Los Angeles. It quickly made many films, mostly short agitprop pieces running from six to twenty-six minutes. To sympathetic audiences, often on college campuses, these seemed to be telling it like it was; to others they seemed merely crude and strident. For example: *Columbia Revolt* (1968) documented an occupation by students of the administration building at Columbia University with great support for the student radicals. In 1971 in the founding New York chapter, after a series of "self-criticism sessions," Newsreel was renamed Third World Newsreel. It decided to focus its efforts on empowering people of color and added media training and audience development to its agenda. Produced during this transition by San Francisco Newsreel was Judy Smith's *The Woman's Film* (1971). Providing a sign of this new direction, it was one of the early feminist documentaries to deal with working-class women and their problems. Third World Newsreel continues to function, carrying on the

A famous shot of napalm victims in *Hearts and Minds*, released theatrically by Warner Brothers (U.S., 1974, Peter Davis). **Museum of Modern Art Film Stills Archive**

progressive vision of the founders. California Newsreel, founded in 1968, is the other remaining pillar. It makes and distributes educational video on "African American life and history, race relations and diversity training, African cinema, media and society, labor studies, campus life, and much more."

Challenge for Change

In 1967 the National Film Board of Canada began a project using documentary in a quite new way. Called Challenge for Change, it was first headed by John Kemeny. In 1968 George Stoney, an American documentarian *(All My Babies,* 1952; *How the Myth Was Made,* 1978), was hired as its head.

The concept behind Challenge for Change was to provide citizens access to the media to express their concerns and needs and to create a dialogue with agencies of government involved in social programs. This, of course, was closer to the Grierson idea of using documentary for social improvement than to the Flaherty one of recording existing cultures—hammer rather than mirror. Grierson, after all, had been the first film commissioner of Canada. But, unlike Grierson, and any other prior program, Challenge for Change was proposing that rather than communicating *to* the people, or even *for* the people, it would at-

A young man burns his draft card in *The War at Home* **(U.S., 1979, Glenn Silber and Barry Alexander Brown). Academy of Motion Picture Arts and Sciences**

tempt to make films *with* the people. Eventually this led to enabling the *people* to make their own films. Grierson characterized this program as "decentralizing the power of propaganda."

The first Challenge for Change project, begun in the summer of 1967, was headed by Colin Low, a seasoned NFB filmmaker (*City of Gold*, 1957; *Universe*, 1960, and later one of the pioneers of large-format filmmaking). The Fogo Island Communications Experiment, as it was called, addressed the economic and social problems of Fogo Island, off the coast of Newfoundland. A high proportion of its inhabitants were on welfare; others were moving out. Sociologists from St. John's Memorial University along with NFB filmmakers studied and recorded the situation, and some twenty hours of footage were shot and made into twenty-eight short films.

Out of a second Challenge for Change project came a film entitled *You Are on Indian Land* (1969). It resulted from the closing of a bridge across the St. Lawrence River at Cornwall Island, Ontario. A treaty in 1794 had given the Mohawk Indians the right to free passage across the river, and they regularly used the bridge. The Indian unit of Challenge for Change instigated a protest demonstration against the closing. While mass media coverage stressed violence in this confrontation, the NFB record shows this view as distorted—that almost everyone behaved humanely. Screenings were held for the Mohawks, the Royal Canadian Mounted Police, the Cornwall police, the city administration, and representatives from Indian Affairs. This was the first time these people had ever sat down together. Subsequent screenings were held in the Parliament Building in Ottawa. Eventually the decision to close the bridge was rescinded.

On the Fogo Island project the NFB crew did all the production. For *You Are on Indian Land* the Indian film unit and the Cornwall Mohawks were involved in the editing as well as the shooting. In subsequent Challenge for Change work, following the introduction of portable ½-inch videotape recorders around 1970, the people involved were taught to use the equipment and made their own tapes.

When George Stoney showed some of this Canadian work to U.S. welfare officials in Washington, they asked two questions: "Does the government know you're doing this sort of thing?" and, "How long do you think you can get away with it?" Eventually Challenge for Change was allowed to wither and die, but not before it had established a precedent for the use of media by citizen organizations.

Public Access Cable

In 1970 Stoney returned to the States to head the undergraduate film program at New York University. One of his first actions there, with colleague Red Burns, was to set up an Alternative Media Center to promote and support the use of public access cable. New York City public access channels began operation in 1971. In 1972 federal legislation reserved public access channels in all new cable installations in the hundred top markets in the country. It has seemed to Stoney, and to other advocates, that public access channels fit within the U.S. tradition of freedom of speech for all the people and nicely accommodated portable video technology. If Stoney can be called the "grandfather" of community access, its "godmother" is Dee Dee Halleck, longtime advocate of the populist voice in public media. Filmmaker and media activist, she was founder of Paper Tiger Television and cofounder of Deep Dish Satellite Network. She has been involved in alternative media since her work in the 1960s with children making their own films to a 1990s' analysis of the media activist phenomenon exploding across the Internet.

Independent documentary video production specifically for community access, often directly inspired by Stoney's teaching, sprang up in the late 1960s and early 1970s. Frequently the work was conceived as alternatives to television shows of the time which, it was felt, had failed to illuminate critical social issues. Many of the alternative media operations were cooperatives bearing names such as Videofreex, Video Free America, Raindance, and Videopolis. Nearly all of these groups saw their mission as one of revolutionary scope: to inform and educate the public toward action and social change. In this sense they were the video successors to anti-Vietnam War 16mm-filmmaking collectives such as Newsreel and California Newsreel, described above.

New York City was a center for this early public access activity, and with later organizations like Paper Tiger Television (founded in 1981) access ethos continued strong there. Among Paper Tiger's best-known programs was *Herbert Schiller Reads the New York Times*, in which the U.C. San Diego professor delivers a funny and sometimes frightening interpretation of "all the news that's fit to print." When public access spread out into other areas of the country, it took on a community focus that has remained characteristic of its use. Ultimately public access produced structures such as Deep Dish TV, a national satellite network, which supports access producers and programmers, independent video makers, activists, and people who believe in a progressive television network. Offering material from producers around the world, Deep Dish transmits to community television stations and home dish owners nationwide. Self-envisioned as an alternative to commercial television, Deep Dish advocates diversity and aims to distribute creative programming that educates and activates. Its alternative to mainstream media approach has continued with coverage of the antiglobalization movement.

On another activist front, in 1971 documentarian Jon Alpert and his wife, Keiko Tsuno, started one of the country's first community media centers—Downtown Community Television Center. Alpert bought a used mail truck for five dollars, installed TV sets in the side, and began showing his videotapes on street corners in New York City's Chinatown. At first nobody watched, but soon their tapes about local issues began to attract small crowds. From the beginning they had a commitment to sharing knowledge.

The newly formed DCTV was the only place in New York City that offered production training and comparable services free. When funding from the New York Department of Cultural Affairs stopped for two years, the workshops went on. Even with the change in arts funding under the Reagan government in the 1980s, DCTV continued to offer free basic video training. Its goal to empower the community through media use remained one of DCTV's top priorities.

Other Emerging Organizations

One of the successes of 16mm, and later video, independent documentary making was the emergence of regional production units across the United States, which often made films on local as well as national or international issues. In the early 1970s a climate of government support in the U.S., fostered to a certain extent by the remains of Lyndon Johnson's "Great Society" programs, was one of the conditions that made such efforts possible. Two examples, in very different social settings, point to the vitality of this grassroots media movement.

Appalshop, a regional media center with strong grassroots activism, was established in 1969 in Whitesburg, Kentucky, with support from the National Endowment for the Arts. An example of its early documentaries is the fourteen-minute black-and-white film by Ben Zickafoose and Dan Moan, *UMWA 1970: A House Divided*. It documents the time when W. A. (Tony) Boyle, president of the United Mine Workers of America, was under indictment for misuse of union funds and suspected of the murder of Jock Yablonski (outspoken advocate for reform of the union) and his family. By inter-cutting a speech given by Boyle at a miners' rally in Virginia with scenes at a mine and interviews with miners, the film contrasts Boyle's statements with those of the reform movement then growing among the union rank and file. The film's point of view is clearly with the workers and ties into another 1970s populist documentary trend, elaborating on labor issues in America, past and present.

Two Appalshop films that were particularly successful are *Coal Mining Women* (1982) and *Strangers and Kin* (1984), the latter by Herb E. Smith. *Strangers and Kin* examines the stereotyping of "hillbillies" through films, television shows, literature, and interviews with contemporary Appalachians. Elizabeth Barrett's *Coal Mining Women* is in the tradition of reclaiming women's history, with personal stories of the women who go into this totally male world. Not directly connected with Appalshop but filming in its region and sharing its concerns on her Academy-Award-winning first film, *Harlan County, USA* (1976), is Barbara Kopple, who has become among the most honored filmmakers to emerge from the social justice filmmaking of the 1970s.

Appalshop remained a viable production entity for regional media makers, with ongoing funding from the NEA. It has continued to produce hundreds of films and trained hundreds more people from Appalachia to use many types of art and mass media to express and share their own life experiences.

In Chicago, in 1970 and 1971, Gordon Quinn and Jerry Blumenthal, as Blumenthal put it, began to gather into their hyperactive, flood-prone basement studio a small band of like-minded progressive-thinking sorts: filmmakers, organizers, teachers, and students. This became the Kartemquin Collective. Kartemquin's reputation and numerous international awards stem from works such as *Home for Life* (1967), its first film. It is an extraordinary feature-length direct-cinema record of two elderly persons entering the Drexel Home for the Aged and adjusting to the changes in their lives. Other noteworthy productions include *The Chicago Maternity Center Story* (1976), about the closing of the service that was the subject of Pare Lorentz's *The Fight for Life*, on the grounds that modern medicine requires high-cost, hospital-based care; and *The Last Pullman Car* (1983), the story of the closing of Pullman Standard's South Chicago plant, the last factory in America to manufacture subway and railroad passenger cars. Working from an agenda of social justice and personal empowerment, Kartemquin has continued to successfully make documentaries, up to and beyond their most noted 1997 phenomenon *Hoop Dreams*, produced by Steve James, Frederick Marx, and Gordon Quinn (discussed in detail in chapter seventeen).

In 2004 Kartemquin made the ambitious series *The New Americans*, executive-produced by Steve James and Gordon Quinn. This truly cooperative series for PBS's *Independent Lens* used multiple filmmakers to document twenty-first century immigration to the United States. The stories of people from Nigeria, Palestine, Dominican Republic, Mexico, and India reveal the ways in which the

The New Americans (U.S., 2004, Steve James and Gordon Quinn, Kartemquin Films).
Kartemquin Films

cultural makeup of the country is rapidly changing. In this seven-hour project Kartemquin brought thirty-plus years of experience in social issue filmmaking to bear with the same thoughtfulness and thoroughness that characterizes all of their work.

By end of the 1970s a fairly broad base of such local grassroots film- and video- making groups existed across the United States. The National Alliance of Media Arts Centers was founded in 1980 by an eclectic group of media activists who felt that by joining together they could create a national organization that would support its institutional members and advocate for the field as a whole. By the late 1980s U.S. national political support for independent regional media all but disappeared, due in no small part to the shift from Democratic to Republican administrations. NAMAC renamed itself the National Alliance of Media Art and Culture, partly in response to such funding shifts, and continued to be an effective force. There remains today a strong twenty-year-plus history of populist activism through regionally based media making as embodied in NAMAC.

Feminist Institutions

One institutional example of rising feminist power was the establishment in 1974 of Studio D at the National Film Board of Canada as a separate woman-oriented production entity. Under the leadership of Kathleen Shannon, Studio D pro-

I'll Find a Way (Canada, 1977, Beverly Shafer). National Film Board of Canada

claimed a strong mandate of serving women, the aged, youth, and nonwhites, with a clearly articulated agenda of "integrated feminism." A direct, if unarticulated, line between Challenge for Change and Studio D is evident in the decision of both to put filmmaking into the hands of the disenfranchised. Shannon insisted that Studio D resources promote only women's perspectives, since she believed that other filmmaking entities already met the interests of white men. One of the studio's earliest successes was Beverly Schaffer's Academy-Award-winning short *I'll Find a Way* (1977). This moving story of a young girl's struggle with the neurological disorder spina bifida was one of a ten-part series, *The Children of Canada*, all directed by Shaffer. Studio D went on to create important work in the 1980s and 1990s, discussed in chapter seventeen. Schaffer has had a continuous career at NFB, including an update to *I'll Find a Way* entitled *Just a Wedding* (1999) and the 2004 release of *Mr. Mergler's Gift*.

Another influential institution reflecting the growing force of women documentarians was the start of the feminist film distribution company Women Make Movies in 1972 "to address the underrepresentation and misrepresentation of women in the media industry." While in Canada government subsidy enabled the Film Board to allocate resources to female and other underserved documentary producers, in the United States it was chiefly the 16mm nontheatrical market that fueled a burgeoning women's documentary movement. Both the Canadian and American entities embodied "liberation" values of the 1960s; and while Studio D eventually became defunct, Women Make Movies continues to be important in the field, led for nearly twenty years by Debra Zimmerman. New Day Films, another institution still operating in the twenty-first century, is a distribution cooperative that grew from meetings at the Flaherty Film Seminars in the early 1970s. Cofounders included filmmakers Amalie Rothschild, Lianne Brandon, Julia Reichert, and Jim Klein. Feminist in origin, New Day was the first distribution company to be run entirely by and for filmmakers. In this it was a unique outgrowth of the empowerment movements of the era. Over fifty independents continue to use the New Day cooperative to market their work.

Historical Documentary

In 1970 previously classified U.S. government footage of the results of the atomic bomb attacks on Hiroshima and Nagasaki, which was originally shot by Japanese cameramen in 1945 for the Japanese government, came to light, due in large part to the work of scholar Erik Barnouw and his colleagues at Columbia University. Suppressed for decades by the Pentagon, the document of destruction was almost unbelievable in its close-up horror. The film made from this declassified material, *Hiroshima-Nagasaki, August 1945* (1970), showed the intimate results of the atomic blast for the first time to the public. This discovery was part of a long visual re-examination of nuclear war and nuclear power that remained a continuing thread in documentary for the next twenty years. The young adults who were making documentaries in the 1970s were the first generation for whom nuclear annihilation was a serious possibility, if not an assumption, and nuclear holocaust became a strong theme in independent documentary in the 1980s.

The repackaging of the A-bomb footage also helped jump-start a late twentieth-century boom in historical archival filmmaking that continues today. Compilation documentaries have a very long history, going back to Esfir Shub's work in the Soviet Union, and extending through the post-WWII reconstitution of combat footage in pieces such as *Victory at Sea* (1952–1953), the success of which inspired a number of successor series on American network television dealt with in chapter 12.

In Britain, in 1964, the BBC produced its first archival-footage-based mega-series for television. The twenty-six episodes of *The Great War*, produced with the Imperial War Museum and narrated by Sir Michael Redgrave, marked the fiftieth anniversary of the outbreak of World War I and helped launch a new channel in Britain: BBC2. Made at a time when many could still recall its events, it evoked deep emotions about the First World War from Britons who were still recovering from the Second. For British television, *The Great War* remained a high point of historical documentary making for a decade. (It was updated, modified for a U.S. audience, and rerun on both BBC and PBS with great success in 2000.)

Although there were other British archival film series, *The World at War* (1975), spearheaded by producer Sir Jeremy Isaacs and narrated by Sir Laurence Olivier, was a landmark in historical television. Using archive film, photographic and other still images, and interviews with eyewitnesses, it broke up historical events into smaller, accessible story lines. These are occasionally supplemented by the use of location shooting to establish atmosphere and to fill a gap where archive footage did not exist. *The World at War* won immense critical acclaim and was highly profitable for Thames Television. It was purchased by broadcasters throughout the world for over twenty years, demonstrating that an historical epic documentary series could be of high quality, attract a large popular audience, and make a great deal of money—very much like the 1950s' *Victory at Sea*.

Born in Glasgow in 1932, Isaacs was educated at Oxford. He joined Granada Television as a producer in 1958 and worked for the BBC on the noted *Panorama* series. In addition to *The World at War* he has produced some of the other most significant British television documentaries. For example, Isaacs was also responsible for *Ireland, A Television History* (1981), and *The Cold War* (1998), made in conjunction with Turner Broadcasting.

Other filmmakers, working independently of major television funding, also turned to archival compilation to make social and political points. In the United States accounts of the labor movement and resurrecting women's history were a big part of the trend, as newly politicized young filmmakers approached history with revisionist eyes. They looked back at the archival record of previous social change and challenged how it had been traditionally presented. The following are some examples.

From 1905 to World War I members of the Industrial Workers of the World (IWW), nicknamed the Wobblies, traveled across the country organizing workers into "One Big Union." The film *The Wobblies* (1978, Deborah Shaffer and Stewart Bird) integrates newsreel footage with music of the period and interviews with IWW members. Cultural, political, and legal events of the time are carefully documented, creating an exceptional record of one of the most exciting periods in American labor history. Another union, the United Auto Workers, which was at one point one of the most powerful in the nation, developed from a series of auto plant strikes in Flint, Michigan, in the 1930s. The women who participated in or supported participants in those strikes tell their story in Academy-Award-nominated *With Babies and Banners* (1978, Lorraine Gray). Again, archival footage from the period of the strike serves to illustrate the women's stories. *Union Maids* (1977, Julia Reichert and Jim Klein), also Academy Award-nominated, is about trade unionism, but it is even more about three extraordinary women. Their stories are intercut with one another and with period newsreel footage as they recall their lives as workers and union organizers in Chicago in the late twenties and thirties. *The Life and Times of Rosie the Riveter* (1980, Connie Field) arguably became the most widely known of these films of labor and women's history, perhaps because it dealt with a past still alive in the memories of many

The Life and Times of Rosie the Riveter (U.S., 1980, Connie Field). OWI photo by Palmer, DCL © 2005, all rights reserved

in its audience. It re-examines the experiences of female war workers in America during the 1940s, especially their struggle for dignity and equality.

It almost seems that for the documentary world, the 1970s slipped into the 1980s unnoticed. Many interesting and important documentaries were being made as the decades changed, most still shot and shown on 16mm film. The aesthetic and ethical considerations of 16mm social issue documentary making had been well honed by filmmakers who came of age with cinéma vérité/direct cinema and who recognized the uses to which archival footage could be put. The social issues that forged identities for these largely college-educated filmmakers from the mid-sixties onward—gay rights, black power, feminism, the American Vietnam War, spiritual enlightenment, environmentalism, drug use, and youth culture—were still the background for many in North America. They learned ways to treat these and other themes in sophisticated films requiring a great deal of technical expertise. It required funding, cooperative work, planning, audience development, and a mastery of many crafts and skills to produce good documentaries. Hundreds of documentary makers had achieved this goal, opening the way for previously unheard voices. The situation in the United Kingdom was somewhat different, as will be explored in chapter seventeen.

The 16mm documentary community, and its public, also had established demanding aesthetic standards for image and sound quality, various editing techniques, music, usefulness of films for education and for entertainment value, originality, and daring. Working with a medium that required intensive technical knowledge of cameras, lighting, sound recording, linear flatbed editing, optical effects, mixing, and laboratory work, meant that documentary filmmaking was by no means a solo or a casual undertaking. Although video pioneers like cable television community access users, Jon Alpert's DCTV, and Alan and Susan Raymond were pushing accepted aesthetics with video, documentary was still basically the machine-based medium that Flaherty had used.

All of this changed dramatically in the 1980s. Video and then digital technologies seemed to sneak up on the documentary, hailed by its prophets and decried by classicists. Many things were gained in the shift away form the film medium, but many other things that had in some cases become the true art of documentary were lost.

Films of the Period

1968

David Holzman's Diary (U.S., Jim McBride and L. M. "Kit" Carson)

1969

High School (U.S., Frederick Wiseman)
In the Year of the Pig (U.S., Emile de Antonio)
Law and Order (Wiseman)

1970

Gimme Shelter (U.S., Albert and David Maysles, and Charlotte Zwerin)
Hiroshima-Nagasaki, August 1945 (U.S., Erik Barnouw)
Sad Song of Yellow Skin (Canada, Michael Rubbo)
Woodstock (U.S., Michael Wadleigh)

1971

Angela: Portrait of a Revolutionary (U.S., Yolanda du Luart)
Gertrude Stein: When This You See, Remember Me (U.S., Perry Miller Adato)
Interviews with My Lai Veterans (U.S., Joseph Strick)
The Murder of Fred Hampton (U.S., Michael Gray and Howard Alk)

1972

Marjoe (U.S., Howard Smith and Sarah Kernochan)

1973

Attica (U.S., Cinda Firestone)
I. F. Stone's Weekly (U.S., Jerry Bruck, Jr.)
. . . No Lies (U.S., Mitchell Block)

1974

Antonia: Portrait of the Woman (U.S., Judy Collins and Jill Godmilow)
Hearts and Minds (U.S., Peter Davis)
Waiting for Fidel (Canada, Rubbo)

1975

Grey Gardens (U.S., Albert and David Maysles, Ellen Hovde, and Muffie Meyer)
The World at War (U.K., Jeremy Isaacs)

1976

The Chicago Maternity Center Story (U.S., Kartemquin Films)
Harlan County, USA (U.S., Barbara Kopple)
Police Tapes (U.S., Alan and Susan Raymond)
Union Maids (U.S., James Klein, Miles Mogulescu, and Julia Reichert)

1977

Georgia O'Keefe (U.S., Adato)
Men of Bronze (U.S., William Miles)
Word Is Out (U.S., Mariposa Film Group)

1978

Daughter Rite (U.S., Michelle Citron)
With Babies and Banners (U.S., Lorraine Gray, Lyn Goldfarb, and Anne Bohlen)

1979

The Wobblies (U.S., Stewart Bird and Deborah Shaffer)

1980

The Life and Times of Rosie the Riveter (U.S., Connie Field)
Model (U.S., Wiseman)
Soldier Girls (U.S., Nick Broomfield and Joan Churchill)

Books on the Period

Anderson, Carolyn and Thomas W. Benson, *Documentary Dilemmas: Frederick Wiseman's* Titicut Follies. Carbondale: University of Southern Illinois Press, 1992.
Atkins, Thomas R., ed., *Frederick Wiseman*. New York: Monarch Press, 1976.
Beattie, Eleanor, *A Handbook of Canadian Film*. Toronto: Peter Martin Associates, 1973.
Benson, Thomas W. and Carolyn Anderson, *Reality Fictions: The Films of Frederick Wiseman*. Carbondale: Southern Illinois University Press, 1989.
Boyle, Deidre, *Subject to Change: Guerilla Television Revisited*. New York: Oxford University Press, 1996.

Ellsworth, Liz, *Frederick Wiseman: A Guide to References and Resources*. Boston: G. K. Hall, 1979.

Evans, Gary, *In the National Interest: A Chronicle of the National Film Board of Canada from 1949 to 1989*. Toronto: University of Toronto Press, 1991.

Feldman, Seth and Joyce Nelson, eds., *Canadian Film Reader*. Toronto: Peter Morris Associates, 1977.

Grant, Barry Keith, *Voyages of Discovery: The Cinema of Frederick Wiseman*. Champaign: University of Illinois Press, 1992.

Halleck, Dee Dee, *Hand-Held Visions: The Impossible Possibilities of Community Media*. New York: Fordham University Press, 2002.

Jones, D. B., *Movies and Memoranda: An Interpretive History of the National Film Board of Canada*. Ottawa: Canadian Film Institute, 1981.

Keller, Douglas and Dan Streible, eds., *Emile de Antonio*, "Visible Evidence" series, vol. 8. Minneapolis: University of Minnesota Press, 2000.

Kolomeychuk, Terry, ed., *Donald Brittain: Never the Ordinary Way*. Winnepeg, Manitoba: National Film Board of Canada, 1991.

Nichols, Bill, *"Newsreel": Documentary Filmmaking on the American Left*. New York: Arno Press, 1980.

Nolan, Brian, *Donald Brittain: Man of film*. DigiWire, e-book, 2005.

Rosenthal, Alan, *The Documentary Conscience: A Casebook in Film Making*. Berkeley: University of California Press, 1980.

Rosenthal, Alan, *New Challenges to Documentary*. Berkeley: University of California Press, 1987.

Steven, Peter, *Brink of Reality: New Canadian Documentary Film and Video*. Toronto: Between the Lines, 1993.

Zaniello, Tom, *Working Stiffs, Union Maids, Reds, and Riffraff: An Expanded Guide to Films about Labor*. Ithaca, NY: Cornell University Press, 2003.

Chapter Sixteen

English-Language Documentary in the 1980s—Video Arrives

As the 1970s progressed into the 1980s a major transition—sometimes threatening to mutate into a battle—took place as technology moved from film to video. Lighter, and easier to learn than 16mm, video did not have to be processed, generally required less light, handled more easily in difficult locations, was felt to be less intrusive in vérité situations, and could capture an image in a continuous shot for much longer than a load of film. Perhaps most important for the ever-money-strapped documentarian was the fact that tape was much, much cheaper than film stock and laboratory processing. The U.S. military (along with the National Football League) had for years been by far the largest consumer of 16mm stock converted to video. The very serious drawbacks of video—lesser image quality and lack of long-term archival stability—did not outweigh its cost-saving benefits, speed, and ease of use.

Even though the first videotape recorder was demonstrated as early as 1956, it wasn't until the 1968 U.S. presidential campaign that a portable video minicam was used in broadcast television. The ½-inch open reel "portapak" became available to consumers around the same time, but not until 1973 did a time-base corrector make ½-inch tape pictures acceptable for commercial broadcast. Video technology refinements continued throughout the 1970s and 1980s. In 1986 Sony introduced digital video recorders, dramatically improving ease of use and image quality. By the end of the twentieth century video had almost completely replaced film for most types of documentary making.

Development of digital editing systems, chiefly the Avid Media Composer, further revolutionized the field by replacing videotapes, which like film had to be wound back and forth, with randomly accessible images on digital hard disks. Fast, relatively simple, and cost effective, Avid became the standard for digital nonlinear editing. At the end of the twentieth century over 80 percent of U.S. television commercials and prime-time programs were edited on this system.

258

These technological advances had numerous effects on documentary production practices as well as esthetics. Shooting ratios could expand exponentially, since the cost of videotape was a fraction of the cost of film. Editors often faced hundreds of hours of videotape material, rather than the dozens of 16mm hours. This was particularly noticeable in vérité-style documentaries and also contributed to the increasing numbers of personal documentaries, which in some ways are an outgrowth of classic vérité. Since it cost virtually nothing to let the camera run, why turn it off? In some cases this led to the capture of wonderful previously unavailable moments; in others it led to overlong navel-gazing of the most boring sort.

The changes in distribution and exhibition brought by video were also dramatic, where technology, economics, and artistry once again converged to rearrange documentary form and content. The nontheatrical educational film field, which was built on a 16mm film marketplace, lost its economic underpinnings to the low-cost availability of videotape. The sale and rental of 16mm films had created an economic base that throughout the 1970s and into the early 1980s generated enough money to support a group of distribution companies, which in turn returned royalties to filmmakers that helped them to continue producing documentaries. The profitability of this business was shattered when a film user (teacher, librarian, film society programmer), who in 1976 had to pay $100 to rent or $800 to buy a 16mm print, could by 1986 purchase a similar videotape for $29. Prerecorded home video was also a blow to art house and cinematheque exhibition, traditional venues for documentaries. So, although the means of production was more affordable and accessible, the economic returns generated by the distribution of video made profits, or even recouping costs, much more difficult.

A major factor in the transition from film to video was a significant change in quality of image and sound recording. Especially in early video work, the poor quality of these, compared to film, caused many serious debates about aesthetic values. From the vantage of the twenty-first century, where crystal-clear digital imagery is available virtually everywhere, it is difficult to understand the heated passion that surrounded the film versus video debates. Advocates of film capture of images and sound were ardent in their beliefs that video degraded the form to an unacceptably low level. Video proponents were just as adamant about the ease of use, cost-savings, and portability of video formats. One of the big problems with video has remained this multiplicity of formats. New video, and later digital, technologies came (and continue to arrive) on the market in such rapid succession that makers, distributors, and audiences all were often spinning in confusion.

The aesthetic effects of video, television, and projected film images are all different, in terms of lighting, depth of field, aspect ration, and even emotional tone, and discussion of these is important. What is just as important, especially for the documentarian, is a consideration of the archival stability of the medium.

Earliest videos have in far too many cases simply disappeared, taped over for other purposes, or just disintegrated. Even when a video exists, the format with which it was recorded and/or shown may no longer exist. Salvaging original two-inch television videotapes is a rarefied art form, and we now witness the phasing out of VHS video, heading the way of beta, one inch, ½ inch, and all the other previous formats. Digital imagery and DVDs are not much more reliable. In fact, the only medium that has proven to last over one hundred years is black-and-white film negative, stored in good conditions. For documentary, this is critical. Not only can historical compilation films be made only when there is historical material to access, but any filmmaker who is producing a document that she hopes will last beyond her lifetime needs to be constantly aware of preservation issues. Without conscious preservation efforts, no documentarian can claim that he is making a contribution to social history.

Cable and Satellite Technology

Another of the big changes to affect documentary making in this period was the growth of multiple cable, and later satellite, television channels that began in the 1970s and exploded in the 1980s. Cable, which originally was intended only to bring a television signal to areas that could not be reached by over-the-air broadcasts, soon presented the possibility of a hugely expanded number of special interest channels. Despite the growth of public-service cable access described in chapter fifteen, the profit-driven nature of U.S. broadcasting assured that most channels, with the exception of public television, were devoted first and foremost to making money. By the end of the eighties there were specialty cable channels for children, every type of sport imaginable, animals, science, home care, history, movies, and more. Documentaries and other varieties of nonfiction programming became more widely distributed than ever before. Ultimately the economics of this mode of distribution had an enormous impact on production. Like the advent of broadcast television, described in chapter twelve, cable television was both a boon and a bane for documentary. There were countless numbers of hours to fill on these new channels but very little money to pay for product to fill them.

One of the more hospitable cable outlets for documentaries was, and remains, HBO. In 1972 HBO went on the air, originally transmitted via terrestrial microwave towers. In 1976 it became the first TV network to broadcast signals via satellite when it showed "The Thrilla from Manila" boxing match between Muhammad Ali and Joe Frazier. Shortly after that other networks also began satellite transmission. HBO, with its subsidiary Cinemax, has both produced and acquired a wide range of documentaries, including an extensive number of works from important independents. Under the long-time leadership of executive Sheila Nevins, HBO has supported work by veterans such as Al Maysles, Alan and Susan Raymond (*Children of War*), Rob Epstein and Jeffrey Friedman (*Para-*

graph 17), and Jon Alpert, as well as newcomers like Jessica Yu (*The Living Museum*), Rory Kennedy (*American Hollow*), Joe Berlinger and Bruce Sinofsky (*Brother's Keeper, Paradise Lost: The Child Murders at Robin Hood Hills*). Due in part to relatively lush production and marketing budgets, HBO helped to create a high television profile for serious documentaries in the 1980s and 1990s. At the same time, it became a cable home for some of the most innovative filmmakers in the United States. HBO creates its share of cable "potboiler" documentaries such as *Real Sex* but, unlike most other cable entities, it offsets these with pieces in which filmmakers retain a great deal of artistic control over their work.

In another vein, Ted Turner launched CNN in 1980, calling it "America's news channel." At that time it reached only about 1.7 million households. By 1985 CNN reached more than 33 million households, nearly 40 percent of all U.S. television homes. In that year Turner combined the U.S. domestic signals of CNN and Headline News to put them on a global satellite system, creating CNN International. In doing so he created a commercial web, outside of old major network control, feeding news images to and from all parts of the world. CNN and TBS (Turner Broadcasting System) have been responsible for numerous documentaries, among the most notable being the continuation of the Cousteau legacy of undersea exploration begun by David Wolper.

The birth and growth of The Discovery Channel provides an interesting example of the shifting relationship between documentaries and television that took place in the 1980s. It is representative of the mass of nonfiction programming that in the twenty-first century occupies most of the time on such networks as A&E, The History Channel, The Learning Channel, House and Garden, American Movie Classics, and others. John S. Hendricks, founder, chairman and until 2004 CEO of Discovery Communications, created the U.S. Discovery Channel in 1982 as a cable network designed to provide documentary programming with a goal of "enabling people to explore their world and satisfy their natural curiosity." By definition, Discovery was all documentary, all the time. In 2003 The Discovery Channel reached over 86 million subscribers in the United States and was the most widely distributed television brand in the world, reaching over 425 million homes in 155 countries. At least nineteen offices outside the United States are part of its extensive infrastructure, enabling Discovery Networks International to create inroads in fast-growing markets from China to India to Mexico.

As a privately held company, Discovery has a strongly unified corporate vision, the primary goal of which is to turn a profit. Its shareholder representatives are the following: Liberty Media (the giant run by John Malone, which also owns Starz!, QVC, The Game Show Network, and Court TV), Cox Communication (one of the highest capability broadband cable networks in the world), Advance/ Newhouse (the Newhouse family's other interests include Condé Nast magazines, *Parade* magazine, daily newspapers serving twenty-two cities, and the American City Business Journals), and John S. Hendricks. Although Discovery began as most cable channels did, by acquiring low-cost programming produced by others, it soon turned to in-house production to fill its ever-expanding schedule. One very early Discovery acquisition, for example, was *Justiceville* (1987), a half-hour video about homeless activists in Los Angeles by Gary Glaser. After Discovery's first months of operation nothing remotely like this subject matter or its rough-hewn treatment (the sound track was by rapper Ice T) would make it into the channel's formula. Instead, Discovery's most successful audience-pleaser by far has been the relentless *Shark Week*.

The methods of production adopted by Discovery became the antithesis of the vision of an independent filmmaker with control over the form and content of his/her work. Rather than presenting a fully formed documentary piece in its entirety, Discovery became most interested in "branding" itself as a cable "destination" and "re-purposing" material contributed by filmmakers to create specifically targeted programs for each of its international markets. In other words, a show about elephants might have one point of view and artistic perspective for audiences in North America, and the same material could be re-edited with a different sound track, aesthetic values, and point of view for an audience in the Middle East. The documentary culture created by these practices is discussed further in chapter 17.

The Personal Essay Film

Some of the same technological factors that led to the production mode of Discovery also contributed to the growth of very individualized films created for opposite reasons. Inexpensive video and the ease of use of digital media led many individuals, who would otherwise never pick up a camera, to create their own documentaries. As Pat Aufderheide, Director for the Center of Social Media at American University, has so clearly pointed out:

> First-person films—diaries, memoirs, home movies, therapeutic records, travelogues—have been part of the audio-visual landscape for decades. But it wasn't until the mid-1980s that the personal essay film became accessible beyond the reaches of film schools and art houses, and began to take a place in the programming diet of television. It was a period of rapid expansion of accessible video technology, and just as rapid cutting back of public resources for independent and experimental use of the medium. Personal essay documentaries were part of a trend in documentary work overall toward a more intimate approach, even in explicitly public affairs subject matter, with the goal of intervening in a shared understanding of meaning. In this documentary genre, the narrator takes clear ownership of the narration, at the same time that the narrator is a character. They are frankly, inevitably personal.

Ross McElwee is the filmmaker perhaps most acclaimed for (or accused of) initiating a flood of self-reflexivity that became known in the 1980s as personal

Ross McElwee in a North Carolina tobacco field with Aaton camera shooting *Bright Leaves* (U.S., 2004, Ross McElwee). Photo by Adrian McElwee

diary or essay documentary. Like Michelle Citron, Mitchell Block, Jim McBride, and Nick Broomfield, McElwee is another of the first film-school-educated generation of documentarians. He began in the mid-1970s, as a graduate student at the Massachusetts Institute of Technology, when Ricky Leacock and Ed Pincus were involved in the documentary film program there. Ten years later McElwee made *Sherman's March: A Meditation on the Possibility of Romantic Love in the South During an Era of Nuclear Weapons Proliferation* (1986). In it McElwee retraces Union General William Tecumseh Sherman's destructive Civil War path, interweaving his journey with vignettes of seven Southern women. The film is not at all about General Sherman. Highly influential among other emerging documentarians of the time and critically applauded, *Sherman's March* was followed by McElwee's continued self-reflection in *Something to Do With the Wall* (1991), *Time Indefinite* (1994), *Six o'Clock News* (1998), and *Bright Leaves* (2004). His films tend toward an almost comic, certainly a self-deprecating, appreciation of life around him.

Alan Berliner, another 1970s film school graduate, merged experimental art with documentary fact in a very personal manner. *Intimate Stranger* (1991) explores the extraordinary life of Berliner's maternal grandfather, a Palestinian Jew raised in Egypt, whose obsession with all things Japanese created confusion and conflict in his post-World War II Brooklyn home. Berliner has said,

Robert S. McNamara speaks to the camera in the Academy Award-winning *The Fog of War: Eleven Lessons From the Life of Robert S. McNamara* (U.S., 2004, Errol Morris). Photo by Claire Folger, Sony Pictures Classics

The truth is I never actually "decided" to become a filmmaker; somehow via a more arduous and circuitous route derived of inner necessity, I grew into one. Much of my adult life has been spent grappling with the conflicts and contradictions of family. With both the presences and absences of memory. When I came upon my family home movies . . . the images I had forgotten about suddenly became triggers for a flood of memories. Using them in my films became a kind of photo-therapy, perhaps even a way towards healing some of the wounds of my childhood.

There are some similarities between Berliner's work and that of Errol Morris. Morris's films are not personal diaries, but they have an unmistakable aura in which the presence of the filmmaker as creator is always evident. His major films have been distributed theatrically to wide critical acclaim. This work includes *Gates of Heaven* (1978), *Vernon, Florida* (1981), *The Thin Blue Line* (1988), A *Brief History of Time* (1992), *Fast, Cheap and Out of Control* (1997), *Stairway to Heaven* (1998), *Dr. Death: The Rise and Fall of Fred E. Leuchter, Jr.* (1999), and *The Fog of War: Eleven Lessons from the Life of Robert S. McNamara* (2002). Morris is drawn to often-eccentric people who talk candidly about their lives while doing what they normally do. In an interview he explained that while he was asked endlessly whether his films are documentaries, "The answer is 'yes' and 'no.' There are elements of fiction and nonfiction in all filmmaking. I use real people. They're not reading a prepared script. They're attempting to talk about themselves. That's real. But I do other things that are closer to fictional films, like I storyboard, for instance."

As a graduate philosophy student Morris spent much of his time at San Francisco's Pacific Film Archives watching movies. After making *Gates of Heaven* and *Vernon, Florida*, he spent two years working as a private detective. Morris's talent for investigating the implied truth of documentary filmmaking, and for appreciating how people reveal themselves to the camera, is at the heart of his art. His first two films became cult favorites. Critic Roger Ebert has said about *Gates of Heaven*: "I believe it is one of the greatest films ever made. Ostensibly a documentary about two pet cemeteries in northern California and the people who owned them, it is in fact one of the most profound, and funniest, films ever made about such subjects as life and death, success and failure, dreams and disappointments, and the role that pets play in our loneliness."

It was the theatrical release of *The Thin Blue Line* that brought Morris popular recognition. The film follows the case of Randall Dale Adams, a man who, it seemed, was falsely accused of the highway murder of a Texas police officer. Morris uses repeated dramatizations of the murder, multiple points of view, talking-heads interviews, and telephone conversations, in concert with Philip Glass's almost eerie score, to create the overriding impression that justice was not served. The film makes a strong case that prejudice and possibly tainted testimony persuaded the jury to find Adams, a drifter from the Midwest, guilty. The "thin blue line" of police officers separating the public from chaos—as the judge, quoting the D.A. in the case, describes them—is shown as ineffective. The police, courts, and prison are seen as putting people at the risk of injustice as often as they protect them. After serving time for a death sentence commuted to life imprisonment, Adams was freed—in no small part because of the impact of the film.

The Historical Film

In almost all subject areas archival compilation films began to multiply. One of the key makers of historical films, Ken Burns, began producing in the 1980s. His work is examined at length in chapter seventeen. For a time in the 1970s and 1980s, before many of the rights-holders realized the economic value of their footage, putting together "clip shows" was relatively inexpensive. Part of the David Wolper empire, discussed in chapter twelve, was built upon popular themes such as *Hollywood and the Stars*, the 1963 clip-filled documentary mini-series on NBC. Other filmmakers used the technique to explore more serious subjects.

America Lost and Found (1980) is a compilation by Tom Johnson and Lance Bird, which conveys the impact of the economic and social collapse of the Great Depression in the United States. The filmmakers spent three and a half years on research and production, assembling period film, photographs, and sounds. Evocative commentary, written by John Crowley, reinforces the images of how the United States reacted to the loss of its dreams of prosperity and how those dreams were slowly rebuilt. This is a deeply psychological presentation of the effects of the Depression, offering persuasive yet emotional contrasts among the images, the hype, and the realities of the era. *The World of Tomorrow* (1985), also by Johnson and Bird and narrated by Jason Robards, is perhaps the most poetic and poignant historical film of the 1980s. Its use of home movies, many in color, as well as promotional films from the 1939 New York World's Fair, captures a precious and precarious moment when the world stood poised between optimism about the fading of the Depression and foreboding occasioned by a looming world war.

Atomic Café (1982), by Jane Loader, Kevin Rafferty, and Pierce Rafferty, is a seriocomic compilation elaborating on the ways that Americans' awestruck celebration of atomic weapons changed to pervasive fear of Soviet nuclear attack. When Kevin Rafferty found a catalog of U.S. government films in a San Francisco bookstore in 1976, he envisioned a film that would utilize such titles to create a satirical documentary on the subject of American propaganda. After six years of work, *Atomic Café* emerged as a successful theatrical feature, partly because the filmmakers abandoned narration and relied on the power of the footage and its often-ludicrous original sound track. The film's footage, much of it produced by the government, follows the development of the bomb through the atomic attacks on Japan to its central role in the cold war. Shown along with the infamous "duck and cover" civil defense films are lesser-known clips, many of which are unintentionally filled with twisted black humor.

Echoing the peace movement's growing concern over the threat of nuclear war in the early 1980s, the National Film Board of Canada commissioned journalist Gwynne Dyer to create the seven-part series *War*, based on his own military experience. The film was a reflection of Dyer's growing concern about the proliferation of new technology, its impact on the changing nature of warfare, and the growing threat of nuclear annihilation. Filmed in ten countries and with the participation of six national armies, it examined the nature, evolution, and consequences of warfare, arguing that in an era of total war, professional armies were no longer able to fulfill their traditional roles. *War* was shown on television around the world to great acclaim but was controversial in Canada. One episode, produced by Michael Bryans and Tina Viljoen, "The Profession of Arms," was nominated for an Academy Award.

Other documentaries responding to the threat of nuclear warfare during these years were *The Day After Trinity* (1980) Jon Else; *Eight Minutes to Midnight* (1981) Mary Benjamin, Suzanne Simpson, Baird Bryant; *If You Love This Planet:*

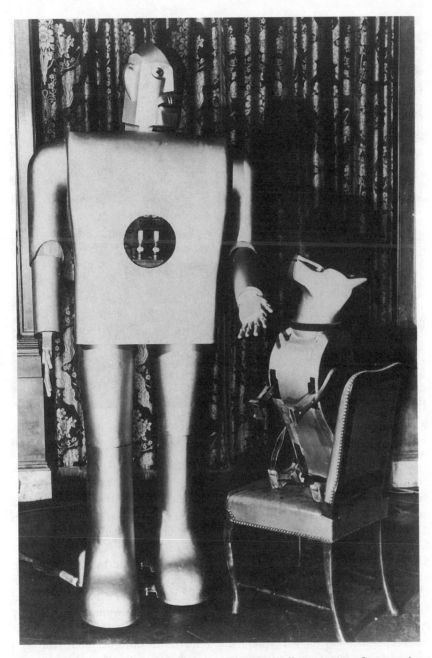

"Electro" the Moto Man and his mechanical dog "Sparko" were among the attractions at the 1939 New York World's Fair, documented in *The World of Tomorrow* (U.S., 1980, Lance Bird and Tom Johnson).

Poster for *If You Love This Planet: Dr. Helen Caldicott on Nuclear War* (Canada, 1982, Terre Nash, Studio D, National Film Board of Canada). DCL © 2005, all rights reserved

Dr. Helen Caldicott on Nuclear War (1982) NFBC Studio D; *Half Life: A Parable for the Nuclear Age* (1985) Dennis O'Rourke; *Radio Bikini* (1987) Robert Stone; and *Dark Circle* (1991) Judy Irving and Chris Beaver. Each of these films makes a strong antinuclear case, although in very different ways. Perhaps the most interesting in political terms is *If You Love This Planet*, produced by Women's Studio at the National Film Board of Canada and directed by Terre Nash. In many ways it is simply a filmed speech by eloquent antinuclear activist Dr. Helen Caldicott. But her message and the delivery of the film are very powerful, and United States nuclear policies are harshly criticized. Before winning an Academy Award as Best Documentary Short, the twenty-minute film was labeled as "political propaganda" by the Reagan-era U.S. Department of Justice under the aegis of a 1930s era law. Copies of the film print shown in the United States were required to carry this warning label, creating a situation in which a documentary from the NFBC was discussed as enemy propaganda.

Terre Nash. National Film Board of Canada

The career of one of the most successful producers of historical/compilation films, Charles Guggenheim, spanned half a century. He made over one hundred documentaries, was nominated for twelve Academy Awards, and won four of them. In 1954 he established his first production company in St. Louis, where he produced a film about the construction of the St. Louis Arch, *Monument to the Dream*. It won the Venice Film Festival's XI Gold Mercury Award, marking the first time in the Festival's history that the award was given to an American. It was in St. Louis that Guggenheim won his first Academy Award, for the film *Nine from Little Rock*, which tells the story of the Arkansas school integration crisis. Later he moved to Washington, D.C., to work with George Stevens, Jr., who headed the film program of the United States Information Agency (USIA) under Edward R. Murrow.

Guggenheim's second Academy Award came from *Robert Kennedy Remembered*, a film biography, which was made in a lightning-fast six weeks after the senator's assassination, in time for the 1968 Democratic Party Convention. This film used extensive footage shot by Drew Associates during the making of *Crisis: Behind a Presidential Commitment* (1963). The third Academy Award went to *The Johnstown Flood* (commemorating the hundredth anniversary of that disaster). Guggenheim's final Oscar was received in 1995 for *A Time for Justice*, a film about the civil rights movement.

As a eulogy noted, despite acclaim, Guggenheim pursued his work with an almost private single-mindedness, developing an unadorned style that seemed to

Charles Guggenheim (second from left) filming the Edward Kennedy Campaign in 1970.

be a reflection of his own personality. In his later films, such as the Academy Award-nominated *D-Day Remembered*, Guggenheim began to explore history from a singular point of view. The struggle and humanity of a few individuals thrown into harrowing circumstances beyond their control was the kind of story that interested him most. This was a theme that would lead him toward his most personal film of all—and his last.

Berga: Soldiers of Another War (2003), made with his daughter Grace Guggenheim, was the first film in fifty years of directing and producing in which Guggenheim included himself in the telling of the story. Many of the American soldiers caught in the Battle of the Bulge were from his 106th Infantry Division. He could have shared their fate if he had not been sidelined by illness. In his narration he remembers quietly, "They went overseas, and I didn't. And some of them didn't come back. And I've been thinking about it for fifty years, wondering why it didn't happen to me. And that's why I had to tell this story."

Strictly Political

The new ease of use and low cost of video production of the seventies made it easier for activists of many stripes to cover situations in remote places. The Central American insurgencies of that era, and U.S. involvement in them, occasioned a number of impassioned exposés. As often happens in documentary, the desire to impress the audience with the importance and/or urgency of the subject sometimes overrides the attention given to craft and artistry. Rarely does someone with the vision of Dziga Vertov use documentary to break aesthetic as well as political ground, but the following documentarians have at least well understood the use of film as political hammer.

Pamela Yates's work in war-torn Central America includes the Academy-Award-winner *Witness to War: Dr. Charlie Clements* (1985, made with David Goodman), as well as *When the Mountains Tremble* (1984), and *Nicaragua: Report from the Front* (1983). Her trilogy *Living Broke in Boom Times* (1990, 1997, 1999 made with Peter Kinoy) describes poverty in America in the 1990s.

Barbara Trent has for many years headed up a Los Angeles-based group, The Empowerment Project, which used agitprop techniques to inform and motivate audiences to speak out. *The Panama Deception* (1992) won the Academy Award with its blunt indictment of U.S. policies in that country. Her other pieces include *Coverup: Behind the Iran Contra Affair* (1988) and *Destination Nicaragua* (1986). Trent's work continues into the twenty-first century with antiglobalism documentaries. Deborah Shaffer, a veteran of the Newsreel Collective, made *Nicaragua: Report from the Front* (1984) with Ana Maria Garcia and Glenn Silber and took another look at the Nicaragua war in 1987 with *Fire from the Mountain*. With David Goodman and Pamela Yates, Shaffer produced *Witness to War* (1985), the story of Dr. Charlie Clements who, as a pilot in the American Vietnam War, refused further combat missions and began to dedicate himself to non-violence and healing. This story of how he ultimately found himself tending to the wounded behind rebel lines in El Salvador won the filmmakers an Academy Award.

Longtime filmmaker and activist Robert Richter has worked in documentary since his days with the Edward R. Murrow team. His career has been dedicated to creating documentary exposés such as *Father Roy: Inside the School of Assassins* (1997), narrated by Susan Sarandon. This film exploring the inner workings of the U.S. Army's School of the Americas recounts the actions of Father Roy Bourgeois, a Vietnam War hero and leader in the campaign to close the school. Non-U.S. operatives were trained at this school for work in Latin America, and Richter documents human rights abuses committed by its graduates. Other productions include the short *School of Assassins* (1994), also narrated by Sarandon, which was nominated for an Academy Award, as was Richter's *Gods of Metal* (1982).

Racial and Ethnic Minorities

William Greaves is a groundbreaking contemporary African-American documentarian in the United States. After beginning in the entertainment industry as a stage actor, he spent a short time at the National Film Board of Canada in the

William Greaves, co-host of the National Educational Television groundbreaking series *Black Journal* (1968–1976). International Film Seminars

early 1960s working with the innovators of cinéma vérité there. He returned to the U.S. and became executive producer (after a controversy in which the white executive producer was removed) and cohost of the pioneering National Educational Television series *Black Journal* (1968–1976), with a mandate to produce "by, for, and about black people." Greaves's best-known documentary work is

Ralph Bunche: An American Odyssey (2001). Among his other documentaries are *From These Roots* (1974), an in-depth study of the Harlem Renaissance, and *Ida B. Wells: A Passion for Justice* (1989). In 1979 eight independent black producers created the National Black Programming Consortium to counter the dearth of African-American programming on PBS. Mabel Haddock has been the continuous driving force behind NBPC, which is committed to positive images of African Americans and the African Diaspora.

Exploring African-American history was Henry Hampton (1940–1998), who established Blackside, Inc., in 1968, the largest African-American-owned film company of its time. As he chronicled political developments of the twentieth century, Hampton became one of the world's most respected documentarians. Hampton as executive producer, with Judith Vecchione as series senior producer, headed production of the massive PBS series *Eyes on the Prize*. The episodes, made over twelve years, followed the pattern of other historical compilations to make its points, using archival footage, interviews with participants, stills, and a strong period musical score. It remains a touchstone in television documentary history in its telling of the story of race relations in the United States.

Eyes on the Prize I: America's Civil Rights Years 1954–1965, narrated by Julian Bond, documents events that helped focus the nation's attention on the oppression of African-American citizens, such as the lynching of fourteen-year-old Emmett Till in 1955, and the Montgomery Bus Boycott. It also covers the key court case *Brown v. the Board of Education* and other milestones. *Eyes on the Prize II: America at the Racial Crossroads (1965–1985)* uses the same formula of mixing present-day interviews and historical footage to examine those years of social unrest. Despite the critical and popular success of the first part, Hampton had difficulty raising the six million dollars needed to fund the sequel. The subjects of *Eyes II*—the rise of the Black Panther party, the Nation of Islam, the Vietnam War, busing, and Affirmative Action—were considered too controversial by many potential funders.

Ironically, this important series is no longer available for purchase or television screening. Only old copies sold chiefly to educational institutions remain in circulation. The complex issues of copyright and clearance of its many archival clips make selling it impossible. As Jon Else, one of its producers and cinematographers, noted in a study by Patricia Aufderheide and Peter Jaszi for the Center for Social Media on rights and clearances for documentary makers,

What happened was the series was done cheaply and had terrible fundraising problems. There was barely enough to purchase the minimum five-year rights of the archive heavy footage. Each episode is 50% archival. And most of the archive shots are derived from commercial sources. The five-year licenses expired and the company that made the film also expired. And now we have this situation where we have this series for which there are no license rights. . . . It will cost

$500,000 to re-up all the rights for this film. This is a piece of landmark TV history that has vanished.

In a television interview Hampton once said that he thought the civil rights movement was often overshadowed by the memory of Martin Luther King, Jr., and that *Eyes on the Prize* was an attempt to tell the stories of lesser-known civil rights activists. He wanted the series to be a testament to the power of ordinary people to effect great changes.

Blackside completed sixty major films and media projects, most exploring the worlds of the poor and disenfranchised. Among the dozens of filmmakers who worked with Hampton in making these films were Orlando Bagwell, Lillian Benson, Callie Crossley, Jim DeVinney, Jon Else, Louis Massiah, Sam Pollard, Judy Richardson, Terry Rockefeller, Paul Stekkler, and Tracy Strain. Their notable titles include *Malcolm X: Make It Plain* (1994), *America's War on Poverty* (1995), and *I'll Make Me a World* (1999).

Marlon Riggs's films explore various aspects of African-American life and culture and earned him wide recognition. In addition to the intrinsic value of his work and his teaching, Riggs will probably be remembered for the controversy surrounding the public television broadcasts of his highly charged productions. *Ethnic Notions: Black People in White Minds* (1987) is an historical compilation examination of mass media stereotypes of African Americans, much like Appalshop's review of hillbilly stereotypes in *Strangers and Kin*. Riggs's *Color Adjustment* (1989) continued the themes of *Ethnic Notions* as it traces forty years of race relations through the lens of TV shows like *Amos and Andy, The Nat King Cole Show, I Spy, Julia, Good Times, Roots,* and *The Cosby Show*. Riggs looks at these familiar favorites in a revealing examination of the interplay between America's racial consciousness and network prime-time programming. His work in another subcategory will be examined later.

Other African-American documentarians of note include St. Clair Bourne, who chronicles African life internationally by finding common links among people of African descent. During the past twenty-five years he has made over forty films, including the feature-length *Half Past Autumn: The Life and Works of Gordon Parks* (2000) for HBO. With actor Wesley Snipes as executive producer, Bourne directed *John Henrik Clarke: A Great and Mighty Walk* (1996), a feature-length documentary about the respected historian and Pan-African activist. He also made *Paul Robeson: Here I Stand!* (1999). For at least forty years filmmaker William Miles has created documentaries such as *Men of Bronze* (1997), the story of the 369th infantry regiment of African-American soldiers that fought under the French flag in World War I, *The Untold West: The Black West* (1994), and *Black Stars in Orbit* (1990), a film about the black astronauts.

In the United Kingdom, Black Audio Film Collective, founded in 1982, was one of the film and video workshops set up in Britain in the aftermath of inner-city protests against institutionalized racism. Best known and most controversial of the collective's work, *Handsworth Songs* (1986), directed by John Akomfrah, uses self-reflexivity and fragmentation to examine the history of contemporary black British experience. Shot in the aftermath of riots against discrimination and unemployment in Handsworth, Birmingham, the film uses images of the violence intercut with interviews with local residents. These are interwoven with archival footage of immigration into Britain, and mainstream media coverage of the riots, along with interior audio monologues. It is part of an emerging history of black people in England in its postcolonial eras. Other documentaries by Akomfrah include *Seven Songs for Malcolm X* (1993), *The Wonderful World of Louis Armstrong* (1991), and *Martin Luther King—Days of Hope* (1997).

In documentary, one of the most successfully organized U.S. racial minorities has been the various coalitions of Asian-Pacific filmmakers. The year 2000 marked the thirtieth anniversary of Los Angeles-based Visual Communications, the twenty-fourth anniversary of Asian Cine Vision (both of these organizations sponsor large film festivals), and the twentieth anniversary of the National Asian American Telecommunications Association (NAATA). These organizations support Asian-American filmmakers and seek to address the need to raise social and cultural awareness of Asian-American experience and history. All three groups played a consistently important role in defining an Asian-Pacific documentary presence.

One of the best-known Asian-American documentarians is Arthur Dong, who is also claimed by the gay film community. His professional career began with *Sewing Woman* (1983), about the life of his grandmother, an immigrant seamstress. Dong's productions also include *Forbidden City U.S.A.* (1989), a musical tribute to Asian-American nightclub performers in the 1940s, and *Licensed to Kill* (1997), a brutal look into the minds of murderers who killed gay men. *Coming Out Under Fire* (1994) chronicles the lives of nine gay and lesbian soldiers during World War II, when the U.S. military established its first explicit anti-gay policies. Dong is an interesting example of a filmmaker who has retained a great deal of independence by self-distributing all of his own work. This distribution income, coupled with grants funding, gives him an autonomy that is very different from that of producers for cable outlets.

Like many Asian-American documentarians, most of the work of Christine Choy deals with social issues directly pertaining to Asian Americans. Choy and partner Rene Tajima made a number of films, including their best known, the Academy-Award-nominated *Who Killed Vincent Chin?* (1988). This is about the murder of a twenty-seven-year-old Chinese American, whose bachelor party turned into an ugly confrontation in a suburban Detroit bar, and later into Chin's fatal beating outside a fast-food restaurant. The incident, on June 19, 1982, was an almost perfect metaphor for then growing anti-Asian sentiment in America. It was ignorant: the attackers presumed Chin was Japanese. It was economically motivated: the two autoworkers blamed the Japanese—and, mistakenly, Chin—for the loss of U.S. auto industry jobs. The crime was horribly

Arthur Dong (left) composes a shot with cinematographer Hiroki Mijano on the set of *The Chinese in Hollywood* (working title) (U.S., 2005, Arthur Dong). Photo by Jon Oh

violent: a baseball bat was used as the murder weapon. The film presents this information in a dispassionate nightly-news manner that serves to make the facts even more shocking.

Other Asian-American documentarians who have left a mark include multi-Academy Award-nominated Freida Lee Mock, *Maya Lin: a Strong Clear Vision*; Rea Tajiri, *History and Memory of Takiko and Takashige* (1991); Jessica Yu, *Breathing Lessons: The Life and Work of Mark O'Brien* (1996); Dai Sil Kim-Gibson, *Silence Broken: Korean Comfort Women* (1999), about Korean victims of WWII Japanese aggression, enslaved as prostitutes for Japanese soldiers; Loni Ding, *The Color of Honor* (1987), on the experiences of Japanese-American soldiers in WWII; and Stephen Okazaki, *Black Tar Heroin: The Dark End of the Street* (1999) and the Academy Award-winning *Days of Waiting* (1990). Spencer Nakasako has worked in the Southeast-Asian community in the Tenderloin district of San Francisco for several years, training at-risk refugee teenagers in video production. He produced and codirected *a.k.a. Don Bonus* (1994), a portrait of a Cambodian family devastated by the pressures of life in their adopted country.

Canadian Abenaki Indian Alanis Obomsawin has had a long career as singer, writer, and storyteller, promoting the history and culture of her people. In 1967,

Jessica Yu with cinematographer Russ Harper on the set of *Realms of the Unreal*, about outsider artist Henry Darger (U.S., 2005, Jessica Yu). International Documentary Association

after being seen in a television profile, *Alanis* (1965), she was invited by the National Film Board to act as a consultant and has since divided her time between filmmaking and performing. In 1971 Obomsawin directed her first film, *Christmas at Moose Factory*, a study of life in a small northern settlement based on children's drawings. Between 1977 and 1994 she made ten films illustrating different aspects of Aboriginal life. Committed to the cause of justice for her people, Obomsawin documented two major confrontations: *Incident at Restigouche* (1984), and *Kanehsatake: 270 Years of Resistance*, her best-known work.

In the United States—unlike Canada, where Indians use the term Aboriginal—the preferred term for American Indians is Native. The Native American Public Broadcasting Consortium was begun in 1974 by a group of six producers, with twenty-six public television stations. Its mission is to support and promote Native-American culture through various media productions. Although it has been involved in numerous documentary works, its greatest successes have been with radio and more recently Internet development. In 1977 Frank Blythe

Alanis Obomsawain. International Documentary Association

opened a national office at the Nebraska Educational Television network head-quarters in Lincoln and was named executive director, a position he held for over twenty-five years.

In the Latino filmmaking community, noteworthy documentarians include Lourdes Portillo, whose *Las Madres: The Mothers of Plaza de Mayo* (1985) was the result of a three-year collaboration with writer/director Susana Muñoz and was nominated for an Academy Award. Portillo's next film, *La Ofrenda: The Days of the Dead* (1989), is a charming look at cultural blending. *La Ofrenda* is set up to challenge the notion that, as Portillo puts it, "documentary is always associated with injustice." In it she celebrates the traditions of a colorful Mexican and Chicano holiday, the November first celebration of *el día de los muertos*. The film relies on a poetic structure that Portillo has used in other work. *Señorita Extraviada, Missing Young Woman* (2001) tells the haunting story of the more than two hundred kidnapped, raped, and murdered young women near the *maquiladoras* of Juárez, Mexico. Like others of the PBS Minority Consortium Groups, there is an organization of Latino Public Broadcasting, although much of its efforts have been focused on fiction works.

Repesenting Gay and Lesbian Culture

As an outgrowth of the social changes and the video technology of the 1970s, various previously disenfranchised groups began to make more documentaries speaking directly to their own concerns. Homosexuals were one large group who found in documentary a powerful way to express a distinctive culture. Many of the advances in gay, later labeled queer, cinema were made in the documentary.

Word Is Out: Some Stories of Our Lives (1977), an early landmark, was pro-duced collectively by the San Francisco-based Mariposa Film Group: Peter Adair, Nancy Adair, Andrew Brown, Veronica Selver, Lucy Phenix, and Rob Epstein. Following videotaped interviews with two hundred gay and lesbian people from across the United States, they focused on a selected group of these individuals. After more than a year of editing, they cut 50 hours of material to a final 135-minute version. *Word Is Out* is divided into three major sections—"The Early Years," "Growing Up," and "From Now On"—although the interviews weave in and out among these with little formal structure. What emerges is a somewhat random, but often moving, collage portrait of the personal stories of gays and lesbians in mid-1970s America.

Before Stonewall (1984), Robert Rosenberg, John Scagliotti, and Greta Schiller (narrated by Rita Mae Brown), chronicles the evolution of gay culture in the United States from the early 1920s to violence in 1969. In that year patrons of the Stonewall Inn in New York's Greenwich Village decided to fight back against ongoing harassment, transforming a police raid into three nights of rioting that signaled the public nature of the new gay liberation movement. Using archival footage and photography from five decades, the film explores the gay under-

Las Madres: The Mothers of the Plaza de Mayo (U.S., 1985, Lourdes Portillo and Susana Muñoz). Direct Cinema, 2005, all rights reserved

COLLEAGUES—
I HOPE THIS SCREENING INTERESTS YOU. WOULD YOU PASS IT
AROUND + POST IT, IF
YOU CAN?
MANY THANKS
AMANDA POPE,
PETER ADAIR

Dear Friends,

        WE WOULD LIKE TO INVITE YOU to attend an investors' screening
of our documentary on gay women and men to be held on Saturday,
June 4 at 10:30 A.M. at the Vanguard Theater, 9014 Melrose Avenue
in Hollywood.
        THE FILM is a series of portraits of twenty-two lesbians and
gay men, edited from forty hours of color footage shot across the
country during the past eighteen months. It is an exploration of
the histories and variety of lifestyles of an emerging, but still
mostly invisible, minority- ten to twenty million people in this
country (according to Kinsey).
        OUR PURPOSE is to begin to counter the pervasive negative
images of "dykes" and "faggots" by presenting a series of intimate
portraits of gay people as people- with all the joys and sorrows
common to everyone. The film will help homosexuals, who themselves
have accepted the negative mythology, begin to feel better about who
they are and who they can be. It will also promote in the country
as a whole a beginning air of acceptance of homosexuality as an
alternative lifestyle.
        OUR AUDIENCE will number in the millions. Following in the
tracks of other recent theatrical documentaries (Harlan County,
Pumping Iron, Antonia, The Sorrow and the Pity, People of the Wind,
etc.), our movie will open first in theaters in large cities this
Fall, then will be televised nationally this Winter (it has already
been sold for four network broadcasts, which guarantees it a minimum
exposure of four million), and then will be available for rental to
colleges, graduate schools, feminist and gay groups, professional
societies, etc.
        FINISHING MONEY is needed in the form of investments. The film
has been produced as a profit-making venture. There are no general
films available about homosexuals, and there is now a tremendous and
growing need for such material. Movies are very expensive to make.
Our budget is $200,000- shoestring by industry standards for a film
of this scope. We have already raised $92,000 from investors and
$50,000 from the television sale. We need $50,000 more to finish.
We're in the final stretch.
        PLEASE COME to this hour-long screening of excerpts from our
film, whether you can consider investing or not. If you are gay or
not, judging from past audience reaction, you will be affected by the
experience.

FEEL FREE TO BRING INTERESTED FRIENDS.

                                                        Yours,

2051 THIRD ST./ SAN FRANCISCO, CA 94107/ (415) 621-6500

A fundraising letter for the film *Word Is Out*. (U.S., 1977, Mariposa Film Group).
Academy of Motion Picture Arts and Sciences

The Mariposa Group of filmmakers who made *Word Is Out,* left to right: Lucy Phenix, Nancy Adair, Peter Adair, Rob Epstein, Andrew Brown, and Veronica Selver.

ground of the twenties and thirties, the rise of gays in the military and workforce during WWII, and their persecution in the U.S. State Department as "subversives" and "sexual perverts" by Senator McCarthy in the 1950s. *After Stonewall* (1999), directed by Scagliotti and narrated by Melissa Etheridge, explores gay and lesbian history from the 1970s through the 1990s. Like its predecessor, it covers a lot of ground in a short time but, since it deals with only three decades, it is more concise.

Other important films of the era dealing in different ways with gay life include Academy Award-winning *The Times of Harvey Milk* (1984), by Rob Epstein and Richard Schmiechen. In 1978 Harvey Milk was elected to the San Francisco city council, becoming the first openly gay person elected to public office in California. One year later he and San Francisco Mayor George Moscone were shot and killed by another council member, former police officer and fireman Dan White. *The Times of Harvey Milk* recreates the story of Milk's grass-roots political organizing and election, through the murders and their repercussions. From the eloquent candlelight memorial joined by tens of thousands of San Franciscans on the evening of the assassinations, to the angry mobs who stormed City Hall, breaking windows and torching police cars in the aftermath of White's lenient sentencing, the film is a revealing analysis of democracy in America. As photographer Andrew Epstein said, "Richard and Robert's vision was, of course,

The Times of Harvey Milk (U.S., 1984, Rob Epstein and Richard Schmiechen).

The AIDS quilt on display in Washington, D.C. in *Common Threads: Stories from the Quilt* (U.S., 1989, Bill Couturié, Rob Epstein, and Jeffrey Friedman). Photo by Marc Geller/HBO, 2005 Direct Cinema

the bigger picture, the whole story in political terms. They reclaimed a queer political history that could have easily been forgotten. They recorded and bore witness. It was our assassination, our Kennedy, our King, our Malcolm X, our bullet."

Common Threads: Stories from the Quilt (1989), by Bill Couturié, Rob Epstein, and Jeffrey Friedman, made for HBO, is one of the most hauntingly beautiful, and accessible to the public, of many films concerning the AIDS crisis. Narrated by Dustin Hoffman, with a score sung by Bobby McFerrin, the film tells the story of the growth of the AIDS epidemic from its mysterious beginnings to the peak of the epidemic in the United States.

Silver Lake Life: The View from Here (1990) is a diary video in which the filmmaker is the subject, at least until he becomes too weak from AIDS to continue shooting. At that point his partner takes up the camera and the work becomes a sometimes harrowing, sometimes tender journey toward death in a most personal, personal essay. In Canada a series that became known as *The Broadcast Tapes of Dr. Peter* aired on the CBC evening news beginning in 1990, made by Dr. Peter Jepson-Young, who had been diagnosed with AIDS in 1986. Each piece chronicled another aspect of his fight for a fulfilling life in the face of the disease. He continued doing segments up until his death in 1992, despite going blind, being disfigured by the cancer Kaposi's sarcoma, and losing his

Silver Lake Life: The View From Here (U.S., 1990, Peter Friedman)

strength from medical treatments. The 111 segments were compiled into a unique forty-five-minute documentary that was broadcast by HBO, creating an emotional and inspiring portrait of the epidemic.

Paris Is Burning (1990, Jennie Livingston) delves colorfully into America's subculture of the urban drag queen. It's a parallel world of bizarre beauty, where "houses" compete for turf and reputation, but instead of street fighting, they vamp down makeshift catwalks in competitive "balls."

Of the gay filmmakers, Barbara Hammer is probably the most prolific. Since the 1970s she has made over eighty films and videos and is considered a pioneer of lesbian-feminist experimental cinema. Her work can be directly related to the experimental art documentaries of the 1920s. One early piece, *Dyketactics* (1974), was the first film about lesbian lovemaking to be made by a lesbian. Her trilogy of documentary essays on lesbian and gay history—*Nitrate Kisses* (1992), *Tender Fictions* (1995), and *History Lessons* (2000)—has been widely acclaimed. Hammer uses an evocative visual and aural style in which, although imagery may not always be instantly readable in a literal sense, its emotional and often sexual power is clearly recognizable. Her films are also laced with a sophisticated humor and sometimes-graphic eroticism.

Hammer's uncompromising work is far from mainstream, like that of African-American filmmaker Marlon Riggs, who pushed the boundaries of conven-

Dr. Peter Jepson reports on his own deterioration from AIDS in *The Broadcast Tapes of Dr. Peter* (1994, Canada, David Paperny).

tional network television. Before his death from AIDS in 1994, Riggs became one of the more controversial figures in recent documentary history. In his second film, *Tongues Untied* (1988), Riggs profiled urban African-American gay men with frank portraits of gay subcultures, complete with explicit language and sexual imagery. The film was partly financed by a $5,000 grant from the National Endowment for the Arts (NEA). When it was about to be broadcast nationally on PBS, descriptions of the film's subject matter touched off a heated debate about government funding of art that some labeled obscene. While artists argued for free speech, government policy makers, especially the politically conservative, engaged in a public discussion about the use of taxpayer money for the funding of such work. Adding to the controversy was the fact that the public television *P.O.V.* (*Point of View*) series, which presented the film, also receives general production funding from the Endowment. Leaders of conservative organizations, many of whom had not seen the film, labeled *Tongues Untied* obscene. When a few public stations decided not to air the program, this self-censorship added to the debate. Although most PBS stations did broadcast the film, controversy surrounding *Tongues Untied* played a key role in the future NEA decision to stop funding individual artists, including individual filmmakers.

Music and Performance

From 1961, when the National Film Board of Canada produced *Lonely Boy*, discussed in chapter 11, through Joe Berlinger and Bruce Sinofsky's 2004 psychological exposé of heavy metal stars Metallica in *Metallica: Some Kind of Monster*, rock and roll and pop music have fascinated documentary makers, and musicians have loved to be filmed. Notable music documentaries are not fiction films that use rock and roll, or straight-ahead filmed concerts, nor are they simply records of performances. These are fully realized creative efforts. Filmmakers such as D. A. Pennebaker (*Don't Look Back*, Bob Dylan, 1967), Martin Scorsese (*The Last Waltz*, The Band, 1979), Taylor Hackford (*Hail, Hail, Rock and Roll*, Chuck Berry, 1987), Penelope Spheeris (*The Decline of Western Civilization*, the punk movement, 1981), Jonathan Demme (*Stop Making Sense*, Talking Heads, 1985), Michael Apted (*Bring on the Night*, Sting, 1985), Wim Wenders (*Buena Vista Social Club*, 1999), and Jason Priestly (*Barenaked in America*, Barenaked Ladies, 2000) are only some of the well-known names who have made notable music films.

For many years the most financially successful theatrically released documentary—rock music or otherwise—was Warner Brothers' *Woodstock* (1970) by Michael Wadleigh. The film devotes almost as much screen time to the audience encamped on Yasgur's farmland in upstate New York as it does to its now legendary musical performances. *Woodstock* thus is an informal sociological study of hippie culture. Its many split-screen images, its (for the time) thundering sound track, and the lure of its carefree approach to "Peace, Love, and Music," as well

Rob Halford, lead singer of Judas Priest in *Dream Deceivers: The Story Behind James Vance vs. Judas Priest?* (U.S., 1992, David Van Taylor). Did subliminal messages in heavy metal music cause two teenagers to fulfill a suicide pact, or was it the hopelessness of a dysfunctional America?

as sex and drugs, made it a landmark and inspiration for millions of young people. The iconography of *Woodstock* remains powerful. New versions of the concert have been staged and new documentaries made about those events, notably Barbara Kopple's *My Generation,* which began as a documentary of Woodstock '94. As she finished editing her Woodstock '94 footage, Woodstock '99 occurred. "I took a deep breath and went and did '99 with a really small crew—one 16mm camera and two DV cameras," she has said. The result was a crossgenerational look at all the factions that participated in the various Woodstocks. Wadleigh's original, which continues to generate income in revamped re-release and home video and DVD sales, remains as a seminal event in the history of American culture.

Wattstax (1973) is a bold documentary directed by Mel Stuart, produced by David Wolper for Warner Brothers. This film of a concert staged in the summer of 1972 that drew over 100,000 people to the Los Angeles Coliseum featured performances by Stax Records soul stars such as Isaac Hayes, Albert King, and the Staples Singers, as well as an appearance by Jesse Jackson. For the African-American community it gained the stature of a black Woodstock. Intercut with

Producer David Wolper and director Mel Stuart on the set of *Wattstax* (U.S., 1973, Mel Stuart). Mel Stuart

the musical numbers are two contrapuntal threads: one of a group of black men discussing life questions in a local bar, another of raw standup comic newcomer Richard Pryor. *Wattstax* is an unusually frank and hip look at the mores and the problems of urban black Americans in the mid-1970s. Stuart, who is white, achieved this insider's perspective by using a crew made up of as many black filmmakers as he could find (an almost unheard of situation for a studio-backed film) and the result is a real-deal celebration of giant afros and swinging dashikis. Stuart's career as a Hollywood-based filmmaker from the Wolper school encompasses decades of durable fiction and documentary works, including the telling portrait *Man Ray: Prophet of the Avant-Garde* made for PBS's *American Masters* series in 1999.

One of the most prolific music documentarians is the iconoclastic Robert Mugge. His film subjects range from the blues to Hawaiian music to entertaining the troops. A graduate of Temple University's film school, his first film was a profile of an avant-garde composer: *George Crumb: Voice of the Whale* (1976). This was followed by his only non-music work, *Amateur Night at City Hall* (1978), about the late mayor of Philadelphia, Frank L. Rizzo. In 1980 Mugge released *Sun Ra: A Joyful Noise*, about Sun Ra and his "Arkestra"; followed by *Black Wax* (1982), a portrait of poet-singer-songwriter Gil Scott-Heron; *Cool*

A murder caught by the cameras in *Gimme Shelter* (U.S., 1970, Albert and David Maysles and Charlotte Zwerin). Maysles Films

Runnings: The Reggae Movie (1983); *The Gospel According to Al Green* (1984); and over a dozen more music profiles continuing through *Blues Breaks* (2003), in which thirteen 60-second mini-movies feature little-known Mississippi blues artists. Mugge's documentaries are in some ways like those of Les Blank (see chapter 17). For both filmmakers, the soul of the subject is the most important element, and Mugge, like Blank, has created an extraordinary record of a part of America often overlooked by the mainstream.

The flip side to *Woodstock*'s sunny view of the world (even during a down-pour) is Albert and David Maysles's, with Charlotte Zwerin, *Gimme Shelter* (1970). Ostensibly the study of a free concert by the Rolling Stones at Altamont Speedway in northern California, *Gimme Shelter* invokes the darkest moments of rock and roll as an enormous crowd surges out of control in response to Mick Jagger's "Sympathy for the Devil" persona. At Altamont two people died in a hit-and-run auto accident, another drowned, and, captured on film, is the knife murder of an eighteen-year-old black spectator by the Hell's Angels, who were hired to provide concert security. Later in the film we see the filmmakers screening, rewinding, and focusing in on this bit of footage as Jagger watches it on a flatbed editing machine. We, the film viewers, watch as the performer watches his performance and the filmmaker watches his own work, while an unknown someone is killed in front of us all. The murder becomes part not only of the filmed record but also of a work of art. In this it presages many controversies about capturing brutality and death on film and so-called reality television. Michael Sragow, writing in 1990 for the magazine of the International Cinematographer's Guild (ICG), made the point that "Pauline Kael and Vincent Canby led the [critical] charge against *Gimme Shelter* as an opportunistic snuff film, essentially saying that the filmmakers were complicit in the murder by having photographed it and subsequently profited from its theatrical release." Their main criticism was that the concert was staged specifically to be filmed—and irresponsibly so. While conceding that the filmmakers had caught Jagger's "feral intensity" with acute "editing of the images to the music," Sragow quotes Kael writing that "the filmed death at Altamont" was part of a "cinéma vérité spectacular." She condemned the movie with rhetorical questions: "If events are created to be photographed, is the movie that records them a documentary, or does it function in a twilight zone? Is it the cinema of fact when the facts are manufactured for the cinema?"

Films of the Period

1980

The Day After Trinity (U.S., Jon Else)
From Mao to Mozart: Isaac Stern in China (U.S., Murray Lerner)
Garlic Is as Good as Ten Mothers (U.S., Les Blank)

1981

Not a Love Story (Canada, Bonnie Sherr Klein)

1982

Atomic Café (U.S., Jane Loader, Kevin Rafferty, and Pierce Rafferty)
The Brooklyn Bridge (U.S., Ken Burns)
Burden of Dreams (U.S., Les Blank)
If You Love This Planet (Canada, Terre Nash)

1983

"The Profession of Arms," *War* (Canada, Gwynne Dyer, Michael Bryans, and Tina Viljoen)

1984

The Times of Harvey Milk (U.S., Rob Epstein and Richard Schmiechen)

1985

Las Madres: The Mothers of the Plaza de Mayo (U.S., Susana Muñoz and Lourdes Portillo)
28 Up (U.K., Michael Apted)

1986

Handsworth Songs (U.K., John Akomfrah)
Sherman's March (U.S., Ross McElwee)
The World of Tomorrow (U.S., Lance Bird and Tom Johnson)

1987

Eyes on the Prize (U.S., Henry Hampton)
To a Safer Place (Canada, Beverly Shaffer)

1988

Lightning Over Braddock: A Rustbowl Fantasy (U.S., Tony Buba)
The Thin Blue Line (U.S., Errol Morris)
Tongues Untied (U.S., Marlon Riggs)
Who Killed Vincent Chin? (U.S., Rene Tajima and Christine Choy)

1989

Common Threads: Stories from the Quilt (U.S., Bill Couturié, Rob Epstein, and Jeffrey Friedman)
Roger & Me (U.S., Michael Moore)

Books on the Period

Bullert, B. J., Public Television: Politics and the Battle over Documentary. New Brunswick, NJ: Rutgers University Press, 1997.

Crittendon, Roger with Cherry Potter, Confronting Reality: Some Perspectives on Documentary. Beaconsfield, England: CILECT Review Clarendon Printers, 1985.

Goldsmith, David A., The Documentary Makers: Interviews with 15 of the Best in the Business. Switzerland: RotoVision, 2003.

Homlund, Chris and Cynthia Fuchs, eds. Between the Sheets, In the Streets: Queer, Lesbian, and Gay Documentary. Minneapolis: University of Minnesota Press, 1997.

Klotman, Phyllis R. and Janet K. Cutler, eds., Struggles for Representation: African American Documentary Film and Video. Bloomington: Indiana University Press, 1999.

Ledbetter, James, Made Possible By: The Death of Public Broadcasting in the United States. London: Verso, 1997.

Rabiger, Michael, Directing the Documentary. London: Focal Press, 1992.

Rosenthal, Alan, The New Challenges for Documentary. Berkeley: University of California Press, 1988.

Stubbs, Liz, Documentary Filmmakers Speak. New York: Allworth Press, 2000.

Waldman, Diane and Janet Walker, eds., Feminism and Documentary. Minneapolis: University of Minnesota Press, 1999.

Zimmerman, Patricia R., States of Emergency: Documentaries, Wars, Democracies. Minneapolis: University of Minnesota Press, 2000.

Chapter Seventeen

English-Language Documentary in the 1990s and Beyond—Reality Bytes

The centennial of cinema, including the one-hundred-year mark for the documentary, was 1995. The date of the first *public* projection of film, which took place on December 28, 1895, in Paris, was settled upon by hundreds of film organizations around the world as the moment when cinema officially began. As described in chapter one, that now famous Lumière brothers exhibition at the Grand Café consisted of an approximately twenty-five-minute program of very short—less than one minute each—films. In that first public screening, the dialectic between the "real" and the "staged," which has continuously been included in discussion of documentary, was already in play. On that occasion, both pre-documentary "actualities" and fiction-based vignettes were shown together without distinction. It is probably safe to say that no one from the Lumière organization stood up and announced: "Here we have a selection of real, unscripted events, and other scenes which are acted for the camera." In fact, those films in the program long deemed "actualities," such as *Workers Leaving the Factory*, on close examination, appear to have been as rehearsed as the "enactment" of the comic *The Hoser Hosed* (*L'Arroseur arrosé*). The Lumière workers were surely told to exit the factory gates as the camera was rolling and not to look at the camera. Different "takes" of this scene, possibly shot months apart, remain extant over a hundred years later. Still, the workers were nonactors engaged in their everyday activities as the Lumière camera recorded them. The people in *The Hoser Hosed* were playacting a comedy.

Over the next one hundred years, as suggested in this book, documentary and fiction filmmakers traveled mostly separate routes. However often the subjects and techniques of the two intersected, documentarians identified themselves as such, often by the social intent of their films. As with all rules, there were exceptions. Still, fiction filmmakers have generally created fictions, usually and primarily meant to entertain. The closing years of the twentieth century, the entury of Cinema, " and the first years of the yet-to-be-named twenty-first century have brought documentary to a place where it sometimes seems more and more difficult to separate the real from the fictional. Technology, economics, and artistic experimentation continue to push and pull the documentary in new directions, and filmmakers themselves more openly challenge the label of "documentarian."

Business and Technology: The Bad and the Good

One of the major trends of the 1980s, the proliferation of cable channels, became even more pervasive in the 1990s. The consequences—ever more hours of television documentary programming, production cost per hour decreasing dramatically, lessening personal control by the individual filmmaker—all continued. What resulted was a marked decline in the overall quality of most televised documentary, even as the number of television hours devoted to nonfiction increased exponentially. This is not to say that there were not notable, even outstanding and groundbreaking, works. There were. But the vast majority of television time devoted to nonfiction was taken up by product whose artistic quality was limited and whose veracity was sometimes questionable. This was increasingly true even before the millennial onslaught of so-called "reality TV." Hours were filled with recycled stock footage on every imaginable subject, accompanied by bland commentary, and the dullest kind of talking-head interviews. Point of view, investigative, and artful filmmaking often went by the wayside as cable channels scurried to fill endless hours.

With advances in technology anyone with a digital camera and a home computer could put together a documentary, and fortunately many more people can tell their own stories. At the same time, the professionalism of documentary craft and artistry, to say nothing of concern for ethical considerations, has suffered. The cost of small-format video is a fraction of that of older technologies. In the twenty-first century one or two people shoot major television documentary projects that once required lavish funding and at least four-plus crew members. When shooting in 16mm, or even Betacam, it was common for makers to travel with twelve to twenty cases of equipment, film, and supplies. The same work can now be done in small-format out of one small suitcase. This crush of quick, and above all cheap, work has considerably lowered the bar as to what television audiences accept as documentary. The speed of this kind of filmmaking, its low cost, and the fact that a person with almost no technical skill can perform it, has opened the field of documentary making to the entire industrialized world.

The need for low-cost programming affected not only documentaries shot mainly in the field. For some cable channels the exigencies of creating mass hours of programming about historical events that had taken place decades ago led to disturbing developments. The slideshow approach, with narration and talking heads, was one consequence. Cost conscious and inexperienced researchers sometimes substituted any available footage for actual shots of the events under discussion. For example, a stock image of a sinking ship has more than once been passed off as a specific sinking ship, whether the ship in the image had actually ever sailed in the same ocean that the documentary claimed. In all too many cases an astonishing disregard for factual rigor overcame historical compilation films. This problem became so widespread that the Association of Moving Image Archivists' newsletter published a column by archivist Jerome Keuhl listing misused footage. His watchful beast, known as the office cat, keeps track of such documentary misadventures and anachronisms and reports to the community when an earnest film researcher starts looking for footage of Lincoln's Gettysburg Address or the sinking of the *Titanic*, events never covered by a camera.

On the commercial front, when the merchandising of documentary tie-in product began in earnest, it became abundantly clear that executives at cable channels were far more interested in "branding" themselves as saleable corporate commodities than in producing meaningful documentaries. A leader in the field was again Discovery Communications, with its Discovery Stores. Using the Discovery name and logos, along with those of its offshoot channels—Animal Planet, Discovery Health, Travel Channel, Discovery Kids, Wings, etc.—stores began to sell everything from plastic sharks to logo shirts, to audio CD, all loosely connected to documentary programming that played on the channels. Starting in 1997 Discovery.com's online store reached out to armchair adventurers with an e-commerce Web site to mirror the Discovery Stores found in retail malls around the world. Eventually most other channels joined in the trend. *National Geographic* magazine redesigned its logo and opened www.shopnationalgeo graphic.com, and public television viewers were now invited continuously to shop the PBS Online Store. The work of Ken Burns in particular was enhanced by astute marketing tie-ins to books and recorded music.

There is nothing inherently evil in selling documentary-linked consumer products. And the cable channels were only adapting the long-time marketing techniques of major Hollywood movie studios in selling theme-related goods. Practices that Hopalong Cassidy and Disney mouse ears pioneered a half-century earlier, and George Lucas and *Star Wars* perfected in the 1970s, simply found expression in the 1990s documentary world. What is insidious for the documentary tradition is that the merchandise in these cases often became far more important to the presenting channel than anything the documentarian might have to say on a subject. Yes, legend has it that chocolate-covered ice cream bars were first marketed as "Eskimo Pies" or "Nanooks" in wake of the success of *Nanook of the North*. "Eskimo Pie" was trademarked in 1922, the same year as *Nanook's* release; prior to that the frozen treat was called "I-Scream-Bar." However, it seems evident that selling ice cream had no bearing on future Flaherty productions.

Great fiscal and artistic consequences have also resulted from the cable industry's contractual practices with individual filmmakers. In the twenty-first century a majority of cable documentaries are works done for hire, in which the film-makers retain little control and hold no rights to their films. This is not the case for those producers who raise money independently and then license their work, but it is true for the majority of hours seen by cable viewers. Whereas at one time independent producers could hope to recoup costs, make a small profit, possibly take some creative risks, and see their work broadcast in a form resem-bling the film they intended, these options, at least in the cable marketplace, are almost nonexistent by the twenty-first century. The big exception remains HBO/Cinemax Documentaries, which is neither product nor advertising but rather subscriber- and awards-driven. In a long-term economic sense, too, the indepen-dent producer is left with little clout. At one time a television mogul like David Wolper chose the subjects and the forms in which he wanted to document them. He amassed capital by retaining the rights to rebroadcast, educational sales, and later home video. To run the *Biography* series and create the Biography Channel, A&E had to pay Wolper. Today's presenting channels demand control of these and any other ancillary rights, leaving the producers with no equity in the work they produced.

On U.S. television there are some alternatives to cable but not at the major broadcast networks. Fighting a defensive battle against the erosion of viewership by cable channels in the 1990s, the networks abandoned documentaries almost entirely. Except for the longstanding success of shows like *60 Minutes* and its spin-offs, the end of the twentieth century brought the demise of what at mid-century had seemed the salvation of serious documentary making (see chapter twelve). No one in network broadcast television was willing to take artistic or content risk, nor even to uphold the investigative reporting traditions of Edward R. Murrow of CBS, or NBC's *Project XX* and *White Paper*. Even Jon Alpert and DCTV's productive twenty-year relationship with NBC ended with the First Gulf War in Iraq. "We were the only independent documentary reporters in Baghdad during the war. But our footage documenting the death and destruction in civil-ian neighborhoods was a shocking message, so instead of broadcasting it, NBC killed the messenger," Alpert says. DCTV formed a new relationship with HBO, producing edgy one-hour investigative programs like *Lock-up: The Prisoners of Riker's Island* (1994), *One Year in a Life of Crime* (1989), *Rape: Cries from the Heartland* (1992), and *High on Crack Street: Lost Live in Lowell* (1995), the last two directed by Maryann De Leo.

Certainly there was high-quality programming on cable other than HBO and its sister channels. A five-part series, *Yugoslavia: Death of a Nation* (1996)—made by the highly respected English documentarian Brian Lapping for the BBC and The Discovery Channel and narrated by CNN's Christiane Amanpour—untangled the political and military events that led to the dismemberment of the country that was Yugoslavia. It integrates video footage of council meetings and other events with interviews of the heads of all six states involved in the resulting war. The series explains how Serbian President Slobodan Milosevic systematically and brutally controlled an entire region.

Another noteworthy film, from the A&E-owned Learning Channel, is Nanette Burstein and Brett Morgan's On the Ropes (1999). It follows three young boxers, in and out of the ring, as they struggle with tough lives in their New York housing projects homes while they train for the Golden Gloves. Even community-activist-based DCTV teamed up in 2003 with Discovery and its New York Times-linked DiscoveryTimes channel to produce programming like Off to War, about the deployment of the Arkansas National Guard to the Second Iraq War. The Sundance and IFC channels program numerous documentaries but their viewership is limited. For the most part, socially critical documentaries were not the province of cable or network television.

American Public Television

There remained public television. Since its beginnings, U.S. public television has struggled, usually desperately, for enough funds to stay in business. The original Corporation for Public Broadcasting (CPB) charter from Congress provided no guarantees of long-term financial support. This has left all three arms of public television—CPB, the PBS network, and the local stations—extremely vulnerable to the changing winds of political practice in Washington and to the vagaries of local tastes. (See the discussion of Tongues Untied in chapter 16.) Pledge drives and corporate underwriting provide most of the money for station operation, while much of the production costs are also dependent on corporate or foundation funding.

In 1988, after years of lobbying by media activists (chief among them Larry Daressa and Larry Sapadin of California Newsreel, theoretical physicist/media advocate Larry Hall, Dee Dee Halleck, and producer Mark Weiss), Congress appropriated funds for an independent PBS production service. Part of that money went to create the Independent Television and Video Service (ITVS). Although it took several years to begin operating effectively, ITVS in the 1990s and into the 2000s has been responsible for some of the more daring programming available on American television. Officially ITVS's mission is to create and present independently produced programs that engage creative risks, advance issues, and represent points of view not usually seen on public or commercial television. ITVS is committed to programming that addresses the needs of underserved and underrepresented audiences and expands civic participation by bringing new voices into public discourse. It divides six or seven million dollars each year among a wide range of producers for all types of work, the majority of which are documentaries. As of 2004, ITVS had partially funded 325 documentaries; 304 documentaries with ITVS funding had aired on some part of the U.S. public television system. Projects produced by minority and underserved makers have been emphasized. It has worked with the minority consortia of PBS (the Native

Frontline, "The Secret Files of J. Edgar Hoover" (U.S., 1993, Bill Cran and Stephanie Tepper). WGBH

American, Latino, African American, Pacific Islander, and Asian American organizations described in chapter 16) and has funded in whole or in part such noted gay-themed documentaries as Arthur Dong's *Coming Out Under Fire* (1995), Meema Spadola's *Our House: A Very Real Documentary About Kids of Gay and Lesbian Families* (1999), and Debra Chasnoff's *It's Elementary: Talking About Gay Issues in School* (1996).

ITVS-funded works that make it to national broadcast generally do so under the umbrella of one of two programming strands: *P.O.V.* or *Independent Lens.* These are limited showcases with twelve to fourteen premieres for *P.O.V.* and twenty-nine for *Independent Lens* each year. This means that on U.S. national public television there are fewer than 50 one- to two-hour time slots open in any year to stand-alone documentaries made by independent filmmakers. All the other documentaries offered for national broadcast are commissioned to order by strands such as *American Experience, American Masters,* and *NOVA.* A big advantage of a PBS broadcast over commercial channels is that producers generally have much more creative control, and the rights to their films revert to them after a period of time. For documentarians seeking to effect social change, a national public television broadcast also delivers a much larger audience than any single cable channel can.

Investigative reporting has remained alive on public television largely on another commissioned strand: through the efforts of WGBH in Boston and producer David Fanning's *Frontline.* A native of South Africa, Fanning came to WGBH from the BBC to start the documentary series *World* in 1977. As executive producer he produced and presented over fifty films for PBS in five years. Fanning conceived, and has executive produced, *Frontline* since it premiered in January 1983. For two decades it has remained America's only regularly scheduled public affairs documentary series on television and has won every major U.S. award for broadcast journalism. *Frontline* has tackled dozens of national and international issues. Important individual *Frontline* broadcasts include "Living Below the Line" (1984), "A Class Divided" (1985), "The Lifer and the Lady" (1985), "High Crimes and Misdemeanors" (1990), "Romeo and Juliet in Sarajevo" (1994), "Ghosts of Rwanda" (2004), and many more.

The Ken Burns Phenomenon

Perhaps the biggest success story for PBS in the past twenty years has been the films made by Ken Burns and company. The multiple broadcasts of *The Civil War*, beginning in 1990, had deep and long-lasting effects on style, funding, and audience development for PBS documentaries. The series changed the way many in America thought about documentary, and it changed the way television executives thought about historical documentaries.

Burns had been making significant documentaries for over fifteen years before *The Civil War*. His first major film, *The Brooklyn Bridge* (1982), remains a graceful, reflective tribute to hard work and engineering genius in America and to many of the traditions of the historical documentary. Burns's output follows in the footsteps of other notable historical documentary makers discussed previously—Charles Guggenheim, Jeremy Isaacs, Lance Bird, and Tom Johnson—particularly in their shared insistence on accuracy and respect for the integrity and beauty of the image. The film that most anticipates the Burns formula is perhaps the National Film Board of Canada's *City of Gold*, made by Colin Low and Wolf Koenig (see discussion in chapter eleven). Like all of Burns's major work, *The Brooklyn Bridge* relies heavily on stills brought to life with a swooping rostrum camera, stunning live-action 16mm cinematography, talking-head interviews with sympathetic experts, and a memorable sound track and score. Burns and a succession of very key coproducers and collaborators were to take this formula and refine it in films such as *The Statue of Liberty* (1985), *The Congress* (1989), and others—a total of seven titles, all shown on PBS before *The Civil War*.

Burns's combination of talent, sincerity, and personality has put him among history's elite group of documentarians whose names are known widely to their contemporary publics. Like Robert Flaherty and John Grierson before him, Burns also developed a bold public persona, which made him and his work fundable from many different arenas. Over the course of making his films he formed highly productive working relationships with his sponsoring PBS station, WETA, Washington, D.C. He also became one of the filmmakers most consistently funded by the National Endowment for the Humanities, which provided

The Brooklyn Bridge commentator and historian Lewis Mumford (lower right) (U.S., 1982, Ken Burns).

money for almost every production, and whose dictates about input from humanities scholars helped shape the form of his work. Burns was also able to cultivate major corporate sponsorship. *The Statue of Liberty*, for example, had funding from Liberty Mutual Insurance, and a later deal with General Motors guaranteed that it would put money into a series of productions following the success of *The Civil War*. Like Grierson or Flaherty, Burns has a strong mission for his work, but his goal is not social change or elegiac poetry. Rather, he considers himself first and foremost an historian, documenting the social and cultural changes of American life through portrayal of its individuals and institutions.

In *The Civil War* Ken Burns used photographs like this one attributed to Mathew Brady, and told an epic story by weaving into it many personal experiences (U.S., 1980, Ken Burns).

The Civil War remains Burns's masterwork. His later, longer films—*Baseball* (1996) and *Jazz* (2001), for instance—suffered somewhat from the lack of control that had been exerted by strong coproducers like his brother Ric Burns, in *The Civil War*, his then wife Amy Steckler Burns, on *Shakers: Hands to Work, Hearts to God* (1974), or Richard Kilberg in *Huey Long* (1985). Collaboration is an important part of Burns's filmmaking technique, and he relies on a crack technical team, including editor Paul Barnes and sound mixer Lee Dichter. Part of the intrinsic beauty of Burns's work has come from an insistence on using film rather than tape or disk, shot by Burns, or more often by cinematographer Buddy Squires. The visual and aural elegance of the films set a high standard for the craft of historical documentary but, perhaps most important, they succeeded in engaging a mass audience in emotional nonfiction experiences.

Direct offshoots of Burns's approach coming from former collaborators include a number of important documentaries: Ric Burns's epic *New York* (1999) and *The Donner Party* (1992); Larry Hott and Diane Gary's *Niagara Falls* (1985), *Sentimental Women Need Not Apply: A History of the American Nurse* (1988), and *Tuberculosis in America: The People's Plague* (1995); Stephen Ives's *The West* (1996, executive-produced by Ken Burns), *Seabiscuit* (2003), and *Reporting America at War* (2003). All of these films were made for PBS broadcast, and each bears the distinctive mark of its makers; still, they follow in the broad form of

Poster for *New York: A Documentary Film* (U.S., 1999, Ric Burns and Lisa Ades)

historical documentary made popular by Ken Burns. Another prolific historical documentary maker for PBS, who works in the same vein but was not a Burns collaborator, is David Grubin. Grubin has made dozens of television documentaries, many with commentator Bill Moyers. His work includes *The Secret Life of the Brain* (2002), *Abraham and Mary Lincoln: A House Divided* (2001), and *Napoleon* (2000).

Canada Soldiers On

Throughout the 1980s and 1990s the National Film Board slowly shifted from a self-contained, government-sponsored production-distribution institution to a hybrid. In 1980 the Canadian government set up a Federal Cultural Policy Review Committee, primarily to study the role of the Board. The committee recommended that it stop producing and distributing films and become, instead, a research and training center. The NFB did not like this recommendation but accepted the cultural thrust of the report, mainly to become "more relevant" to Canadians. While the NFB enjoyed a stellar reputation outside Canada throughout its history, to a large part of the Canadian public it had come to represent stodgy instructional films.

In 1984 the Minister of Communications' National Film and Video Policy redefined the NFB's mandate. Substantial changes in production and distribution activities followed, with savings from distribution reinvested in production. The plan also suggested a reduction in permanent personnel and the increased use of freelance filmmakers. In 1982 the NFB, in collaboration with the Canadian

Film Development Corporation, set up the Film Canada Program to support private producers; by the end of the 1980s freelancers accounted for 70 percent of production. This led in the early 1990s to works like the gay-themed documentaries of David Adkin's *Out: Stories of Lesbian and Gay Youth* (1994), and Aerlyn Weissman and Lynne Fernie's *Forbidden Love: The Unashamed Stories of Lesbian Lives* (1992).

More restructurings—which reflected budget reductions, technological changes, and a 1996 Mandate Review Committee's Report—again changed the form of the NFB. It slashed its infrastructure, with far-reaching results. Based on the report, a new long-range plan was put in place by 2000, which emphasized coproductions with independent Canadian producers and international coproductions. It also reaffirmed the NFB's commitment to ethnic diversity, particularly to supporting work by aboriginal peoples. Early in the twenty-first century, the Canadian Department of Communications dedicated $25 million for the NFB to undertake coproductions with independent producers. Additionally it mandated that 35 percent of funding go to new, emerging filmmakers. Tangible results of these policies are only beginning to emerge.

Other outlets for documentaries in Canada were principally on television. The History Channel in Canada is a completely separate entity from The History Channel in the United States. The state-run Canadian Broadcasting Corporation (CBC) has long produced and shown documentaries. In 2000 the NFB joined with the CBC and several private partners to create The Documentary Channel, Canada, based on the observation that "Canadians have a special fondness for the documentary form." TVOntario, a private television network, has aired many acclaimed social issue documentaries. Rudy Buttignol, the Creative Head of Documentaries, Drama, and Network at TVO, was formerly an independent producer, director, and writer of documentaries. He has created a for-profit television home for independent documentarians in Canada.

The documentary spirit of individual Canadian filmmakers has remained vital. Vancouver documentarian Nettie Wild has created a number of ardent political films. From revolutionary guerilla armies in the Philippines and Mexico, to confrontations over heroin use in Vancouver's East End, Wild's films tend to focus on the flashpoints of social conflicts. Her work includes *A Rustling of Leaves* (1988), *Blockade* (1993), *A Place Called Chiapas* (1998), perhaps the most telling document about the situation of indigenous people in Chiapas, Mexico, and *FIX: The Story of an Addicted City* (2002).

Ron Mann has made mostly compilation documentaries for more than twenty years. An historian and educator as well as an experimenter with technique, Mann has primarily targeted areas of cultural interest. His first international recognition came with *Comic Book Confidential* (1988); he went on to make the definitive film on the *Twist* (1992), and explored marijuana use in North America with *Grass* (1999). Mann has made his technological interests evident in his work as well, with collage, archival footage, and animation used to

Go Further (Canada, 2004, Ron Mann). Home Vision Entertainment

recount the history of pop culture. Following the popular success of *Grass*, which was narrated by actor/activist Woody Harrelson, Mann focused on him in *Go Further* (2003), which follows Harrelson as he embarks on his Simply Organic Living Tour.

In some ways the Canadian documentary scene presents a middle ground between that of the United States and the United Kingdom. Canada has a much stronger system of public funding support for its documentarians than does the U.S. The NFB, even with the changes that took place in the past two decades, along with the government-supported CBC, provide a base from which filmmakers can build a budget. In the U.S., public funding is almost nonexistent. But like the U.S., Canadian documentary has embraced diversity in style, content, and in welcoming new kinds of filmmakers, particularly women. In the U.K., where public funding is strongest, the productions have remained largely in the hands of the traditional white male media stakeholders.

Developments in the United Kingdom

Unlike the often chaotic diversity of documentary in the United States, many of the filmmakers working in the United Kingdom come from a common background, university education at the "right" schools leading directly into apprenticeship programs in television. This has led to a very high quality of craftsmanship but also to a somewhat homogenized product. Unlike public broadcasting in the U.S., however, the government-supported broadcasting tradition in Britain does allow many socially critical documentaries to appear regularly on television. There are series such as producer Nick Fraser's BBC *Storyville*, which funds some works and acquires others, including some of the best North American independent documentaries. Fraser, a filmmaker in his own right, is one of the most astute and articulate of commissioning editors active in the twenty-first century. He works with a range of filmmakers, from venerable British documentarian Leslie Woodhead, who was awarded an OBE in 1994 (Order of the British Empire, which Grierson had received in 1971) for "Services to Television," to startling newcomers like Luke Holland, whose films include *I Was a Slave Labourer* (1999) and *More Than a Life* (2002).

Woodhead joined Granada Television as a graduate trainee in 1961, after Cambridge University, and in the mid-1960s worked on the series *World in Action*. During the early 1970s he pioneered the development of docudramas on British television, specializing in investigative reconstructions of major East European stories. His extensive filmography includes a documentary about the Iranian hostage crisis of 1979, the first on this subject shot inside Iran, a film about the Srebrenica massacre, *A Cry from the Grave*, and the dramatized reconstruction *The Holocaust on Trial*, about the trial of Holocaust denier David Irving. Other recent films include a documentary about a Russian nuclear missile base, a film about Slobodan Milosevic, and the autobiographical *my life as a spy* for *Storyville*.

Clive Gordon is one of England's prolific investigative documentarians. His work ranges from the tragedy of *Children of Chernoble* (1991), to the horrors of war in *The Unforgiving* (1993) or *The Betrayed* (1995), to the violence and misogyny of the Milwaukee, Wisconsin, vice trade in *Pimp Snooky* (2000). In *The Mission* (2000), his third film about civil wars, Gordon focused on the conflict in Central Africa and exploitation of children.

John Pilger is an Australian-born investigative journalist/documentarian who works in England, where he developed a reputation as a television polemicist. For example, his Carlton Television documentary *Palestine Is Still the Issue* (2003) analyzes the Israeli-Palestinian conflict, condemning Israel's injustices toward the Palestinians and arguing that Israelis were at the root of the Middle East conflict. The public outcry about this view was considerable. Pilger, a writer and presenter, was previously in the spotlight for his antiglobalization work, *The New Ruler of the World* (2001), which links economic globalization with mass abuses of human rights.

Among the very few women who have penetrated the male domain of the British documentary tradition is Molly Dineen. Born in Canada, she is a graduate of the U.K.'s National Film and Television School and has made a series of documentaries that, in a self-reflexive mode, make evident the filmmaker in the making. The first of these, her student production, was *Home from the Hill* (1985), about retired soldier and safari operator Colonel Hook, returning from Kenya to England. She went on to make *My African Farm* (1988), a portrait of Sylvia Richardson and her servants on a farm in Kenya, and *The Ark* (1993), a series of four one-hour programs about the London Zoo, filmed during a six-month period of internal crisis. More recent films include the sponsored promotional *Tony Blair*, a ten-minute portrait of Prime Minister Blair, screened across all four television channels just prior to the election campaign of 1997. (Dineen publicly disavowed support of Blair during the Second Iraq War.) *Geri* (1999) presents a portrait of the predicament of modern celebrity by following Geri Halliwell (aka Ginger Spice) in the three months after her departure from the popular singing group the Spice Girls.

Dineen is a recurring presence in her films, although not on camera. It is her voice, heard asking questions offscreen, which integrates the filmmaker in the works. In the earlier films, her questioning depicts the subject in ways the subject likes, while later films contain more of the filmmaker. In *Geri*, Dineen adds her own commentary as a voice-over, in addition to probing the celebrity subject with questions about who is in control of this documentary. In 2003 the Grierson Memorial Trust presented its first Trustees Award, which recognizes an outstanding contribution to the art of documentary, to Dineen, whose films also include *The Pick, The Shovel and the Open Road* (1991) and *Heart of the Angel* (1989).

Angela Holdsworth, a seasoned television journalist and BBC producer, conceived *Out of the Doll's House*, an eight-part BBC series, broadcast in 1988. It aimed to "allow women of all ages and social backgrounds to tell their story in their own words." Relying heavily on personal recollections and oral testimony, the series tackled themes including home, work, health, sex, marriage, motherhood, fashion, education, and politics. Holdsworth's profile of the eighteenth-century media darling Lady Georgia Spencer, *The People's Duchess* (1999), drew comparisons with one of her descendants—Diana, Princess of Wales. Another woman who has recently made a mark in the U.K., doing both documentary and docudramas, is Philippa Lowthorpe, whose films include *Three Salons at Seaside* (2002) and *Remember the Family* (2003) for BBC's *Storyville*.

Nick Broomfield continued to press onward in the 1990s with the development of his own screen persona, to the extent of starring as himself in a Volkswagen television commercial. In this, and in other film projects, he and Joan Churchill again successfully collaborated professionally. Although his work sometimes veered over the top, a more insightful balance seemed to take hold with 2003's *Aileen: Life and Death of a Serial Killer*, made collaboratively with Churchill. This follow-up to *Aileen Wuornos: The Selling of a Serial Killer* (1992) pulls back a bit from the filmmaker as subject to convey the banal horror of a woman facing execution. Broomfield is still there onscreen, but seems less sure of the moral righteousness of his presence than in his other films, especially in the face of a clearly unstable woman about to be executed. At the close of the film, Broomfield holds a press conference in the parking lot of the state penitentiary as Wuoronos is executed. He and Churchill were the only journalists with whom Wuoronos would speak in the final days before her death.

From *Night Mail* onward the poetic documentary in Britain has had a long history. In the 1990s director Brian Hill collaborated with poet Simon Armitage in a number of unusual poetic works. *Drinking for England* (1998) is a documen-

Nick Broomfield   **Joan Churchill**

tary on alcoholism, and *Saturday Night* (1996) a commentary about nightlife in Leeds. These can be called "film poems," which evolved from Armitage's work. Some critics have called their later collaborations documentary musicals. In *Feltham Sings* (2002), producer Roger Graef provided Hill and Armitage access to Feltham Prison in the hope that their film might make the public look more closely at young criminals. Hill has said, "Feltham is grim; youth crime is serious; some of these kids have very tragic lives. But I don't think doing it as a musical belittles the problem. And some of the lads at Feltham have more talent than a lot of people who've got recording contracts. . . . I don't think any subjects are off limits." The lyrics are by Armitage, who fashioned them from months of interviews with the inmates, although some prisoners insisted on writing their own songs. Most of the film was shot inside cells; all of it behind the prison's bars. Hill and Armitage pushed the documentary musical format even further with *Pornography: the Musical* (2003). In it, porn actresses sing and talk about their lives in a mix of staged studio/musical numbers, interviews, and glimpses into their daily jobs.

The *Connection* (1996), produced by Marc de Beaufort for Carlton Television about drug traffic between Colombia and the United Kingdom, in 1998 created a stir about ethics in British documentaries. Reporters from *The Guardian* newspaper revealed that many elements in the film were reconstructed, staged, and faked. The Independent Television Commission, the body responsible for the control and regulation of British commercial television, picked up the allegations. The ITC condemned the film for its techniques, while supporters of the film argued that using reconstruction was a general documentary practice that the ITC had turned into a crime. Like other works, this one raises, but doesn't necessarily answer, many questions about documentary ethics.

Kevin Macdonald, a Scotsman, has become a very visible force in the U.K. during the past decade with a variety of documentaries. *Touching the Void* (2003), with its tagline "The closer you are to death, the more you realize you are alive," became an international theatrical success. Its story is of two young climbers, Joe Simpson and Simon Yates, who become the first people ever to scale the summit of Siula Grande in Peru. An accident during their descent left Simpson with three breaks in his leg. While trying to lower him down the nearly 90-degree face of the mountain, Yates was forced to cut Simpson's line in order to prevent them both from falling to their deaths, Yates assumed that the fall killed Simpson. Simpson, however, continued to crawl his way down the mountain back to the base camp just a few hours before Yates was set to leave. Macdonald takes the two back to Siula Grande to recount their adventure in a manner that includes many re-enactments as well as storytelling.

Macdonald's other films evince a wide-ranging sense of style and subject matter. *Humphrey Jennings: The Man Who Listened to Britain* (2000) is of particular interest in its sympathetic and penetrating portrayal of one of England's most artful filmmakers. Others on film subjects include *Chaplin's Goliath* (1996), *Howard Hawks: An American Artist* (1997), and *A Brief History of Errol Morris* (2000). *One Day in September* (2000), made with Arthur Cohn, deals with the terrorist attack at the 1972 Munich Olympics. Its careful recounting of the act at a time when few expected or knew how to deal with such a thing won the Academy Award for Best Documentary Feature.

Michael Apted studied law at Cambridge before joining the BBC. He began his film career in 1963 with a Manchester-based training program for Granada Television. He is a prime example of the English system for turning out filmmakers highly skilled in craft, who can move freely from one genre to another. (His fiction work ranges from *Nell* to the James Bond film *The World Is Not Enough*.) One of his first assignments was to research a film entitled *Seven Up* for producer Tim Hewet, whose idea it was to take a survey of English society from the eyes of a group of seven-year-old children. Following the Jesuit saying, "Give me the child until he is seven, and I will show you the man" as a theme, Apted spent three weeks selecting fourteen children from a range of class backgrounds. He has since returned every seven years to visit the same individuals, and in the process has created one of the most remarkable phenomena ever in English-language documentary. He has been a dignified champion of the documentary form in Hollywood throughout ups and downs of its popularity.

The films, known as the "Up Series"—*14 Up, 21 Up, 28 Up, 35 Up, 42 Up,* and *49 Up* (due in 2005)—have documented the personal and social changes in

Jackie, Lynn, and Sue in various stages of Michael Apted's *The Up Series*. Michael Apted

this small sample of English people for over forty years. The only comparable documentary exercise is John Marshall's ethnography of the Kung! people, an African tribe whom he has revisited regularly for fifty years, recording the vast changes in their lifestyle. The characters of the "Up Series" have not been subjected to the immense physical upheavals of the Kung!, but their stories weave both engrossing personal drama and a broad sociological tapestry. Apted has also made other significant documentaries, among them *Incident at Ogallala* (1992), *Inspirations (Me and Isaac Newton)* (1999), *Married in America* (2002), and *Bring on the Night* (1985).

American Independents

Given the state of public and corporate funding for documentaries, American independents have resorted to a wide variety of means to make and exhibit their projects. The innovations that have emerged are as diverse as the many populations of the United States. San-Francisco-Bay-Area-based Les Blank is a man of few words and many films. It has been said by fans that with Les you get less. With over thirty self-made films to his credit, he has continuously explored American subcultures, finding revelation and celebration in life's ordinary details. Blank captures on film the sensual human spirit, often seen through the cultures of music and food. Born in 1935 in Florida, Blank attended film school at the University of Southern California. His first personal films were on Texas blues singer Lightnin' Hopkins—*The Blues Accordin' to Lightnin' Hopkins* (1970)—and the hippie subculture—*God Respects Us When We Work, But Loves Us When We Dance* (1968). To finance these and other projects, he made industrial and promotional films, generally working as cameraman.

Blank's work continued with a series of intimate glimpses into the lives of passionate people who live at the periphery of American society—a series that grew to include rural Louisiana French musicians and cooks in *Yum, Yum, Yum!* (1990), *J'ai Eté au Bal—I Went to the Dance* (1989), *Hot Pepper and Dry Wood* (1973), and *Marc and Ann* (1991); Mexican Americans in *Chulas Fronteras, Del Mero Corazon* (1979); New Orleans music and Mardi Gras in *Always for Pleasure* (1978); chef Alice Waters and other San Francisco Bay Area garlic fanatics in *Garlic Is as Good as Ten Mothers* (1980); filmmaker Werner Herzog in *Burden of Dreams* (1982) and *Werner Herzog Eats His Shoe* (1980); Appalachian fiddlers in *Sprout Wings and Fly* (1983); Polish-American polka dancers in *In Heaven There Is No Beer?* (1984); Serbian-American music and religion in *Ziveli!: Medicine for the Heart* (1987); Hawaiian music and family traditions in *Puamana* (1991); Afro-Cuban drumming and religious tradition in *Sworn to the Drum* (1995); East Texas bluesmen Mance Lipscomb in *A Well Spent Life* (1972) and *Cigarette Blues* (1985) with Sonny Rhodes; and the extraordinary *Gap-Toothed Women* (1987). Several of these were made with collaborator and editor Maureen Gosling, whose work apart from Blank includes *Blossoms of Fire* (2002).

Blank is perhaps the most independent American documentarian. His films have been financed by the sale of previous films through his distribution company, Flower Films, by lecture and screening fees, and by selling T-shirts and tapes from the trunk of his car. Every one of his works bears his own definitive stamp. The subjects are allowed to speak for themselves; the camera is respectful, not intrusive. The editing is not jarring or flamboyant, and the music flows naturally from the situation at hand. Blank is not an invisible filmmaker, the subjects often speak directly to the camera, but he is one who becomes a part of people's lives. His documents are important as ethnographic evidence, but they are just as important for the singular artistic worldview they create. If Ken Burns captures the realities of American history with the accuracy of detailed research and minute exactness, Les Blank captures it simply by witnessing.

Among the many independent American documentarians to begin creating significant work in the late 1990s and the earliest part of the twenty-first century, Judith Helfand is one who has most obviously combined the personal self-reflexive mode with a Griersonian dedication to education and social change. She coproduced and codirected, with George Stoney, along with Susanne Rostock, *The Uprising of '34* (1995), a documentary that draws on the hidden history of the General Textile Strike of 1934 to explore labor, power, and economics in the South at the time.

Cleveland Chenier in *Dry Wood and Hot Pepper* (U.S., 1973, Les Blank). Flower Films

Helfand was working for other producers when at twenty-five she was diagnosed with DES-related cervical cancer. In 1963 Helfand's mother, pregnant with
Judith, had been prescribed the ineffective, carcinogenic synthetic hormone di-
ethylstilbestrol (DES), meant to prevent miscarriage and ensure a healthy baby.
After a radical hysterectomy Helfand went to her family's home to heal and
picked up her camera. The resulting video-diary is an exploration of how science,

marketing, and corporate power can affect our deepest relationships. Shot over five years, *A Healthy Baby Girl* (1997) tells a story of survival, mother-daughter love, family renewal, and community activism. Continuing to combine the personal and the political, Helfand teamed up with Daniel B. Gold to make the "toxic comedy" *Blue Vinyl* (2002), which addresses the complex issue of toxins in vinyl production by bringing viewers into her parents' home, recently resided with blue vinyl. The film balances Helfand's efforts to convince her parents to have the siding, which is "embossed to look like wood," removed, and her detective work to discover the conspiracy by the vinyl industry to conceal its knowledge of highly harmful toxic byproducts affecting workers in the factory and the surrounding environment.

Another example of the personal diary film that became a powerful public document is Deborah Hoffmann's *Complaints of a Dutiful Daughter* (1995). Nominated for an Academy Award, the film uses both humor and insight to explain how Hoffmann comes to terms with her mother's deterioration from Alzheimer's disease. A more traditional documentary made by Hoffmann, along with Frances Reid, is *Long Night's Journey into Day* (1999), which follows the stories of four individuals whose cases come before South Africa's Truth and Reconciliation Commission following the abolition of apartheid. This film, too, was nominated for an Academy Award.

Reid and Hoffmann are both documentary veterans from the Bay Area, as is Jon Else, another independent who believes firmly in using media for social change. Else, who was series producer and cinematographer for *Eyes on the Prize: America's Civil Rights Years,* teaches documentary filmmaking at the University of California at Berkeley's Graduate School of Journalism. He directed the first three parts of the four-part PBS series *Cadillac Desert: Water and the Transformation of Nature* (1997), which examines the history and struggle for water in the American West. His Academy-Award-nominated *The Day After Trinity* (1980) looks at the life of J. Robert Oppenheimer and the Manhattan Project at Los Alamos, while *Sing Faster: The Stagehands Ring Cycle* (1998) views Wagner's operas from the point of view of people backstage. Else also has a career as an accomplished cinematographer, working on everything from commercials and music videos to feature-length documentaries such as John Korty's *Who Are the DeBolts? And Where Did They Get Nineteen Kids?* (1977), and Lauren Lazin's *Tupac Shakur: Resurrection* (2003). After being frustrated with the amount of time and effort it requires an independent filmmaker to raise money through grant writing (310 funding proposals for *Cadillac Desert*), Else launched a program to make documentaries using very low-cost technology, providing access to a wide range of young would-be documentary makers.

Formerly the co-curator of the Margaret Mead Film Festival, Jonathan Stack began his filmmaking career in 1991, forming Gabriel Films, "an independent documentary film company that specializes in social issue storytelling." His first production was *One Generation More* with the BBC, about the resurgence of Jewish culture in Estonia. He was nominated for an Academy Award for his

The view from behind the curtains in opera in *Sing Faster: The Stagehand's Ring Cycle* (U.S., 2001, Jon Else).

documentary, produced with Liz Garbus, *The Farm: Angola USA* (1998), and was nominated a second time for *The Wildest Show in the South: The Angola Prison Rodeo* (1999), produced with Simon Soffer. Both of these films deal with Angola Prison in Louisiana, the largest maximum-security penitentiary in the U.S., which houses around 5,000 men, three quarters of whom are black and 85 percent of whom die within its walls. Stack is a filmmaker who works very much in the Griersonian tradition of explaining social problems that general audiences might not fully understand, with an aim of bettering social conditions. His 2004 film, made with James Brabazon, *Liberia: An Uncivil War*, takes a very hard look at a brutal African war that few people wanted to know existed.

It is also important to remember that many of the stalwarts of American independent documentary filmmaking remained vitally active in the 1990s and into the twenty-first century. Verité pioneers such as Robert Drew, Albert Maysles (David Maysles died in 1987), D. A. Pennebaker, Ricky Leacock, and Frederick Wiseman all continued to make important contributions. For Pennebaker, the 1990s was a prolific time, greatly enhanced by his personal and professional partnership with filmmaker Chris Hegedus. Their film (with R. J. Cutler) *The War Room* (1993) was one of the most fascinating studies of a political campaign ever undertaken. It presents a classic vérité chronology of the 1992 presidential campaign waged by candidate Bill Clinton, and among other things made a media star of campaign manager James Carville. *Down from the Moun-*

George Stephanopoulos and James Carville in *The War Room* (U.S., 1993, Chris Hege-dus and D. A. Pennebaker). Pennebaker-Hegedus Films

tain (2000), which Hegedus and Pennebaker made with Chris Doob, is a concert documentary and historical document of American bluegrass music. In 2001 Hegedus, working without Pennebaker but with Jehane Noujaim, made *Startup .com*, which traces the rise and fall of a new media company during the "dot com" business craze of the 1990s.

Al Maysles teamed with Susan Fromke and Bob Eisenhardt to make *Concert of Wills: Making the Getty Center* (1997). Filmed over twelve years, it documents the conception, construction, and completion of the Los Angeles "Parthenon": the Getty Center. Fromke and Maysles also made, with Deborah Dickson, the Academy-Award-nominated *Lalee's Kin: The Legacy of Cotton* in 2001. Robert Drew continued making films in the cinema vérité/direct tradition almost non-stop for over forty years, often working with his wife and partner, Anne. Among the many titles are shows for PBS's *Frontline* and stand-alone pieces for PBS such as *For Auction: An American Hero* (1986). In the twenty-first century Drew made a radical departure to create a personal film using recreations and a poetic histor-ical style to tell the story of his own experiences as a WWII fighter pilot shot down behind enemy lines in nazi Italy. *Two Men and a War* (2005) explores not only a dramatic adventure but the origins of Drew's thinking about filmmaking. Frederick Wiseman remained true to his format throughout a career that in-cludes over thirty-five films. *High School II* (1994), *Ballet* (1995), *Public Housing* (1997), *Belfast, Maine* (1999), *Domestic Violence* (2001), and *The Garden* (2004)

Robert Drew (far left) and his family during World War II, from *Two Men and a War* (U.S., 2005, Robert and Anne Drew). Drew Associates

about Madison Square Garden are only some of the more recent titles. Continuing to examine American institutions in his own distinctive style, and continuing to have his films broadcast on PBS, Wiseman has himself become something of an institution. Leacock's latest work in progress is one of his many performance films, *A Musical Adventure in Siberia*, about opera impresario Sarah Caldwell.

Theatrical Documentary

The first years of the twenty-first century were good for the theatrical exhibition of documentaries, but it would be wrong to think that the theatrical documentary had ever completely vanished. In the 1920s Flaherty's *Nanook of the North* was such a financial success in theaters that Jesse Lasky, at Paramount Pictures, decided to finance Flaherty's next effort (*Moana*). In the 1930s Pare Lorentz's *The River* and *The Plow That Broke the Plains* played to enthusiastic audiences in mainstream movie theaters across the country. WWII documentaries were featured theatrically. It was through theatrical newsreels that people knew about that war, and "The March of Time" appeared on the marquees once a month, sometimes above the feature. It was not until the advent of television in the 1950s that it, and nontheatrical distribution, replaced theaters for documentary exhibition. In the 1950s and most of the 1960s documentaries were almost entirely absent from the big screen. Exceptions were *Kon Tiki* (1951), *Sky Above,*

Mud Below (1961), The Endless Summer (1966) or, perhaps most typically Holly-wood, This Is Cinerama (1952). Those were difficult years for the film industry as a whole as it struggled to find a way to compete with television for audiences. The end of the 1960s and the 1970s brought something of a change. The independent cinema, which emerged from the social and political upheaval of that era, gave rise not only to a group of new fiction filmmakers but also to documentarians whose work was shown in theaters. The rock-and-roll and music films such as Don't Look Back, Gimme Shelter, Monterey Pop and, most significant, Woodstock were treated as major theatrical events. Emile de Antonio had his theatrical heyday with In the Year of the Pig (1969). In addition to many more music films, the 1970s saw the release of theatrical documentaries such as The Hellstrom Chronicle (1970), Marjoe (1972), and Hearts and Minds (1974)—all of which won Academy Awards. In 1972 The Man Who Skied Down Everest, The California Reich, and Shirley MacLaine's The Other Half of the Sky: A China Memoir all played in theaters. Errol Morris first appeared in theaters in 1978 with Gates of Heaven, as did the now somewhat discredited Arnold Schwarzeneg-ger profile Pumping Iron (1976). Other theatrically exhibited documentaries included The Secret Life of Plants (1978) and On Any Sunday (1970). Warner Brothers released Malcolm X in 1971, the same year that Manson was in theaters.

In the 1980s the following were only some of the documentaries released theatrically in the United States: This Is Elvis (1981), From Mao to Mozart: Isaac Stern in China (1981), The Weavers: Wasn't That a Time! (1982), Seeing Red (1982), Streetwise (1983), The Times of Harvey Milk (1983), Sixteen Days of Glory (1985), Pumping Iron II (1985), Shoah (1986), Imagine: John Lennon (1988), U2: Rattle and Hum (1988), The Thin Blue Line (1988), Broken Noses (1988), Let's Get Lost (1989), Nobody Listened (1988), For All Mankind (1989), Roger & Me (1989), and Paris Is Burning (1989). The list in the 1990s and early part of the 2000s is even longer.

The film that turned the steady stream of theatrical documentaries into a wider river was Hoop Dreams (1994). Its three principal filmmakers were all film-school graduates based in Chicago. Peter Gilbert, Steve James, and Frederick Marx approached Gordon Quinn of Kartemquin Films with the basic idea for the film in 1986. Their objective was to create a short about the street culture of basketball in inner city neighborhoods. Quinn moved the project in the direction of PBS funding and broadcast. Two of the boys selected by the filmmakers, William and Arthur, became the focus, and as time went on, it was obvious that a longer, far more complex film was needed. Shooting, and funding, continued on and off for five years. Hoop Dreams won the Audience Award for Best Documentary at the 1994 Sundance Film Festival. With the success at Sundance, PBS agreed to delay broadcast until Fall 1995 so that the film could be released in theaters. Fine Line Features bought the theatrical distribution rights after the Sundance success, and Hoop Dreams, originally shot mostly in Beta, was blown up to 35mm and remixed in Dolby Stereo and Surround sound. The cost of the

Shadow (left) and Shellie in *Streetwise*, a theatrical release in 1983 (U.S., Martin Bell, Mary Ellen Mark, and Cheryl McCall). Photo by Mary Ellen Mark

Hoop Dreams (U.S., 1994, Peter Gilbert, Steve James, and Frederick Marx). Kartem-quin Films

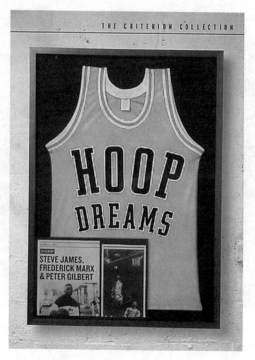

The DVD box cover for *Hoop Dreams.* **Home Vision Entertainment**

film, up through its screening at Sundance, was about $400,000. The cost of its preparation for theatrical distribution was roughly an additional $150,000. Some of these costs were borne by Fine Line, the rest by the producers.

The theatrical success of the film was propelled by rave critical responses. Roger Ebert again lead the way for a documentary by writing in the *Chicago Sun Times*: "'Hoop Dreams,' however, is not only a documentary. It is also poetry and prose, muckraking and expose, journalism and polemic. It is one of the great moviegoing experiences of my lifetime." The film eventually grossed over $7 million at the U.S. box office, although, as always, it is not clear how much was ever returned to the filmmakers. The gross in this case is important because the sense that *Hoop Dreams* was making money was one of the reasons more attention was brought to theatrical release for documentaries. And unlike Michael Moore's 1988 *Roger & Me*, *Hoop Dreams* is a documentary in very traditional ways. It uses vérité and interviews to tell personal stories having wide social implications. The warmth and value placed on the human spirit caused people to tell others to see the film, at the same time that it exposed the brutal nature of high-stakes high school athletics. *Hoop Dreams* showed that serious and thoughtful social-issue documentary could become a success at the box office.

A secret service officer and Michael Moore confront one another in *Fahrenheit 9/11* (U.S., 2004, Michael Moore). Dog Eat Dog Films

Michael Moore confirmed that sensationalism and humor used in documentary could also capture a crowd. Legions of fans have made his books and films runaway best-sellers and box-office successes. This has been accomplished by the marketing departments of some of the very conglomerates Moore attacks as being at the root of America's troubles. His book *Stupid White Men* was published by HarperCollins Regan Books (owned, along with Twentieth Century Fox, by Rupert Murdoch), and remained on the *New York Times* best-seller list more than fourteen weeks—without ever being reviewed in the paper! *Dude, Where's My Country?* was published in 2002 by the former AOL Time Warner. Warner Brothers released *Roger & Me*; MGM distributed *Bowling for Columbine*.

The distribution of *Fahrenheit 9/11* (2004), about the unholy business ties between the Bush and bin Laden dynasties, became one of Moore's better publicity moves when a hue and cry was raised about Disney's refusal to release the picture through its subsidiary Miramax for political reasons. The buzz surrounding this film created a singular moment in documentary history, pushing the form to the forefront of popular Western culture. For at least a week Michael Moore and the documentary were a primary focus of many news outlets. Individuals and organizations rallied to both support and decry Moore's anti-Bush exposé of the war on terrorism and the war in Iraq. The film won the Palme d'Or at the 2004 Cannes festival. This was an astonishing feat that reflected—aside from the merits of the film—not only the anti-American sentiment of Europe at the time but the fact that director Quentin Tarrantino, the head of the Cannes jury, owed much of his career success to Miramax Film Corporation, the distributor for *Fahrenheit 9/11*. As a theatrical documentary phenomenon,

Fahrenheit 9/11 is unmatched. In its opening weekend in the United States it grossed $21.8 million at the box office in over 800 theaters; $10 million was spent on release advertising; more than 2,000 35mm prints were eventually struck. The film's intent was to mobilize the American public to vote President George Bush out of office. Although it failed to do that it took the role of the socially conscious documentarian to its logical democratic conclusion.

The cultural celebrity Moore has gained through the documentary medium is perhaps fitting for his times. His muckraking "average Joe" persona (complete with baseball cap and unfashionable girth) struck a responsive chord in a public grown cynical about its own institutions. Michael Moore's films raise innumerable questions about documentary ethics, but there is no denying that they present serious issues in an unusual and effective form—that of seriocomic entertainment.

Moore charged onto the American documentary scene in 1989 when Warner Brothers agreed to distribute his debut feature *Roger & Me*. Ostensibly it told the story of muckraking journalist Moore attempting to track down the head of the General Motors Corporation to get him to explain plant closings in Moore's (and GM's) hometown of Flint, Michigan. This narrative device allowed Moore to show the economic hardships and very real personal pain of ordinary people who suffered from the loss of tens of thousands of blue-collar jobs. It also allowed Moore to create situations in which his chief targets—big business, callous rich people, ignorant bureaucrats—could look genuinely foolish in front of the camera. This formula served Moore well in all of his subsequent work. *Roger & Me* was the first in a number of antiglobalization-themed documentaries that appeared in the middle of the first decade of the twenty-first century. It bridges the gap between serious labor films such as Barbara Kopple's *American Dream* and the personal documentary. *Roger & Me* also gave new meaning to self-reflexivity in the cinema, turning it from introspection to broad comedy. The film did well at the box office and Moore was able to capitalize on the fact that the Academy of Motion Picture Arts and Sciences failed to nominate it, the year's most commercially successful documentary, for an Oscar, despite the fact that the Academy claimed to support theatrical exhibition of documentary.

Moore's propensity for inflaming media controversy also served him well in his next work, *Bowling for Columbine* (2002), about the tragic Colorado high school massacre. Taking the title from the fact that the teenage murderers were enrolled in a bowling class, Moore takes on the issue of guns and violence in America with mixed results. His confrontational approach is nothing short of brilliant when he visits K Mart headquarters with students shot in the attack who still carry in their bodies bullets purchased at K Mart. Its shortcomings are painfully evident when Moore stalks National Rifle Association President Charlton Heston in Heston's home. By this time the Academy had changed its rules (again) for awarding documentary Oscars, and Michael Moore created another media stunt when he accepted the Oscar for Best Documentary Feature.

Moore's brand of political filmmaking did not spring full-blown to the screen on its own. It has a direct antecedent in the work of a much less well-known proletarian documentary maker, Tony Buba, who has been making documentaries through his western Pennsylvania based company, Braddock Films, since 1974. After spending time on a factory assembly line and then attending college to study film, Buba's initial work consisted of a dozen black-and-white shorts known collectively as *The Braddock Chronicles*. These are portraits and vignettes of life in his own community, the dying mill town of Braddock, Pennsylvania. *Voices From a Steeltown* (1983) followed in this vein. Buba becomes an often-comic onscreen guide in this and other films. His first feature was *Lightning Over Braddock: A Rustbowl Fantasy* (1988). It mixes outlandish fictional fantasy sequences with serious footage of the problems of daily life for deindustrialized blue-collar workers. Buba and coproducer Raymond Henderson made *Struggles in Steel: A Story of African American Steel Workers* (1996). A documentary of industrial racism, the film has as its core a series of interviews with over seventy African-American workers whose stories had never before been told. Michael Moore was obviously familiar with Buba's films before he made *Roger & Me*. In fact, according to Buba, Moore contacted him to work as an editorial consultant on that film and eventually hired Buba's editor to work on the project.

Other documentaries of various types have played their way into theaters. It would be remiss to discuss theatrical exhibition of documentaries without noting the importance of large-format (IMAX) films. Although few large-format documentaries take a strong social position, very many of them use the beauty of nature and the adventures of humankind in a manner reminiscent of Flaherty's legacy. And perhaps more important, the vast majority of films made for large-format screens are documentaries, not fiction.

The creators of the IMAX film system, Canadians Graeme Ferguson, Roman Kroiter, and Robert Kerr, came together at "EXPO '67" in Montreal and went on to premiere their system at the Fuji Pavilion of "EXPO '70" in Osaka, Japan. Permanent IMAX theaters started being constructed in the early 1970s (primarily in museum and science park settings). Now a public corporation, IMAX continues to introduce evolutionary changes (such as 3D and high-definition versions) at World's Fairs, and several other companies produce large-format films. The technology creates an image of unsurpassed clarity and impact by using 70-mm film stock that runs horizontally through a massive projection system. Specially designed large-format cameras record images with much greater detail than do 35mm motion picture cameras. The projected area can be up to twenty-five times larger than conventional screens and can stand up to eight stories high and over 100 feet across.

Large-format films have been very good at educating people about scientific achievements and natural wonders. They have been less good at developing narrative capabilities. Like the history of all moving image technologies, it has taken experimentation and time for large-format makers to master their craft. And working in large format is many times more expensive than any other technology. There have been successful large-format films since the early 1970s, but it was not until *Everest* (1998) that there was a documentary blockbuster. It is the most financially successful large-format film ever made, having grossed over $125,700,000. It could also be considered the most financially successful documentary ever made, since in many ways it fits the classic definition of documentary. A MacGillivray Freeman production, *Everest* is the story of a team of climbers who triumph in the wake of tragedy. Their 1996 successful ascent of Mount Everest, just days after fellow mountaineers and friends died there, is a compelling tale, witnessed by the large-format camera. Producer Greg MacGillivray said, "Great fictional films impart an emotional story of a life-and-death struggle. Our large format films, being nonfiction, have never before had that same urgency and poignancy. But with *Everest* we have these powerful story elements in a real, nonfiction film, photographed . . . in the most realistic format yet invented."

As a specialized category of documentaries, large-format films can perhaps be considered akin to the "actualities" of one hundred years ago. They, too, were the beginnings of a new form of nonfiction. Both intended to show audiences the world around them in a new way. The same can also be said of the tiniest of formats, the use of computer and Internet technology to spread the documentary movement, a subject that is addressed in the final chapter of this book.

Films of the Period

1990

Berkeley in the Sixties (U.S., Mark Kitchell)
The Civil War (U.S., Ken Burns)

1991

American Dream (U.S., Barbara Kopple)
Brother's Keeper (U.S., Joe Berlinger and Bruce Sinofsky)

1992

A Brief History of Time (U.S., Errol Morris)
Forbidden Love: The Unashamed Stories of Lesbian Love (Canada, Lynne Fernie and Aerlyn Weissman)
Nitrate Kisses (U.S., Barbara Hammer)
The Panama Deception (U.S., Barbara Trent)

1993

The War Room (U.S., D. A. Pennebaker, Chris Hegedus, and R. J. Cutler)

1994

D-Day Remembered (U.S., Charles Guggenheim)
Hoop Dreams (U.S., Peter Gilbert, Steve James, Frederick Marx, and Gordon Quinn)
Lock-up: The Prisoners of Riker's Island (U.S., Jon Alpert)

1995

Complaints of a Dutiful Daughter (U.S., Deborah Hoffmann)
Crumb (U.S., Terry Zwigoff)

1996

When We Were Kings (U.S., Leon Gast)
Yugoslavia: Death of a Nation (U.K., Brian Lapping)

1997

Cadillac Desert (U.S., Jon Else)
Concert of the Wills: Making the Getty Center (U.S., Susan Fromke, Bob Eisenhardt, and
    Albert Maysles)
Four Little Girls (U.S., Spike Lee and Sam Pollard)
A Healthy Baby Girl (U.S., Judith Helfand)
Licensed to Kill (U.S., Arthur Dong)
Waco: The Rules of Engagement (U.S., Dan Gifford and William Gazeccki)

1998

The Cold War (U.S./U.K., Jeremy Isaacs)
Everest (U.S., MacGillivray, Freeman Films)
The Farm (U.S., Jonathan Stack and Liz Garbus)
42 Up (U.K., Michael Apted)
Human Remains (U.S., Jay Rosenblatt)
A Place Called Chiapas (Canada, Nettie Wild)

1999

Belfast, Maine (U.S., Frederick Wiseman)
Geri (U.K., Molly Dineen)

2001

Domestic Violence (U.S., Wiseman)
Startup.com (U.S., Hegedus and Jehane Noujaim)

Filmmakers Joe Berlinger (left) and Bruce Sinofsky with cinematographer Bob Richman filming *Metallica: Some Kind of Monster* (U.S., 2004, Joe Berlinger and Bruce Sinofsky). Photo by Annamaria DiSanto

2002

Dogtown and Z Boys (U.S., Stacy Peralta)
Feltham Sings (U.K., Roger Graef, Brian Hill, and Simon Armitage)
The Fog of War (U.S., Morris)

2003

Aileen: Life and Death of a Serial Killer (U.S., Nick Broomfield and Joan Churchill)
Bowling for Columbine (U.S., Michael Moore)
Capturing the Friedmans (U.S., Andrew Jarecki)

2004

Fahrenheit 9/11 (U.S., Moore)
Metallica: Some Kind of Monster (U.S., Berlinger and Sinofsky)
Super Size Me (U.S., Morgan Spurlock)

Books on the Period

Bullert, B. J., *Public Television: Politics and the Battle Over Documentary Film*. Rutgers, NJ: Rutgers University Press, 1997.
Bruzzi, Stella, *New Documentary: A Critical Introduction*. London: Routledge, 2000.

Corner, John, *The Art of Record: A Critical Introduction to Documentary*. Manchester, U.K.: Manchester University Press, 1996.

Edgerton, Garry R., *Ken Burns's America*. New York: St. Martin's Press, 2001.

Goldsmith, David A., *The Documentary Makers: Interviews with 15 of the Best in the Business*. Switzerland: Rotovision, 2003.

Hogarth, David, *Documentary Television in Canada: From National Public Service to Global Marketplace*. Montreal: McGill-Queen's University Press, 2002.

Kilborn, Richard and John Izod, *An Introduction to Television Documentary: Confronting Reality*. Manchester, U.K.: Manchester University Press, 1997.

Macdonald, Kevin and Mark Cousins, *Imagining Reality: The Faber Book of the Documentary*. London: Faber and Faber, 1996.

Sights of the Turn of the Century: New Tendencies in Documentary Cinema: lectures. CILECT, 1996.

Singer, Bennett, ed., *42 Up: A Book Based on Michael Apted's Award-Winning Documentary Series*. New York: Free Press, 1998.

Steven, Peter, *Brink of Reality: New Canadian Documentary Film and Video*. Toronto: Between the Lines Press, 1993.

Stubbs, Liz, *Documentary Filmmakers Speak*. New York: Allworth Press, 2002.

Vaughn, Dai. *For Documentary: Twelve Essays*. Berkeley: University of California Press, 1999.

Waldman, Diane and Janet Walker, eds., *Feminism and Documentary*. Minneapolis: University of Minnesota Press, 2000.

Winston, Brian, *Lies, Damn Lies and Documentaries*. Berkeley: University of California Press, 2000.

Zimmerman, Patricia R., *States of Emergency: Documentaries, Wars, Democracies*. Minneapolis: University of Minnesota Press, 2000.

Chapter Eighteen

Some Other Ways to Think About Documentary

D uring its century-long journey from a single screening to blanketing the world with information and opinion, documentary has given voice to both charlatans and truth-tellers; it has gathered acolytes and debunkers, shaken up populations, and kept them in line. The history of documentary is far from simple or straightforward, even though this book presents an organized chronicle of the major works and trends that shaped the field. The complexity of that field has become ever more pronounced as the twenty-first century begins. There are so many types of work laying claim to the term *documentary*, so many practitioners of the form, and so many ancillary "documentary" activities, that the more one examines it, the more confused the label "documentary" might seem. In this, documentary is much like other aspects of our postmodern world: extremely rich in data and nuance. It is different, however, from everything else because the driving force of social documentary has always been, and remains, a deep desire on the part of its makers to shed light on the very issues, people, places, and processes that make the world so complex. Grierson or Flaherty might not recognize the technology or the politics at work, but they would certainly identify with filmmakers' motivations in the 2000s. As individuals who belong to this increasingly global society, we can best affect what we best understand, and we bear an increasing responsibility for the ways our actions affect the entire world. In terms of promoting social change, documentary film remains one of the most effective ways to enhance understanding on a mass level. For this reason, if for no other, it is worth the effort to make sense of the documentary now, to linger on the history that shaped it, and to dwell for a while on its possible future.

Even though this book deals primarily with Great Britain, the United States, and Canada, documentary has long been a much more global form than suggested by these geographical/political entities. Globalization has made what was always an international movement the province of every part of the earth. Worldwide access to documentary is due in no small part to the same technological, economic, and artistic changes that brought documentary making into the hands of women, minorities, and other disenfranchised groups in North America in the 1970s. Similar forces have been at work worldwide in the 1990s and 2000s. Now images originate almost everywhere. There has always been a somewhat irregular triangle of elements operating on documentaries. The points of this triangle might be thought of as technology/invention, artistry/aesthetics, and money/economic systems. In the past they could be studied as developments that took place mostly within the confines of separate nation-states and then spread to other places. National and regional distinctions do remain, but media making (especially funding) and viewing now take place across national borders. It is beyond the scope of this book to detail developments worldwide, but to understand the current state of the documentary form, even within the parameters in play here, it is necessary to look at documentary as a more global system.

Technological Promises

The trends that began with cinéma vérité in the early 1960s toward lighter, less expensive, and easier to use equipment continued to build at an ever-accelerating rate for the next forty years. The pace shows no sign of abating. Consider the following about video equipment, true as of 2003 according to Jim Feely, editor of *Digital Video* (DV) magazine (which began publication in 1993): "Hi8 and S-VHS have been dumped into the dustbin of history. VHS is hanging on as a distribution format, but it should be erased from memory soon. Betacam SP and Digital Betacam still rule the broadcast market, but they are losing market share to DV25 formats, DVCPROHD, and HDCAM. DV50 and MPEG production formats hold promise." Not withstanding the alphabet soup, the message is clear: image capture technology changes at a rate so rapid that even well-funded professionals must be constantly ready to adapt to new formats. For documentarians, often working with limited funding, technological flexibility in shooting is key.

The same is true for postproduction. In the early 2000s Apple accelerated the digital editing revolution (begun by AVID) with Final Cut Pro, a nonlinear editing software package. Any editor with a Mac could afford a high-quality editing solution, and every desktop could be an editing station. Many middle-class homes and schools in North America have digital "movie" DV cameras, easy-to-use editing software, and computers on which to run them, as well as access to disc-making and/or the Internet, where almost anyone can share their "movies" with whomever they choose.

Rapid changes have also affected distribution and exhibition. High-definition television, hundreds of cable and satellite channels, Internet exhibition, and video on demand are all realities. At the same time that Hollywood spends more and more millions for fictional effects spectacle in fiction features, documentaries of all kinds are made with this low-cost "prosumer" equipment. Some, on the level of 2004's theatrical success *Super Size Me*, are produced for $100,000 or less and screen at festivals and in cinemas. Many others, made with much smaller budgets, reach much smaller audiences. All are giving voice to documentary makers who have never before been heard.

As access to equipment for production, distribution, and exhibition becomes more universal, the documentary world expands and reconfigures in surprising ways. Just as many third-world countries skipped the second stage of the tele-communications chain—jumping from no telephones at all to mobile phones, without ever stopping at landline phones—some filmmakers leapt from no access to media making to complete access to a world stage. In 2004 Arab Muslim terrorists filmed the beheading of foreign hostages and put the images on the Internet for all to see, creating a few moments of "actualities" indeed. It is absurd to think of these terrorists having the access or ability to do the same with 35mm or 16mm cameras, or without the Internet as a distribution mechanism.

An interesting sidelight to the jumps in technology is the fact that in most Eastern European countries, the domination of the Soviet system of centralized filmmaking through the 1980s dictated that most documentaries there were made with 35mm equipment. Documentary production, distribution, and exhibition was heavily supported by the communist systems, but in Eastern bloc countries the leap was from 35mm to portable video with little stopover at 16mm. The 16mm television documentaries of Marina Goldovskaya were an unusual exception to this.

The Internet is vital now to documentary. Most working documentarians and many individual films have their own Web sites, but these still remain ancillary to the main works. Historically no new technology immediately begets great artistry. It always takes some time, and trial and error, to find the best uses for new equipment and new means of expression. Internet documentaries have progressed little further than snippets, most thankfully more productive than terrorist acts, but, as in the large-format technologies discussed in the previous chapter, better Internet documentaries will surely arrive.

Aesthetics and Content

The aesthetic questions that always arise with the introduction of new technologies also continue to shift. It is often claimed that much is lost—visually, aurally, and artistically—with the cheaper, easier-to-use equipment. That is true in many cases. *Super Size Me* feels more like a home movie than a finished work meant to be screened in theaters, although it was successful there, grossing over $7 million. Perhaps the home-movie aesthetic was the intention of the filmmaker, Morgan Spurlock. Probably this story—of the consequences of its maker eating nothing but fast food from McDonald's for a month—would not have been made without the cheap technology. Would it have been better not to tackle this

Super Size Me (U.S., 2004, Morgan Spurlock). International Documentary Association

issue at all than to have it exist in a rough form? Is it better to drink wine from a poor vintage than to drink no wine at all? The answer perhaps is that every vintner must take care to do the best job possible with the grapes at hand. The danger for the documentary lies not in using the newest, most accessible technologies but in being careless with their use. Just because something seems simple does not mean that it does not deserve to be used with care and respect. It is possible, for example, to light beautifully for mini DV, just as it is possible to shoot without any regard for the lighting.

Audiences have been conditioned for several generations now to accept certain aesthetic qualities as part of documentary. They are unlikely to reject a nonfiction film simply because it has less-than-perfect image quality, sound or editing techniques, or because it promotes a first-person point of view. In fact, documentaries have long been victim to being judged solely for their content rather than for their skillful use of film techniques. It is almost axiomatic that the perfectly produced documentary on a less than emotionally compelling subject will be bested in competition for prizes and audience acceptance by the less-well-made film that moves an audience to tears. The best documentaries, just as the best of fiction films, manage to combine both skill and emotion. Although Grierson sometimes decried the artifice of technique, great documentarians try very hard to combine the best of available technique with a passion for their subject.

Contentwise there have also been shifts toward globalization and democratization of documentary. In some cases this has meant a move to better understanding the complexities of our linked globe. *Frontline/World*, for example, is a U.S. public TV series that seeks to profile countries and cultures seldom seen on American television. Springing from the original WGBH *Frontline*, each episode of *Frontline/World* features two or three short stories told by an ethnically diverse group of video journalists. With portable digital cameras, these correspondents roam the world, observing and filming, sometimes surreptitiously. According to the *Frontline/World* Web site, "The goal is to not only help fill the void in international news coverage but also to engage the American public in global stories that resonate in their own lives."

In other cases globalization of documentary has meant a diminished level of understanding among cultures. The subjects most easily transported to all parts of the world are often those that are least offensive to mass audiences. Nature documentaries, because they rely on no human language, have an international currency that transcends any border. Stories of adventure, ancient civilizations, natural wonders, and unexplained phenomena are also easier to sell cross-culturally, and fascination with every detail of World War II seems to permeate the globe, sixty years after it ended. It is the politically and personally challenging analyses of recent historical and current events that are hard to explain across cultures. These are the documentaries that create the most controversy.

Finance

International coproduction became a buzzword in the documentary field of the 1990s. In most cases the term meant international cofinancing rather than actual production. In its simplest form, broadcast entities from various countries invest money with a production company (usually based in only one country) to buy the rights to telecast a film that has yet to be made—in effect, presales. The finished documentary takes shape dependent upon the amounts of monies involved and the varying power of the investors and the production company. In Europe this system was a fairly natural outgrowth of the meshing of separate countries into the European Union. The National Film Board of Canada has, as it tends to do with all development, institutionalized the globalization trend with a mandate decreeing that a specific percentage of all its productions be made with international cofinancing monies.

For U.S. producers, operating independently, the challenge is often far greater. While European coproductions are facilitated by European Union incentives, documentarians in the United States are both aided and penalized by international coproduction. Although enterprising producers are savvy enough to try to find financing from any place on earth, trade laws and cultural quotas of other

Surrounded by the children of prostitutes in India, filmmaker Ross Kauffman shares the mysteries of a camera in *Born into Brothels* (U.S., 2005, Zana Briski and Ross Kauffman). International Documentary Association

nations do not always facilitate the funding of U.S. production companies. Many nations mandate that the majority of their media funding go to "native" producers. Conversely U.S. television entities, even public television, have no restrictions about paying for programming from foreign sources. These policies make sense in the Hollywood-dominated fiction and reality genres. The hegemony of U.S. media giants is well documented and fought by those who wish to retain separate cultural identities. However, the same exclusionary formulas are also often applied to independent U.S. documentarians who do not have the same economic clout as major corporate producers.

The market for completed documentaries on television internationally is large. Networks and stations around the world buy thousands of nonfiction shows. According to the trade publication *The Hollywood Reporter* in October 2003, prices to license documentaries (of all types) for broadcast ranged from $2,000 to $5,000 U.S. in the Middle East, $1,000 to $7,500 in Eastern Europe, $5,000 to $15,000 in Japan, and a high of $25,000 to $50,000 in the U.K. The films are sold by a variety of individual producers, sales representatives, television networks, and large production entities at markets like Docs for Sale at IDFA (International Documentary Film Festival Amsterdam) and Sunny Side of the Doc in Marseilles, France. The traditional international television market MIP, which takes place each year in Cannes, added a special separate two-day MIP-

DOC session in the mid-1990s specifically for the buying and selling of documentaries. Many of these are nature films and other types of nonfiction that might well not be categorized as documentary (cooking shows or travelogues, for example), but important social issue documentaries, too, are almost all ultimately sold to international television. International television sales are the largest source of revenue for the majority of these documentaries.

Today's international documentary scene also includes a large number of public pitching events and conferences designed to help filmmakers coproduce their work with partners from different countries. These emerged from concepts such as the Amsterdam Forum, running within IDFA, and from the three International Documentary Congresses organized in the late 1990s by the Academy of Motion Picture Arts and Sciences and the International Documentary Association in Los Angeles. There are documentary training initiatives funded by the European Union's MEDIA (e.g., Eurodoc), Discovery Campus Master schools, the Banff Television Festival in Canada, etc. The original pitching Forum was so popular in Amsterdam that it successfully expanded to a sister Forum at the Hot Docs Festival in Toronto, Canada. There are also specialized multiday conferences for history documentary producers, science documentary producers, wildlife documentary producers, and the like.

Articulating the flip side to the argument that an increasingly global culture and international funding results in a healthier production landscape for documentaries, Leslie Woodhead, in a critique for the Web site Docos.com in 2001, said:

> In his remarkable series of diaries recording the subtle corruptions of daily life in Nazi Germany, Victor Klemperer notes how curious it is that at the moment when modern technology annuls frontiers and distances (flying, wireless, television, economic interdependence) the most extreme nationalism is raging. They (these words) were written more than 60 years ago, in 1938. At the beginning of the 21st century, it is hard to avoid the evidence that those same forces of new technology and international business, far from extending our understanding and our tolerances, are shutting down our horizons. More and more, it seems, the Global Village is patrolled and ring-fenced by the Global Market. The evidence for that mounting insularity is clear and disturbing in the tough new environment for television documentary. Commissioners and schedulers regret that international stories don't get the big audiences; ratings-hungry networks gorge on the overnight returns for material, which exploits the most intimate doings of the people closest to home. In a time when even the most public-spirited broadcasters seem frozen in the headlights of ratings and profits, the space for documentary to explore difficult issues in faraway places shrinks every year.

Intimate Doings of Reality

It has been posited that part of the wide audience enthusiasm for documentaries in theaters at the start of the twenty-first century in America lies in the fact that commercial television so embraced "reality" shows like MTV's *Real World*, *Survivor*, *Big Brother*, and on downward to *Extreme Makeover*, that a ready-made audience accepted the conventions of Michael Moore and other first-person documentarians as ordinary entertainment. There is a devolving and skewed road leading from the founders of cinéma vérité to the frenzy of TV reality shows, with many stops of self-reflexivity on the way. An example of such begins with Frederick Wiseman's *Law and Order* (see chapter fifteen), plus John Marshall's 1969–1970 series of cv/d films on the Pittsburgh Police Department, continues with Alan (who worked for Drew Associates) and Susan Raymond's *Police Tapes*, which foreshadows Malcolm Barbour and John Langley's *COPS*. Wiseman looks at the institution of the police with his distanced vérité approach. *Police Tapes* is a serious, yet character-driven, personal and sobering vérité view of the very real threats to policemen. *COPS*, on the other hand, earned an online review in which it was observed that "*COPS* is always more fun when you are a tad inebriated yourself, this collection (*COPS: Caught in the Act*, 1989) can be enjoyed simply for the fact that some people can be very, very stupid, and, as a bonus, these people are not you." *COPS* has played successfully on the FOX network for over fifteen years and has generated numerous spin-offs and copycats around the world. *COPS* is often cited as the progenitor of reality shows, but it sprang from a documentary impulse. One of its creators and its longtime executive producer, John Langely, came to the documentary world with a master's degree in English. He worked with Alan Landsberg Productions and always had an interest in crime documentary. Langely and partner Malcolm Barbour happened to pitch the *COPS* concept to FOX at a time when the network was new and very hungry for inexpensive programming.

It sometimes seems that every boundary of documentary ethics has been crossed by reality TV. Following the success of its U.S. broadcast of the BBC's *Victorian House* (a show in which middle-class people from the twenty-first century attempt to dress and live as Victorians), PBS got into the reality show business with a series that began with *Frontier House* in 2003. This eventually produced the spin-off *Colonial House* (2004), in which rich and famous television talk show host Oprah Winfrey arrived via rowboat at the colonial outpost, fully dressed in colonial garb. Few would claim that this is documentary.

Other documentary-heavy channels followed the network trend. Cheap and easy-to-produce reality shows even joined the globalization trend by mid-decade. The Reality Channel itself, featuring mainly reruns of old reality shows, was in full swing by 2004. The cross-cultural reality series *Worlds Apart* was generated in 2004 for the U.S. National Geographic Channel. Plopping urban American families into remote locales around the world for ten-day periods, it aired in the U.K., Brazil, and the Middle Eastern channel Al-Hurra, Goodlife Channel in Israel, Australia's ABC, and National Geographic Channel Canada. Promoting the show, Gary Lico, the president and CEO of CABLEready, said, "The drama caused by the intermingling of cultures in *Worlds Apart* has proven to have wide appeal around the globe. Viewers in North and South America, the U.K., the Middle East and Australia will be able to see these entertaining examples of how people overcome their differences to eventually arrive at enlightenment." This series combines reality television, globalization, new technology, and perhaps, despite itself, a traditional documentary impulse to educate and broaden the public's horizons.

Newer Theory

Intellectual debate and discussion of theoretical issues surrounding the documentary has continued since John Grierson first used the "D" word in 1926. Grierson and Flaherty, Drew and Leacock, George Stoney and Barbara Kopple, have all spent hours in debate and discussion over issues of documentary form. As a rule, documentarians love to gather to discuss the ethical and practical aspects of their work. After all, these are people who have strong opinions about the subjects of their films and very strong opinions about the ways they should be made. As is evident in this text, the British documentary movement founded by Grierson has received the most attention in critical and historical writings, followed later by debates about the nature of cinéma vérité. Discussion of practice and ethics continues today with vigor.

For much of its early history film was written about chiefly in the form of popular criticism in general interest publications. While film theory in general grew rapidly as a field of serious study in the late 1960s and throughout the 1970s, it was not until later that documentary emerged as a subcategory in the newly academicized field of film theory. Feminist theorists were among the first to turn their attention to the subject, in part because documentary was a field in which many women gained access to filmmaking as early as the 1970s. Today there is lively scholarly debate about documentary theory in journals and specialized conferences.

Teachers and writers who helped to shape the emerging field include Jay Ruby, Cal Pryluck, Henry Breitrose, and, especially, Brian Winston. Much credit for the strength of documentary theoretical thought in the twenty-first century goes to Bill Nichols and Michael Renov, two scholars whose wide-ranging writings and work have influenced many others. Nichols has an organic approach to the development of various kinds of documentaries that sees new works growing out of existing examples in the categories he calls Expository, Observational, Interactive, Reflexive, and Performative modes, suggesting a chronology of linear development. Renov argues that documentary is the cinematic idiom most actively promoting the illusion of immediacy insofar as it forswears "realism" in favor of a direct, ontological claim to the "real." This approach has influenced the way that many recent film theorists attack the problems of documentary.

Women have added significantly to the development of theories about documentary, among them Jane Gaines, Patricia Zimmerman, and Pat Aufderheide.

English scholar Stella Bruzzi has produced an argument about contemporary documentary theory that involves a polemic against some of the traditional ways of discussing the form and advocating an analysis of newer films that are "familiar and relevant" rather than the canon of older classics. However useful they may be for viewers seeking a deep understanding of the films, the academic writings of film theorists are not very much a part of the world of documentary making and watching. It is without a doubt fascinating and instructive to think about, read about, and discuss film theory. Its impact on the vast majority of documentaries made and seen is minor, because it is a specialized field with its own language, its own arguments, and its own self-limited audience. There are documentary makers, such as Jill Godmilow, Barbara Hammer, Dennis O'Rourke in Australia, Jay Rosenblatt, and most notably Chris Marker in France, who employ preconceived formal theoretical constructs in their work. Most makers, however, are driven principally by issues that put documentary theory, when it is considered, in service to a larger idea.

The Future

What do we see, then, when we look at a documentary at the beginning of this century? One answer for a new form lies in the media response to the 2001 terrorist attack on New York City's World Trade Center. Because it was unexpected and took place in a world media hub, this became the most documented event in human history. Many of the twentieth-century trends of documentary development reached a natural apotheosis in coverage of the attack and its aftermath. Not only was the technology portable, lightweight, intimate, and immediate, the event was observed by hundreds of individually owned and operated still and motion cameras. Access to many versions of the visual record of this attack could not be effectively limited by anyone; there were just too many people with too many cameras for authorities to control. Many recorded their own reactions to the events in an unself-conscious outpouring of self-reflexivity.

It was the financial and production resources of HBO that focused this mass of imagery to produce a new kind of documentary with *In Memoriam: New York 9/11/01*. When the World Trade Center was attacked within view of HBO's midtown Manhattan headquarters, Sheila Nevins and her team created a response that has become a milestone. This film is revolutionary because the 9/11 attack was recorded on film and video from hundreds of perspectives, all of which were made within the same time frame of a few hours. Never before has any event been photographed from so many angles by so many different kinds of people with different kinds of cameras. Still and moving images were edited together with a soundtrack by the HBO team, to create an almost unbelievable record of the shattering events of that day. The "Rashomon effect" was realized in a way that fiction makers could never equal. Here was the visual and aural evidence of an event seen from many points of view. The editing, narration,

In Memorium: New York City 9/11/01 (U.S., 2002, Brad Grey, Sheila Nevins, John Hoff-man). International Documentary Association

music, and the narrative focus on Mayor Giuliani represent elements that colored the film, but it is the intimacy and immediacy of the first-person accounts that make the work compelling. The sheer number of media witnesses to the attack made the points of view in *In Memoriam* something new under the cinematic sun.

September 11, 2001, was important for documentary, but other less noble, if no less imaginative, forces were also at work. In fall of 2004 Discovery Channels around the world aired a show entitled *Virtual History: The Secret Plot to Kill Hitler*, using animation technique to "bring to life" events for which no actual film footage exists. In this first effort, the faces of historical figures, copied from archival footage, were melded onto actors to recreate July 20, 1944, showing viewers a day in the lives of Franklin D. Roosevelt, Josef Stalin, and Adolf Hitler. After every commercial break a disclaimer was shown on screen along with a visual that showed a wire frame becoming a face, so real was the effect that Discovery wanted to make certain people knew it was computer generated. The notion of documentary as "a truth," even if not "the truth," has in this instance been deeply called into question. Filmmakers, or perhaps *technicians* is a better

Sheila Nevins. Photo by Tom LeGoff. HBO

word, can recreate an image of Hitler, undistinguishable from a genuine image of Hitler, and then have the recreated Hitler say whatever words the filmmaker chooses. The possibilities for exploitation of the technique are innumerable and perhaps even unfathomable from our current vantage point.

Conclusion

Our history of social documentary is a story of determined individuals who overcame every kind of obstacle to put their messages on the screen. That message may be one of artistic experimentation, political consciousness, personal triumph over adversity, or historical record. Documentarians can choose among dozens of available technologies and techniques to get their messages seen and heard. However, what was once a manageable number of documentary films to see and evaluate every year is now a cacophony of sounds and images, sometimes seeming relentless. There are animated documentaries, computer-generated documentaries, IMAX documentaries, Internet documentaries, scripted documentaries, video diaries, vérité documentaries, investigative news documentaries, and all of their hybrids.

In this first decade of a new century, documentary is livelier and more complex than ever. This book devotes more than one chapter to the thirty-odd films per year of the British documentary heyday in the 1930s and 1940s. Today, thirty English-language documentaries premiere on television, in theaters, or at festivals every month. Making sense of this panoply of product is, at the very least, a challenge. Not only do more people make documentaries, more people than ever before watch and talk about documentaries. Perhaps this is inevitable simply because there are many more people, but it also has to do with worldwide access to production, distribution and exhibition mechanisms, and, more important, to the strength and flexibility of the "documentary impulse."

Although there is always discussion about and debunking of documentary, many, many people want to make documentaries. It has been suggested, more than once, that the term is obsolete and the form too defiled to have meaning. The ongoing and sometimes heated debates about documentary, however, indicate that the term is too meaningful and too powerful to abandon. People are always interested in seeing their, and other, realities reflected back to them through any medium. The proof is in the history of the form. From the astonishing successes of the Lumiéres' *The Arrival of a Train at the Station*, Flaherty's *Nanook of the North*, Capra's "Why We Fight," Murrow's "Harvest of Shame," Pennebaker's *Don't Look Back*, IMAX's *To Fly*, Burns's *The Civil War,* and Moore's *Fahrenheit 9/11*, among many others, we know that people love documentaries. Filmmakers will continue to produce, audiences will watch, the world will debate, and our culture will remain richer, not only for the magnificent legacy of this form that tries to explain some truths, but also for its present and its future. Our world today without the debate of documentary is hard to imagine, and a future without its questioning energy is a place where few of us would want to live.

Books on the Period

Beattie, Keith, *Documentary Screens: Nonfiction Film and Television*. Houndsmill, Basingstoke, Hampshire: Palgrave Macmillan, 2004.

Bruzzi, Stella, *New Documentary: A Critical Introduction*. London: Routledge, 2000.

Covert, Nadine, ed., *Fifty Years of Flaherty: Inspired Filmmaking*. Canada: International Film Seminars, Inc., 2004.

Hogarth, David, *Documentary Television in Canada: From National Public Service to Global Marketplace*, Montreal: McGill-Queen's University Press, 2002.

Kilborn, Richard and John Izod, *An Introduction to Television Documentary: Confronting Reality*. Manchester, U.K.: Manchester University Press, 1997.

Sights of the Turn of the Century: New Tendencies in Documentary Cinema, lectures. CILECT, 1996.

Renov, Michael, *The Subject of Documentary*. Minneapolis: University of Minnesota Press, 2003.

Waldman, Diane and Janet Walker, eds., *Feminism and Documentary*. Minneapolis: University of Minnesota Press, 1999.

Zimmerman, Patricia R., *States of Emergency: Documentaries, Wars, Democracies*. Minneapolis: University of Minnesota Press, 2000.

Appendix One

Film Festivals

The increased screening of documentaries in commercial theaters discussed in chapter seventeen owes not a little to the rise in the number and quality of film festivals that showcase the form. There is a natural symbiosis between the popularity of documentaries and the popularity of documentary films in festivals. One aids the other. During the first half of the 2000s, the growing interest in documentaries swept many titles from film festivals into multiplexes, where the number of small screens for specialized product was also increasing. The late 1990s and early 2000s saw an exponential growth in the sheer number of festivals put on worldwide, and in the United States in particular. It is possible to be at a film festival in some part of the globe every day of the year. It is probably possible to be at a film festival in the United States every day of the year. These festivals in themselves create a niche market for documentaries, since every festival programmer is competing with others to have the premiere showing of any given film. Navigating and exploiting these festivals is something that savvy documentary makers must now understand.

Documentaries have been a part of film festivals as long as there have been film festivals. There have also long been festivals devoted to documentary. Nyon, Switzerland was one of the first modern festivals to focus on the documentary. Originating in a trend for ciné-clubs, the Nyon Festival started in 1969, and by the end of the 1970s was well established. Other important festivals for documentary in the twentieth century were Rotterdam, Holland, and in the U.S. the Margaret Mead Film Festival, held at New York's Metropolitan Museum. Although its focus was on the anthropological film, it was a serious showcase for many varieties of documentary long before other film festivals celebrated the form, and it remains an important venue.

In the past decade in the United States, no festival has been more responsible for the explosion of interest and commercial exposure for documentaries than Sundance. "Robert Redford [its founder and patron saint] has always supported, talked about and embraced documentaries," according to festival director Geoff Gilmore. Sundance eventually provided the same legitimization to documentaries that it had for years bestowed on independent fiction films. In 2004, Stacy Peralta's *Riding Giants*, an exploration of surfing culture, was the first documentary to ever be the opening night film. Peralta had a previous hit at Sundance and in theaters with *Dogtown and Z Boys* (2002), his homage to the skateboarding culture of his youth in Santa Monica, California. This opening night was

Frances Flaherty listens to Willard Van Dyke during a Flaherty Film Seminar, the institution she founded after Robert Flaherty's 1951 death to perpetuate the meaningful discussion of documentaries and to keep Flaherty's ideas alive. International Film Seminars

another signal that the documentary had arrived in terms of Hollywood's independent film scene.

Five hundred and forty documentaries were submitted to Sundance in 2004, up ten percent from 2003, which was ten percent greater than the 2002 submissions. Of these, only a handful of these were screened during the festival. That means that each year hundreds of U.S.-made documentaries are floating around seeking a festival home. An example of a documentary greatly helped by Sundance was *Capturing the Friedmans*, which was awarded the grand prize for documentaries in 2004. Later it was shown on HBO and released in theaters. Because it deals with the sensitive issue of child molestation in an ambiguous, non-traditional way, the film was not a likely candidate for theatrical release. Its somewhat controversial approach, in which the filmmaker does not take a clear stand on the guilt or innocence of the convicted child molesters, led to critical debate in the press. "Winning the prize got the film invited to other festivals. And it hiked up the profile a notch, which is very important for difficult films with difficult subjects that are hard enough to sell," said director Andrew Jarecki. The list of significant North American documentaries that have premiered at Sundance is impressive. It includes, among many others, Joel DeMott and Jeff Kreined's *Seventeen* (1985), Ross McElwee's *Sherman's March* (1987), Al Reinerd's *For All Mankind* (1989), Mark Kitchell's *Berkeley in the Sixties* (1990), Barbara Kopple's *American Dream* (1991), Joe Berlinger and Bruce Sinofsky's *Brothers Keeper* (1992), Terry Zwigoff's *Crumb* (1995), Leon Gast's *When We Were Kings* (1996), Kirby Dick's *Sick* (1997), Liz Garbus and Jonathan Stack's *The Farm* (1998), Jef-

Ricky Leacock (left), Robert Drew, and Al Maysles at the International Documentary Film Festival, Amsterdam, in late 2004. Photo by Anne Drew

frey Friedman and Rob Epstein's *Paragraph 175* (2000), Chris Smith's *Home Movie* (2001), Doug Pray's *Scratch* (2002), Steve James's *Stevie* (2003), Ross Kauffman and Zana Briski's *Born Into Brothels* (2004), and Eugene Jarecki's *Why We Fight* (2005). Starting in 2003, Sundance, which had traditionally been limited to mostly U.S.-made films, introduced a world documentary section, reflecting the globalization of the field.

Festivals in North America devoted exclusively to the documentary include The Hot Springs (Arkansas) Documentary Film Festival, Full Frame (New York), Hot Docs in Toronto, and many others. Historically, the festival situation in Europe is different. Documentaries and documentarians have generally been more respected there, and the tradition of festivals that showcase documentaries is long. The most significant nonfiction festival in Europe in the twenty-first century is the International Documentary Film Festival Amsterdam, run by Ally Derks. It is a huge, comprehensive world festival that attracts public and professionals alike to almost two weeks of screenings in six theaters. It also includes an important film market and the original "Forum" pitching sessions. In Asia, the Yamagata Documentary Film festival, held every other year in Japan, is perhaps the most prestigious. The leading documentary film festival in Latin America is called "It's All True." Held in Brazil in Rio de Janeiro and Sao Paulo, it is considered to be the most important in Latin America. There are presently over twenty film festivals devoted to documentary around the world. A more complete list can be found at www.documentary diva.com.

Winner of an Academy Award for Best Documentary Short, *Number Our Days* (U.S., 1977, Lynne Littman)

Woodstock (U.S., 1970, Michael Wadleigh). Warner Brothers Pictures

Appendix Two

Academy Award®-Winning Documentaries

1941 (14th)
Churchill's Island National Film Board of Canada

1942 (15th)
The Battle of Midway United States Navy
Kokoda Front Line! Australian News and Information Bureau
Moscow Strikes Back Artkino
Prelude to War United States Army Special Services

1943 (16th)
Feature: **Desert Victory** British Ministry of Information
Short Subject: **December 7th** United States Navy

1944 (17th)
Feature: **The Fighting Lady** United States Navy
Short Subject: **With the Marines at Tarawa** United States Marine Corps

1945 (18th)
Feature: **The True Glory** The Governments of Great Britain and the United States of
    America
Short Subject: **Hitler Lives?** Gordon Hollingshead, Producer

1946 (19th)
(no feature this year)
Short Subject: **Seeds of Destiny** United States Department of War

1947 (20th)
Feature: **Design for Death** Sid Rogell, Executive Producer; Theron Warth and Richard O.
    Fleischer, Producers
Short Subject: **First Steps** United Nations Division of Films and Visual Information

1948 (21st)
Feature: **The Secret Land** Orville O. Dull, Producer
Short Subject: **Toward Independence** United States Army

1949 (22nd)
Feature: **Daybreak in Udi** Crown Film Unit
Short Subject (tie): **A Chance to Live** Richard de Rochemont, Producer
So Much for So Little Edward Selzer, Producer

1950 (23rd)
Feature: **The Titan: Story of Michelangelo** Robert Snyder, Producer
Short Subject: **Why Korea?** Edmund Reek, Producer

1951 (24th)
Feature: **Kon-Tiki** Olle Nordemar, Producer
Short Subject: **Benjy** "Made by Fred Zinnemann with the cooperation of Paramount
    Pictures Corporation for the Los Angeles Orthopaedic Hospital"

1952 (25th)
Feature: **The Sea Around Us** Irwin Allen, Producer
Short Subject: **Neighbours** Norman McLaren, Producer

1953 (26th)
Feature: **The Living Desert** Walt Disney, Producer
Short Subject: **The Alaskan Eskimo** Walt Disney, Producer

1954 (27th)
Feature: **The Vanishing Prairie** Walt Disney, Producer
Short Subject: **Thursday's Children** World Wide Pictures and Morse Films, Producers

1955 (28th)
Feature: **Helen Keller in Her Story** Nancy Hamilton, Producer
Short Subject: **Men Against the Arctic** Walt Disney, Producer

1956 (29th)
Feature: **The Silent World** Jacques-Yves Cousteau, Producer
Short Subject: **The True Story of the Civil War** Louis Clyde Stoumen, Producer

1957 (30th)
Feature: **Albert Schweitzer** Jerome Hill, Producer

1958 (31st)
Feature: **White Wilderness** Ben Sharpsteen, Producer
Short Subject: **Ama Girls** Ben Sharpsteen, Producer

1959 (32nd)
Feature: **Serengeti Shall Not Die** Bernhard Grzimek, Producer
Short Subject: **Glass** Bert Haanstra, Producer

1960 (33rd)
Feature: **The Horse with the Flying Tail** Larry Lansburgh, Producer
Short Subject: **Giuseppina** James Hill, Producer

1961 (34th)
Feature: **Le Ciel et la Boue (Sky Above and Mud Beneath)** Arthur Cohn and René
    Lafuite, Producers
Short Subject: **Project Hope** Frank P. Bibas, Producer

1962 (35th)
Feature: **Black Fox** Louis Clyde Stoumen, Producer
Short Subject: **Dylan Thomas** Jack Howells, Producer

1963 (36th)
Feature: **Robert Frost: A Lover's Quarrel with the World** Robert Hughes, Producer
Short Subject: **Chagall** Simon Schiffrin, Producer

1964 (37th)
Feature: **Jacques-Yves Cousteau's World without Sun** Jacques-Yves Cousteau, Producer
Short Subject: **Nine from Little Rock** Charles Guggenheim, Producer

1965 (38th)
Feature: **The Eleanor Roosevelt Story** Sidney Glazier, Producer
Short Subject: **To Be Alive!** Francis Thompson, Producer

1966 (39th)
Feature: **The War Game** Peter Watkins, Producer
Short Subject: **A Year Toward Tomorrow** Edmond A. Levy, Producer

1967 (40th)
Feature: **The Anderson Platoon** Pierre Schoendoerffer, Producer
Short Subject: **The Redwoods** Mark Harris and Trevor Greenwood, Producers

1968 (41st)
Feature: **Journey into Self** Bill McGaw, Producer
Short Subject: **Why Man Creates** Saul Bass, Producer

1969 (42nd)
Feature: **Arthur Rubinstein: The Love of Life** Bernard Chevry, Producer
Short Subject: **Czechoslovakia 1968** Denis Sanders and Robert M. Fresco, Producers

1970 (43rd)
Feature: **Woodstock** Bob Maurice, Producer
Short Subject: **Interviews with My Lai Veterans** Joseph Strick, Producer

1971 (44th)
Feature: **The Hellstrom Chronicle** Walon Green, Producer
Short Subject: **Sentinels of Silence** Manuel Arango and Robert Amram, Producers

1972 (45th)
Feature: **Marjoe** Howard Smith and Sarah Kernochan, Producers
Short Subject: **This Tiny World** Charles Huguenot van der Linden and Martina Huguenot van der Linden, Producers

1973 (46th)
Feature: **The Great American Cowboy** Kieth Merrill, Producer
Short Subject: **Princeton: A Search for Answers** Julian Krainin and DeWitt L. Sage, Jr., Producers

1974 (47th)
Feature: **Hearts and Minds** Peter Davis and Bert Schneider, Producers
Short Subject: **Don't** Robin Lehman, Producer

1975 (48th)
Feature: **The Man Who Skied Down Everest** F. R. Crawley, James Hager, and Dale Hartleben, Producers
Short Subject: **The End of the Game** Claire Wilbur and Robin Lehman, Producers

1976 (49th)
Feature: **Harlan County, USA** Barbara Kopple, Producer
Short Subject: **Number Our Days** Lynne Littman, Producer

1977 (50th)
Feature: **Who Are the DeBolts? And Where Did They Get Nineteen Kids?** John Korty, Dan McCann, and Warren L. Lockhart, Producers (Henry Winkler was Executive Producer)
Short Subject: **Gravity Is My Enemy** John Joseph and Jan Stussy, Producers

1978 (51st)
Feature: **Scared Straight!** Arnold Shapiro, Producer
Short Subject: **The Flight of the Gossamer Condor** Jacqueline Phillips Shedd and Ben Shedd, Producers

1979 (52nd)
Feature: **Best Boy** Ira Wohl, Producer
Short Subject: **Paul Robeson: Tribute to an Artist** Saul J. Turell, Producer

1980 (53rd)
Feature: **From Mao to Mozart: Isaac Stern in China** Murray Lerner, Producer
Short Subject: **Karl Hess: Toward Liberty** Roland Hallé and Peter W. Ladue, Producers

1981 (54th)
Feature: **Genocide** Arnold Schwartzman and Rabbi Marvin Hier, Producers
Short Subject: **Close Harmony** Nigel Noble, Producer

1982 (55th)
Feature: **Just Another Missing Kid** John Zaritsky, Producer
Short Subject: **If You Love This Planet** Edward Le Lorrain and Terre Nash, Producers

1983 (56th)
Feature: **He Makes Me Feel Like Dancin'** Emile Ardolino, Producer
Short Subject: **Flamenco at 5:15** Cynthia Scott and Adam Symansky, Producers

1984 (57th)
Feature: **The Times of Harvey Milk** Robert Epstein and Richard Schmiechen, Producers
Short Subject: **The Stone Carvers** Marjorie Hunt and Paul Wagner, Producers

1985 (58th)
Feature: **Broken Rainbow** Maria Florio and Victoria Mudd, Producers
Short Subject: **Witness to War: Dr. Charlie Clements** David Goodman, Producer

1986 (59th)
Feature (tie): **Artie Shaw: Time Is All You've Got** Brigitte Berman, Producer
Down and Out in America Joseph Feury and Milton Justice, Producers
Short Subject: **Women—For America, for the World** Vivienne Verdon-Roe, Producer

1987 (60th)
Feature: **The Ten-Year Lunch: The Wit and Legend of the Algonquin Round Table**
Aviva Slesin, Producer
Short Subject: **Young at Heart** Sue Marx and Pamela Conn, Producers

1988 (61st)
Feature: **Hotel Terminus: The Life and Times of Klaus Barbie** Marcel Ophuls, Producer
Short Subject: **You Don't Have to Die** William Guttentag and Malcolm Clarke, Producers

1989 (62nd)
Feature: **Common Threads: Stories from the Quilt** Robert Epstein and Bill Couturié,
Producers
Short Subject: **The Johnstown Flood** Charles Guggenheim, Producer

1990 (63rd)
Feature: **American Dream** Barbara Kopple and Arthur Cohn, Producers
Short Subject: **Days of Waiting** Steven Okazaki, Producer

1991 (64th)
Feature: **In the Shadow of the Stars** Allie Light and Irving Saraf, Producers
Short Subject: **Deadly Deception: General Electric, Nuclear Weapons and Our Environment** Debra Chasnoff, Producer

1992 (65th)
Feature: **The Panama Deception** Barbara Trent and David Kasper, Producers
Short Subject: **Educating Peter** Thomas C. Goodwin and Gerardine Wurzburg, Producers

1993 (66th)
Feature: **I Am a Promise: The Children of Stanton Elementary School** Susan Raymond
and Alan Raymond, Producers
Short Subject: **Defending Our Lives** Margaret Lazarus and Renner Wunderlich, Producers

1994 (67th)
Feature: **Maya Lin: A Strong Clear Vision** Freida Lee Mock and Terry Sanders, Producers
Short Subject: **A Time for Justice** Charles Guggenheim, Producers

1995 (68th)
Feature: **Anne Frank Remembered** Jon Blair, Producer
Short Subject: **One Survivor Remembers** Kary Antholis, Producer

1996 (69th)
Feature: **When We Were Kings** Leon Gast and David Sonenberg, Producers
Short Subject: **Breathing Lessons: The Life and Work of Mark O'Brien** Jessica Yu, Producer

1997 (70th)
Feature: **The Long Way Home** Rabbi Marvin Hier and Richard Trank, Producers
Short Subject: **A Story of Healing** Donna Dewey and Carol Pasternak, Producers

1998 (71st)
Feature: **The Last Days** James Moll and Ken Lipper, Producers
Short Subject: **The Personals: Improvisations on Romance in the Golden Years** Keiko
Ibi, Producer

1999 (72nd)
Feature: **One Day in September** Arthur Cohn and Kevin Macdonald, Producers
Short Subject: **King Gimp** Susan Hannah Hadary and William A. Whiteford, Producers

2000 (73rd)
Feature: **Into the Arms of Strangers: Stories of the Kindertransport** Mark Jonathan Harris and Deborah Oppenheimer, Producers
Short Subject: **Big Mama** Tracy Seretean, Producer

2001 (74th)
Feature: **Murder on a Sunday Morning** Jean-Xavier de Lestrade and Denis Poncet, Producers
Short Subject: **Thoth** Sarah Kernochan and Lynn Appelle, Producers

2002 (75th)
Feature: **Bowling for Columbine** Michael Moore and Michael Donovan, Producers
Short Subject: **Twin Towers** Bill Guttentag and Robert David Port, Producers

2003 (76th)
Feature: **The Fog of War** Errol Morris and Michael Williams, Producers
Short Subject: **Chernobyl Heart** Maryann DeLeo, Producer

2004 (77th)
Feature: **Born Into Brothels** Ross Kauffman and Zana Briski
Short Subject: **Mighty Times: The Children's March** Robert Hudson and Bobby Houston

Appendix Three

The National Film Registry

The National Film Preservation Board (NFPB), authorized and established by the National Film Preservation Act of 1996 (Public Law 104–285; 2 U.S.C. 179), serves as a public advisory group to the Librarian of Congress. The Board consists of forty members and alternates representing the film industry, archives, scholars, filmmakers, and others who make up the diverse American motion picture community. As its primary mission, the Board works to ensure the survival, conservation, and increased public availability of America's film heritage, including: advising the Librarian on the annual selection of films to the National Film Registry, and counseling the Librarian. To be eligible for the Registry, a film must be at least ten years old and be "culturally, historically, or aesthetically significant." The 375 films chosen during the first fifteen years illustrate the vibrant diversity of American filmmaking, and range from well-known Hollywood classics (*Casablanca*, *The African Queen*, and *A Night at the Opera*) to landmark independent, documentary, and avant-garde masterpieces (*Nothing But a Man*, *Louisiana Story*, and *Meshes of the Afternoon*) (Source: *www.loc.gov.film*).

Documentaries Selected for the National Film Registry (in order by date of release) are:
Blacksmithing Scene, Thomas Edison, 1893
President MacKinley Inauguration footage, 1901
Westinghouse Works, G.W. Bitzer, 1904
In the Land of the Head Hunters /aka In the Land of the War Canoes, Edward S. Curtis, 1914
Manhattan, Charles Sheeler, Paul Strand, 1921
Nanook of the North, Robert Flaherty, 1922
Grass: A Nation's Battle for Life, Ernest B. Schoedsack, 1925
Jenkins Orphanage Band, Fox Movietone Newsreel, 1928
From Stump to Ship, Alfred Ames, 1930
A Bronx Morning, Jay Leyda, 1931
The Forgotten Frontier, Mary Marvin Breckinridge Paterson, 1931
The Plow That Broke The Plains, Pare Lorentz, 1934
Republic Steel Strike Newsreel footage, 1935
Master Hands, Chevrolet Motor Company, 1936
Trance and Dance in Bali, Margaret Mead, 1936–1939

Hindenberg Disaster Newsreel footage, 1937
The River, Pare Lorentz, 1937
March of Time: Inside Nazi Germany, Louis de Rochemont, 1938
Marian Anderson: The Lincoln Memorial Concert, 1939
The City, Ralph Steiner, Willard Van Dyke, 1939
Cologne: From the Diary of Ray and Esther (home movie), 1939
Tacoma Narows Bridge Collapse Footage, 1940
Memphis Belle, William Wyler, 1943
Why We Fight (series) 1943–1945 Frank Capra, Anatole Litvak, Anthony Veiller
Jammin' the Blues, Gjon Mili, 1944
Battle of San Pietro, John Huston, 1945
Louisiana Story, Pare Lorentz, 1948
Duck and Cover, U.S. Federal Civil Defense Administration, Anthony Rizzo, 1951
All My Babies, George Stoney, 1953
House in the Middle, Federal Civil Defense Administration, 1953
The Hunters, John Marshall, 1957
The Living Desert, Walt Disney Studios, James Algar, 1957
Jazz on a Summer's Day, Aram Avakian, Bert Stern, 1959
Primary, Robert Drew, Richard Leacock, Al Maysles, D.A. Pennebaker, 1960
Zapruder footage, 1963
Dead Birds, Robert Gardner, 1964
Point of Order, Emile de Antonio, 1964
The Endless Summer, Bruce Brown, 1966
Through Navajo Eyes (series), Mike Anderson, Susie Benally, Al Clah, 1966
Don't Look Back, D.A. Pennebaker, 1967
Czechoslovakia, Dennis Sanders, 1968
Why Man Creates, Saul and Elaine Bass, 1968
High School, Frederick Wiseman, 1968
Woodstock, Michael Wadleigh, 1969
Salesman, Albert and David Maysles, 1969
Hospital, Frederick Wiseman, 1970
King, A Filmed Record, Sidney Lumet, 1970
Antonia, Portrait of a Woman, Jill Godmilow and Judy Collins, 1974
Chulas Fronteras, Les Blank, 1976
Harlan County, USA, Barbara Kopple, 1976
Topaz 1943–45 (home movie footage taken at Japanese American Internment Camp)
To Fly, Greg MacGillivray, 1976
Garlic is as Good as Ten Mothers, Les Blank, 1980
Life and Times of Rosie the Riveter, Connie Field, 1980
Sherman's March, Ross McElwee, 1986
The Thin Blue Line, Errol Morris, 1988

The Grierson Award

The Grierson Trust commemorates the pioneering Scottish documentary maker John Grierson (1898–1972), famous for *Drifters* and *Night Mail* and the man widely regarded as the father of the documentary. Each year, the Trust recognizes the best documentary filmmaking from Britain and abroad through the Grierson Awards. The Grierson Award for the best documentary film of the year was established by the British Federation of Film Societies (BFFS) in 1972, a few months after the death of John Grierson, who had been associated with the film society movement from its earliest days.

Later the Grierson Award was taken under the wing of the British Film Institute as part of its BFI Awards, which were presented between 1980 and 1995. A single award was given every year until 1998, when a Trustees' Award was also introduced. A grant from the U.K. Film Council in 2000 made possible a three-year program designed to recognize, promote, and celebrate excellence in all forms of documentary production. As a result, awards were given in five categories in 2001, eight in 2002, and eleven in 2003. There are now ten categories including the Trustees' Award, given to an individual who has made a significant contribution to the art of the documentary (source: www.griersontrust.org).

Grierson Award and Grierson Trust award winners are:

2004
Best International Television Documentary: **To Live is Better than to Die** Weijun Chen
Best Documentary on the Arts: **George Orwell: A Life in Pictures** Chris Durlacher
Best International Cinema Documentary: **Capturing the Friedmans** Andrew Jarecki
Most Entertaining Documentary: **The Prince, The Showgirl and Me** Clare Beavan
Best Newcomer: **The Boy Whose Skin Fell Off** Patrick Collerton
Best Series or Strand: **National Trust** Patrick Forbes, Clare Kavanah
Best Documentary on Science or the Natural World: **Project Poltergeist** David Sington
Best Historical Documentary: **Dunkirk: The Soldier's Story** Peter Gordon
Best Documentary on a Contemporary Issue: **Terror in Moscow** Dan Reed

2003
Trustees' Award: Molly Dineen
Best Documentary on the Arts: **Antoni Gaudi: God's Architect** Mandy Chang
Best Newcomer: **Chavez: Inside the Coup** Donnacha O Briain, Kim Bartley

Most Entertaining Documentary: **Jamie's Kitchen** Sandi Scott
Best Documentary Series: **The Last Peasants** Angus MacQueen
Best Documentary on Science or the Natural World: **DNA: The Future** David Glover
Best Historical Documentary: **SAS Embassy Siege** Bruce Goodison
Best Documentary on a Contemporary Issue: **Crackhouse** Laurence Turnbull, Carl John,
    Martin Fuller

2002
International Documentary: **Southern Comfort** Kate Davis, Elizabeth Adams
Most Entertaining Documentary: **Faking It: Burger Man to Chef** Jamie Simpson, Harry
    Lansdown
Best Documentary Series: **The Trust** Jenny Crowther, Jonathan Smith
Best Historical Documentary: **Ceaucescu: The King of Communism** Ben Lewis, Richard
    Klein
Best Documentary on the Arts: **Omnibus: David Hockney's Secret Knowledge** Randall
    Wright, Andrea Miller
Best Documentary on a Contemporary Issue: **Kelly and Her Sisters** Marilyn Gaunt

2001
Premiere Grierson and Best Documentary on a Contemporary Subject: **Correspondent:
    Killers Don't Cry**
Best Historical Documentary: **Britain at War in Colour: Darkest Hour** Stewart Binns
Best Documentary Series: **Indian Journeys** William Dalrymple
Best Newcomer: **Fifteen** Daisy Asquith

2000: No awards given
1999: **Gulag: Enemy of the People** Angus Macqueen
    Trustees' Awards: Philip Donnellan and David Munro
1998: **Inside Story: Tongue Tied** Olivia Lichtenstein
    Trustees' Award: Michael Apted
1997: **The System: The Nature of the Beast** Peter Dale
1996: **Man and Animal** Antony Thomas
1995: **Tripping with Zhirinovsky** Paul Pawlikowski
1994: **Beyond the Clouds** Philip Agland
1993: **Aileen Wuornos: The Selling of a Serial Killer** Nick Broomfield
1992: **Children of Chernobyl** Clive Gordon
1991: **Absurdistan** John Whiston
1990: **Four Hours in Mai Lai** Kevin Sim
1989: **Concerning Cancer** John Morgan
1988: **Fourteen Days in May** Paul Hamann
1987: **Handsworth Songs** John Akomfrah
1986: **From the Cradle to the Grave** John Willis
1985: **Miners Campaign Tapes** Platform Films/National Union of Mine Workers
1984: **Framed Youth** Lesbian and Gay Youth Video Project/GLAA
1983: **Give Us This Day** Phil Mulloy
1981/2: **Rough Cut and Ready Dubbed** Hasan Shah
1980: *joint winners* **Josef** Jerzy Kaszubowski & **The Tom Machine** Paul Bamborough
1979: **Fred Dibnah—Steeplejack** Don Haworth

1978: **Begging the Ring** Colin Gregg
1977: **Tom Phillips** David Rowan
1976: **Devices and Desires** Giles Foster
1975: **Drive Carefully Darling** John Krish
1974: **Butterfly Ball** Lee Mishkin
1973: **Like Other People** Paul Morrison
1972: **The Wind in the Wires**

Appendix Five

The IDA Awards

The IDA Awards were created in 1985 by the then two-year-old International Documentary Association. In an era before awards for documentarians were common, IDA honored those in the field in a variety of categories, none more prestigious than the Career Achievement Award. The following is the list of IDA Career Achievement Award winners. Pictured is Pare Lorentz with the Award, designed by filmmaker Harrison Engle.

1985   Pare Lorentz
1985   Fred W. Friendly
1985   Richard Leacock
1985   David L. Wolper
1985   Jacques-Yves Cousteau
1985   Frederick Wiseman
1985   Bill Moyers
1985   Walter Cronkite
1985   Robert Drew
1985   Albert and David Maysles
1985   Marcel Ophuls
1985   Ted Turner
1985   Henry Hampton
1985   Sheila Nevins
1985   Michael Apted
1985   Charles Guggenheim
1985   Jean Rouch
2002   Ken Burns
2002   Sir David Attenborough
2004   William Greaves

INDEX

Acknowledgments from Betsy A. McLane

T here are many individuals and institutions that made this work possible. It was first and foremost an honor and a pleasure to be able to work with a scholar and a true gentleman such as Jack C. Ellis. I learned from him more than only film history.

Two teachers at USC School of Cinema Television who most inspired me and who deserve recognition for much-overlooked contributions to film studies are Drew Casper and the late Arthur Knight.

I would like to thank especially the following: Tomm Carroll, Grace Ouchida, and Joan Von Herrmann who read many drafts and guided me personally over the years; for photographic assistance Mitchell W. Block, the Margaret Herrick Library at the Academy of Motion Picture Arts and Sciences, Tracie Lewis at the International Documentary Association, and the Photo/Stills Department of the National Film Board of Canada were more than professionally accommodating; enormous financial and moral support came from Gary Shafner and Pete Zachary. A tireless and high-voltage cheerleading section, led by my sister Janice McLane includes: Charles Benton, Michael Bryans, Ed Carter, Danise Delgado, Michael Demirjian, Anne Drew, Audrey Zaun Ferraro, Tom Gianakopoulos, Ed Landler, Drew Leder, William T. Murphy, Stephanie Mardesich, Lindsay and Robyn Sharp, and Mark Zuniga.

Most significantly, my thanks and love to Frank J. Delany, Esq.

Betsy A. McLane

Essential CG Lighting Techniques with 3ds Max

Dedication

To all the friends and family who continue to support me through the many years of my abnormally circuitous career and to Georgina for keeping me in check.